Henry Lansdell

Chinese Central Asia

A ride to Little Tibet

Henry Lansdell

Chinese Central Asia
A ride to Little Tibet

ISBN/EAN: 9783742840998

Manufactured in Europe, USA, Canada, Australia, Japa

Cover: Foto ©Andreas Hilbeck / pixelio.de

Manufactured and distributed by brebook publishing software (www.brebook.com)

Henry Lansdell

Chinese Central Asia

BY

HENRY LANSDELL, D.D.

M.R.A.S., F.R.G.S.

AUTHOR OF "THROUGH SIBERIA," "RUSSIAN CENTRAL ASIA,"
"THROUGH CENTRAL ASIA," ETC.

With Three Maps and Eighty Illustrations

IN TWO VOLUMES

Vol. I.

London

SAMPSON LOW, MARSTON, & COMPANY, Limited

ST DUNSTAN'S HOUSE, FETTER LANE, E.C.

1893

[*All rights reserved*]

To His August and Imperial Majesty
The Emperor of China,

ETC., ETC., ETC.

SIRE,
Seeing that my work on "*Russian Central Asia*" was dedicated by permission to His Imperial Majesty the Emperor of Russia, I desired that these volumes on "*Chinese Central Asia*" should be dedicated to His Imperial Majesty the Emperor of China. To this end permission was asked on my behalf of the Imperial Government in Peking by Her Britannic Majesty's Envoy Extraordinary and Minister Plenipotentiary, Sir John Walsham, Baronet; and the answer of the Yamen, telegraphed by him to the Foreign Office in London, was to the effect that no foreign work could be presented or dedicated to the Emperor until it had been translated into Chinese, and examined by the responsible ministers.

A few weeks later, however, letters arrived from Peking telling me more fully what had been done, and inclosing a translation of a letter from the Secretaries of the Yamen to Mr Jordan, Oriental Secretary at the British Embassy at Peking. In this translation I read that "*The Prince and Ministers consider Dr Lansdell has done a very praiseworthy work indeed in making a special study of the habits and customs of the people among whom he travelled, and in compiling a book which he wishes to see widely circulated in China.*" I gather also that

DEDICATION.

the Secretaries of the Yamen on one occasion verbally requested Mr Jordan to inform Sir John Walsham that you, Sire, were graciously disposed to accept the proposed dedication (which I esteemed a great kindness on the part of your Majesty), though the letter referred to affirms the general rule in regard to works of foreign origin and language.

Seeing then, Sire, that my linguistic attainments do not enable me to translate my work into Chinese, and that I cannot delay its publication in England, and hoping further that I have at least your good-will and favour in the matter, I trust I shall not be committing an unpardonable crime if I venture here to offer my book to your Imperial Majesty as a humble token of thankfulness for protection and safe conduct whilst travelling through a remote portion of your Majesty's dominions.

I confess to having been gratified, on crossing the Chinese frontier at Kuldja, to find my coming expected, and at Kashgar my reception provided for. Much assistance was afforded me in the Ili valley by the provision of suitable interpreters for the little-known languages of some of the peoples with whom I was brought into contact. Moreover, in preparing for my journey across the Muzart Pass, the greatest care was taken of my person, and my comfort studied, whilst as I continued round Chinese Turkistan I received from your Majesty's officials repeated manifestations of hospitality and good-will. All this made my journey less arduous than I expected, and greatly mitigated what were to me the privations of the way.

Chinamen, I believe, usually travel for one of three reasons—namely, on Government service, commerce, or religion. It was the last of these, Sire, that led me to travel in China, and from the following pages it will be seen that my object was to spread the knowledge of the supreme God. I am aware that when an Englishman thus approaches the Chinese, he approaches an ancient nation with a literature much older than his own; a people which numbers perhaps a third of the population of the globe, and whose armies, through many centuries, were ever victorious. I have heard, too, of Chinese prejudice against the religion and ways of foreigners; but I do not forget that Buddhism, now so widely spread throughout the empire, was originally imported from abroad, and that an illustrious Emperor of China, more than a thousand years ago, gave a respectful hearing to a Nestorian teacher of Christianity, and, after raising him to high religious office, appointed him "Great Conservator of Doctrine for the preservation of the State." Others of your Imperial Majesty's august predecessors have similarly shown favour to Christianity (some of them by building Christian churches), and only within the last few years an edict has been issued enjoining the Chinese people to respect Christians and praising their teaching as promoting peace and good living.

These things lead us in England to hope that some, at least, in China are willing to give to Christianity a fair hearing. And this, Sire, is precisely what we ask for. We do not seek to force our religion upon your Majesty's subjects (as the Muhammadans have often done in the Tarim valley) by the power of the sword. We are willing that the superiority of our religion should be tested by its fruits, feeling sure that Christianity, rightly taught, can do as much for the happiness of the Chinese as it has done for the English. To this end there are some hundreds of my countrymen and countrywomen who are nobly and unselfishly spending their lives for the good of China. For these may I ask your Majesty's favour and encouragement, feeling as I do that they are deserving of kindness and consideration? Most of them have sundered, wholly or in part, family ties, which are deemed sacred all the world over. Not a few have relinquished positions of comparative ease and comfort, in order to be of use to the people amongst whom they have come to live. And although, lastly, my own little effort is not worthy of mention in comparison with theirs, yet, inasmuch as the journey recorded in these volumes was by far the hardest I have known, I hope that the record of what has been attempted may be regarded as some little indication of my desire for what I believe to be the good of your Majesty's empire.

It is with these sentiments, Sire, of thankful appreciation of kindness shown to me in Chinese Turkistan, and with every good wish for the highest welfare of your Majesty and the people of your vast dominions, that I venture respectfully to subscribe myself,

Your Imperial Majesty's very humble Servant,

THE AUTHOR.

PREFACE.

THIS book is intended to be a companion and complement to my *Russian Central Asia*. The area covered by the two works extends all across the continent from the Caspian to the Pacific, whilst my *Through Siberia* deals with the rest of Asia, northward, to the Arctic Ocean. By *Chinese Central Asia* is meant that portion of the Celestial Empire lying outside the Great Wall—that is to say, external or extra-mural China; but not all parts thereof are here treated with equal fulness.

In the chapters concerning Chinese Turkistan I have endeavoured to be fairly thorough, if only because we have no standard work treating of this country as a whole. In saying this I do not forget the contributions of Sir Douglas Forsyth, Surgeon-General Bellew, and others, to whose valuable reports and writings, published and unpublished, in connection with the Yarkand Missions, I am greatly indebted. Names of other writers also on certain parts of the country, to whom I owe much, are given in the Bibliography.

The main object of my journey was to spy out the

land for missionary purposes. If, however, the lover of missionary information should think that I did little or no work of a missionary kind myself, I would remind him that as a preacher I was dumb; as a distributer of literature I had not the proper translations; whilst as a pioneer I conceived it my chief task to observe what openings existed, or could be made, for qualified evangelists to follow.

The book has been longer in making its appearance than I intended. As a matter of fact the word "Finis" was written on my rough manuscript more than a year ago, but the work of revision and printing has been delayed by private affairs with which it is not necessary to trouble the reader.

A preface, though coming in a book first, is written last, and therefore may be regarded in more senses than one as a suitable place for thanksgiving. Several old friends who aided me with my earlier books have again come to my assistance; such as Mr Glaisher, F.R.S., in meteorology, and Professor Bonney, F.R.S., in geology. Mr Dresser, F.Z.S., determined and arranged such of my birds as are here presented; whilst Mr Bethune-Baker, F.L.S., F.E.S., and Mr Western, F.E.S., kindly made lists of my *lepidoptera* and *coleoptera*. In literary matters, Lieut. W. H. Cromie and Mrs Bell have again helped in Russian translation, and the Rev. W. W. Tyler, B.D., has done much by way of revision. To all of the foregoing my thanks are due, as also to my wife, who has penned the whole of the Bibliography, and the Chronology.

Most of the illustrations are from my own photographs, and have been drawn to illustrate articles in *Harper's* and *Scribner's Magazines*, the *Graphic*, the *Fishing Gazette*, and *Black and White*, as well as a series of letters on "A Ride to Little Tibet" in the *Daily Graphic*. If the illustrations from the last of these should appear somewhat rough and unfinished, the reader will kindly remember that the blocks were not prepared for this book, but for the exigencies of rapid newspaper printing. They are, however, so true to nature and what actually occurred that it was deemed desirable not to omit them. To the editors of the above-mentioned periodicals I am indebted for electrotypes. Still more perhaps am I indebted to Dr Lindsay Johnson, the oculist, who not only urged my taking a camera, but with excellent judgment selected my apparatus, and gave me lessons in photography.

The foregoing may be called home thanksgivings. It is with difficulty that I mention names of those who helped me abroad; for if I begin, where shall I stop? As I did not rely in vain upon the assistance of the Foreign Office, the Russian Embassy, or the Chinese Legation at home, so was I similarly favoured at the Russian capital, where his Excellency M. Pobedonostzeff and various Ministers of State lent me their important aid, so that between St Petersburg and the Chinese frontier the Russians outdid all they have ever done for me in smoothing my way.

In India, again, the Marquis of Lansdowne, as Viceroy, and several heads of departments, not only lent me valuable books and maps, but gave me letters, and showed me an amount of attention out of all proportion to my claims or deservings. I was favoured for the entire journey with from three to four hundred introductions—official, social, religious, scientific, literary, and general. What they did for me may be surmised when it is added that, though I set foot in every country of Asia, I was permitted to go there to scarcely a dozen hotels.

In sending forth this book, I do so with hearty greetings to those who, in various parts of the world, have perused my former works. If it shall further interest or instruct them, I shall be glad; but my greatest happiness would be that the work may in some way call attention to the need, and help in further opening up the remote parts of China to the influence of the Gospel.

H. L.

Morden College,
Blackheath, London, S.E.
11th November, 1893.

P.S.—Within a few days of sending this sheet to press, my attention has been called to a new map of the Pamir regions by Messrs Constable & Co., who state that it embodies the latest information published (besides much of value that is unpublished) on the region in question. I have accordingly inserted the map in Volume II., to illustrate further my chapter on the Pamirs, and my route over the adjacent mountains.

CONTENTS.

	PAGES
DEDICATION	iii
PREFACE	vii
CONTENTS OF CHAPTERS	xi
LIST OF ILLUSTRATIONS IN VOLUME I.	xxii
THE AUTHOR'S ITINERARY	xxiv
OBSERVANDA	xxx
INTRODUCTION	xxxi

CHAPTER I.

FROM LONDON TO MOSCOW.

The start, and Author's forebodings, 1.—Delayed arrival at Berlin ; Visit to the Chinese Embassy, 2.—Custom-house at Wirballen ; Arrival at St Petersburg, and objects of visit; Request to travel by Trans-Caspian Railway, 3.—Calls on Sir Robert Morier and M. Pobedonostzeff; Acceptance by Emperor of *Through Central Asia*, 4.—Promise of help from Minister of Interior; Scientists visited ; Social gatherings, and dinner at Embassy, 5.—Visit to M. Vlangali, Assistant-Minister for Foreign Affairs ; Reception by Prince Dondukoff-Korsakoff, and recommendation to General Annenkoff; Visit to the Minister for War, 6.—My programme, 8. —Meeting with General Kostenko, 9.—Departure for Moscow ; Travelling acquaintances, Dr Alexéef and Count Bobrinsky, junr, 10.— Arrival in Moscow, and call on Count Leo Tolstoi, 11.— Departure southwards, 12 . . . . . 1 12

CHAPTER II.

FROM MOSCOW TO THE CASPIAN.

PAGES

Railway dangers ahead; Pleasant fellow-passengers, and offers of hospitality, 13.—Arrival at Kursk; Arrival and enforced stoppage at Kharkof, 14.—Former visit to town prison, 15.—Departure from Kharkof, and arrival in Crimea, 16.—Improved weather at Sevastopol; Sunday service, 17.—Departure for Batoum; H.B.M. Consul; Departure across Caucasus, and arrival at Tiflis; Sir Drummond Wolff and Col. Stewart; Presentation of introductory letters, 18.—Dr Radde and M. Hedjouboff; Departure from Tiflis to Baku, 20 . . . . 13—20

CHAPTER III.

FROM THE CASPIAN TO MERV.

"Wanted" by the Police-master; Call on the Governor, 21.—Comforts on steamer to Uzun Ada; Landing at railway terminus, 22. —Trans-Caspian stations to oasis of Akhal Tekke, 25.—Kizil Arvat, 26. Arrival at Geok Tepe, 28.—My coming to Askhabad expected, 30.—Continuation of journey to Dushak, 32.—Arrival at Merv, 35.—Hospitality of Colonel Alikhanoff; Modern Merv, 36.— Oriental carpets and embroidery, 37.—Alikhanoff's successful administration; Quiet and order of Panjdeh, 38.—A visit to Old Merv, 39.—Ruins on site of Merv; Arab and Persian remains, 41.—Russian annexation of Merv, 43.—How brought about, 44.— Liberation of slaves, 46 . . . 21—46

CHAPTER IV.

FROM MERV TO THE OXUS.

Further railway favours, 47.—Journey through sand barkhans and desert stations, 48.—Guest at Amu-daria with Colonel Tcharykoff, 50.—Reforms by new Emir of Bokhara, 51.—Dinner-party at Colonel Tcharykoff's, 52.—Visit to Bek of Charjui; Murder of previous Bek, and lynching the murderer, 54.—The prison revisited, 55.—The gallows, 57.—Journey continued in a rolling maisonette, 58.—Bridge over the Oxus, 59.—Inn at Bokhara station, 60. . . . . 47—60

CHAPTER V.

BOKHARA.

Drive to the town, 61.—Fellow-guests and repeated experiences; Madame Klemm's hospitality, 62.—Russian ladies in Bokhara, 63.—Espionage and suspicion of natives; Visit to bazaar and Kalan Mosque; Photography allowed but suspected, 64.—House of the Ishan and maniacs, 65.—Picture-taking under difficulties; Visit to Jewish synagogue, 67.—Morning prayers and circumcision, 68.—Jewish oppression in Bokhara, 69.—Visit to city prison, 70.—Lepers' quarter, 72.—Audience with the Emir, 73.—" A bargain's a bargain"; Political influence of Russian Residency, 77.—Rides about the town, 78 . . . . . . 61—79

CHAPTER VI.

SAMARKAND.

Departure from Bokhara, 80.—Arrival at head of the line; Guest of General Annenkoff, 81.—M. Rubenstein and Dr Heyfelder, 84.—Drive to Katte Kurgan; Custom-house; A banquet anticipated, 85.—Departure by post-horses, 86.—Farewell to General Annenkoff; Bridges prepared for railway, 87.—Approach to Samarkand; Guest with M. Tolpygo; Dinner at Government House, 88.—Condition of former acquaintances; Sights revisited; Tamerlane's Mausoleum, 89.—Synagogue, and visits from Jews; Farewell to M. Tolpygo and Samarkand, 91 . . . . . 80—91

CHAPTER VII.

TASHKEND.

Crossing the Zarafshan to the bridge of Shadman-Malik; Route to Jizak, 92.—Across the "Hungry" Steppe to Chinaz, 93.—Tashkend, 94.—Dinner with Governor-General Rosenbach; Help from Captain Blinoff, 95.—Easter services, and subsequent reception at Government House; Lutherans' request for a service and Easter communion; Withdrawal of money from bank, 96.—Arrangements for communication with Kashgar, 97.—Improvements in Tashkend and purchases, 99.—Russian lady nurses, 101.—An open-air bazaar; Further visits to Government House, and parting amenities, 102 . . . . . . 92—102

CHAPTER VIII.

FROM TASHKEND TO ISSIK-KUL.

                                                                                                 PAGES

Departure from Tashkend; Arrival at Chimkend, 103.—Passing through Aulie-Ata; Previous visit remembered at stations beyond, 104.—Region of "Ming-bulak"; Out of General Government of Turkistan into that of the "Steppe"; Telegrams to and from General Kolpakovsky; Arrival at Pishpek, 105.—Should I visit Issik-Kul? 106.—Start with a Colonel; Arrival at Tokmak, and excursion to the Burana Tower, 107.—Recent discovery of Nestorian cemeteries, 109.—Two graves opened, 110.—Traces of surrounding habitations; Tokmak cemetery; Inscriptions and decipherment, 112.—Departure from Tokmak; The Buam defile; Crossing the Chu to Kok-Mainak, 114.—Northern chain of the Tian Shan; The Ala-Tau and Alexander ranges; Basin of Issik-Kul, 115.—Description of the lake; Road along its northern shore; A narrow escape; Arrival at Kara-Kol, 116 . . . . . 103—116

CHAPTER IX.

FROM ISSIK-KUL TO VIERNY.

A previous traveller to Issik-Kul; Scenery of Kara-Kol, 117.—Attentions from Colonel Vaouline; Arrangements of Chief of the District on my behalf, 118.—Change of plans, 119.—The Kara-Kirghese; their districts, origin, and costume, 120.—How far Muhammadans; Missions among them of Russian Church, 121.—Kirghese modes of treating disease; Fish, for specimens, 124.—Passing through Pishpek, 125.—The Chu river and the Aral depression; Our wheel fallen to pieces, 126.—Arrival at Otar, and repair of tarantass, 127.—Arrival at Uzun-Agatch, and escort to Vierny, 128 . 117—128

CHAPTER X.

VIERNY AFTER AN EARTHQUAKE.

Vierny pleasantly situated, 129.—Eye-witnesses' description of earthquake, 130.—Houses of burnt brick most damaged; Destruction around town; Mud streams from the mountains, 131.—Losses of life, 132.—Removal of inhabitants; Author taken to Governor's temporary abode; Lodged in M. Gourdet's new house, 133.—Money sent to Kashgar, 134.—Anniversary of earthquake, and Memorial Chapel; Seismic record of earthquake shocks, 135.—Baggage delayed; Remissness of Russian Society for Transport, 137.—*Douceur* given and misappropriated, 138.—Arrival of baggage; Luggage forwarded to Jarkend, 139 . . . 129—139

CHAPTER XI.

FROM VIERNY TO THE CHINESE FRONTIER.

PAGES

Departure from Vierny, and meeting an Englishman at Ilisk, 140.—A gang of Siberian exiles; False statement as to their chains, 141.—Altitude of Ilisk, 142.—Crossing bridge; Geology of the road; Need of sound wheels; Road to Jarkend, 143.—Hospitality provided, 144.—Introduction to a rich native; Offers of service from Prjevalsky's guides, 145.—Arrangements for money, and modes of conveyance; Purchase of cart and horses, 146.—Kindness of Yuldasheff; Departure from Jarkend, and review of Russian favours, 147.—Driving towards the frontier, and warnings as to being stopped, 148.—Advised to approach from Peking, 149.—Deprived of interpreter, 150.—Cossacks for escort, and "success number one"; Site of ancient Almalik; Martyrdom of mediæval Christians; To and at Suiting; Arrival at Kuldja, 151 . 140—151

CHAPTER XII.

MANCHURIA, MONGOLIA, SUNGARIA.

China within and beyond the Wall; Outer China girdled by mountains; Former extent of China's dominion; Character of surface, 153.—Political divisions of Outer China, 154.—Manchuria; its boundaries, dimensions, mountains, and rivers; its provinces, government, and population, 155.—Our knowledge of Manchuria, and whence acquired; Nomad tribes, their Shamanism, and partial conversion, 156.—Manchuria colonised by Chinese; Manchu, the court and official language of China; Efforts to Christianise Manchuria, 158.—Mongolia; its dimensions and climate, 160.—Divisions and towns of Mongolia; Kiakhta, and tea route; Inhabitants of Mongolia, 161.—The Mongols, lamaists, 162.—Missionaries' translation of Bible still in use; Baptisms by Russian missionaries; Missions to southern Mongols, 163.—A difficult but open field, 164.—Sungaria; its depressions a highway to and from the Turkistan plains; Three districts of Sungaria, 165. Chuguchak; its troops and trade, 166.—District of Kara-kur-usu; its lakes and towns; The imperial high road to Hami, 168.—History of the Sungars, and their approximate extermination; Sungaria repeopled by various nationalities, 169.—Translation of Scriptures into Kalmuk; Another field for missionary effort, 170 . . . 152—170

CHAPTER XIII.
CHINESE OFFICIAL PRELIMINARIES.

Lodgings at Kuldja, 171.—Book-post parcels not opened by Censor, 172.- Packages from Russian Consul; Visit to M. Uspensky, 173.— Changed appearance of Kuldja under Chinese, 175.—Arrival of horses, 176.- Paucity of public buildings; Call from Lutheran postmaster, 177.—Letter from the *Tsian-Tsiun*; Excursion to Suiting, 178.—Appearance of Suiting, 179.—Chinese inn; Intruding natives and distracting noises, 181.—Called to breakfast with Kah; A score of dishes, 182.- Chinese table etiquette and conversation, 184.—Return call from Kah; his Manchu agility; Audience with the *Tsian-Tsiun*, 185.—Presents to *Tsian-Tsiun* and Kah; Calls from and upon Mattie, a former acquaintance, 186.—Presents from *Tsian-Tsiun*, including a sucking-pig; Disgust of Muhammadan innkeeper; Return to Kuldja, 187 . . . 171—187

CHAPTER XIV.
PREPARATIONS AT KULDJA.

My impedimenta, 188.—Food, physic, and clothing, 189.—Furniture, books, and instruments, 190.—Presents; Visit from a blind native, 192.—Call on Roman missionaries, 193.—Their assistance sought by Chinese; Ill effects of child-marriage, 194.—Shelter given to the girl by missionaries; Names added to roll of adherents; Chinese quarter of Kuldja and magistrate's procession, 195.— Instruments of punishment, 196.—Intended route changed, 197.— Interpreter into Chinese unwilling to proceed, 198.—Withdrawal of interpreter into Turki; Perplexing, but subsequently proving well; Objections to route *via* Urumtsi; Consideration as to mountain roads, 199.—The Muzart Pass, 200.—A caravan leader willing to attempt it; How affecting main object of journey; Where to find interpreter? 201 —Another excursion to Suiting, 202.—Chinese temple and theatre, 203.—Change of route sanctioned and arranged for, 204—Return to Kuldja; Interpreter sent for to Kashgar, 205.—My Tatar hostess, 206.—Farewell visit to Suiting and Chinese officials, 207. . . . . . . 188—207

CHAPTER XV.
FROM KULDJA TO THE PASS OF CHAPCHAL.

Caravan travel by horses; M. Bornemann and his linguistic abilities, 208.—Caravan leader and negotiations; Text of contract, 210.— Departure from Kuldja, 212.—Swollen condition of river; Escort of four, 213.—Jing's pretensions; Whipping the ferryman, 214.—

The Ili, and how crossed ; Bivouac, and departure next morning,
215.—*Personnel* of caravan, 216.—A Sibo village ; Solon colonists,
217.—Reception at Kalmuk encampment, 218.—Shooting grouse,
and ride to Damarchi ; Taranchi inhabitants, 219.—Hospitality at
Damarchi ; Ride along the Uzun-Tau Mountains, 220.—Arrival at
gorge of Chapchal, 221 . . . . 208—221

CHAPTER XVI.

THE TEKES VALLEY.

First Sunday in camp, 222.—Lodging in Kalmuk tent, 223.—Breakfast *menu*, 224.—Review of month, 225.—My servant Joseph, 226.—Lack of efficient interpreter, 227.—Altitude and temperature of Chapchal ; Visit to Kalmuk tents, 228.—Pass of Chapchal ; Defile of Sua-Chow ; Geology of Uzun-Tau, 229.—Altitude of Pass, 230.—Descent to Booghru ; Cattle of the Kalmuks, and dogs, 231.—March from Booghru and butterfly hunt, 233.—Manchu larking on horseback ; Caution against spirit-drinking, 234.—Arrival at Khanakai, 235.—Taking photographs ; Departure to the Tekes ; its rise and course, 236.—Impracticable ford at Geelan and *détour* to Narin-Kol ; Welcome at Russian picket, and help of Cossacks, 238.—Fording the Tekes, 239.—Another night on river bank ; Awakened by Lama's prayers ; Departure for Muzart defile, 240 . . . . 222—240

CHAPTER XVII.

UP THE MUZ-TAG MOUNTAINS.

Orography of Tian Shan system, 241.—Abundance of glaciers, but few rivers, 242.—Sources of our knowledge of the Tian Shan ; the Muz-Tag range, 243.—Fording the Urten Muzart, 244.—Absence of Kirghese ; Entrance to Muzart defile ; A quiet Sunday, 245.—Remains of stone fort ; Starting-point of Shepeleff ; Kostenko's route, 246.—Departure from Shattoo ; Inscription on granite rock ; Forest zone of birch, fir, etc., 247.—Beauty of path, 248.—Butterfly-hunting on horseback, 249.—Arrival at Udungei ; Chinese picket, and Kalmuk tents ; Kalmuk food, 250.—Osman Bai's orthodoxy as to food, 251.—Departure to Khan-Yailak, 252.—Visit to last Kalmuk tent ; Comparison of *koumiss* of Orenburg and farther east, 253.—Kalmuk photographs and anthropological remarks, 254.—Dress, numbers, and administration, 256.—Russian education of Kalmuks ; their intellectual capacities, 257.—Buddhist objects of worship ; Kalmuk women, marriage customs, and morals, 258.—Features of nomad life ; Chinese picket, 259.—Willingness of Jing and Tor-jee to proceed ; other two attendants sent back, 260 . . 241—261

b

CHAPTER XVIII.

OVER THE MUZ-DAVAN, OR ICE PASS.

From Khan-Yailak to bed of Muzart, 262.—View of Archali-Karachat glacier; Camp at Toghri-su, 263.—Stir at daybreak, 264.—Basin receiving five glaciers, 265.—Photograph of the "White Mountain," 266. Kaulbars' remarks on Jalyn-Khatsyr glacier, 268.—Ice-tables and stony roads; View of *mer-de-glace*, 272.—Ice-hummocks, crevasses, grottoes, and pinnacles; Difficulties of pack animals, 274.—Fall over precipice of horse and baggage; Mazar-bash; former hermitage, and fort, 275.—Soldiers' provisions and horses hauled up an ice-cliff, 276.—Scrambling down the Muz-davan, 277.—Road over rocks and stones, 278.—From Mazar-bash to Tamgha-tash; End of glacier, and superb ice-cavern; Hiuen Tsiang's description, 279.—Frequent loss of horses; Good fortune of first European in completely crossing the Pass, 281 . . . . 262—281

CHAPTER XIX.

DOWN THE MUZART VALLEY.

Tamgha-tash station unapproachable; Waiting for baggage, and supperless to bed in the open, 283.—A remarkable day, 284.—Arrival next morning of Osman Bai; Military insignificance of Tamgha-tash, 285.—Departure southwards; A marble monument, 286.—Fine view from Balguluk; Professor Bonney's note on Romanovsky's geological map; Kungei Ala-Tau range; Rocks east, south, and west of Issik-Kul, 287.—Shaping of mountains, and suggested periods of earth movements, 288.—Alexander chain compared with Swiss Oberland; Complicated orographical structure at Kara-Kol watershed, 289.—The Ferghana mountains and their characteristic rocks extending to Pamirs; Geology of route southwards, 290.—Three lines of orographical folding; Continuation of author's route, 291.—Accident in fording river; Camera washed away; Attendants' pursuit, and success in recovering baggage, 292.—Arrival at Kailek, 294.—Breaking into a post-station, 295.—To Tuprak; An afternoon's shooting, 296.—Purchase of an eagle, 297.—Joseph's taxidermical masterpiece, 298.—Departure from Tuprak, and pursuit of partridges; Narrow escape from homicide; Arrival at Muzart-Kurgan, 299 . . 282—299

CHAPTER XX.

FROM MUZART-KURGAN TO AKSU.

Lodging at Muzart-Kurgan, 300.—Objections to Customs examination; Advice concerning Chinese officials, 301.—Standing on one's rights, 302.—Visit of Customs official, 303.—Inspection of Muzart-Kurgan; Nimrod's cunning, 304.—Route continued over undulating tableland; Dust columns, 305.—Kizil-Bulak; Route southwards over curious geological formation, 306.—Messenger from Aksu; Stay at Auvat, and ride to Jam, 307.—Southern view of Tian Shan, 308.—Khan Tengri, visible 100 miles off, 309.—Glaciers and crests westwards; From Jam to Tash-Lianger, 310.—Death of a horse and dog, 311.—Thermometrical observations between Kuldja and Aksu; Arrival of Madamin Bai from Russian Consul, 312.—A minatory letter, 314.—Escorted into Aksu, 316 . 300—316

CHAPTER XXI.

CHINESE TURKISTAN.

Chinese Turkistan; its boundaries and varying names, 318.—The Sin Kiang, or New Frontier; its eastern boundary and latest cartography, 319.—Its dimensions, mountains, rivers, and lakes, 320.—Surface and communications, 322.—The country described as approached from Peking by northern route, and by southern route, to Hami, 323.—Hami; its history, European visitors, and present condition, 326.—Roads from Hami to Kobdo, Barkul, and Guchen, 329.—Urumtsi; its history and situation as headquarters town of the Sin Kiang, 330.—Route via Toksun to Pishan and Turfan, 333.—History of Turfan; its sacred mountain and latest European visitors, 334.—Karashar and its Kalmuks, 337.—Kurla, Kuchar, and Bai, 338 . . . . . 317—339

CHAPTER XXII.

OUR STAY AT AKSU.

Aksu; its history and area, 340.—Our arrival and lodging, 341.—Intricacies of Chinese money; shoes, tengas, and cash, 343.—Visits from merchants; Distribution of Scriptures, 345.—Reward offered for Dalgleish's murderer, 346.—Aksu bazaar, 347.—Riding round the town; its buildings, cemetery, and mode of burial, 348.—Repair of camera, 349.—Visit to Chinese Aksu; Reception of official visits, 351.—Inspection of prison, 352.—Preparations for departure, and payment to Osman Bai; Presents to Monkey-face and Tor-jee; Letters despatched to Kuldja, 354.—Cart-driver taken before the magistrate, 355 . . 340—355

CHAPTER XXIII.

THE SOURCES OF OUR KNOWLEDGE OF CHINESE CENTRAL ASIA.

PAGES

Meaning of "Chinese Central Asia," anciently "Cathay," 356.—How regarded by Greeks and Romans; Ptolemy's "Serica"; Chinese historians, 357.—The Buddhist pilgrims, 359.—Arabian knowledge of the "Seres"; Armenian and Persian intercourse with China, 360.—Nestorian and Roman missionaries, 361.—Marco Polo, 362. —Benedict Goes; Translations from Chinese records and from Tchuen-yuen, 364.—Russian contact with Mongols; Missions to Peking and Yarkand, 368.—Advances to Sungaria and Kashgar, 370.—Prjevalsky's journeys in Mongolia, 371.—Renat's map of Sungaria, 372.—English explorers in Sungaria, and in Tarim basin, 374.—Forsyth's missions to Kashgar, 375.—Later travellers in Chinese Turkistan, 376 . . . . . . 356—376

CHAPTER XXIV.

FROM AKSU TO MARALBASHI.

Two roads to Kashgar; Northern through Ush-Turfan, followed by Younghusband, 377.—District of Ush-Turfan; its people and capital, 378.—Aksai valley and Kirghese nomads, 379.—Our departure by southern route, 380.—March to Chinese city of Aksu, 381.—Fording the Janart river, and shooting birds, 383.—Ride to Sai-Aryk, 384.—Stormy weather, 385.—Night travel through Chilan to district of Maralbashi, 386.—Sunday at Yaka Kuduk; A Chinese official, 387.—Undesirable companions, 388.—March to Chadir-Kul, 389.—Its birds and buildings, 390.—Pheasants and Podoces, 391.—Scriptures at Tum Chuk, 393.—Arrival at Charwagh, visited by Biddulph for shooting, 394.—Antiquities between Charwagh and Maralbashi, 395 . . . 377—395

CHAPTER XXV.

THE INHABITANTS OF CHINESE TURKISTAN.

Chinese Central Asia and its inhabitants; Manchus in Ili and Pelu towns, 396.—Kalmuks in Sungaria and Karashar, 397.—Kirghese; their anthropological characteristics, diseases, morals, and occupation, 398.—Scarcely subjected by Chinese; Turkish inhabitants of plains, 405.—Their alleged Aryan descent, 406.—Lack of physical strength; The Turks hard-working and honest; Weak points of urban character; Lack of baths; Abuse of narcotics, 408.—Sexual depravity, 409.—Piteous story of a female prisoner, 410.—Degradation of country through Muhammadanism; The Chinese, "strangers and foreigners"; their mandarins and soldiery, 412.—Chinese garrisons and traders; Total population, 414 . . . . 396—414

CHAPTER XXVI.

FROM MARALBASHI TO KASHGAR.

An early welcome, 415.—Call on the mandarin; The bazaar, 416.—Visited by mandarin, 417.—Photography, and consequent excitement, 418.—The fortress and its features, 420.—General character of forts in Chinese Turkistan; Maralbashi, a strategical position; Road southwards to Yarkand, 422.—Dolan shepherds and their underground dwellings, 423.—Departure from Maralbashi, 424.—A trot to Urdaklik, 425.—Caught in a quagmire, 426.—A neighbourhood of wild-boars and deer, 427.—March to Faizabad; Visited by Chinese general, 428.—Features of the town, 429.—Limits of Kashgar district; March to the Yengi-shahr, 430.—March through fortress to old town of Kashgar, 431 . 415—432

CHAPTER XXVII.

OUR STAY AT KASHGAR.

Ride to Russian Consulate, 433.—Ascent of city wall, 434.—M. Nicolas Petrovsky and his Consular staff, 435.—His hospitality and intellectual tastes, 436.—Miscarriage of letters; Visited by local authorities, 437.—Taking photographs, 438.—Trade of Chinese Turkistan and its ramifications, 439.—Calls and presents from the *Tautai*, 440.—Visit to prison, 441.—Three homicides, and instruments of torture, 442.—Uncertainty as to route; Thoughts of Kafiristan, 444.—Preparations for Karakoram route; Osman Bai paid off, and three carts engaged; Lack of antiquities in Kashgar, 446.—Ruin of Aski Shahr; Present town of Kashgar; Visit to shrine of Khoja Aphak, 447.—Rifled grave of Yakub Khan, 449.—The Mausoleum, 450.—The Golden Mosque; The Consul's photography and Muhammadan prejudice, 451 . . 433—451

CHRONOLOGY OF CHINESE CENTRAL ASIA . 452

LIST OF ILLUSTRATIONS IN VOL. I.

	PAGE
FORDING THE MUZART-NIN-SU (*See page* 291) . . . . *Frontispiece*	
MAP OF CHINESE CENTRAL ASIA, WITH AUTHOR'S ROUTE . . *To face*	1
GENERAL L. M. ANNENKOFF, CONSTRUCTOR OF THE TRANS-CASPIAN RAILWAY	7
UZUN ADA, THE WESTERN TERMINUS OF THE TRANS-CASPIAN RAILWAY .	24
KODJ STATION IN THE AKHAL TEKKE OASIS	26
A BROKEN ICE-HOUSE ON THE PERSIAN FRONTIER . . .	27
THE STATION AT GEOK TEPE	28
TEKKE FORTRESS OF GEOK TEPE, SHOWING THE HOLES IN WHICH THE TURKOMANS HID THEMSELVES FOR PROTECTION FROM THE RUSSIAN MISSILES	29
RAILWAY STATION AT ASKHABAD . . .	30
GARDEN OF THE MILITARY CLUB, ASKHABAD .	31
THE TOMB OF CAIN AT SARAKHS	33
STATION AT DUSHAK, THE FARTHEST POINT SOUTH, WHENCE THE RAILWAY MAY BE CONTINUED TO THE AFGHAN FRONTIER . .	34
NEW BRIDGE AT MERV	35
THE PRINCIPAL GATEWAY OF BAIRAM ALI	42
A RUSSIAN OFFICER NEGOTIATING WITH TURKOMAN CHIEFS; TURKOMAN WOMEN WITH SPINNING WHEEL; A TEKKE BEAUTY IN FESTAL ARRAY	44
RESERVOIR AT BAIRAM ALI, OR OLD MERV	48
RAILWAY DEPÔT AT AMU-DARIA	50
BATCHAS, OR DANCING BOYS, WITH MUSICIANS AND SINGERS .	53
CEMETERY, AND MODE OF EXECUTION IN BOKHARA AND KHIVA .	56
OPENING OF THE BRIDGE ACROSS THE OXUS AT CHARJUI . .	57
BRIDGE OVER THE OXUS, 6,230 FEET, THE LONGEST IN THE WORLD .	58, 59
JEWS OF BOKHARA	70
THE EMIR OF BOKHARA AND HIS TREASURER	75
COLLEGE OF DIVAN-BEGGI .	78
AT THE HEAD OF THE LINE .	81

LIST OF ILLUSTRATIONS.   xxiii

	PAGE
A LOCOMOTIVE HABITATION FOR GENERAL ANNENKOFF, PART OF HIS STAFF, AND SERVANTS	82
LAYING RAILS AT THE RATE OF FOUR MILES A DAY	83
MAKING A CUTTING—ASSES TAKING AWAY THE EARTH IN PANNIERS	84
CONSTRUCTION OF A BRIDGE NEAR SAMARKAND	87
THE GUR-EMIR, OR MAUSOLEUM OF TAMERLANE, AT SAMARKAND	90
WELLS IN THE "HUNGRY" STEPPE	93
COSTUMES OF CENTRAL ASIAN WOMEN IN THE STREET	100
A WOMAN OF CENTRAL ASIA AT HOME	101
THE SOURCE OF THE KOPA	127
A MUD-STREAM AFTER AN EARTHQUAKE	132
A CONVICT WITH HALF-SHAVEN HEAD	141
CHAINS AND SUMMER COSTUME OF A SIBERIAN PRISONER	142
A GROUP OF GOLDI CHRISTIANS	157
MANCHU SOLDIERS AT SWORD DRILL, AT DURBULJIN, NEAR CHUGUCHAK	166, 167
THE TARANCHI MARKET AT KULDJA	175
THE DISCOMFORTS OF A CHINESE INN AT SUITING—PREPARING A ROOM FOR THE AUTHOR	180
BREAKFAST WITH THE COMMISSARY OF RUSSO-CHINESE AFFAIRS AT SUITING	183
A TATAR WOMAN	206
VAN, A KALMUK KHAN, WITH HIS SUITE, AT BARATOLA	209
ON THE WAY TO THE MUZART PASS—THE AUTHOR'S CARAVAN	217
BAGGAGE TENT AND "PALATKA" AT KHANAKAI	244
A GROUP OF MONGOLS IN CHINESE TURKISTAN	255
SUNRISE ON A PEAK IN THE MUZART PASS, LOOKING SOUTH-WEST FROM TOGHRI-SU	265
THE "WHITE MOUNTAIN" IN THE MUZART PASS, AS SEEN WHEN APPROACHING FROM THE NORTH	267
THE DORGA GLACIER IN THE MUZART PASS	272
COMING DOWN THE ICE-CLIFF AT MAZAR-BASH	278
NEARING AKSU—TEA BY THE WAY	315
IN THE PRISON AT AKSU—METHODS OF PUNISHING THE PRISONERS	353
A KIRGHESE IN "MALAKHAI," OR TRAVELLING HOOD	399
A KIRGHESE BRIDE	401
INTERIOR OF A KARA-KIRGHESE TENT	403
CHINESE WOMEN AT KASHGAR	413
TAKING PHOTOGRAPHS IN THE BAZAAR	419
TAKING A PHOTOGRAPH FROM THE ROOF OF THE CARAVANSERAI	421
AT KASHGAR—THE "TAUTAI" ON HIS WAY TO VISIT DR LANSDELL	440
DERVISH SHAH ISMAIL, A KALENDAR OF THE APHAK MONASTERY	448
AT KASHGAR—MULLAHS INDICATING THE RIFLED GRAVE OF YAKUB KHAN	450

THE AUTHOR'S ITINERARY.

The following shows the Author's departures and arrivals, and where described; the number of stationary and travelling days, and miles traversed.

A stationary day signifies one on which there was no travelling forward on the expedition, though there may have been thereon excursions from headquarters. A travelling day (beginning at midnight) signifies one whereon there was movement forward on the expedition.

Miles by "riding and driving" signifies alternate riding with travelling on wheels, generally in native carts.

DATES IN 1888.	JOURNEYS AND WHERE DESCRIBED.		Stationary Days.	Travelling Days.	Rail.	Water.	Driving.	Riding.	Driving and Riding.
Feb. 17 to 19	London to Berlin	Vol. I. 1	1	3	663	23	...	...	...
,, 21 ,, 23	Berlin to Pskoff	,, 3	...	3	849	...	...	...	...
,, 23 ,, 24	Pskoff to St Petersburg	,, 5	13	1	171	...	...	...	...
Mar. 9 ,, 10	St Petersburg to Moscow	,, 10	3	2	406	...	...	...	...
,, 14 ,, 15	Moscow to Kharkof	,, 13	...	2	488	...	...	...	...
,, 16 ,, 18	Kharkof to Sevastopol	,, 16	1	3	468	...	...	...	...
,, 20 ,, 23	Sevastopol to Batoum	,, 18	...	4	...	618	...	...	...
,, 24	Batoum to Tiflis	,, 18	5	1	220	...	...	...	...
,, 30 ,, 31	Tiflis to Baku	,, 20	1	2	343	...	...	...	...
April 2 ,, 5	Baku to Merv	,, 22	2	4	513	195	...	...	...
,, 6 ,,	Merv to Bairam Ali and back	,, 39	...	...	...	...	40	5	...
,, 8 ,, 9	Merv to Amu-daria	,, 47	2	2	152	...	...	...	...
,, 10	Amu-daria to Charjui and back	,, 54	...	...	...	...	20	2	...
,, 12 ,, 13	Amu-daria to Bokhara	,, 58	8	2	73	...	9	...	...
,, 22 ,, 23	Bokhara to Togai Robat	,, 80	...	2	91	...	...	...	...

Dates in 1886.	Journeys and where Described.		Stationary Days.	Travelling Days.	Rail.	Water.	Driving.	Riding.	Driving and Riding.
April 24	Togai Robat to Katte Kurgan	Vol. I. 85	...	1	...	...	18	...	...
,, 25	Katte Kurgan to Samarkand	,, 86	4	1	...	...	44	...	...
,, 30	Samarkand to Jizak	,, 92	...	1	...	...	65	...	...
May 1	Jizak to Chinaz	,, 93	...	1	...	...	83	...	...
,, 2	Chinaz to Tashkend	,, 94	14	1	...	...	43	...	...
,, 17 to 20	Tashkend to Pishpek	,, 103	...	4	...	...	373	...	...
,, 20 ,, 26	Pishpek to Kara-Kol and back	,, 107	...	6	...	...	251	...	...
,, 21	Tokmak to Burana Tower	,, 107	...	...	...	...	16	...	...
,, 26 ,, 28	Pishpek to Vierny	,, 126	15	2	...	...	157	...	...
June 13	Vierny to Ilisk	,, 140	...	1	...	...	46	...	...
,, 14 ,, 16	Ilisk to Jarkend	,, 142	3	3	...	...	167	...	...
,, 20 ,, 21	Jarkend to Kuldja	,, 148	22	2	...	...	87	...	...
,, 28 ,, Jy 2	Kuldja to Suiting and back	,, 178	3	2	...	...	...	...	52
July 9 ,, 13	,, ,, ,,	,, 202	3	2	...	...	...	...	52
,, 23 ,, 24	,, ,, ,,	,, 207	...	2	...	...	...	...	52
,, 26	Kuldja to River Ili	,, 211	...	1	...	...	...	6*	...
,, 27	Ili to Ghaljat	,, 216	...	1	...	...	...	15	...
,, 28	Ghaljat to Chapchal	,, 219	1	1	...	...	...	21	...
,, 30	Chapchal to Booghru	,, 229	...	1	...	...	...	21	...
,, 31	Booghru to Khanakai	,, 233	1	1	...	...	...	24	...
Aug. 2	Khanakai to Geelan	,, 236	...	1	...	...	...	27	...
,, 3	Geelan to Tekes Picket	,, 238	...	1	...	...	...	24	...
,, 4	Tekes Picket to Shattoo	,, 244	1	1	...	...	...	24	...

* From Kuldja to Leh, the mileage is reckoned at 3 miles per hour of caravan travel.

Dates in 1885.	Journeys and where described.	Stationary Days.	Travelling Days.	Rail.	Water.	Driving.	Riding.	Driving and Riding.
Aug. 6	Shattoo to Udungei		1				18*	
„ 7	Udungei to Toghri-su		1				15	
„ 8	Toghri-su to Tamgha-tash		1				36	
„ 9	Tamgha-tash to Kailek		1				36	
„ 10	Kailek to Tuprak		1				9	
„ 11	Tuprak to Muzart-Kurgan	1					18	
„ 13	Muzart-Kurgan to Auvat		1				24	
„ 14	Auvat to Lianger		1				21	
„ 15	Lianger to Aksu	5					12	
„ 21	Aksu to Choktal		1					15
„ 22	Choktal to Kumbash		1					15
„ 23	Kumbash to Sai-Aryk		1					9
„ 24	Sai-Aryk to Chilan		1					33
„ 25	Chilan to Yaka Kuduk	1						30
„ 27	Yaka Kuduk to Chadir-Kul		1					12
„ 28	Chadir-Kul to Charwagh		1					30
„ 29	Charwagh to Marallbashi	2						18
Sept. 1	Marallbashi to Kara-Kuchan	1						30
„ 3	Kara-Kuchan to Urdaklik		1					18
„ 4	Urdaklik to Lungur		1					27
„ 5	Lungur to Faizabad		1					30
„ 6	Faizabad to Yaman Yar		1					27
„ 7	Yaman Yar to Kashgar	10	1					24

* From Kuldja to Leh, the mileage is reckoned at 3 miles per hour of caravan travel.

Dates in 1888.	Journeys and where Described.		Stationary Days.	Travelling Days.	Rail.	Water.	Driving.
Sept. 18	Kashgar to Yapchan	Vol. II. 43	...	1	...		...
,, 19	Yapchan to Yengi Hissar	,, 45	...	1	...		...
,, 20	Yengi Hissar to Kok-Robat	,, 76	...	1	...		...
,, 21	Kok-Robat to Yarkand	,, 78	3	1	...		...
,, 25	Yarkand to Posgam	,, 135	...	1	...		...
,, 26	Posgam to Karghalik	,, 139	...	1	...		...
,, 27	Karghalik to Kosh Langar	,, 149	...	1	...		...
,, 28	Kosh Langar to Guma	,, 150	...	1	...		...
,, 29	Guma to Moji	,, 151	...	1	...		...
,, 30	Moji to Janghuia	,, 156	...	1	...		...
Oct. 1	Janghuia to Pialma	,, 156	...	1	...		...
,, 2	Pialma to Zawa Kurghan	,, 157	...	1	...		...
,, 3	Zawa Kurghan to Khotan	,, 162	5	1	...		...
,, 9	Khotan to Zawa Kurghan	,, 221	...	1	...		...
,, 10	Zawa Kurghan to Pialma	,, 223	...	1	...		...
,, 11	Pialma to Janghuia	,, 223	...	1	...		...
,, 12	Janghuia to Guma	,, 223	1	1	...		...
,, 13	Guma to Chulak Langar	,, 223	...	1	...		...
,, 15	Chulak Langar to Karghalik	,, 224	...	1	...		...
,, 16	Karghalik to Posgam	,, 224	...	1	...		...
,, 17	Posgam to Yarkand	,, 225	4	1	...		...
,, 22	Yarkand to Seh-Shambeh	,, 232	...	1	...		...
,, 23	Seh-Shambeh to Yak-Shambeh	,, 232	...	1	...		...
,, 24	Yak-Shambeh to Besh-Aryk	,, 233	...	1	...		...
,, 25	Besh-Aryk to Bora	,, 236	...	1	...		...

DATES IN 1886.	JOURNEYS AND WHERE DESCRIBED.		Stationary Days.	Travelling Days.	Rail.	Water.	Driving.	Riding.	Driving and Riding.
Oct. 26	Bora to Bash Langar	Vol. II. 237	...	1				18	
,, 27	Bash Langar to Kilian	,, 237	1					18	
,, 29	Kilian to Ak-Shor	,, 263	...	1				24	
,, 30	Ak-Shor to Chiguluk Aghse	,, 266		1				18	
,, 31	Chiguluk Aghse to Basilik Aghse	,,	...	1			...	18	...
Nov. 1	Basilik Aghse to Tschkun	,, 267	...	1				12	
,, 2	Tschkun to Kara Chaglan Aiaghe	,,	...	1		...	...	27	...
,, 3	Kara Chaglan Aiaghe to Bostan	,, 273	1			...	...	27	...
,, 5	Bostan to Aibuk	,, 275	...	1	...	...	...	18	...
,, 6	Aibuk to Suget	,, 314	...	1	...	...	...	18	...
,, 7	Suget to Khotan Jilga	,, 315	...	1	...	...	...	18	...
,, 8	Khotan Jilga to Darwaz Surgut	,, 315	...	1	...	...	...	33	...
,, 9	Darwaz Surgut to Balti Brangsa	,, 317	...	1				21	...
,, 10	Balti Brangsa to Chougeh Jilga	,, 322	...	1				21	...
,, 11	Chougeh Jilga to Gyapshan	,, 324	...	1				27	...
,, 12	Gyapshan to Saser Tschkun	,, 324	...	1				24	...
,, 13	Saser Tschkun to Tut Vailak	,, 326	...	1				27	...
,, 14	Tut Vailak to Changlung	,, 327	...	1				21	...
,, 15	Changlung to Panamik	,, 329	...	1			...	15	...
,, 16	Panamik to Tirit	,, 332	...	1			...	24	...
,, 17	Tirit to Khardung	,, 333	1	1			...	24	...
,, 19	Khardung to Leh	,, 336	6	1			...	42*	...

* From Kuldja to Leh, the mileage is reckoned at 3 miles per hour of caravan travel.

Nov. 26	Leh to Basgo	.	*Vol. II.* 374				24
,, 27	Basgo to Nurla	.	,,				24
,, 28	Nurla to Lama Yuru	.	,,				18
,, 29	Lama Yuru to Mulbek	.	,,				30
,, 30	Mulbek to Kargil	.	,,				24
Dec. 1	Kargil to Tashgam	.	,,	1			24
,, 3	Tashgam to Dras	.	,,				15
,, 4	Dras to Matayan	.	,,	1			15
,, 5	Matayan to Sonamarg	.	,, 385				26
				146	147	4,437 836 1,419 1,129	1,092
						8,913	

The above Itinerary shows 146 stationary days, and 147 of travel, thus indicating movement forward on the average every other day; namely:—

25 days by Rail at a mean rate of 174 miles a day.
6 ,, ,, Water ,, 152 ,, ,,
116 ,, ,, Horses ,, 31 ,, ,,

Total 147 days by Rail, Water, and Horses at an average of 60 miles a day.

OBSERVANDA.

IN proper names the letters should be pronounced as follows :—
a as in f*a*ther ; *e* as in th*e*re ; *i* as in rav*i*ne ; *o* as in g*o* ; *u* as in l*u*nar ; and the diphthongs *ai* and *ei* as *i* in pr*i*de.

The consonants are pronounced as in English, save that *tch* is guttural, as *ch* in the Scotch lo*ch*.

Unless otherwise stated :—

English weights and measures are to be understood.

Degrees of temperature are expressed according to the scale of Fahrenheit.

The Chinese *yamb* (50 *taels*) is reckoned at £11 5s. 0d. English.
,,	*tael, liang,* or *ser* of silver is reckoned at 4s. 6d.			,,
,,	*cash*	,,	$\frac{1}{10}d.$	,,
,,	*catty*	,,	$1\frac{1}{3}$ lb.	,,
,,	*jing*	,,	$1\frac{1}{4}$ lb.	,,
,,	*li* (1825·25 English feet)	,,	$\frac{1}{3}$ mile	,,
The Turkish *tenga*		,,	$2\frac{1}{2}d.$	,,
,,	*pul*	,,	$\frac{1}{12}d.$	,,
The Russian *rouble* (paper)		,,	2s.	,,
,,	*verst*	,,	$\frac{2}{3}$ mile	,,
,,	*pound*	,,	14·43 oz.	,,
,,	*pood*	,,	36 lbs.	,,
The Indian *rupee*		,,	1s. 6d.	,,

INTRODUCTION.

I PURPOSE, in the present work, to treat in general of Chinese Central Asia, and, more particularly, my journey from London to Little Tibet.

As to the reasons and motives for the expedition, especially those of a personal character, I might prefer quietly to pass them over; but they are of interest to some, who like to "begin at the beginning," and experience has taught me that if, on such points, I keep silence, others undertake to speak, but not always so accurately as I could wish.

Thus, one newspaper, during my absence, flatteringly designated me as a "useful and enterprising agent of the Bible Society"; and I have been frequently connected in a similar manner with the Religious Tract Society; the fact being that I have never acted as an agent of either, albeit that both Societies, as well as the Society for Promoting Christian Knowledge, have accorded me grants of religious literature for distribution.

Again, another newspaper, during my absence from England, informed its readers that I "went out more than a year ago with a sort of roving commission from the Church Missionary Society," which is so wide of the mark that the Committee felt obliged to decline my two requests for co-operation.

The story of my going is simply this. When proceeding to Russian Central Asia in 1882, I received from the Marquis Tseng letters to the Governors of Ili and the New Dominion, on the remote possibility of my wishing to cross the Chinese frontier near Kuldja. Time did not permit of my doing so; but I made the remark, I think at the dinner-table of the Governor-General of Turkistan—Colonel Poukaloff, six years afterwards, reminded me of it—how interesting a journey it would be to cross the Tian Shan Mountains to Kashgar, Yarkand, and Khotan. My fellow-guests, who were officers, agreed as to the interest of the journey, but thought it would be difficult to accomplish.

Nine months afterwards, at the Mildmay Conference, I found myself seated next to the Rev. Hudson Taylor, Founder of the China Inland Mission; and, upon making his acquaintance, I asked what they were doing for Western China, and broached the thought of my possibly some day going there through Mongolia. He readily favoured the idea, and offered to do all he could to help me, by advice or letters, or possibly by sending a man to accompany me.

This was kind and encouraging, as Mr Hudson Taylor has been ever since; but he rather damped my ardour when he went on to say that his Society had a man on the frontier of Tibet, learning the language, and ready to go in when permitted.

What need, then, I thought, to pursue the matter?

On the same day I went to the Chinese Legation, where I had promised to give information about travelling to Kuldja through Russia; and took the opportunity to inquire about the possibility of going to Mongolia. I learnt that the country was free to travellers, and was promised such help as could be given.

Two days later, on meeting a scientific acquaintance, he said that a journey across Mongolia would present facilities for useful investigations in almost every department of Natural History.

These considerations, with the foregoing, I thought over

on the morrow, and, for the time being, put the matter to sleep. This was in June 1883, when I was busy writing *Russian Central Asia*.

My diary for the following September and December shows that the idea was not abandoned, however; nor, on the other hand, in April of the following year, was it growing, for I thought the China Inland Mission had the business in hand. In 1885 I was invited to take temporary charge of St Peter's Church, Eltham, and became so happily engaged in parochial work that I thought my long journeys were over.

Nor was this equanimity disturbed in the following year on receiving a letter from an American named Crossett, lately arrived from Peking, who at Tientsin had been reading my *Through Siberia*. He thanked me for what I had done for that country, and, on obtaining an interview, intimated that he would like me to go to Mongolia and Tibet, whilst in the coolest manner possible he took out his pocket-book and gave me the names of two or three persons for interpreters. Not wishing to appear rude or indifferent, I wrote them down, but told him I had no thought of going.

Nor had I; though in a few weeks things were changed. My temporary engagement came to an end; the Church Homiletical Society, of which I had been Honorary Secretary, was dissolved, and I had just given up the editorship of the *Clergyman's Magazine*, when I received another note from Mr Crossett, this time asking for linguistic information, after which he added, "I am hoping that the way will be opened soon for a pioneering tour into the eastern and northern borders of Tibet from Peking. Will you come out and lead the way?"

Such a bald question, put by a stranger, would ordinarily have cost me but a few moments' consideration; but on this occasion the thought occurred to me, Is this a call,

"Come over and help us"? I felt I could not summarily dismiss the matter, and on the following Sunday, after carefully seeking for guidance, determined that I must not say "no" without further inquiry.

On my going next day to Mr Hudson Taylor, he surprised me by showing that I had previously misunderstood him, in supposing that the China Inland Mission had the matter in hand. Their plan, he said, was to go forward stage by stage, establishing a line of missions behind; and in this way, he said, it would take them many years to reach Western Mongolia. But he thoroughly welcomed the idea of my going as a pioneer, and again offered such help as his Society could render.

I had the good fortune to make the acquaintance on the day following of Mr Ney Elias, who kindly furnished me with a good deal of information on the region in question, and added that, in taking the Scriptures to Chinese Turkistan, I should be doing a work hitherto unattempted.

With such data, then, as had been gathered, I set apart the next day to consider the question of a journey through Mongolia to Chinese Turkistan. I traced in my diaries what had been written thereon since 1882, and then put down what seemed to me the arguments for and against the undertaking.

On the one hand, my friends thought I ought to be settled in a parochial charge. I had the disqualification of not speaking the requisite languages, and prudential considerations naturally suggested that my going would mean loss of income, perhaps loss of life, and that, in any case, there would be some danger and certainly many difficulties.

On the other hand, the peoples of Chinese Turkistan, I thought, have not probably a Bible among them, and certainly have never seen the face of a Protestant missionary. Translations of the Bible, or parts of it, are ready in Persian,

Kirghese, and Chinese. The country, from a missionary point of view, is unknown; no other pioneer appears to be in the field; and I have at least the advantage of previous experience in Siberia and Russian Central Asia.

Both religion and science might be advanced by such a journey, and, for the moment, I am free from definite responsibilities at home. If I lose my life no one is dependent on me, whilst certain facilities germane to the situation appear within my reach, and there does seem a definite call to the work. Finally, I asked myself whether Mr Crossett's question was from God, and said, " If it be, and if God will provide the means, not for stipend, but for cost of travel, etc., then my answer shall be, ' Here am I ; send me ! ' "

This is easy to write, still easier to read, but it was not easy to resolve. It looked like breaking up one's nest for nearly three years, and going forth presumably assured of food and raiment only, besides putting oneself further out of the way of clerical preferment at home. With the murders before me of Stoddart, Conolly, Schlagintweit, and Hayward, the danger to life did not, at this stage, present itself as a trifle, and I fully realised that it was by far the biggest leap in the dark that I had ever ventured on.

To make open confession, however, I had recently read a paper by Dr Cust[*] on the heroic conduct of the native Christians among the Melanesians; how, in their zeal to spread their new religion, some of them faced the extreme probability of being eaten by their cannibal tribesmen ; and then the writer drew the contrast so obvious to every one who will honestly think of it, how microscopically little average Christians in England do by way of personal service or self-sacrifice for the spread of the religion they profess to believe and love.

[*] " How Native Teachers Evangelised Polynesia and Melanesia " (*Church Missionary Intelligencer*, 1887).

This consideration helped me in resolving to take my leap, and the following shows how all this theory, as some will call it, was converted into action.

I set to work by speaking in private to sundry acquaintances and friends who had seats on Committees of our great Church Missionary Societies. The manifesto placed before them was headed, "A Projected Expedition to Chinese Turkistan"; its object being to distribute Scriptures and other religious literature, and to study as a pioneer the religious condition and needs of the people.

To this was added : " Among the results wholly or partially due to my former journeys, has been the supply by sale or gift of Scriptures, and religious literature, to the number of 150,000 copies, to the prisons, hospitals, and people generally of Scandinavia, South-Eastern Europe, Finland, the Caucasus, a large portion of European Russia, and the whole of Siberia and Russian Central Asia. The value of this work has been recognised by the Christian Church and the reports of the Bible and Tract Societies, and similar advantages might reasonably be expected from similar work on the virgin soil of China. A country so little known as Chinese Turkistan presents, moreover, a field of inquiry upon many topics of scientific and general, as well as missionary, interest ; and of these I should make note, as opportunity might serve, for the use of those who may follow."

The manifesto went on to state that to carry out my project thoroughly might take from one and a half to three years. For this I asked no salary, but inquired of various societies whether they could contribute towards what I was advised, and what my previous experience led me to estimate, would be the cost of the expedition.

The individuals spoken to, for the most part, seemed interested, and some—the Archbishop of Canterbury among them—promised support, if possible, in committee. As for the secretaries of the societies, I found most of them sympathetic, some of them very much so; but I do not remember one of them who held out hope that I should get from his committee the help I needed.

I continued trying in vain for three months, after which the time to start was rapidly approaching, if, that is, I was to be in Peking by the autumn, as suggested; so that, had I staked everything upon the great English societies, my projected expedition would now probably have collapsed.

But light was arising in another quarter. One of the first persons I had communicated with was Dr Robert Needham Cust, who more than once, on meeting me in the street and elsewhere, had casually asked, "When are you going on another journey?" volunteering on one occasion the remark, "I shall ask the committee of the Bible Society to send you somewhere," to which I then replied neither yea nor nay.

Now that I had such a journey in prospect Dr Cust suggested my writing, and using his name, to a certain gentleman who had given large sums for the distribution of the Bible in Africa, and who perhaps might be taken with my scheme.

I did so, and received for reply a suggestion that I should approach Mongolia from the west, getting my funds from the same sources as for previous journeys; whilst my correspondent, for a simultaneous work, should send £200 to the China Inland Mission for the visitation, with appropriate Scriptures, of the eastern half of Chinese Turkistan. Subsequently, he enlarged his proposed area to the whole of Mongolia, and sent the £200 to Mr Hudson Taylor.

At this time, and previously, I had several interviews with Mr Hudson Taylor, and I have a pleasant recollection of the patience with which he listened and entered into my plans. Once he was ill, always he was busy, on one occasion just returned from a long journey, on another wanted here and there after a public meeting, but ever treating my little affair, not as something to be got rid of as quickly as decorum would allow, but as if he thought it of importance.

In making arrangements it was necessary to look far ahead, and, before a penny was promised, he wrote in faith and hope to China as to who should accompany me, and also asked whether the American Bible Society at Shanghai would be likely to aid in my project.

This elicited a kind reply from the Secretary of the Society in New York, who wrote thus to Mr Taylor:—

"If in the present case the explorer were unknown or inexperienced, there would be reasons for hesitation and delay, which do not now exist, but Dr Lansdell's journey through Siberia has already given proof of his qualities, and exhibited a measure of philanthropy which we admire and honour."

After which he went on to say that his Board had authorised the expenditure of 500 dollars a year, for a period not exceeding three years, for the exploration of Central Asia and Tibet, with a view of promoting there the circulation of the Scriptures, particulars to be learned from their agent at Shanghai.

This reached me on July 23rd, after I had come to the conclusion, three weeks before, that my way to Chinese Turkistan through Peking was blocked. Whether I could enter from the west, in the following Spring, was doubtful, and might remain in abeyance, I thought, till September, when I had been invited to speak of my journeys at a Convention in Dublin; and I wondered whether anything to the point might transpire there.

Accordingly, when the time came, I stated publicly in Dublin my willingness to go another journey; and at Old Connaught, in the drawing-room of the Archbishop of Dublin, with whom I had the privilege of staying, I remarked, at a private lecture on my travels, that I thought my amended scheme would cost a thousand pounds; but I did not invite contributions. An Irish rector's wife, however, volunteered to give 10s., and afterwards Lady Cochrane sent a cheque, saying that of the needed thousand pounds she should like to give one, which was the first brick of my building really laid.

But things did not look very bright. Mr Hudson Taylor had tried to cheer me by saying, "Don't be discouraged; the devil will be sure to hinder"; and I confess to having carried sometimes a heavy heart. I had met with many disappointments and discouragements, and was beginning to wonder whether I had mistaken my call, insomuch that, on October 25th, I went to Mr Hudson Taylor with the question:—

"Why should *I* go at all? Why not let the two men we have in view, instead of accompanying me, go by themselves, and leave me out of the question?"

Had he humoured this mood I think I should have been willing, at this period, to withdraw; but he thought it decidedly better that I should go, and offered me half of the £200 sent to him for Mongolia. To this I mentally added what looked, at first sight, a promise of £300 from the American Bible Society; resolved to submit the matter to a few persons of means likely to be interested therein; and if sufficient promises for the remaining £600 were not forthcoming before the end of November, then to interpret it as God's will that I was not to go.

Accordingly I corrected the manifesto to altered circumstances, mentioned one and a half or two years instead of three, a greatly shortened journey, and an estimate of expenses cut down by half. On November 8th I began to send out letters, not in hundreds and thousands to the public generally, but three or four at a time to names from my address book.

And now the tide completely turned. Within a week I heard from Mr Blackstone, of Illinois, who had from the outset warmly encouraged my scheme, and now promised £100. The post, one morning, brought two letters of curiously opposite character. In the first, the writer spoke of the contemplated journey as "serious and perilous," to which he could not contribute; whilst in the second, the late Mr R. C. L. Bevan "thought the enterprise very hopeful and feasible," and promised £100.

And so cloud alternated with sunshine, and I was wondering on the 24th whether the £130 lacking would come. On the 28th arrived a note from the Archbishop of Canterbury, inclosing a "cheque of nominal value only, but as a token of good will," which helped to raise my spirits, if not greatly to increase my pile, whilst my friend Miss Peache and the late Mr Allcroft sent £50 each, so that by the 29th I regarded the matter as pecuniarily settled, and began to think of a day for the start. I was afterwards found to have been precipitate in reckoning on £300 from the American Bible Society, for they now felt obliged to limit the amount to £200; but the late Sir William Mackinnon came to the rescue with £50, and smaller sums made up the total to £1,000 10s. 4d.

How a few hundred pounds in addition were raised for an attempt to travel in Tibet proper will be found stated in Chapter XLVIII., on "Plans Concerning Lassa." Meanwhile, my purse being made up, I learned from the Russian Embassy that, in the event of my wishing to travel by the Trans-Caspian railway, it would be wise on my part, instead of proceeding there direct, to go for permission to St Petersburg, which accordingly I proceeded to do.

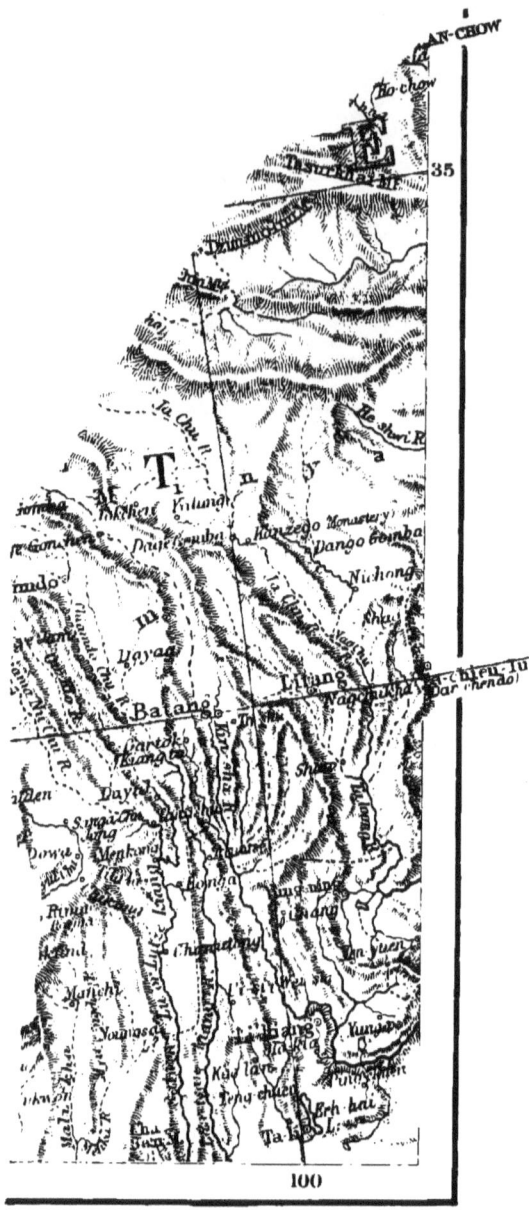

CHINESE CENTRAL ASIA:

A RIDE TO LITTLE TIBET.

CHAPTER I.

FROM LONDON TO MOSCOW.

The start, and Author's forebodings, 1.—Delayed arrival at Berlin; Visit to the Chinese Embassy, 2.—Custom-house at Wirballen; Arrival at St Petersburg, and objects of visit; Request to travel by Trans-Caspian Railway, 3.—Calls on Sir Robert Morier and M. Pobedonostzeff; Acceptance by Emperor of *Through Central Asia*, 4.—Promise of help from Minister of Interior; Scientists visited; Social gatherings, and dinner at Embassy, 5.—Visit to M. Vlangali, Assistant-Minister for Foreign Affairs; Reception by Prince Dondukoff-Korsakoff, and recommendation to General Annenkoff; Visit to the Minister for War, 6.—My programme, 8.—Meeting with General Kostenko, 9.—Departure for Moscow; Travelling acquaintances, Dr Alexéef and Count Bobrinsky, junr, 10.—Arrival in Moscow, and call on Count Leo Tolstoi, 11.—Departure southwards, 12.

IT was a dirty night on February 19th, 1888, when I left London for St Petersburg; and my spirits were somewhat in harmony with my environment. I did not forget, when planning to enter Bokhara, that Stoddart and Conolly, the last Englishmen there, had been put to death by the Emir, and now I was meditating Kashgar, where Schlagintweit had by order of the ruler been killed. I will not say that I had anything so strong as a foreboding that such might be my own fate; but I acted as if it were to be, and so arranged my home affairs as if I were never to return, hoping, of course, for the best.

Friday night is the time for packing off the Indian mail. This delayed us at Cannon Street; and the rough state of the Channel after a hurricane increased the delay, so that we arrived at Calais to find the express gone, and the ground covered with snow. Slow trains, and waiting at Cologne, brought me early on Sunday morning, instead of Saturday, as planned, to Berlin. This was to be my first halting-place, for here I hoped to see Hung Ta-jen, the Chinese Minister.

Going on Sunday evening to St George's English Church, where they pounced upon me to preach, I was not a little surprised to see in the porch, and afterwards at the service, a Chinaman in full costume and pigtail, who, though not a member of the Legation, gave me sundry pieces of minor information anent thereto, and I drove there on Monday morning by appointment.

A change had been made only a few weeks previously in the Chinese diplomatic arrangements. Formerly, the Minister who resided in London looked also after Chinese interests at St Petersburg, and the Minister at Paris had Berlin under his charge. Now London and Paris are under one diplomatic Minister, and Berlin and St Petersburg under another.

I therefore showed his Excellency what had been given me by the Minister in London, told him what I received when going to Kuldja before, and said that as I was now about to pass through Russia, to which he had been recently accredited, I begged of him also a letter, and if possible an open one. An open letter, he observed, was not necessary—my passport would be sufficient—but he would give me a letter to the Governor-General of Ili. The ambassadorial seal on this, he said, would be useful, and it should be sent to me on the morrow.

On the day following the promised letter arrived by the hand of an English-speaking servant, and I left the Central Hotel in Berlin the same night for Russia. My luggage, having been booked through to St Petersburg, had preceded me, and I wrote from Cologne to the officials of the Russian Custom-house explaining why my baggage would appear without its owner.

On arriving, therefore, at Wirballen, I was expected, and met with nothing but smiles and every possible assistance, which was very gratifying, seeing that I had more than 3 cwt of luggage in eight cases, the extra carriage of which had already cost me more than half the price of my ticket. Besides these eight packages I had sent 19 others by sea to Batoum. Thus my total luggage weighed already 16 cwt.

Most English travellers rush from the German frontier to the Russian capital without breaking the journey. I did the same three times without knowing what I lost thereby. On the present occasion, after travelling through the night, I determined to stop for a day at Pskoff, which I did, and arrived at eight o'clock on the following morning at St Petersburg.

The objects that took me to the Russian capital might be termed diplomatic, administrative, and financial. The first thing to be asked for, and that of prime importance, was permission to travel as far as possible towards Kuldja by the new Trans-Caspian railway. Not that this was the only way of reaching Kuldja from St Petersburg, for there was the summer route of rail, river, and road by which I proceeded there before, and the post route, through Orenburg and the Syr-daria province; but on both these routes frost and snow were now supreme. Accordingly, a few hours after my arrival, I called at the British Embassy, and found Sir Robert Morier ready to help in every way.

I had, besides, the advantage of acquaintance with his Excellency M. Pobedonostzeff, the Chief Procurator of the Holy Synod. To this gentleman I drove next, and received a welcome. He had seen my *Through Central Asia*, then recently published; and, the Emperor having intimated his pleasure to accept a copy, I told the Procurator I had brought it to St Petersburg.

The proper person through whom the presentation should have been made was the Minister for Foreign Affairs, but M. Pobedonostzeff volunteered, without further ceremony, to send the copy direct. I forwarded it to him that afternoon; it was sent to the palace in the evening, and at midnight his Majesty sent to M. Pobedonostzeff a kind message of appreciative thanks. As for my needed permissions, M. Pobedonostzeff handed me over to his assistant, M. Sabler, the Secretary to the Synod, and on the morrow we set to work with a will.

I called, alone, on M. Plevé, Assistant to the Minister of the Interior, who, if I did not remember him, speedily showed that he had not forgotten me; for, opening a drawer, he drew forth my portrait, which I had presented to him when, six years before, he was in the police department. He was good enough to say that he appreciated my works on Russia as of scientific value, promised me another open letter such as I had been furnished with on previous occasions, and added that he would write to the several departments and do all he could to forward my wish to travel by the new railway.

I had also to call on sundry persons—scientific, literary, and otherwise—for introductions, information, and advice. Dr Bretschneider, who spent many years at the Russian Legation in Peking, has published several interesting books on the geography of Central Asia as known to the Chinese in mediæval times. I was glad, therefore, to call upon this savant and sinologue, and talk of some of the places I was about to visit.

Running hither and thither left little time for sight-seeing or social intercourse. I was present one evening at a meeting of the Imperial Geographical Society, which was well attended, for public meetings in Russia are rare; but it struck me as tame and somewhat gloomy by comparison with the gatherings of our Geographical Society in London.

On another evening I dined at the British Embassy, where Sir Robert Morier was rejoicing in an exceptionally able Russian-speaking staff. Amongst the party I met Lord (now the Duke of) Fife and Colonel Herbert, the Military attaché, a Mr Harford, and some others. Sir Robert promised to get me official letters to the Russian consuls at Kuldja and Kashgar, and to add one from himself to Governor-General Rosenbach at Tashkend. From various other sources also promises of introductions were received, and my way was becoming clearer, though I dared not yet take for granted that I might do all I wished in proceeding by the Trans-Caspian railway.

A few days after seeing M. Plevé, I had taken a letter from M. Sabler to M. Vlangali, the Assistant-Minister for Foreign Affairs, who asked me to write definitely what I wanted, and he would then try to get me the needed permissions. Accordingly, in addition to the railway journey, I asked that, if it should for any reason seem desirable, after entering Chinese Turkistan, for me to return to Russia instead of proceeding south to India, I might have the option of crossing the Pamirs into Ferghana.

Some thought that in this I had asked a hard thing and had better withdraw it, since no Englishman had, up to that time, been allowed so to do; and no answer coming for a day or two, I feared this might partly account for the silence; but soon it seemed that the carriage for the Minister of War blocked the way, inasmuch as he had not answered M. Plevé's letter.

M. Plevé had, however, heard favourably from Prince Dondukoff-Korsakoff, then Lieutenant of the Caucasus, as to my crossing the Caspian, and as the Prince happened to be staying, as I was, at the Hôtel d'Angleterre, I waited on him. He had lately been reading my *Through Siberia*, gave me an excellent reception, and promised all I asked for; told me whom to see at Tiflis; and for General Annenkoff, the constructor of the Trans-Caspian line, he gave me his card with the following words thereon: "*Prince Dondukoff-Korsakoff, Aide-de-Camp Général, recommande chaleureusement à la bienveillance et aux soins du Général Annenkoff, Dr Lansdell si connu par ses voyages, et ses sympathies pour la Russie.*"

I then went all in a glow to General Obrucheff, the

Chief of the Staff of the Minister for War, but was received at first, I thought, with martial rigour and without a smile or anything that savoured of the milk of human kindness, being formally and coldly asked what I wanted. Having briefly replied, I was told

GENERAL L. M. ANNENKOFF.

that I must make out my line of march, since it might be necessary in some places to divert my course. I had never before been asked to do such a thing, and did not know whether to suspect a trap wherein to catch and defeat my plans, or the furnishing a clue whereby my steps might be watched.

I was conducted through room after room and passage after passage of that huge building the "Etat Major" to what I now suppose was the head office of the Asiatic section, where, among several officers, I was seated at a table with paper and pens that revived the long-passed anxieties of college examinations.

I thought it would not do to be too general in my statements, lest vagueness should leave room for suspicion that I was keeping something in the background, nor too minute, lest, if I did not hereafter keep exactly to the programme, I might be charged with breaking faith. So I wrote as follows—

"St Petersburg, *February 23rd, March 6th,* 1888.

"I expect to leave St Petersburg to-morrow, or soon after, for Moscow; to stay not more than a week (for banking arrangements, etc.), then proceed direct to Batoum; from Batoum to Tiflis (stay 2 or 3 days), then to Baku and Askhabad (stay 1 or 2 days, perhaps), Merv (2 or 3 days), Charjui (1 or 2 days, to get, if possible, fishes, pheasants, etc., for specimens), Bokhara (about a week, to see places once again that I visited in 1882), Samarkand (3 or 4 days), Tashkend (about a week, to purchase various necessaries), Vierny (2 or 3 days, to receive my luggage, sent forward from Batoum), Kuldja. I hope to arrive at Kuldja by May 1st (N.S.), and at Urumtsi by June 1st (N.S.), there to meet my English interpreter into Chinese. If news reaches me that he arrives earlier, I shall hasten forwards; if I learn that he will come later, then I need not go through Turkistan quite so fast. I should like to arrive at Yarkand by September 1st, and cross the

Himalayas, and it is only in case of accident, sickness, or something important and unforeseen, that I should wish to return to Russia from Kashgar to Ferghana.

"(*Signed*) HENRY LANSDELL, D.D."

This declaration had now to be translated into Russian by one of the officers present, and I meanwhile had time to breathe and observe, though my spirits were not high. Every face was strange to me, but one officer in a general's uniform spoke as if I were not entirely unknown to him. He was short in stature, sallow in complexion, and I could not make out whether I was speaking to one who had power to decide the matter, or whether he was collecting and preparing information about me to submit to a council, presumably sitting in the adjoining room.

Presently something revealed his name—Kostenko—and my thermometer began to rise. Could it be, I asked, the author of *The Turkistan Region*, whose book, whilst I was writing *Russian Central Asia*, was scarcely out of my hands? It was the very same, and I saw one whom, quite apart from the present business, it gave me the greatest delight to meet, for we were fellow-writers upon the same ground. He recognised me as such, knew my volumes, told me he was chief of the Asiatic section, and volunteered that if I got into any difficulty I might telegraph to him.

My spirits now were jubilant, and spread to the officers near; for when they became acquainted with my projected journey one of them said they were quite excited. What was better, they brought in Captain Grombchevsky, who had recently made the journey from Kashgar to Khokand, and who gave me much pertinent information.

Looking round, I noticed on the wall a map of the region about the head-waters of the Oxus, and comprising much of the territory I was going to. It was newer and better than any I had seen, and like a spoiled child I wanted it, and asked where a similar one could be purchased. I was told that " it was not on sale," being, I suppose, " secret and confidential." Some whispering, however, went on between one and another, and then I was asked to accept a copy, which I congratulate myself upon possessing.

It was presently intimated that the letter desired would be given, and thus before I left the " Etat Major" I had received all I had asked for, and more than all, for General Mirkhovitz favoured me with an invitation I gladly accepted for the morrow, to meet Madame Mirkhovitz, and see from the windows of the House of the Staff a parade of troops before the Emperor.

On the day following, March 9th, after taking luncheon with Princess Lieven, who had heard of my being in St Petersburg, and sought me out at the Bible Society, I left for Moscow.

" A good name " Solomon affirms to be better than riches, and a fellow-passenger in the train seeing mine on the label of my portmanteau, forthwith claimed acquaintance on the ground that when recently in England he was to have had an introduction to me.

This little incident gave me a pleasant travelling companion and occasional interpreter; my fellow-passenger being Dr P. Alexéef, who had lately been studying the temperance question in America, and in England had heard of me at the Church of England Temperance Society.

On being addressed by another passenger in the

same carriage, a young soldier in uniform, I asked where he had learned such excellent English.

"Near Edinburgh," said he.

"Why, then," I replied, "you must be one of the sons of Count Bobrinsky?" to which he answered in the affirmative, but appeared rather surprised till I gave my name, and mentioned my having met his family in London.

The young Count and some of his sisters were on their way to a wedding in the family of Count Leo Tolstoi, upon whom Dr Alexéef proposed that we should call to talk upon matters teetotal.

Accordingly, after a somewhat uncomfortable night in a second-class sleeping carriage, we reached Moscow, and I accompanied my friend to the study of the novelist, who recently had taken up the temperance crusade and was trying to work it in Russia, where, notwithstanding the crying need of it, the movement has reached only to the stage at which it remained some years in England, when silly people dismissed the matter with a laugh or a sneer, but failed to recognise their lack of philanthropy and self-denial in doing nothing to oppose a curse which ruins so many.

Understanding that I was going to Chinese Turkistan to circulate the Scriptures, the Count said he envied my work and would gladly go too, but for his wife and a dozen or so of children, some of whom we presently met round the family *samovar*; and thus finished a pleasant visit to the house of this celebrated Russian nobleman.

On the next day I preached at the English Church, and on Monday was no more successful than I had been in St Petersburg in making banking arrangements for Kashgar. I determined, therefore, to push forward on the Tuesday, but news came that the line southwards was snow-blocked.

The same afternoon, on the introduction of Madame Alexéef, I drank tea with Princess Mestchertsky, and afterwards had some hours of quiet rest, for, sooth to say, the incessant strain upon mind and body of the previous three months, in preparing, planning, and packing, had sent me away from London much fatigued. Then, what with the excessive cold, continued worries, and the water of the capital relaxing my physical powers still more, I reached Moscow so weak and weary that I requested Dr Alexéef to prescribe for me.

He, however, said there was nothing organically wrong, that my condition was merely the result of fatigue and change of atmosphere, and that with less strain recovery would soon follow, which, I am thankful to say, was speedily the case.

CHAPTER II.

FROM MOSCOW TO THE CASPIAN.

Railway dangers ahead; Pleasant fellow-passengers, and offers of hospitality, 13.—Arrival at Kursk; Arrival and enforced stoppage at Kharkof, 14.—Former visit to town prison, 15.—Departure from Kharkof, and arrival in Crimea, 16.—Improved weather at Sevastopol; Sunday service, 17.—Departure for Batoum; H.B.M. Consul; Departure across Caucasus, and arrival at Tiflis; Sir Drummond Wolff and Col. Stewart; Presentation of introductory letters, 18.—Dr Radde and M. Hedjouboff; Departure from Tiflis to Baku, 20.

WHEN ready to journey southwards to the Crimea, there were afloat ugly rumours and warnings of trains being stopped and snowed up for days together, to the great inconvenience of passengers not provisioned for such little emergencies. I therefore looked to the commissariat, and as a concession to my jaded condition indulged in a first-class ticket, which took me away from Moscow at all events in comfort, a snowstorm notwithstanding.

One of my fellow-passengers was a pleasant Russian lady, daughter of an ambassador, who in the course of the day not only offered help in translation, but before we parted invited me to pay her a visit at her country house. This generously offered hospitality was of a piece with that I had received on the same line on a previous occasion, when happening, near Tula, to meet Prince Dmitry Obolensky; and it is illustrative of the kindness with which educated Russians hasten to receive an English stranger.

From Moscow Tula is only 120 miles distant, but this took us at least six hours to accomplish. We passed through a uniform undulating plain, traversed by low hills with little wood, and no remarkable scenery, but having boundless cornfields and meadows, for the province is one of the best cultivated and most populous in the empire. The chief railway stations are Podolsk and Serpukhov, the latter possessing a large river traffic, some tanneries, and calico works.

We were timed to arrive at the station of Tula about six o'clock in the afternoon, and allowed a quarter of an hour for refreshment, after which I set about making myself comfortable for the night. In this there was every prospect of success, for I had the compartment all to myself, and it was furnished in a manner than which we have nothing better, if so good, in England. Our next important stopping-place was Orel, passed in the middle of the night, and early next morning I awoke to find that we were at Kursk, but only about 350 miles from Moscow, the train being shunted into a siding because the road some few stations beyond was blocked by snow.

On arriving at Kharkof, which was only 150 miles from Kursk, but took about eight hours, it was announced that no trains were yet running southwards, which did not greatly disappoint me, for I was glad of an enforced stoppage, and drove to the Hôtel de l'Europe.

My numerous packages were somewhat suggestive perhaps of commercial pursuits, since, on asking for a room, the waiter took me to a huge, grandly furnished apartment, which I said was too large.

"But," said the man, evidently mistaking me for a commercial traveller, "will you not want to exhibit your patterns?"

He then appeared quite disappointed at not letting his show-room, and landed me in a much less pretentious chamber, where I determined on the morrow to read, write, and rest.

Kharkof has a population of 160,000, of whom I presume an appreciable number must be Germans, since I remember, on a previous visit, attending the Lutheran Church and calling upon the pastor. It was during that same visit, on my way to the Caucasus, that I first made the acquaintance of Prince Dondukoff-Korsakoff. He was at that time Governor-General, and gave me permission to visit the town prison and distribute copies of the Scriptures.*

* My notes, taken on the spot, record "352 prisoners in 48 rooms, including 22 cells. Cells of political prisoners (of whom there were 29 under trial) are large; food and accommodation better than in the case of criminals; and politicals have more than one hour a day for exercise. The amount of daily bread for each prisoner is two and a half pounds, Russian. *Kvas*, or small beer, is allowed *ad libitum*."

In the punishment ward were five men, who a few days previously had attempted to escape, by making a ladder of their bedding with which they scaled the wall close to a sentry, who was also under arrest. One of those under correction came to the door, and through the hole in it spat at us defiantly.

Corporal punishment was not allowed, the dark cell being the severest form of correction, and even that might not extend beyond six days. The sick list stood at 52, but I am not sure whether this might not have represented the remnants of a former *régime*, inasmuch as they spoke of none now being there for a longer term than three years.

My notes mention no library or books for the prisoners. Probably I found none, and as a friend of mine had offered to bear the expense, I asked the General if he would allow me to place a copy of the New Testament in each room of every prison under his charge. He thanked me for the proposal, entered readily into my plans, asked me to write

I was attempting nothing of this kind in Kharkof on the present occasion, and did not leave the hotel until the next evening, when it was announced that the line farther south was cleared.

Kharkof is at the head of three main routes to the Sea of Azof, to Odessa, and the Crimea; but no trains had been running south for several days. It was not surprising, therefore, that on reaching the station confusion prevailed. I asked for a ticket for Sevastopol, and, without looking carefully at what was given me, handed it to the baggage clerk, whereupon it was discovered only just in time that my luggage was registered for Rostoff, and put in a train which was on the point of departure. This would have separated me and my belongings, on our respective arrivals, a trifle of 400 miles, and perhaps delayed me a week, so that I was not a little thankful to get the mistake rectified.

At length I found myself in a through sleeping carriage to the Black Sea. The distance to be traversed was nearly 500 miles, through a dull, flat, snow-covered country without a station of interest until we reached Baghchiserai, a name which calls to mind the days when the Tatars of Central Asia pushed their conquests into Russia, and made also the Crimea their own.

my wishes and directions, which he promised to see carried out, and then volunteered, for some reason I did not understand, to publish my letter in the Journals.

It only remained, therefore, to calculate the number required. He was Governor-General of six provinces or more, in which were six Government or capital towns, with 150 rooms in each for what we should call county prisoners, besides which there were 200 rooms for Government prisoners. Altogether, therefore, I sent to him on the following day, for his prisons and hospitals, 2,700 tracts, pictures, and journals, and ordered to follow 1,500 New Testaments.

Although the line south of this was clear of snow, the train was six hours late; but we were entering a milder climate. My seven previous visits to Russia had all been in summer, and I had looked forward with pleasure to seeing St Petersburg in its winter dress. Perhaps in my fatigued condition I did not do so to advantage; at any rate experience compels me to pronounce one winter visit enough, and it was a relief, when awaking the next morning but one in the Crimea, to be able to look once more upon Mother Earth, whose face had been snow-veiled all the way from Calais, now 3,000 miles in the rear.

Abundance of mud and water covered the plains, but as we approached the lofty rocks of Inkerman surroundings improved, and the air of Sevastopol was so balmy as to render agreeable a drive through the dry streets in an open carriage with one's fur coat thrown open.

Happening to pass our Consulate, and thinking it was Saturday morning, it occurred to me to call on Captain Harford, with whom I was acquainted, and offer to conduct a service on the morrow. I was a day out in my reckoning, however, for it was already Sunday, but it was early, and whilst I went to the hotel and made preparations, notice was sent round by Mr Grierson, the British Pro-Consul, with the result of gathering a congregation of about 20 persons, who met at the Consulate.

An English service is a rare thing in Sevastopol, there being no chaplain, and it was entered into with a zest that spoke of appreciation. I was, however, told of one stumbling-block to a larger attendance—namely, that English steamers come into port and employ labour on Sundays; for some London firms, who would not dream of opening their offices or employing their clerks in the "City" on a Sunday, do permit their captains when abroad to do so. It is proper, however, to add that in some cases the captains themselves are at fault, and act thus in direct contravention to their employers' orders.

On the third day after my arrival at Sevastopol, Mr Grierson, having laden me with such things as I had need of, accompanied me with his wife and little ones to the ship. We left the port about eleven in the morning, and by five in the afternoon reached Yalta, which I had seen before, so that I was not tempted to land; but on reaching Kertch on the following afternoon, I found time to call on our Consul, Mr Hunt (whom I had met at Odessa in 1882), and to telegraph my coming to Batoum, where we arrived, after a run of about 36 hours, early on Friday morning, March 23rd.

The first person to meet me was my servant Joseph, who had come from London by steamer with the heavy baggage. Soon after Joseph came Mr D. R. Peacock, at that time the Vice-Consul, and whose brother I had met in Siberia. If pleasure had been my pursuit, Mr Peacock would have prevailed upon me to visit a native (I think Ghurian) prince at his castle in the mountains, to whom he had mentioned my coming. But I felt obliged to content myself with a view of Batoum, its picturesque mountains with verdant slopes, its naphtha stores and oil waggons, and the native bazaars.

Next morning we started for Tiflis, and having reached our destination late on Saturday evening, we put up at the Hôtel de Londres, where I was glad to find my friend Colonel Stewart, and Sir Drummond

Wolff and suite, on the way to take up their respective appointments in Persia. Like myself, they were seeking information as to the movements of steamers on the Caspian; and finding that I had four days to wait, it seemed better to remain at the capital than to go forward to Baku.

The number of Englishmen at Tiflis was less than I had seen on the previous Sunday at Sevastopol, and they have no Sunday service in English, so we had one in the hotel; and I visited in the afternoon a German Bible-class, attended by a dozen youths and conducted by a Swede named Hoijer, to whom I had an introduction from Finland.

I had also a dozen introductions to other persons in Tiflis. On the chance of my meeting Russian officers with whom they had served on the Afghan Boundary Commission, Sir West Ridgeway and Colonel Holdich had given me letters, and these brought me into contact with Colonel Paul Kuhlberg, Chief of the Topographical Staff, who seemed to cherish a pleasant recollection of his English comrades, and by whose help I got some excellent maps of the Trans-Caspian region.

He kindly invited me to meet General Zelenoy, another celebrity in connection with the Afghan Boundary Commission, and General Jdanow, Chief of the *Etat Major*, at dinner. These gentlemen were much interested in my projected journey to Chinese Turkistan, and wished to bespeak a paper from me, if I came back that way, at the Tiflis branch of the Imperial Geographical Society.

Prince Dondukoff-Korsakoff, Lieutenant of the Caucasus, had desired me to call upon his *locum tenens*, General Sheremetieff, which I did, and I was also successful in finding at home Dr Radde, the founder and curator of the excellent and well-arranged Tiflis Museum.

Dr Radde was kind enough to give me sundry hints as to what I might hope to do in collecting specimens of fauna, and I was indebted also for various attentions and assistance to M. George Hedjouboff, an Armenian, to whom I had an introduction.

I took occasion before leaving Tiflis to purchase of the Bible Society a few copies of the Scriptures in Hebrew. I also found an agreeable photographer in M. Yermakoff, who accompanied me to make a trial of my apparatus, and developed for me the negatives with such success as gave me hope for the future, when, beyond the Caspian, I should be thrown on my own resources.

We left Tiflis a little before ten on Friday night for Baku, expecting to cover 340 miles in 17 hours—not a furious rate of travelling, but quick in comparison with the four days required for the journey in 1882, when, before the line was open to the public, I travelled the distance in a horse-box. That journey, however, gave opportunities for seeing the country which darkness now denied.

For the last 50 miles of the way the train runs along the coast of the Caspian, for the most part through a desert, in the midst of which we reached Baku, about three o'clock on Saturday afternoon.

CHAPTER III.

FROM THE CASPIAN TO MERV.

"Wanted" by the Police-master; Call on the Governor, 21.—Comforts on steamer to Uzun Ada; Landing at railway terminus, 22.—Trans-Caspian stations to oasis of Akhal Tekke, 25.—Kizil Arvat, 26.—Arrival at Geok Tepe, 28.—My coming to Askhabad expected, 30.—Continuation of journey to Dushak, 32.—Arrival at Merv, 35.—Hospitality of Colonel Alikhanoff; Modern Merv, 36.—Oriental carpets and embroidery, 37.—Alikhanoff's successful administration; Quiet and order of Panjdeh, 38.—A visit to Old Merv, 39.—Ruins on site of Merv; Arab and Persian remains, 41.—Russian annexation of Merv, 43.—How brought about, 44.—Liberation of slaves, 46.

THERE was little to detain us at Baku, for I had previously seen its oil wells and the temple of the fire-worshippers. Notice came, however, to the Grand Hotel that, my passport having been sent to the authorities, the police-master required to see me. Now I had heard of this man, rightly or wrongly, that he was obstructive to English travellers, and apt to give them trouble; so I thought it better to take the wind out of his sails by paying a visit to his chief, which I accordingly did, and received from the acting Governor, M. Osit Augustovitch Beneslavsky, a welcome, and an invitation to dinner.

As Sir Drummond Wolff and Colonel Stewart, moreover, were expected to arrive in the afternoon and start at night by steamer, they were also to be invited. "Ask them to come," said the Governor, "*sans cérémonie—en petit costume de voyage.*" Neither of the travellers, however, was thus to be seduced in the midst of a journey to something like a dinner-party. I had therefore to go alone, and found myself the only guest.

The local authorities were very obliging in providing on the steamer for the comfort of the English travellers. The Ambassador's party was proceeding south to Resht, and most, if not all, of the berths being taken, some Russian passengers were, I believe, invited to give up to the foreigners the accommodation which, by priority of arrival, they had secured, whilst, in my own case—proceeding east—I was accommodated, thanks to the Governor's introduction, with a cabin for three. The passage across the Caspian, in good weather, takes only 20 hours for the 195 miles between Baku and Uzun Ada, where we arrived on Tuesday at noon.

In my *Russian Central Asia* four chapters are devoted to Turkmenia, so that for the general characteristics of the country it may here suffice to say that the train runs, from the Caspian to the Oxus, through a desert that is enlivened by the four oases of Akhal, Attek, Tejend, and Merv.

Uzun Ada, or "Long Island," is the terminus at which the traveller arrives on the Caspian littoral, and a more desolate landing-place I never beheld. Siberia is a paradise to it. Nevertheless, one fellow-passenger, looking on the bright side of things, observed to me that less than ten years ago there was nothing on the island but sand, whereas now there is a harbour, a railway station, reservoirs of naphtha, a church, hospital, doctor's residence, and a few houses, these last having been imported ready-made from Russia.

Not a blade of grass could I see, though it was now the beginning of April, and two cows, wandering amongst the water-carts near an enclosure behind the station, suggested the reflection that, under similar circumstances in England, they might be " run in " by the police for going about " without any visible means of support."

The train was not to start for six hours, but carriages were sent to the shore end of the jetty to take passengers and luggage, there being no lack of Tatar porters. I had heard at Tiflis of the prodigious strength of these men, and at Baku one of them gave proof of it by carrying on his back to the ship four of my packages, weighing 2½ cwt, and then taking in his hand a bag of ½ cwt more.

At the station I fell at once on my feet, and received the first of a succession of kindnesses and acts of attention, that continued in Asiatic Russia till I passed beyond the frontier.

Showing the letter of the Minister of the Interior to a military officer on the platform, he bowed himself "*votre serviteur*," as he meant to say ; but, his French being rather shaky, he substituted "*votre domestique*," and immediately assigned me for my three days' journey a small compartment to myself, nor would he allow me to be displaced when the conductor of the train wished to turn me out in favour of some of his friends.

We started about six in the evening, the train crossing an embankment, about three-quarters of a mile long, which connects the island with the mainland, and then plunged into the desert, the chief

UZUN ADA, THE WESTERN TERMINUS OF THE TRANS-CASPIAN RAILWAY.

feature of which is sand, sand everywhere, without water or food for man or beast.

At the first station, Mikhailovsk, at the head of Balkan Bay, which was formerly the starting-point of the line, and whither passengers were brought in craft of light draught from Krasnovodsk, we reached the Uzboi, one of the old beds by which the Oxus entered the Caspian. The railway skirts this channel for about 30 miles.

At the next station, Mulla Kara, we passed from sand to an alluvial plain, and at the fourth station, Bala Ishem, large tuns on wheels reminded us that enormous quantities of water were distilled from the brine of the Caspian at Mikhailovsk, and sent along the line to the waterless districts, whilst at the same place we were also reminded, by naphtha tanks or trucks, like steam boilers on wheels, that the fuel of our engine was not coal or wood, but petroleum refuse, which is brought to Bala Ishem from oil wells in the neighbourhood.

Near this place is a salt marsh, some 15 miles long by half as broad, and also a salt station on the branch line between Bala Ishem and the naphtha wells. The night was passed in crossing this alluvial desert, which was without inhabitants, even at the stations, other than the railway officials. It is also without water, except at the little village of Kazandjik, where there is a potable spring and a little verdure.

And thus we went on for 140 miles to Ushak, where the small station is surmounted by a tower of observation, and where we arrived at sunrise. Here the Muhammadans got out of the train to wash themselves and pray, whilst the lark rose in the heavens, as the poets will have it, to sing his hymn.

was somewhat like that of the lily of the valley; but the villages, dependent on rivulets at the foot of

From a photograph by] [Gov.-Gen. Komaroff.
A BROKEN ICE-HOUSE ON THE PERSIAN FRONTIER.

the mountains, were remote from the line and few and far between.

Passing three more stations brought us to the vicinity of Durun, where there are a very unpretending telegraph station, something between a Russian *izba* and a Turkoman tent, and a ruined Tekke village of mud houses, which gave a good idea of the local native dwellings, the domed roofs being so constructed probably for coolness, as are the huge domes erected

THE STATION AT GEOK TEPE.

over the ice-cellars, several of which may be seen in approaching the Persian frontier.

Soon after midday we arrived at Geok Tepe, where the train stopped long enough to allow of my scaling the walls of the famous fortress whose defenders offered such stubborn resistance to Skobeleff. The wall in some places is completely broken down, but enough remains to show what crude ideas of fortification the Turkomans possessed.

Imagine a bank of earth 30 feet thick, finished on

the top with breast-high inner and outer walls, and running for nearly three miles round a quadrilateral area like that of Hyde Park or Blackheath, but without their verdure, and you will have some idea of the proportions of the "fortress" of Geok Tepe. Many

TEKKE FORTRESS OF GEOK TEPE, SHOWING THE HOLES IN WHICH THE TURKOMANS HID THEMSELVES FOR PROTECTION FROM THE RUSSIAN MISSILES.

holes were still visible, made perhaps by Russian shells, or dug by the besieged as hiding-places from the balls of the besiegers; but there was not a structure or building of any kind within. I saw there only a few camels grazing on the scanty herbage kept alive by a brook

Beyond Geok Tepe the train passed through a somewhat richer country, and about four in the afternoon we reached Askhabad.

Askhabad is the capital of the Trans-Caspian province, a place, it is said, of 10,000 inhabitants, including perhaps the soldiery, for whom there is a military club and garden.

The market-place is exposed to the full glare of the sun, but affords the visitor an opportunity of studying

RAILWAY STATION AT ASKHABAD.

Russian and native life together, whilst not far distant is a Persian ice-cellar, built of rammed mud in the form of a cone, such as I have not observed in other countries.

My coming to Askhabad was expected, officially—probably, privately—certainly; for on the evening of my departure from Tiflis M. George Nicolaivitch Milutin, entering the hotel and seeing my name on the guest-board, wondered if it were that of the author whose book he had read.

Seating himself at a dinner-table near me, and scanning my countenance hard, he presently ventured to introduce himself, saying that he should invite me to drink wine with him, only that he had read that I was an abstainer, and telling me that he had been engaged on General Annenkoff's staff on the Trans-Caspian railway.

On learning that it was for that very region I was to start in an hour or two, his friendliness at once rose

GARDEN OF THE MILITARY CLUB, ASKHABAD.

to the emergency. "I will telegraph," said he, "to my friends to assist you"; and, then and there, he drafted a despatch to Colonel Alikhanoff and Count Mouravieff at Merv, to General Annenkoff and others of his friends, named Kulkevitch and Sabouroff, saying, "The celebrated traveller Lansdell is leaving Tiflis to-night for the Trans-Caspian region; please help him."

This unexpected and unsought kindness, in addition

to other introductions, bore ample fruit, and I found awaiting me at the Askhabad station Colonel Levashoff, the acting Governor, who had brought to meet me a countrywoman, Mrs Harfeld, married to a Russian officer on the line, and a Finnish gentleman, M. Carl Constantinovitch von Schultz, Controller-in-Chief of the Trans-Caspian railway.

According to my official programme written at St Petersburg, I expected to stay two or three days at Askhabad, and they had prepared accordingly; but I afterwards determined to push on, and so my friends did the next best thing by giving me a capital dinner at the station, which is of first rank and European proportions, and sped me forward, telegraphing my approach to Colonel Alikhanoff at Merv.

About eight miles from Askhabad the train passes a fine old ruined mosque at Anau, and over a tongue of sand to Giaurs, which may be regarded as the end of the Akhal oasis.

Then we traversed an alluvial desert to Baba-Durmaz, between which and the next station, Artyk, lies, somewhat to the north, a salt tract. Over a portion of this the train passes, and enters beyond Artyk the Attek oasis.

Stretching along the Persian mountains as far as Sarakhs, the Attek, though not so long as the oasis we had traversed, is greener and less bare of trees. Its chief town is Luftabad, and there is a considerable ruin at Shilgan, whilst the ardent lover of antiquity who will make a pilgrimage to Sarakhs will be shown the tomb of Cain.

The sixth stopping-place beyond Askhabad is Dushak; at present only a station with a few dwellings for the officials and workmen and a pile or two of firewood, but which has a certain importance in British minds because, situated at 400 miles from

THE TOMB OF CAIN AT SARAKHS.

the Caspian, it is the nearest point to our Indian railways, the distance from Dushak to the Afghan frontier being only as far as from London to Doncaster.*

The line had run from the Caspian nearly straight to the south-west, but at Dushak turned at a sharp angle to the east, leaving the mountains in the rear,

STATION AT DUSHAK, THE FARTHEST POINT SOUTH, WHENCE THE RAILWAY MAY BE CONTINUED TO THE AFGHAN FRONTIER.

and passing from the Attek oasis to that of the Tejend.

* On my way homeward through India I ran up to Quetta and pushed on to New Chaman, beyond the Khojak tunnel, to the extreme end of the Indian line, on the southern frontier of Afghanistan; whence to the northern frontier just mentioned is about 500 miles, or the distance from London to Aberdeen.

At last, after passing over an uncultivated district for nearly 50 miles, towards the station Karab-Ata, we entered the oasis of Merv. Here daylight found us on the morning of the third day from the Caspian; and at length, about half-past eight, we steamed into Merv station.

The commercial and native parts of the town are situated on the left bank of the Murghab, where also

NEW BRIDGE AT MERV.

is the railway station and its buildings. On the right bank is the Turkoman inclosure called Kaushid Khan Kala, within which are a dozen houses of brick, occupied by civil and military officers, a temporary church, and barracks.

The two portions are connected by a wooden railway bridge, 150 feet long, of about a dozen spans, the woodwork resting on piles driven into the sand; and across the bridge I drove in a station cab or phaeton through the wide opening in the fortress walls to the house of Colonel Alikhanoff, the Governor, or more accurately *Nachalnik*, or Chief of the District.

The Colonel was busy in his garden, in which he said he took great delight, though it had not long been planted. Then, taking me indoors, he pointed out that all his bedrooms were occupied, but that I should be welcome to such accommodation as he could offer, which was to be that of the best room in the house by night and the run of the premises by day.

Needless to say I thankfully accepted his hospitality; for though Merv possesses a third or fourth class establishment, decorated in front with the Persian Lion and Sun, and dubbed "The Imperial Hotel," yet I was only too pleased to stay for a day or two with a man of whom I had both written and read, and who played so important a part in bringing about the submission of the Mervis, and figured so prominently during the labours of the Afghan Boundary Commission.

The next acquaintance I made was Colonel Mouravieff, who took me off the same morning to the Turkoman bazaar, or market, then being held, where from 3,000 to 5,000 persons assemble twice a week, to deal in horses, asses, camels, and sheep.

We mounted the walls of the fortress, which is similar in character to that of Geok Tepe. After lunch we visited the town that has sprung up since the foreign occupation. I was much struck with the large number of drinking-places, the stock-in-trade of the distilleries, brandy, beer, and wine shops being more than double that of all the grocers, pastrycooks, bakers, butchers, and vendors of lemonade.*

One has a good opportunity to study certain features of native life in the caravanserais or native inns of Merv, where the men appear in sheepskin coats and hats, and occasionally mounted on good Turkoman horses, but more frequently on donkeys, their baggage being carried on Bactrian camels. I was delighted to find in the shops of Merv in April melons of the last season, some of which we took home for dessert to the Colonel's house.

Here I observed that the Colonel, Moslem though he was, provided wine for his guests, whilst abstaining himself. It seemed also somewhat paradoxical to hear him zealously advocating the building of a fine cathedral at Merv. "We have so many thousand roubles," he said, with the air of an enthusiastic member of a church building committee, "but we must have more, in order to erect such a building as will excite the admiration and respect of the natives."

To a connoisseur in carpets and embroidery my room was a perfect museum of Central Asian handiwork. The long wall facing the windows was covered in Oriental fashion with an immense Persian carpet, as was the broad divan running along it, whilst suspended

---

* The figures were given me as follows, in roubles :—

Manufacturers	205,000	Distillery	10,560
Brickmakers	62,070	Brandy shops	29,000
Bokhara manufacturers	150,000	Wine shops	82,000
Smallware shops	80,260	Beer shops	45,700
Iron shops	12,320	Eating-houses	52,800
Timber shops	36,000	Tea-houses	19,760
Transport Company	35,000	Inns	60,500
Grocers	30,670	Baths	18,000
Pastrycooks	8,500	Caravanserai	22,500
Bakers	18,000	Lodging-houses	7,800
Butchers	12,500		
Seltzer and lemonade	4,000	Roubles	1,002,940

from the cornice all round the room was an ornamental hanging of tassel work, specially made for the Colonel by the Sariks of Panjdeh. At the end where I slept the wall and divan were adorned with exquisite Tekke carpets and tent bands, with abundance of cushions of Bokhara velvet, displaying various specimens of Central Asian silk embroidery.

In excellent agreement with all this, each of the upper window curtains consisted of a rich Bokhariot saddle-cloth embroidered in silver and gold. The floor was covered with Persian carpets, and over the Colonel's study door were hangings of Indian embroidered silk.

But more interesting than these was their owner, who, fortunately for me, spoke French, and gave me a good deal of information concerning the affairs of Turkmenia. An Asiatic by descent, a Muhammadan by birth, and of the same religion as those over whom he rules, Colonel Alikhanoff appeared to be the right man in the right place. In a surprisingly short time he had reduced to order the most turbulent and blood-thirsty of the tribes of Central Asia. Not more than four or five cases of robbery a month, he told me, came before him, but sometimes as many as five or six murders—the frequent result of quarrels. He gave me several instances of his rough-and-ready fashion of administering punishments and rewards, by which he seemed to have quieted and gained the goodwill of the people.

In harmony with the foregoing was the testimony of a Russian Colonel who dined with us, and had ridden on the morning of the same day from Yulatan, on the Murghab, in the direction of Panjdeh, where he was administering a district of 30,000 persons, who quite recently were robbers and thieves by profession, but amongst whom he was living as the only European, and undefended, save by eight native *djiguitts*, or mounted attendants.

This Colonel told me that at Panjdeh he had entered some ancient catacombs of the fire-worshippers, dated back vaguely to the time of Zoroaster, one of them having receptacles for 200 bodies. Of these receptacles he saw 40, and showed me a sketch of the entrance to one of the catacombs.

The great event of the morrow was to be a drive to Old Merv, which for a traveller to omit is as culpable as to visit London and not see Westminster Abbey. For this the Colonel kindly ordered a carriage and mounted attendants, arranging that we should lunch on the way at the historic dwelling of Yusuf Khan, one of the four who negotiated the submission of Merv; and word was sent to his mother, in whose tent the critical meeting was held, that an Englishman desired the favour of an interview.

I was accompanied by Count Mouravieff and M. Guillaume, who was teaching the Colonel the French language, and in other ways making himself useful. It was a bright spring morning when we started, and pleasantly warm. A drive of two or three hours brought us to the *aul* or collection of tents of Yusuf, and whilst lunch was being prepared I looked about the premises and picked up information.

Presently we were regaled with a *dostarkhan*—that is, a tablecloth—and with something on it in the shape of meat, as well as (though tell it not in Mecca!) wine and *vodka* to drink. Lemonade, too, and tea were served, the tables being turned for the nonce, the Muhammadan drinking wine and the Christian water.

In the course of conversation it transpired that

Yusuf Khan, though only 20 years old, had under his authority 2,000 "souls" (that is to say, men, for the Russians do not reckon women as "souls"), with the rank of a Russian captain and pay of £120 a year. His mother, Gur Jemal, widow of Nur Verdi Khan, was enjoying a pension of £100 a year, and, in addition, she had received from the Emperor handsome presents of clothing and jewels.

Arrayed in these, she received us after lunch, and our eyes were dazzled by a *khalat*, or dress of silver and gold brocade, edged with sable fur. Her waistband was of gold and turquoise, and she wore a necklace of precious stones, as well as numerous rings; whilst her head was covered with three handkerchiefs.

Her age was said to be 47, but, like all Turkoman women thus far advanced, she appeared very much more—60 at the least, though her good looks had not quite left her. She had less to say than to show, behaved with becoming dignity, and on her thanking us for our visit, I felt glad to have been favoured with admission to the presence of a Turkoman lady.

She is considered rich, which Alikhanoff accounted for by her possessing a canal of water. "When," said he, "the Russians wished to reward me I received the first-class Cross of St George" (of which, by the way, I fancy he is the only man in the empire to possess two), "but when the Turkomans wished to recompense Gur Jemal they gave her not only acres of land, which are plentiful enough, but a canal of water to keep them fruitful." *

---

* Hence we see the propriety of Achsah asking of her father as dowry, not only a field, but springs to water it. Joshua xv. 18, 19; Judges i. 14, 15.

We had still some few miles to drive, our coachman being not too nice in the choice of his roads, where road indeed there was none. Our party was now increased by the Khan and several more *djiguitts*, who rushed forward to show and clear the way. Hitherto I had suspected that those words in the " Burial of Sir John Moore "—

"The sods with our bayonets turning,"

were a poet's trope, but on our way they were very closely illustrated; for, coming to a ditch deepened by recent rains, the *djiguitts* dismounted, turned their swords into spades, and speedily levelled the ground for our vehicle to pass. On nearer approach to the ruins we were provided with saddle horses, and in this way viewed the lions.

No less than four cities have flourished on or near the site of what is now called Old Merv. The most ancient is called Giaour Kala, and is said to date from the time of Zoroaster.

The ruins of the city next in antiquity are called Iskander Kala, after Alexander the Great, who made it one of his colonies. To this Merv Christianity was introduced about 200 A.D. It subsequently became the seat of an archbishop, and in 420 was made a metropolitan see. Of these two cities little now remains above ground except some high walls, though one cannot but surmise that the spade might bring to light some antiquarian treasures.

The third of the cities alluded to was built by the Arabs who conquered the place in the seventh century, and of this Merv, now called Sandjar Kala, there remain two or three monuments indicative of considerable greatness.

The structures mentioned are the chief survivors of the Arab city. In the sixteenth century the Persians

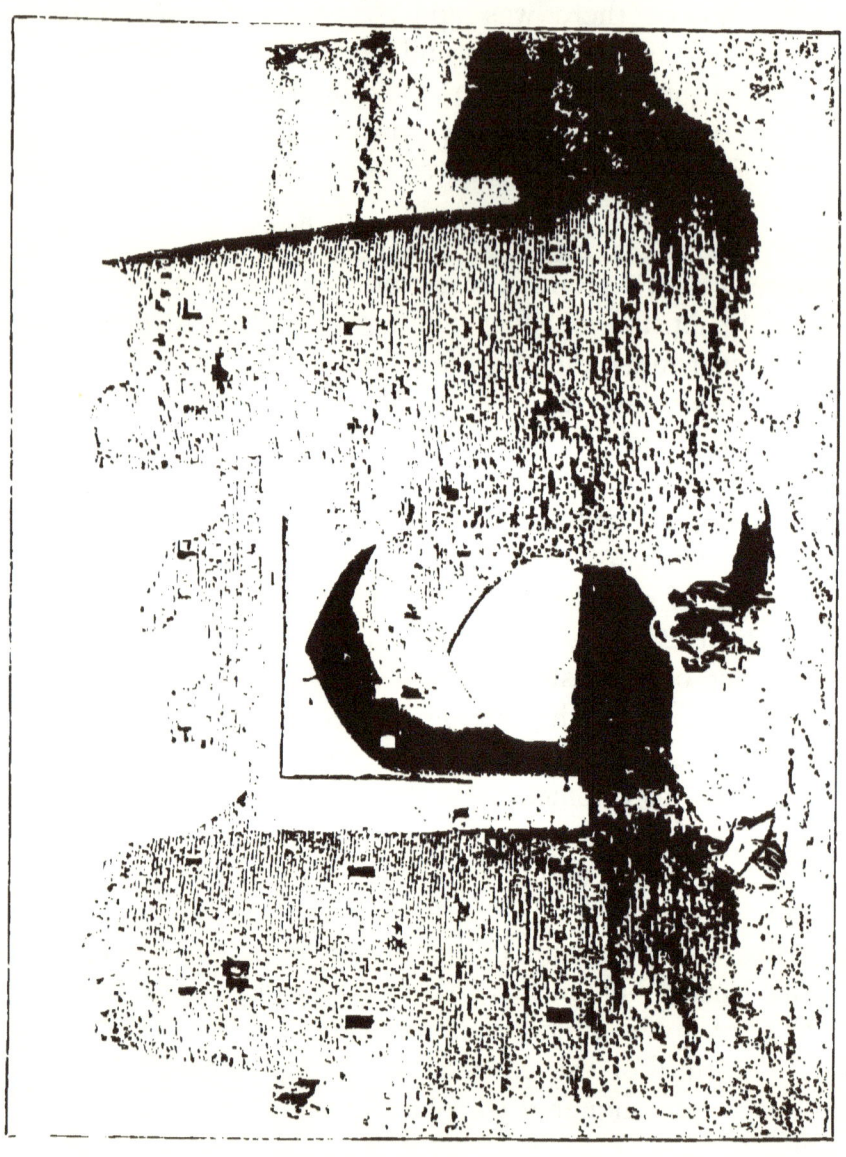

THE PRINCIPAL GATEWAY OF BAIRAM ALI.

took the place and built a city, the walls of which, flanked with semicircular towers and possibly measuring from two to three miles round, are now called Bairam Ali, and here it was we found the ruins most plentiful, though few, if any of them, could be called beautiful. A distant view of Bairam Ali presented to the visitor a gateway of fine proportions, though looking very dilapidated from the rear. On approaching the principal entrance to the citadel, the flanking towers were seen to be of sun-dried brick, as were also the remains of the lesser mosque.

Our host and chaperon, being determined that we should not starve, regaled us among the ruins with sweetmeats and drinks, as well as conversation, so that before I left Merv I was much pleased to have had the opportunity of getting at first-hand, and from various persons who took part therein, sundry pieces of information concerning its annexation.

When England was startled in February 1884 by the telegram received in St Petersburg from Askhabad to the effect that the Turkomans had declared themselves subjects of the Czar, there was no lack of English newspapers charging Russia with perfidy in having stolen Merv, whilst British hands were full in Upper Egypt and incapable of interfering.

Personally, I never joined in this hue and cry: first, for lack of what seemed to me adequate proof; and next, because from what I had heard at Khiva, less than twelve months before, of the lawless condition of Merv, it seemed to me that the Russians had only to wait, and Merv must fall into their hands without their even asking for it.

The telegram stated that "this decision was arrived at by the Turkomans of Merv because they were assured of their incapability of governing themselves." This, in England, was laughed at, but was strictly in keeping with what I had heard from the Khan of Khiva and others in the neighbourhood; as also with the testimony of the Baron Benoist-Méchin, who visited Khiva six months after me, and, proceeding thence to Merv, found, the Baron said, " such an absence of all government that after our arrival in the month of July we did not hesitate to write to General Chernaieff it seemed to us that the Merv oasis would submit without fighting at no distant date "—which is precisely what happened a few months later.

Accordingly, I felt unable, from such facts as had come to my knowledge, to adopt and to write upon an engraving which appeared in the *Graphic* of April 25th, 1885. It represented the interior of a Turkoman hut, copied from a photograph I lent to the editor, whilst seated around were Turkoman chiefs inserted from another of my photographs; but there was added also what was not in mine—a Russian officer in the attitude of an envoy exhorting the chiefs to submission, and for this I felt I could not with a good conscience stand sponsor, having no proof that such a conference had ever taken place.

So nearly, however, do truth and error often lie together, that I afterwards learned the editor was right, and so, too, was I.

The true story as to how the submission of Merv was effected was given me as follows:—Colonel Alikhanoff, as is well known, entered the Russian army early in life, became major, and in 1875 was degraded to the ranks for fighting a duel. In 1879 he took part in the Turkoman campaigns, gradually rose again, and in 1882, for a secret reconnaissance of the oasis of Merv, was promoted to a captaincy.

It was not long after this that some Turkoman

raiders, approaching the Persian frontier near Askhabad, carried off some natives who were Russian subjects, and their sheep. This could not, of course, be allowed to pass unnoticed, and a volunteer was called for who would undertake the difficult work of proceeding to Merv, and demanding the restitution of both persons and cattle.

Alikhanoff offered to go, and when warned of danger and the possibility of losing his life, he persisted, and finally started, but with a certain number of soldiers, whom, if I mistake not, he left on the borders of the Merv oasis, and proceeded alone to play his game in his own way.

It was no part of his commission, so I was told, to broach the question of annexation, but he saw therein a means of regaining perhaps his old laurels, and possibly fresh ones besides. Going from *aul* to *aul*, he pointed out to this and the other chief that a great power like Russia could not possibly allow brigandage on her borders, and that the Turkomans would do well to become Russian subjects.

Their apprehension, that they should be obliged to give up their Muhammadanism, he was able to allay by pointing out that his father before him and he, too, though both Russian officers, had nevertheless continued Muhammadans; and other objections he similarly met, speaking to them in their own tongue.

The lawlessness then prevalent inclined those who had anything to lose to wish heartily for a better state of things. To my own knowledge they had sent three times to Khiva and Petro Alexandrovsk asking for a Governor of their own nationality. But this move had not been successful.

Some of them told Alikhanoff that, if they must

have foreign rule, they would prefer that of the English, whilst others preferred that of Russia, and some of Persia.

Amidst these divided counsels Alikhanoff came to the spot where we had lunched—the *aul* of Yusuf Khan—where were assembled some 600 people, to whom he said: " It is impossible for me to confer with so great a crowd; I will give you half an hour to decide whether or not you will become Russian subjects, and, if you decide in the affirmative, to choose four persons as representatives by whom the business can be negotiated."

And thereupon he left them to deliberate, retiring to the tent, if I remember rightly, of Gur Jemal.

In 15 minutes they came to say they had decided; and Alikhanoff despatched a messenger to Askhabad; but so taken aback were the authorities there that they refused to believe, and Alikhanoff had to send a second time for arrangements to be made whereby the chiefs could proceed and swear their allegiance before the Governor-General.

Thus, if the foregoing account is true,—as I, for one, believe it to be,—the submission of Merv was brought about by the diplomacy of an officer in the Russian service, but upon his own responsibility, and in excess of the orders with which he was entrusted.

The rest is a matter of history, but the Colonel told me he had the satisfaction of liberating 700 slaves in the Turkoman oasis, and among them a Russian colonel.

CHAPTER IV.

FROM MERV TO THE OXUS.

Further railway favours, 47.—Journey through sand barkhans and desert stations, 48.—Guest at Amu-daria with Colonel Tcharykoff, 50.—Reforms by new Emir of Bokhara, 51.—Dinner-party at Colonel Tcharykoff's, 52.—Visit to Bek of Charjui; Murder of previous Bek, and lynching the murderer, 54.—The prison revisited, 55.—The gallows, 57.—Journey continued in a rolling maisonette, 58.—Bridge over the Oxus, 59.—Inn at Bokhara station, 60.

MY journey from the Caspian to Merv was travelled with the maximum comfort the line could afford—namely, a separate compartment in the one second-class carriage in the train, for of first-class as yet there was none. The remainder of the passenger accommodation consisted of third-class carriages, and of fourth-class, if they may be so called, without seats or benches, for natives. A second-class carriage was attached to the train only twice a week, and when starting afresh towards the Oxus I happened to fix on a non-second-class day.

The kindness of the railway officials, however, with that of Colonel Alikhanoff, who accompanied me to the station, proved equal to the occasion; for, seeing that there were many passengers, the station-master was good enough to place at my disposal a whole third-class carriage, wherein, if there was lack of cushions, there certainly was not of room, my only companions being my servant Joseph and a messenger whom Colonel Alikhanoff was sending on business to Bokhara, and who he thought might be useful on the way.

The first station eastwards is named after the neighbouring ruins, Bairam Ali, where water is stored in a tank alongside the railway, and supplied to the engine from a tun raised on logs of wood. Between this and

RESERVOIR AT BAIRAM ALI, OR OLD MERV.

the next station, at a distance of about 27 miles from Merv, the line enters upon the outer fringe of the most terrible desert, I suppose, crossed by any railway in the world.

This desert is not merely sandy, but of sand entirely, with this additional drawback, that whereas the sands on the coast of the Caspian may by labour be half fixed, those near the Oxus are at the mercy of every wind that blows. They cover the face of the country in *barkhans*, or sickle-shaped hills, varying in height up to 100 feet.

In certain places plantations of bushes suitable to the soil have been placed beside the railway; but until these grow it seems inevitable that from time to time, after strong winds, the rails will need to be cleared as after a snowstorm. It was by reason of this uncertainty as to what might be the condition of the road that our train, though arriving at Merv in the morning, did not leave until nearly midnight, so as to traverse the worst part of the sandy desert by day.

In the grey dawn of very early morning we reached a station significantly named Pesky, in allusion to the surrounding sand. Here we bade farewell to the few tokens remaining of the Merv oasis, after which sunrise found us at Repetek, where was a refreshment station, with only brackish water for making tea, and then we plunged in among the sand barkhans. At Karaul-Kuyu no station was yet erected, but a few tents pitched and a hut constructed of railway sleepers, out of which the drifting sand was kept with difficulty.

From the next station, Barkhan—again named after its local surroundings—there was nothing visible all round but sand-hills, whilst a more desolate outlook than we had from the carriage windows in steaming along could hardly be imagined.

Finally, about six miles west of the Amu-daria, cultivation reappeared, with fortified mud houses and walls and trees, the last somewhat larger than those of Merv. We had now entered the oasis of Charjui, a narrow strip of cultivated land belonging to Bokhara on the west bank of the Oxus; and at ten o'clock we arrived at the station Amu-daria, thus completing a journey of 670 miles from the Caspian in 60 hours of actual travel.

The local railway potentate for this part of the line was Prince Khilkoff, who had been kind enough to send to the station General Annenkoff's carriage to

RAILWAY DEPÔT AT AMU-DARIA.

take me to be the guest of Colonel Nicholas Tcharykoff, the Russian Political Agent (or "Resident," as the English would call him) in Bokhara, who for the moment was laid up here with a broken ankle.

The Colonel spoke English fluently, having received a part of his early education in Edinburgh, and proved to be one of the most polished and gentlemanly Russian officers I have ever met. Though unable to go out, he made my stay thoroughly enjoyable; and knowing well my writings on Bokhara, he was able to confirm or correct what had been written.

Since my previous visit the Emir Muzaffar-ed-din had died, and had been succeeded by his fourth son, Seid Abdul Ahad, of whom it was pleasant to hear that he had introduced certain reforms and improvements, as, for instance, that on coming to the throne he had proclaimed throughout the country liberty to slaves.

Nominally, the slave markets of Bokhara, under compulsion from the Russians, had long been closed; and when I was at Charjui in 1882 I did not suspect the trade to be going on, but that Persian girls were brought by the Turkomans and sold there I learned after my return to England from Colonel Stewart, who had left Eastern Persia only a few weeks previously, and I thereupon, with his consent, published his statement by way of confirmation of M. Stremoukhoff's letters to the *St Petersburg Gazette* stating that the odious trade was not completely stamped out in Bokhara.

It was a wise and humane policy, therefore, of the Russians to "advise" (which meant to command) the young Emir not merely to prohibit the trade, but to set at liberty those already bound, and to send special orders to the frontier towns that if any slaves were imported there they should be immediately set at liberty.

Thus, whatever may be said in disfavour of Russia's annexations, it should not be forgotten that she has by this last measure completed the extirpation of slavery from the shores of the Caspian to China.

The new Emir was said to have made other attempts to improve public morality. Mr Curzon, who accompanied a party of tourists to Bokhara at the time of the opening of the railway, writing afterwards of the Emir's court, says: "*Batchas*, or dancing boys, are among the inseparable accessories of the palace, and represent a Bokharan taste as effeminate as it is depraved." *

But Colonel Tcharykoff informed me, in answer to my question on the subject, that the new Emir, instead of providing boys with their tambourine music for the public entertainment of guests as did his father, had forbidden *batchas*, and ordered them to enlist in the army, though it might be that they were in some cases tolerated in private.†

On my second evening at the Amu-daria, Colonel Tcharykoff gave a dinner, and invited me to meet the officers of the garrison, and Captain Loewenhagen, the commander of the steamer *Czar*, then in course of construction on the river, and also an English engineer named Boots.

Next morning I went by invitation of Captain Loewenhagen to see the *Czar*, then lying below the bridge alongside of the barge or lighter she was intended to tow, after which Colonel Tcharykoff kindly arranged that I should drive to the town of Charjui, and pay a complimentary call on the native Bek or Governor.

* *Russia in Central Asia*, p. 200.
† Something similar may be said with regard to prostitution in Bokhara, for, whatever may be done secretly, the Muhammadan law regarding its prohibition remains in force; and a case having at the time of my visit recently come to light of two parents selling their daughter for an immoral purpose, the father's throat was cut, and the mother shot, which in Bokhara is a common method of capital punishment for offences of this class.

BATCHAS, OR DANCING BOYS, WITH MUSICIANS AND SINGERS.

I was well pleased thus to revisit a place that had interested me exceedingly, six years before, as a frontier outpost, whence one looked into the desert towards Merv, and longed to go but dared not, there being then no security for a foreigner's life.

Outside the citadel, instead of inside, as one would expect, is arranged under a shed a very small park of antiquated artillery, which the Charjui natives, I suppose, used to fancy brought them abreast of the times. So ignorant were they on my former visit, that on my thinking to surprise the young Bek by describing our hundred-ton guns and their enormous projectiles, he replied, "Yes, ours are like them too."

This young Bek was a younger brother of the present Emir. At my reception in 1882 he had got himself up in a dandy turban and gorgeous robes, but he lost his post at his father's death, and his successor had now been summoned to court to take the place of the Kush-beggi's son, whom I had seen when calling on his father, and whom I had mentally dubbed the greatest nincompoop in the kingdom. But this was by no means the estimate put upon him in Bokhara, for the new Emir had taken him to his cabinet as Divan-beggi, or Minister of Finance. Colonel Tcharykoff also spoke well of him, saying that he had been a favourite with the people.

No small indignation, therefore, had been recently aroused when, the Divan-beggi serving a warrant for the sale of the goods of a man who had embezzled money, the culprit shot the Divan-beggi with two bullets, who after lingering 20 hours died, but not before he had expressed a wish that his murderer might not be put to death.

But the Emir condemned the culprit, and handed

him over to the dead man's relatives to do with him what they liked. This was, first, to break his bones; next, to drag him through the donkey market (some said at the tail of an ass); thirdly, to behead him; and lastly, to cast his body outside the city to the dogs.

On my present visit to Charjui I was received in the usual reception room by the acting Bek and his staff, robed in their gaily coloured *khalats* and white turbans, and, after speaking of my former visit, and partaking of light refreshment and sweetmeats, I returned towards the outer gateway between lines of soldiers and a native band.

Being anxious to revisit the prison, and remembering that it was under a chamber at the gate of the citadel, I stopped opposite the entrance and asked to be allowed to go in. My gaining admission six years previously was a great triumph, because at Bokhara they had done their best to keep me from seeing their prisons, and I then discovered at Charjui not only a near approach to the "Black Hole of Calcutta," but men wearing iron collars, through the ends of which was passed a chain to secure them all together, as well as a long beam, wherein the prisoners' feet were made fast, placed across the centre of the chamber.

This beam I could not help thinking was anciently an ordinary piece of furniture in prisons, similar perhaps to that in which the Philippian jailer thrust the feet of Paul and Silas (Acts xvi. 24), and I was anxious on the present occasion to take a photograph of it.

But the hot and fusty chamber, without windows or ventilation, and measuring only six paces by four, was too dark and the space too contracted to allow of operating satisfactorily; so, putting a bold face on the matter, I asked that the prisoners might be brought out into the yard, and the beam too, which was accordingly done, for the police-master looked afraid to refuse. Then I sent to the bazaar for refreshments,

CEMETERY, AND MODE OF EXECUTION IN BOKHARA AND KHIVA.

which the prisoners partook of before they were posed and photographed, much to their astonishment, but on terms they evidently approved.

In addition to the chamber already described, I found, on this visit, another on the opposite side of the citadel gateway, circular in form and measuring four paces across. In the former place were four prisoners chained by the neck together; in the latter were eight, one of whom had been confined for a year, others for a longer period, together with a boy of 13, whose tale was a pitiful one.

It appeared that his father had struck him, and afterwards the son, finding his parent asleep, retaliated by dealing him a blow which proved fatal. The young parricide had already been in confinement for nearly a

OPENING OF THE BRIDGE ACROSS THE OXUS AT CHARJUI.

year, but I could not make out what they intended to do with him.

On passing the gallows they told me that, previous to the advent of the Russians, they used to hang from five to six hundred Turkomans a year, but that this state of things had now passed away.*

* Among sundry photographs kindly given me by Colonel Tcharykoff is one of the gallows at Khiva, not as when I was there, in front of the Khan's palace, but in a cemetery, with a felon supposed to be

Before leaving the Amu-daria railway station, or depôt, as they called it, I attempted a photograph of the curious vehicle in which we were to go forward to Bokhara. We had come by payment as far as the line was available to the public, and the ceremony of opening the bridge had taken place only a few weeks previously, but the rails were placed and trucks were running for another 80 miles.

BRIDGE OVER THE OXUS, 6,230 FEET.

Accordingly, Prince Khilkoff assigned me, free of charge, a wooden hut or maisonette, with slanting roof, built on a wheeled platform, and introduced, if I mistake not, by himself, from his experience in railway

suspended. His foot, however, is suspiciously near a mud wall, on which it looks as if the man might be posing for the photographer; but whether it be so or not, the picture illustrates the primitive character of the Turkistan gallows, consisting simply of two posts and a cross beam.

making in America. It consisted of two chambers about 10 feet long by 9 wide. In each room was a bedstead, a table, and two candlesticks. The walls were lined with striped cotton, the windows and doorways were curtained, and there was a lavatory intervening, so that all that was needed was the Russian *samovar* and a lunch-basket to enable one to travel as many miles as one pleased.

THE LONGEST IN THE WORLD.

It was in this fashion we crossed the Oxus, whose bed is here more than two miles wide, with many sandbanks, and occasionally islands pastured by cattle; whilst so changeable was the course of the current that a place measuring 20 feet deep at the time of the erection of the bridge, and chosen as the spot for steamers to pass, had now silted up to a depth of two feet only.

The bridge is, I suppose, the longest in the world—so long that, when standing at one end, the other is not visible, especially on such a day as we crossed, with sand in the air blown by a strong east wind, and when the train—going very slowly, it is true—took 26 minutes to go the entire length of the railings. The bridge is constructed lightly of wood, and is not intended to be other than temporary. Tubs of water with pails attached, in case of fire, are placed upon it at intervals, and on the bridge itself occurs the one thousandth verst post from the Caspian.

Immediately east of the river we passed over cultivated land and through trees to Farab, our first stopping-place, where there was a garden laid out, but no station built; and this was the usual condition of things till we reached the stopping-place for Bokhara, where, after a heavy rainfall at night, I made my first acquaintance with Central Asian mud, into which, from its slippery character, I fell.

An enterprising Armenian, or Jew, if I remember rightly, had built at the station a small inn; and here I was called upon by the station-master, Colonel Popoff, and the local engineer, Ivanoffsky, who had heard about me from General Annenkoff, and suggested that I should sleep the remaining hours of the night, and in the morning they would see me started for the town.

CHAPTER V.

BOKHARA.

Drive to the town, 61.—Fellow-guests and repeated experiences; Madame Klemm's hospitality, 62.—Russian ladies in Bokhara, 63.—Espionage and suspicion of natives; Visit to bazaar and Kalan Mosque; Photography allowed but suspected, 64.—House of the Ishan and maniacs, 65.—Picture-taking under difficulties; Visit to Jewish synagogue, 67.—Morning prayers and circumcision, 68.—Jewish oppression in Bokhara, 69.—Visit to city prison, 70.—Lepers' quarter, 72.—Audience with the Emir, 73.—"A bargain's a bargain"; Political influence of Russian Residency, 77.—Rides about the town, 78.

WHEN the carriage arrived for the nine miles' drive between the station and the town of Bokhara, I recognised it as the *calèche* in which, six years previously, I was drawn by two artillery horses from Kitab to Karshi. I recognised, too, one of the postillions, but not the line of country through which we now drove, on a beautiful spring morning. It presented a very different aspect from the parched appearance of the Khanate as I had last seen it in autumn.

On arriving before the grim and sombre-looking walls and towers of Bokhara, we were taken to what was formerly the harem or women's apartments of the house assigned me in 1882, which the Emir had now lent for the Russian Residency, pending the building of a suitable dwelling for the Political Agent near the railway station.

The rooms I occupied before, in the principal court, were now inhabited by Colonel Tcharykoff, and in the same court were the treasury, guarded by Cossacks, and the apartments of M. Basil Oskapovitch Klemm, Secretary-dragoman to the Political Agency at Bokhara, and his family, with whom were staying Madame Klemm's mother and sister, Madame Olga and Mdlle Aphekhtine, on a visit from Moscow.

There was also lodging on the premises a Russified native officer and interpreter named Mirbadaleff, whose brother I met at Petro-Alexandrovsk. To complete the list of visitors must be added a Spanish gentleman and his wife, of whom mention had been made by the Governor at Baku as coming after me, who passed under the name of Juan de Chelva, from Valencia, but who were said to be none other than the brother of Don Carlos of Spain, and his wife, the Duchess of Montpensier.

An American fellow-traveller once, inviting me to come and stay at his house, added, "We will take you in, you know, boots and all"; and in this fashion, on my first visit to the Khanate, from the moment of crossing the frontier, I was regarded as the Emir's guest, and supplied with lodging, servants, food, and raiment, and all that was necessary for myself and attendants.

Something of the same sort was observed on this second visit, though I could not at first make out whether I was a guest of the Emir or of the Russian Residency. The lunch brought daily to my room was of native preparation, but in the evening Madame Klemm entertained us at dinner; and, considering the difficulty of getting variety of food for European palates, and serving it in anything like Western fashion, in the midst of a city where foreigners were so few, it was not an undeserved compliment the duchess paid one evening to our hostess in observing, "*Comment on mange bien, Madame, chez vous !*"

This paucity of Europeans in the town contributed largely towards making prisoners of the ladies of the Residency, for at first their appearance in the bazaar, unveiled, drew together a crowd to admire or to stare, as the case might be, and this was intensified when Mdlle Aphekhtine appeared on horseback with a lady's saddle.

Accustomed, like all Muhammadans, to degrade their wives into drudges or toys, it seemed to the natives a bold thing for women thus to appear in public; and that these sentiments were not those of the vulgar only, came out on the day of the opening railway *fête*, when the Residency was decked out with flags and carpets, and the nobles of Bokhara were invited to dine with Russian officers and their wives, perceiving which, one of the Bokhariots, high in dignity, remarked that he thought the Russian ladies were not kept sufficiently in subjection!

On the birth of Madame Klemm's first baby there was much rejoicing and passing of compliments and presents, and the young boy was forthwith dubbed a " bek " in honour of having been born in " Bokhara the Noble"; but I could not gather that, even with the best of Russian desires to that end, there could be maintained anything like family intercourse or intimacy between Muscovite and Bokhariot ladies, so great was the ignorance of the latter, and so little did they understand each other's customs; added to which the natives were intensely suspicious that beneath every proffered kindness there lay concealed a snare.

To me these indications of suspicion were not new, for so rampant were they at the time of my previous visit, that our deeds and words, and taking of notes especially, were reported to the Emir—an undoubted fact, because some of my retainers one day heard two of the spies reading over what they intended to report. On this second visit I was less tightly in their grasp, but I recognised one of our old spies among three native officials who remained on the premises nominally, and to a considerable extent really, to look after the Emir's guests, but also, of course, to espy.

On the day after our arrival the Kush-beggi, or Prime Minister, sent a Karaul-beggi to show me the bazaar, where things were going on as of old. From the bazaar the Karaul-beggi took me to the Kalan Minaret, said to have been built by the Arabs in the ninth century, and to the Great Mosque adjoining, out of which I had formerly been hurried in fear lest I should be set upon as an unbeliever, whereas now I was allowed to examine everything at leisure, and even to photograph the *Mihrab*, or sanctuary towards which Muhammadans pray, and the *Sakka-khana*, or place for drinking water.

Had I brought a camera six years before, its use would undoubtedly have been forbidden, but now they had seen some of the Russians practising their "black art." This had to some extent softened prejudice, so that when in the mosque one of the natives was about to object, the Karaul-beggi overruled that I should be allowed to proceed. On another day, however, one old simpleton, and a great obstructionist on my first visit, after seeing me take a photograph of a tomb in the cemetery, thought the proceeding so mysterious and uncanny that he declared next day it had caused him a sleepless night!

I photographed this place of sepulture because the cemeteries of Bokhara and Khiva give the best illustration that I have seen how those possessed of devils (which in Bokhara would mean the insane) had their dwellings in the tombs.* These tombs are built of clay, the ends presenting the form of a triangle with the sides bent out. Beneath this the corpse is laid, often on the surface of the ground, divested of all clothing, except a turban, and the tomb plastered up. In course of time, however, the heat of summer causes the clay to crack, and, the ends having fallen, disclose the dry bones and skull within. Thus is formed a place wherein friendless maniacs, turned loose to provide for themselves (as I heard they sometimes were in Bokhara), might easily take refuge.

I had heard on my previous visit of the barbarous manner in which the insane were kept and treated, being beaten whilst prayers were read over them from the Koran, and then picketed, like horses, to posts in the yard of a mullah called the Ishan, but I did not then succeed in witnessing it. This house of the Ishan, therefore, was one of the places I asked now to be taken to see.

It was an ordinary native dwelling, presided over by a sort of mullah-doctor, who was treating his insane patients as "possessed of the devil," and was dealing largely in charms for all comers, consisting of extracts from the Koran, placed in receptacles to be worn on

* Matthew viii. 28.

the afflicted part of the body. He sat in his room near a window, and outside was a little crowd of ignorant women, many of them said to be childless, who had come to consult this man in their troubles and pay for his nostrums.

This was sad enough, but the sight of the maniacs was pitiable; the case of one man especially, Akhmet Kul, from Karshi, who had been there six months, and, although chained by the ankles, kept violently jumping and dancing about. Unlike some of the others, when I gave him money or sweets he threw them into the air, and appeared decidedly combative. Near him, chained to the wall, was a youth who had been there ten days only.

"What is the matter with him?" I asked.

"Oh!" said they, "he has a devil." Whereupon I took from his legs the chains, which they allowed me to purchase.

Passing through a doorway, I found myself in a stable in which was a donkey, and, seemingly as little cared for, two maniacs, one of whom was jumping and crying, the place looking indescribably miserable, and filthily dirty. Sitting outside in the sun, but chained, was an Afghan, and another man of unknown nationality who was evidently vain of his appearance, for, before a small looking-glass, he was continually combing his long and plentiful hair and beard. There were others on a loft who had been there three months, but some only 15 days, and in all cases their stay was intended to be temporary.

Of course I wanted to photograph this sad and strange, but instructive scene, for it connected itself in my mind with further characteristics of those we read of as possessed with devils. I accordingly began to put up my apparatus, the Ishan not expressing any objection.

Some of his subordinates, however, did not like it, but being too timid to stop me, and thinking perhaps to escape responsibility themselves, let loose the Karshi maniac, who came dancing before the camera, crying out, as interpreted to me, "We don't want to be photographed! we don't want to be photographed!" Upon this I desisted, and, by permission, returned a few days afterwards to accomplish my purpose.

On this second occasion there were ten patients, and Akhmet Kul, a man of middle age who told me he was three years old, made no objection to having his portrait taken, showing the charm he wore on his shoulder, which seemed to be the only thing they were applying for his recovery. Whether he had been beaten I have no record; some were so treated, and some, they said, beat themselves.

I paid a third visit to the Ishan's house on my last Sunday in Bokhara, thinking to give the poor creatures a dinner of *pilau*, which being announced to the old obstructionist, he said, rightly or wrongly, the needed quantity of *pilau* could not be had in the bazaar at so short a notice. "Very well," I said, "then we will give them bread and sweets, as before," which accordingly was done, much to the satisfaction of the patients; and the Ishan gave me, I suppose as a compliment, one of his charms or slips of writing.*

On our third day in Bokhara, accompanied by one of the Emir's officials, I revisited the Jews' synagogue,

* The text, kindly translated for me by Sir Henry Rawlinson, reads, "In the name of God, the Most Merciful, the Great and True," after which it appears to continue, "A charm by the truth of the Gospel of Jesus, and what God made to descend upon Jesus. Mary was daughter," etc., the remainder being illegible.

anxious to thoroughly overhaul a number of manuscripts and disused rolls of the Law which, six years before, were stowed away in dust and disorder in a loft. But the spirit of church restoration had been abroad—the loft was removed, and the old rolls were now arranged in order in niches in the walls and in cupboards.

On asking for the most ancient, a Torah, or copy of the Pentateuch, was shown, said to have been given by Abdurrahman Kalan, the Israelite patron or founder of the synagogue, four or five hundred years ago. Just before my previous visit a woman in Bokhara had parted with a manuscript I was shown at Moscow on its way to London, and which, when sold to the British Museum, turned out to be of importance both for textual criticism and for illustration of the art of Jewish illumination — to be pronounced, in fact, the most richly illuminated Hebrew manuscript of the Old Testament extant.

On applying a few tests on this second visit, as to the form of certain letters, I could not make out that this oldest copy in the synagogue would be regarded by an expert as very ancient, or perhaps remarkable, though the writing was larger than usual, and carefully penned.

On the next morning at sunrise I was taken again to the synagogue to witness a circumcision. Many men were assembled wearing phylacteries and prayer shawls or scarves, called locally *sisid*, but in Hebrew *talith*, some of which were ornamented with strips of silver and gold. The congregation sat on the ground, but sprang to their feet at the repetition of the *Kodesh*, or " Holy, Holy, Holy !" and from time to time they turned towards Jerusalem.

After the usual daily morning prayers, which last for about three-quarters of an hour, two chairs were brought into the midst of the congregation near a stone lectern, said to be 400 years old, and covered with cloths of silk. The officiating rabbi or priest then took in his hand a silver rod, called the rod of Elijah, and the child was brought in by the father amid shouting and recitation of prayers by the congregation. A prayer was said by the rabbi, after which the infant, held by two aged men, was circumcised according to the law.

The usual offering given to the priest on such occasions is from four to ten shillings, or more perhaps from the rich. To what extent, and in what numbers, their rich men exist is not easy to tell at a glance, since many years of oppression and extortion have made them careful to hide their wealth.

In Bokhara the Jews still labour under many restrictions. They may not wear a garment of silk, for instance, with a belt and a turban, but are compelled to wear a cotton *khalat* and black calico cap, and to be girded only with a piece of string. Again, they may not ride a horse in the city, and in the fields are made to dismount from an ass before a mounted Muhammadan, who, if he choose, may smite a Jew, but the Jew must not retaliate.

The boys, many of whom, like their mothers, were extremely good-looking, at first were terrified at me if only I patted them on the head. Meanwhile they showed themselves well disposed towards me, some of them remembering my former visit, especially one boy to whom I had given a Hebrew New Testament. Moreover, true to their character, the Jews were not above turning a penny where possible. The rabbi sold me a small manuscript roll of the Book of Esther ;

and coins and precious stones were brought for my selection, as also old embroidery. Some of the last I purchased, and now value highly.

JEWS OF BOKHARA.

I expressed a strong desire to see also the Zindan or city prison of Bokhara, which they asked me not to photograph. It was a wretched place, of which they might well be ashamed, consisting of two rooms, not too large for four persons, but into which they had crammed 47. The first room was ten paces long, the ceiling almost within reach, and contained 25 prisoners, one poor fellow crying because sick, and apparently broken-hearted. The second chamber was six paces square, without boards or ceiling, the domed roof opening to the sky, and containing 22 prisoners, of whom six were Persians.

There was no furniture in the rooms, except a piece or two of matting on the bare earth, a water vessel, and the most wretched sanitary arrangements. They said the man longest there had been imprisoned 18 months; and it is proper to remember that imprisonment as such, for a term of years, for instance, is not a recognised form of Bokhara punishment, but men are put in prison until their cases can be dealt with and disposed of in a summary fashion, which may be anything between a thrashing and being put to death.

Joseph, my servant, had brought an armful of bread, which I would not entrust to the keepers, but distributed myself; and on going again on a subsequent day for a similar purpose I perceived, in the centre of the chamber, open to the sky, a hole covered over with earth and sticks, which I learned was the entrance to the bottle-shaped dungeon, into which prisoners could be lowered by cords.

Here it was, I make no doubt, that the English Colonel Stoddart was at first placed by Nasr-ullah, the present Emir's grandfather, and afterwards removed to another prison within the palace, where he and Captain Conolly were said to have been persecuted by sheepticks.

However that may be, I had heard from Colonel

Tcharykoff that, before he came to the Residency, it was hinted to the new Emir that such abominations could not be allowed in a city inhabited by a representative of the Czar, in deference to which desire of his friends the Russians the Emir had covered up the underground dungeon, and released, or otherwise disposed of, more than 100 prisoners confined therein at the death of his father.

I brought away a souvenir of the Zindan in the form of a hand-drum such as is used by the master of a hawking party. There it was beaten by the Zindan watchman walking round the walls at night. It was given me by the jailer, into whose apartments we went when looking at the kitchen, near to which was the tomb of a mullah of repute.

Another place I thought it might be a charity to visit was the lepers' quarter, which before at Karshi they refused to allow me to see, nor did I subsequently get more than a passing glimpse of it, and that by stealth, at Bokhara. I now said that I wished to give a dinner to the lunatics, the prisoners, and the lepers; and we rode out to a village where were reported to be 200 persons, or houses of the infected. They were not congregated in any one building, so that all we could do was to gather a few together, ask for their head-man, and give him some money to distribute.

I heard of no hospital of any kind in Bokhara, though Dr Heyfelder, on the railway staff of General Annenkoff, when resident in the city, had given the natives much medical assistance, and made many friends thereby. He told me, quite feelingly, that the Divan-beggi, when shot, sent for his assistance, but he was too far off to arrive in time to be of use.*

It is not customary in Bokhara that visitors be admitted to the presence of the Emir until they have remained in the city a few days, at the least three: it was said on my former visit, and during that interval they would not, at Shahr-i-Sabz, let me go off the premises. On the present occasion the staying within was not exacted, but on the fifth day after my arrival my Spanish fellow-guest and I were to be presented to the Emir, who was staying in his summer palace at Shirbadan, a few miles out of the city.

His Highness sent repeated invitations to M. Klemm, desiring that he also would come. Accordingly, we drove in a *calèche* through the streets, preceded by a cavalcade of numerous outriders and servants, and after them, to do honour to the occasion, the Minister of Finance, lately Bek of Charjui. Added to this the people along the route were *en fête*, keeping the Muhammadan New Year, the festivities of which had been postponed on account of the Emir's absence in March. As we approached Shirbadan the crowds increased, for they were expecting to scramble for presents, and, in addition, soldiers were drawn up to salute.

The palace, with a fairly good entrance approached by four steps from the court, and covered with an awning supported by two slender wooden columns, stands in a garden of a hundred acres, and the

* This was the more remarkable when a surgical operation might be necessary, because it was said that the Bokhariots will not submit to amputation, thinking that, unless whole at the time of death, they cannot enter heaven. I heard too that the bodies of Persian subjects in Russia are not subjected to post-mortem examination, in deference perhaps to the same superstition.

Reception Hall, with its pool of water in front, is ornamented on the exterior with arabesque painting in no way remarkable. It was otherwise with the ceiling within, which had been painted only a year before, and was, I think, the prettiest work of art we saw in Bokhara. The room had glazed windows, testifying to contact with Russia, as did also the three chairs placed for the visitors and a fourth occupied by the Emir; but I remember no other furniture in the room, which was richly carpeted.

I had been requested not to ask permission to take his Highness's portrait, though I managed otherwise to secure his photograph in full dress, wearing a richly embroidered velvet *khalat* and trousers, with a sword and a highly ornamented turban, and attended by one of his ministers. On the present occasion he was less gorgeously dressed, and displayed the insignia of four or five Russian and Bokhariot orders.

It was pleasant for us that M. Klemm could speak to the Emir direct in Persian, and thus kindly act as interpreter. After sundry remarks of a formal character, and passing of compliments, we attempted to interest him with the recital of some of our travels. But geography, if existent at all, occupies a poor place in the Muhammadan curriculum, and it was somewhat difficult to find subjects for conversation of mutual interest. I thought the present Emir, however, more intelligent than his father, and after a few more speeches he invited us to walk in his flower garden and take refreshment in an adjoining room.

This tea-room, as it was called, was said to be 50 years old. It was less brilliant than the one we left, and here was spread for us the usual *dostarkhan* of fruits and sweets and *pilau*, of which they pressed us

THE EMIR OF BOKHARA AND HIS TREASURER.

much to eat abundantly. Then we adjourned to the gardens, which were in no way beautiful to an English eye.

After awhile we returned, and to our surprise found awaiting us a number of presents that were quite embarrassing. Mine consisted of a horse with turquoise-mounted bridle, a silver- and spangle-embroidered saddle-cloth, and ten *khalats* or changes of raiment. Two were of woollen stuff, one of them real kashmir, which Paisley shawls are made to imitate, and the other coarser; a third was of gold and satin damask; a fourth of scarlet silk velvet; a fifth of striped satin; and others of silk and cotton native materials and mixtures. Besides these were three *khalats* of inferior quality for my servant.

The presents given to my fellow-guest and to M. Klemm resembled my own, and took me somewhat aback; for, remembering how kindly the late Emir had entertained me, I had brought with me some few presents I thought his son might appreciate. But M. Klemm informed me they had altered the custom, so that I expected not to receive since I was not allowed to give, and afterwards I was further dissuaded on the ground that presents were received by the Emir only from the Russian Emperor, the Governor-General, etc.

On our return to the Residency I was glad to keep the robes of honour, but was not so clear what to do with the horse, which, when the saddle-cloth was taken off, proved a sorry steed, and to take it with me was pronounced impossible. A dealer accordingly was brought from the market who offered me 50*s*. as its value, and I took the man at his price, thereby giving rise on the morrow to a somewhat unusual exhibition of commercial dealing, for the Emir's officer at the Residency, hearing the price quoted, insisted that the man should give more, and I was offered some few roubles in addition.

I judged it right, however, not to be outdone, and said, "No, a bargain's a bargain. Had the man come saying that he found the price given too much, he would not have had money returned, and I do not think that now I ought to receive more." This remark they approved, and were content to abide by; but the incident reminded me how, continually, in the bazaar and elsewhere, the Emir's men had asked the price I gave for my purchases, which they do in the case of strangers, it was said, in order to prevent their being cheated.

All at the Residency were foreigners, but it was interesting to see how important an influence they wielded in the city, and how well the Resident and his Secretary were suited to their posts. Colonel Tcharykoff struck me as an able diplomatist, and the Secretary as thoroughly industrious, and better acquainted with Oriental languages than most Russians I met.

Hence the people, whether Jews or natives, could come with their grievances, which they frequently did, hoping that the Russians would gain them redress. Slaves sometimes came asking to be freed. Fathers complained of the treatment of their daughters by the Emir, and some of the discontented occasionally were bold enough to ask that the Czar would take possession of the country.

It was not the policy of the Resident, however, to interfere more than was necessary in the domestic affairs of the Khanate, except when they related to

Russian subjects; and as for annexing the Khanate, "Why," as one asked of me, "should they do that?" To administer the country in Muscovite fashion would cost a great deal more than the taxes would pay for, and if the Russians want anything done, they have

COLLEGE OF DIVAN-BEGGI.

simply to nod to the Emir, and he does it. They are much too wise, therefore, to annex Bokhara; but if need arises, it can, of course, be done at any moment.

During our stay at Bokhara, I went sometimes for a drive with M. Mirbadaleff, or for a ride with him and Mdlle Aphekhtine, which gave opportunities for seeing the town and noticing the curious customs in its narrow, old-fashioned streets. I visited some of the Medresses or Colleges, of which that of the Divan-beggi, with its pool in front, and shaded by mulberry trees a century old, is one of the best.

A smaller one called Chuchugoim, near the Residency, was inhabited by 13 students only. One had been there three years, and intended to stay much longer, but was so poor as to be thankful for alms, which Joseph asked on his behalf, saying that the scholar could not beg. I gave, therefore, like a good Mussulman for the nonce, and in accordance with the teaching of the Koran, which prescribes giving not only " to him who asks," but " to him who is ashamed to ask "—a very good maxim for countries where primitive manners obtain, and begging has not become a trade.

M. Klemm, arriving one evening, brought intelligence that General Annenkoff wished to see me, and would arrive in two or three days; but as during that time he did not come, I judged it better to go forwards towards Samarkand, examining on my way the railway operations at the head of the line.

CHAPTER VI.

SAMARKAND.

Departure from Bokhara, 80.—Arrival at head of the line; Guest of General Annenkoff, 81.—M. Rubenstein and Dr Heyfelder, 84.—Drive to Katte Kurgan; Custom-house; A banquet anticipated, 85.—Departure by post-horses, 86.—Farewell to General Annenkoff; Bridges prepared for railway, 87.—Approach to Samarkand; Guest with M. Tolpygo; Dinner at Government House, 88.—Condition of former acquaintances; Sights revisited; Tamerlane's Mausoleum, 89.—Synagogue, and visits from Jews; Farewell to M. Tolpygo and Samarkand, 91.

WE left Bokhara a little before midnight on April 22nd, after trying to sleep for an hour or two at the station inn, this establishment being impressed on my memory because it was the only hotel to which the hospitality of the Russians allowed me to go whilst passing through their territory east of the Caspian.

We passed at Kuyuk Mazar, the first station, from the cultivation of Bokhara to the uncultivated Steppe, and early in the morning reached Malik, the next station beyond being Kermine, the bekship of which was usually held, as in the case of the present Emir, by the heir-apparent to the Bokhara throne. Here we caught our first glimpse of the Central Asian mountains, and, after proceeding another 16 miles, reached Zia-eddin or Ziat-din, one of the principal towns of the bekship. After this we arrived about noon, at a distance of 91 miles from Bokhara and 828 from the Caspian, at an open place called Tugai Robat, which was for the moment the end of the line.

I was glad of the opportunity of being the guest of

AT THE HEAD OF THE LINE.

the General, of whom one had heard so much, and of seeing his famous train of two-storied railway waggons, a veritable movable village of 1,500 persons. Calling upon his Excellency in his own waggon, which he had inhabited for about three years, it was found to consist of office and bedroom, lavatory, etc., for himself and his immediate staff of officers, whilst in the upper story was accommodation for servants.

This train was never allowed to be very far from the head of the line, which meant, of course, that it frequently moved, since, when the weather was good and all went well, the rails were being laid at the rate of four miles a day, the embankment being prepared beforehand, and the metals brought alongside on a

A LOCOMOTIVE HABITATION FOR GENERAL ANNENKOFF, PART OF HIS STAFF, AND SERVANTS.

narrow movable Decauville railway, as imported twice a day on trains from the Caspian.

I stayed only a day at Tugai Robat, but had time to see the principal features of the rolling community, which necessitated, at its various stopping-places, the erection of tents, the creation of a temporary "bazaar," and a brisk trade with the natives of the locality. In the evening I dined with the General's staff, almost all of whom were very young.

LAYING RAILS AT THE RATE OF FOUR MILES A DAY.

Among the staff was M. Rubenstein, son of the well-known musician of that name. The General bade him help me forward on the morrow. Another officer on the staff was Dr Heyfelder, to whom my name was known through my books. He had published an

MAKING A CUTTING—ASSES TAKING AWAY THE EARTH IN PANNIERS.

excellent little work, *Transkaspien und seine Eisenbahn*. He was on the staff of Skobeleff at the taking of Geok Tepe, and, being of an inquiring turn of mind, had studied the people and things about him, and knew Turkmenia well. I thought myself fortunate when he proposed that on the morrow we should travel together to Katte Kurgan.

M. Rubenstein arranged that one of the General's carriages should be placed at our disposal, and in this, with a *troika* of horses, we set out on what proved a pretty and interesting, but extremely dirty drive. As we proceeded alongside the embankment we had opportunity of seeing a cutting here and there, in which the labour of asses taking away the earth in panniers was a feature not usual on English railways. For the most part the ground to Katte Kurgan was level.

We passed the Custom-house on the frontier. M. Klemm had kindly telegraphed on my account from Bokhara that my baggage should not be stopped or examined, and Dr. Heyfelder now told the officials that my servant was following in an *arba*,—all of which seemed very simple; but I subsequently learned that lacking these favours, the passing out of Bokhara into Russian Turkistan might have given me some little trouble and perhaps expense.

We finished our drive of 18 miles, and arrived early in the afternoon at Katte Kurgan, where I was taken to be the guest of Mr. Engineer Timashhovsky. Dr. Heyfelder introduced me also to some of the inhabitants of this frontier Russian town, which just now was all in a ferment expecting within a day or two the first appearance of the train, when the coming of General Annenkoff was to be celebrated with a banquet.

The General had kindly expressed a wish that I should be present at the grandest fête of all, to be held on a day fixed in the near future at Samarkand; but of this I could hold out no hope nor intention. Still I wait at Katte Kurgan for the minor festival. I called on Colonel Voisekovitch, the chief of the district, to whom I presented M. Klemm's card, and asked for a *padarojna*, or ticket to travel by post-horses to the frontier near Kuldja.

I was too old a traveller by Russian post not to know how many conveniences would be given or denied me, according to whether I received an ordinary traveller's ticket, or a crown *padarojna* such as is usually reserved for officials, since the latter gives the first claim to post-horses and sundry other advantages.

Remembering, therefore, the value of quoting a good precedent, I produced an old crown *padarojna* showing how I had been indulged on my former visit, and was not a little pleased when the Colonel informed me I should be so indulged again, and that I could have my horses early on the morrow.

On driving next morning out of Katte Kurgan, we left the tourist world behind, with its comfortable carriages and cushions, for the sterner mode of progression in Russia implied by the word *pericladnoi*, or rough springless post-cart supplied to travellers who have no tarantass or carriage of their own. Arrangements had been made for me to have a tarantass farther on; but as Samarkand was only 43 miles distant, a large post-cart, good of its kind, was supplied, into which my baggage was packed, myself seated thereon, and Joseph with the driver perched on the box.

We had not gone very far when we met General Annenkoff, who had been obliged to leave Tugai Robat on the day of my arrival, and was now returning. Seeing my rough vehicle, he asked, half apologetically, if I was comfortable, and on being answered in the affirmative, he gave me his card to M. Tolpygo, another of his engineer officers at Samarkand, with whom I might lodge.

Having thus multiplied his kindnesses in favour of a passing traveller, we parted—he to return for a few weeks longer to his little carriage-home, and I

CONSTRUCTION OF A BRIDGE NEAR SAMARKAND.

to continue my journey eastwards, gratified at having met a man whose name will not soon be forgotten in the history of railroad making.

We did not see much of the preparations for the railway beyond Katte Kurgan, but were given to understand that the last bridge was finished, the embankment made, and all in readiness for the sleepers and rails. The number of small bridges required near Samarkand was enormously increased, in passing over cultivated land, by reason of the irrigation canals, whereby the water is led from the Zarafshan.

We approached Samarkand by a road I remembered well, with the military cantonment lying off to the right, and shaded by numerous trees, such as the Russians have planted by thousands both within and without the capital. These excited the admiration of Joseph not a little; for though he knew Western Asia, including Persia and Afghanistan, he had never seen a town with streets so full of poplars, sometimes three and four deep, growing beside watercourses, and suggesting the delights of a Muhammadan paradise.

On reaching the house of Mr Engineer Tolpygo, it was found to be a large building of one story, embowered in tall trees, and having a covered portico or platform admirably adapted for the outdoor meals that the Russian loves, and in a hot place like Samarkand in summer, exceedingly agreeable. Here a welcome was accorded me, and a room placed at my disposal, whilst my host, living *en garçon*, entertained me at meals with some of his fellow-engineers.

I proceeded, within a few hours of my arrival in Samarkand, to call on the Governor, General Yaphimovitch. I remembered well the approach to the Government House, for it was there I stayed on my previous visit, though not with its present occupant. I soon found that I was no stranger, and dining there the same evening, I met Colonel Poukaloff, who in 1882 had been chief of the town of Tashkend, and reminded me of my inquiries and of the remarks then made as to the possibility of crossing into Chinese

Turkistan, a feat that neither he nor I then thought it likely I should ever accomplish.

The Colonel was now promoted to be Vice-Governor of Samarkand, and I had heard of other acquaintances who, in six years, had climbed the ladder a few steps higher; but things were not all on the bright side.

On calling next morning on the chief of the district, George Arendarenko, I learned that Yakoob, who accompanied me as interpreter to Khiva, was dead. Also a gentleman who had shown me great attention and kindness in one of the towns of Turkistan, had got his official accounts wrong, and been under judgment; whilst another case more painful still was that of a highly intellectual young fellow, with whom I had stayed, and who struck me as extremely well educated and gentlemanly, but who had succumbed to the fascination of the card-table and wine-cup, and become a moral and social wreck.

As for the two *djiguitts* who accompanied me from Samarkand to the Oxus, one of them, Kolutch, was gone for the moment to Kerki, whilst Fazul was now told off to accompany me about the town.

I have described elsewhere a former stay in Samarkand, but there were certain places that one could not do otherwise than re-visit, notably the Mausoleum of Tamerlane. The building is too far gone for restoration to anything like its original beauty, nor will its present condition stand comparison with the antique monuments of India and the care bestowed on them by the Indian Government; but on entering the tomb of Tamerlane I found it swept and garnished, its marbles polished, and the whole kept in a better condition than in 1882; whilst by contrast with the disgraceful manner in which the natives had allowed this venerable pile of their ancestors to fall into neglect and ruin, the Russians have expended an amount of care upon it that is fairly puzzling to the Muhammadans.

THE GUR-EMIR, OR MAUSOLEUM OF TAMERLANE AT SAMARKAND.

On emerging from the Gur-Emir we passed up the splendid avenue leading to the Rhigistan, an improvement, needless to say, of the Russians.

I visited again the synagogue of the Jews, and found that they had a new one in course of building, thereby showing the greater liberty they enjoy under Russian rule than their brethren at Bokhara under the Emir, who, like his father before him, has persistently refused to allow them to build a new synagogue.

I told the Jews of Samarkand that at the close of my journey in Bokhara in 1882, when writing to thank the Emir for his kindness, I had asked him to mitigate the oppressed condition of his Jewish subjects, which they heard with satisfaction, and the Rabbi invited me to his house for further conversation.

Later, on a Sunday morning, two Jews called on me, showing a portrait of myself as clean and fresh almost as when received from me six years before. One of them had been reading the New Testament, and the copy I had given to the other had been handed down to his son. Thinking to apply a money test to his sincerity, I offered a further copy of the Hebrew New Testament for 20 kopecks, which he immediately gave, and both seemed interested to see me again.

On the Saturday after my arrival, M. Tolpygo had to leave me for Katte Kurgan, of which I took advantage to send by him a letter of thanks to General Annenkoff for all his attention.

M. Tolpygo also laid me under other obligations by his additions to my collection of photographs. Further, the Governor volunteered to lend me a tarantass wherein to travel to Tashkend; so that, after spending a good part of Palm Sunday with the Vice-Governor, who took me after dinner to the Ivanoff Park, we left Samarkand on Monday morning.

CHAPTER VII.

TASHKEND.

Crossing the Zarafshan to the bridge of Shadman-Malik; Route to Jizak, 92.—Across the "Hungry" Steppe to Chinaz, 93.—Tashkend, 94.—Dinner with Governor-General Rosenbach; Help from Captain Blinoff, 95.—Easter services, and subsequent reception at Government House; Lutherans' request for a service and Easter communion; Withdrawal of money from bank, 96.—Arrangements for communication with Kashgar, 97.—Improvements in Tashkend and purchases, 99.—Russian lady nurses, 101.—An open-air bazaar; Further visits to Government House, and parting amenities, 102.

ALTHOUGH it was now the last day of April, by which date in Turkistan the warm weather has usually set in, we found it chilly at half-past six in the morning when driving out of Samarkand. The water of the Zarafshan was sufficiently low to allow of its being forded, without having our baggage and selves transferred into a tall *arba*, as had been the case when I crossed before. Having gained the northern bank, we turned aside to look for a few minutes at the two arches of the ruined bridge of Shadman-Malik.

We had before us a journey of 190 miles to Tashkend, and it had been arranged that I should sleep the first night at Jizak. My host was Colonel Alexander Mikhailovitch Sunarguloff, a native who did not speak French, in consequence of which Captain Goujouss came to the rescue as interpreter. On this my first day's travel for the season in a tarantass proper, I had been incautious enough to lay by my side a bag containing an india-rubber washing basin, and Galton's *Art of Travel*. These in the course of the journey had jolted out of the vehicle, and inquiries were set on foot by my host

WELLS IN THE "HUNGRY" STEPPE.

for their recovery, but in vain. Happily it was my only loss of the kind whilst posting, and, by the kindness of friends, I was able afterwards to replace both the missing articles.

Next morning, early, we started to cross the "Hungry" Steppe, passing in the course of the day, and changing horses at, four stations, of which the most remarkable was Murza-Rabat. Here stands an old ruin of a caravanserai supposed to date from the sixteenth century. It is built of large square bricks, and consists of a central chamber covered by a dome, as are several smaller chambers adjoining.*

Towards evening we finished our 80 miles of Steppe, and approached the Syr-daria river, crossed by a large rude ferry-boat, and soon after dark reached Chinaz. It would have been easy to post the remaining 40 miles during the night, but I preferred to rest at the post-house. Next morning we passed the station of Old Tashkend, drove along the valley of the Chirchik, with snow mountains in front of us, and soon after midday arrived at Tashkend.

In Tashkend there was obligingly placed at my disposal a furnished house in Romanoff Street, wherein are usually lodged embassies from Bokhara. This was far more comfortable than what I remembered of the local hotels, my small meals being provided by the caretaker, his wife, and my servant, whilst Prince Cantakouzine introduced me at the military club, where I could lunch and dine, and meet officers who were ready in various ways to advise and assist in my projected expedition.

Calling the day of my arrival on General Rosenbach, the Governor-General, in his modest and unpretending palace, where so little state was kept up that the front entrance was not used except on special occasions, I found my coming expected and my name known, thanks partly to Miss Hay, an English lady living in the family, who had translated to them some of my writings.

* It has no doubt afforded a place of refuge to many a caravan in days when an escort was necessary in crossing the dreary waste. The road is now perfectly safe from robbers, as are all the post-roads of Russian Turkistan, thereby presenting a striking contrast to those I subsequently travelled on in Asiatic Turkey.

The General invited me to dinner the same evening, and at once expressed his willingness to help me in everything I asked, not excepting even my return, if necessary, over the Terek Pass into Ferghana. In fact, his Excellency seemed in no way inclined to follow an exclusive policy in keeping Englishmen and other foreigners out of Turkistan.

" Why should we ? " said Madame, as we discussed the subject at table. " We have nothing to hide or be ashamed of foreigners seeing here, but rather something to be proud of!" whereupon I put in a good word for Mr St George Littledale, who I knew was just about to ask permission to pass through Turkistan to the Russian Pamirs for a season's shooting of wild sheep, and on whose behalf I had written to M. Vlangali. Subsequently the General's sincerity was proven, as I judged on receipt of a telegram from Mr Littledale in one word, which the telegraph clerk in Kuldja spelt " Komming."

I perceived much appreciation by the Governor-General of English people and things, and it was amusing on a subsequent visit to discover that his sister was known to me by reputation, and had been living within a mile or two of my home at Blackheath.

On the day after our arrival an officer named Blinoff called, whose duty it seemed to be to look after the material comforts of guests, which he did thoroughly, and sent to me a M. Feodoroff, who took me to see M. Klemm's tarantass, wherein I was to go forward to Kuldja, the vehicle being first put in thorough repair.

I had arrived, however, in Passion Week, and the near approach of festivities did not promise well for my getting away quickly, though, on the other hand,

I was glad to have reached the capital, wherein to witness for the first time a Russian Easter.

On Good Friday evening I attended, in the cathedral, the *Vuinos*, or ceremony of the entombment, and was present also at a gorgeous spectacle in the same building on Easter Eve.

I had been specially invited to go from the church to the Government House, where was held a select official reception, and where I met again Colonel Tcharykoff, from Bokhara, in court costume, with many others, who, after conversation and walking about for an hour, sat down to an ample Easter supper, and towards three in the morning made their way home.

Meanwhile I had been asked by Colonel Lilienfeld if I would not give the Lutherans a service, they having no resident pastor, and several of them being desirous to partake of an Easter communion. But my German was weak, English was useless, and, though able to speak, I had never attempted to preach, in French. This last seemed, however, to be the only way out of the difficulty, and as it came before me in the way of a plain duty, I resolved to try, and gave them both service and sermon in the house of a M. Pfennig.

An important transaction, for me, in Tashkend was the withdrawal from the State Bank of roubles forwarded there, as the *ultima thule* in this direction of the banking world. How to carry my money had been a puzzle from the outset. For civilised regions Messrs Brown, Shipley, & Co. supplied a single letter of credit, by means of which I could draw upon their correspondents any amount up to a certain sum named; and this was preferable to the usual way of carrying a number of circular letters for £10 each, which, when numerous, became bulky.

As for the little-known regions whither I was proceeding, I had gathered from Mr Carey's paper, read not long before at the Royal Geographical Society, that he exchanged rupee notes at a discount in parts of the Tarim valley, and I accordingly purchased as many of these as just then could be found in London, but vainly inquired in the great city for any one who could give me a letter of credit for Chinese Turkistan; and upon asking if the General Post Office could inform or assist me, they replied that the department possessed no information whatever as to the places I mentioned, since they were quite beyond the recognised region of regular postal communication. It seemed not unreasonable to hope that some of the merchants in St Petersburg could furnish a letter of credit upon Kashgar, but it was not so.

At Junker's bank they advised taking to Turkistan Russian gold coins. Perhaps they had some to sell, for they quoted as a price nearly two roubles paper for one of gold. Fortunately for me, I did not take their advice. To have done so would have been a blunder, and costly to boot. With the pride pardonable in an Englishman, I had thought that her Majesty's countenance on a clean Jubilee sovereign could not fail anywhere to command respect, and I had taken 50; but that proved a delusion.

Another adviser in St Petersburg said that the people of Chinese Turkistan were unaccustomed to gold coins, and that lumps of brute silver were the proper thing. This was true, but to have turned my sterling into lump silver, even had it been possible at the Russian capital, would have added more than three hundredweight to my baggage!

In doubt, therefore, I telegraphed to Kuldja whether one should bring Russian gold, silver roubles, or paper roubles, and was told the last. The condition of the Russian money market was just then in my favour, for there was a panic on their exchange, and, whilst gold had advanced in price, and in quantities was not even to be had, paper fell 2*d*. below what I had given for the rouble in England, and enabled me to purchase more, at about 1*s*. 8*d*. each.

Accordingly, with some thousands of these in my pocket, my London letter, 50 sovereigns, some rupee notes, and a London cheque, I determined to try again in Moscow and Tiflis for the needed letter of credit on Kashgar. But Moscow proved no better in this respect than St Petersburg ; and at Tiflis, where my cheque was changed for more paper roubles, I found the only way to avoid carrying the money about me was to place it in the State Bank to be transferred to Tashkend, payable at call.

This was a temporary lessening of responsibility, which returned, however, on receiving my deposit in notes of 100 roubles each, which a St Petersburg adviser had specially urged should, according to Chinese taste, be clean and new.

Among various persons upon whom I called in Tashkend was M. Pomerantzoff, at the Observatory, who showed me some of his instruments and gave me local barometrical and thermometrical observations. I saw, too, Brigadier-General Levashoff, who was acquainted with the Kuldja district, and gave information respecting Sungaria.

He deemed that my route, as then projected from

Kuldja to Kashgar, might take four months and cost £600; whilst another adviser, who had been a good deal on the Chinese frontier, put the time at three months and the cost at £200, thus leaving an ample margin between the two estimates for the teaching of experience.

I called likewise on the Princess Vziemskiy to see her sister, Miss Petrovsky, just finishing her education at Tashkend, and about to leave for her father's house at Kashgar by way of Osh, in Ferghana. Up to this point there was a regular postal service, letters for Kashgar being forwarded once a month by a *djiguitt*, who made the journey in eight or ten days, except in April and May, when the flooded rivers were impassable.

The Governor-General promised to write to Colonel Deibner, in command at Osh, to forward my letters and telegrams to Kashgar; also to arrange that I might from that place, and if needed, re-enter Russian territory.

I have not thought it necessary to say much about Tashkend itself, because it has been already treated of in my *Russian Central Asia*. Speaking generally, marks of improvement were visible in many quarters, specially in the new bazaar, recently built.

I was able to procure therefrom some embroidery worked by Central Asian women, and such as they love to spread about the house when assembled for drinking tea and smoking the *chilim*, or pipe. To see such parties is not permitted, of course, to the English visitor of the male sex, who has to be content in such matters with what he can see of old women who go about unveiled, or with such furtive glances at female faces as may be gained among the lower classes, washing perchance at the side of a stream, or engaged in household employment near their homes. I secured, nevertheless, photographs of native women as they appear in the street and in private.*

When visiting the hospitals for natives on my first journey to Turkistan, it was pointed out that the native

COSTUMES OF CENTRAL ASIAN WOMEN IN THE STREET.

* I heard from Miss Hay, who supplied me with a miniature suit of female attire, that the younger women are very Jezebels in the use of paint and powder, making their coloured eyebrows meet above the nose, and plaiting the hair in numerous small braids. Over the head is worn a white handkerchief, above it a black *kokoshnik*, or head-dress, and over these, when out of doors, a thick black horsehair veil, which is the only thing visible in the region of the face over the few inches left uncovered by a large *khalat*, or mantle, enveloping all from the crown of the head to the feet; whilst beneath that garment are seen the boots, frequently of scarlet, into the top of which are tucked wide drawers.

women were utterly averse to coming to the instructions; but this time I was glad to hear from the Governor-General that he had enlisted the help of Russian lady nurses, for which he was rather disposed to claim credit

A WOMAN OF CENTRAL ASIA AT HOME.

as of something new in the history of philanthropic or missionary effort in Asia.

On being appealed to at the General's table as to whether we had not the like in India, I was able to answer generally in the affirmative, but not so definitely, I am ashamed to say, as I ought to have been able to do, seeing I am a life-member of the Church of England Zenana Missionary Society, which has more than a hundred female missionaries in the field.

It was a step in the right direction, however, to find Russian women beginning thus to take up what is so essentially woman's work amongst her native fellow-subjects in Central Asia, and one hopes for greater things hereafter.

Madame Rosenbach presided at an open-air *fête* or bazaar held during our stay in Tashkend, on behalf of some charitable object, and on the following day, with the General, showed me their garden, in the cultivation of which they took much pleasure, having introduced with success English strawberries.

This gave opportunity, as on other occasions, for further conversation with the Governor-General, in the course of which I mentioned to him what I had seen of the horrors of the Bokhariot prisons, and ventured to express the hope, as I had done to Colonel Tcharykoff, that if they saw their way they would do something when opportunity offered to ameliorate the prisoners' condition.

Thus a fortnight slipped by before all was in order for our travelling forward. My newly-mended tarantass was then packed, the Governor-General kindly telegraphed my coming to the chief of the district at Chimkend, and on Thursday, May 17th, M. Bartsch, the agent of the Bible Society, came in the early morning to see me start. Madame Rosenbach also, mindful of my weakness for fruit, sent down as a parting present a dish of delicious strawberries surrounded with roses—a real treat.

Thus ended my halt in Tashkend, the longest I had yet made since leaving London.

CHAPTER VIII.

FROM TASHKEND TO ISSIK-KUL.

Departure from Tashkend; Arrival at Chimkend, 103.—Passing through Aulie-Ata; Previous visit remembered at stations beyond, 104.—Region of " Ming-bulak "; Out of General Government of Turkistan into that of the "Steppe"; Telegrams to and from General Kolpakovsky; Arrival at Pishpek, 105.—Should I visit Issik-Kul? 106.—Start with a Colonel; Arrival at Tokmak, and excursion to the Burana Tower, 107.—Recent discovery of Nestorian cemeteries, 109.—Two graves opened, 110.—Traces of surrounding habitations; Tokmak cemetery; Inscriptions and decipherment, 112.—Departure from Tokmak; The Buam defile; Crossing the Chu to Kok-Mainak, 114.—Northern chain of the Tian Shan; The Ala-Tau and Alexander ranges; Basin of Issik-Kul, 115.—Description of the lake; Road along its northern shore; A narrow escape; Arrival at Kara-Kol, 116.

ON setting out from Tashkend for a posting journey eastward, the weather was now perfection, not too hot, and without dust, whilst the road was sufficiently hilly to give variety of pleasing landscape. I noticed this especially in the extensive view from Bekler-Bek, where we crossed the watershed between the valleys of the Keles and the Aris, and where I remembered well the old *medresse*, now turned into a Russian post-house.

Two stations beyond was Chimkend, which we reached after 14 hours of travel, and where Colonel

Blagovidoff, the *Uyezdi-nachalnik*, or chief of the district, had kindly prepared a bed for me; but I preferred after supper at his house to push forward, posting, as the local manner is, through the night. In so doing we passed out of the basin of the Syr-daria system into that of the Chu and minor streams which run down from the Alexander Mountains into the sandy desert west of Lake Balkash.

We had a lovely view of the mountains all the next day. The range was still snow-capped, presenting a very different appearance from what it did in the autumn of 1882; whilst the abundance of water fructified the steppe with the poppy and other flowers, and brought forth pasture for vast herds of cattle not yet driven to the mountains by the heat of summer. Thus by posting all day we accomplished about 120 miles in 24 hours, and drove at night into Aulie-Ata, with nothing worse than breaking the hood of the tarantass against the gatepost of the station yard.

Aulie-Ata might be called the capital of the Kirghese, since they form so large a proportion of its inhabitants. The place had increased considerably since my previous visit, and now was all ablaze with illuminations during the Muhammadan fast of Ramazan. I did not stay, however, hoping that I might reach Pishpek on Saturday evening and rest there on Sunday.

The fourth station beyond Aulie-Ata was Maldabaevskaia, where, on my previous visit, a horse kicked a poor *yemstchik*, or postillion, and broke his leg, whereupon my interpreter, like a good Samaritan, set the bone, and we left the man with some pence in charge of the postmaster to be taken care of. The present whereabouts of the patient I could not learn, but at another station, Akir-Tiube, the incident seemed to be remembered by one of the men, who added that the *yemstchik* had since died.

We were now passing through the historical region of Ming-bulak, or the land of a " thousand springs" mentioned by mediæval travellers in Central Asia, where the season was not so advanced as we had found it at Tashkend. The nights were rather cold, and though we had entered the second half of May, I was not too warm sleeping in my fur-lined ulster. Besides this, it did not improve matters that I had to get out of the tarantass at several stations to pay the fare, Joseph's Russian being almost *nil*, and his Uzbeg not always understood by the postmaster.

At Merke, 104 miles from Aulie-Ata, we had passed out of the General Government of Turkistan into that of the Steppe, over which rules General Kolpakovsky. Remembering the kind reception this gentleman had previously given me, and with a lively hope of favours to come, I telegraphed from Tashkend to his Excellency, giving the date when I expected to leave, and intimating that I might like to make a *détour* to Issik-Kul; and in that case asking his assistance at Pishpek, where the road turns off to the mountains.

On the next day came a telegram from the General, according me a welcome to Central Asia, and saying that he had asked the Governor of Semirechia to help me towards Issik-Kul, Kuldja, and Kashgar. In accordance with this I telegraphed on Saturday afternoon from Merke to Colonel Pushchin, the chief of the district at Pishpek, to say that I was coming, and then set out once more to post all night.

Arrived at Pishpek early next morning, we were speedily inquired for by Colonel Pushchin, upon whom, after a few hours' sleep and breakfast, I called, and was introduced to his mother, who spoke German, and to a brother-officer, Gedyuonoff, who talked French.

The Colonel said he had sent a messenger to Kara-Kol, the seat of administration, 250 miles distant, at the extreme east of Lake Issik-Kul, to make special arrangements whereby I should pass from thence to Vierny, and he was now ready to change my *padarojna* accordingly, and to accompany me for a few days' journey. This was all very kind, but was a little more than I had asked, since I had not finally decided to go thus far out of my way.

Before leaving England I had asked for hints and suggestions from that prince of Central Asian geographers, the late Colonel Sir Henry Yule, whom I was privileged to number among my literary friends, and who looked over for me some of the proof-sheets of my *Russian Central Asia*. He replied that he had not many things to advise, but suggested my seeing as much as possible of the Tian Shan Mountains and Lake Issik-Kul.

In St Petersburg they told me there are but few specimens of fish or fauna from this region in the museums of Europe, and they spoke of the desirability of my getting more; added to which, M. Oshanin had told me that he had once proceeded from Pishpek to Kara-Kol by post, and thence, by hire of private horses, to Zaitefska, and so forward by *zemstvo* or municipal post to Vierny, for which last stage, however, it was necessary to have an *okriti list*, or official permit.

It was, therefore, on the possibility of my wishing to make this novel *détour* that I had telegraphed to General Kolpakovsky that I might like to go to Issik-Kul. What, then, was now to be done?

From information gathered on the way, it had been ascertained that my baggage could not reach Vierny for several days, and that it was undesirable for us to arrive there much beforehand, because Vierny had not yet recovered from the effects of an earthquake which had turned the people out of their houses into tents, and destroyed the hotel.

Also the Colonel mentioned amongst the interesting points of the proposed journey that I might photograph an ancient tower near Tokmak; and when to these considerations it was added that all the necessary preparations had been made, it seemed to me that I could not do better than take advantage of time and opportunity to proceed by this longer and more difficult, though, as I hoped, more interesting and profitable, route to Vierny.

After continuous travel of three days and nights it would have been pleasant to rest; but the Colonel's business required haste, and after entertaining me at dinner, he suggested that we should start the same evening, and sleep 40 miles distant, at Tokmak.

We set out accordingly in our two vehicles at dusk, all going well until, about midnight, my Jehu drove into a ditch, where we stuck so fast that neither coaxing nor whip would get us out. We had therefore to wait until the Colonel sped forward to the station and sent back help, after which we reached the Russian village of Tokmak, and slept in a semi-official rest-house.

Early next morning we started for an excursion of eight miles southwards, over a plain, to the Burana, a small stream running from the mountains into the Chu. Near to this was the Burana Tower, of burnt bricks, nonagonal at the base, but circular above, with six ornamental bands of bricks laid in arabesques, though not coloured or in the form of letters.

The tower had no chamber within. I stepped round the base in 44 paces; but a peasant among the company, who professed to have measured it, said the tower was 84 feet round and 210 feet high, though I should think the latter an exaggeration. Some 15 or 20 feet above the ground was a doorway, with a lintel of rotten wood, leading by a staircase to the top, up to which eminence, when I was about to take a photograph of the tower, one of the natives climbed, to be immortalised, as the Colonel told him, in a never-dying picture.

No one on the spot could give information as to the origin of the structure. Some attributed it, like other great and unknown things in Turkistan, to Tamerlane, and said that the Kirghese had found here gold coins which had been sent to the Archæological Commission at St Petersburg. For my own part, it reminded me of very similar towers I had seen, without gallery, finish, or finial at the summit, among the ruins of Old Khiva, as well as a later attempt to build one of like character at Modern Khiva.*

At the time of my visit a discovery had recently

* For illustrations of these minarets, see *Russian Central Asia*, vol. ii., pp. 291, 306, 343, and vol. i., p. 586. There is no lack of slender minarets in Central Asia, as in Samarkand, to say nothing of the one already alluded to at Bokhara; but all of these are, if I mistake not, smaller in girth than those of the two Khivas and this one at Tokmak. Is it that the larger ones are more ancient, and the slender forms, with projecting gallery at the top, a supposed later improvement? Those at Ancient Khiva are not probably less than seven centuries old, since it was in 1220 Kunia Urgenj was destroyed by the sons of Jinghiz Khan, and, so far as one can judge by the present state of the brickwork, I venture to think this tower at Tokmak quite as old, if not older; and we know there was a city in this locality at least 500 years earlier. In the seventh century the Chinese traveller Hiuen Tsiang passed

been made of Christian cemeteries near Tokmak and Pishpek, which give us dates and suggest the former populousness of these localities. A pamphlet entitled *Christian Monuments in Semirechia* was given me by Mr Nicholson when passing through St Petersburg. This pamphlet Lieutenant Cromie has helped me by translating, whence it appears that the description therein of the cemetery near Pishpek is written by M. Pantusoff (upon whom I called in Vierny, and who supplied me with rubbings of some of the tombstones). Professor D. A. Chvolson, a well-known Russian scholar, has supplemented the description by remarks on the inscriptions discovered, as well as by a short account of Nestorian Christianity in Central Asia. This will no doubt interest antiquarian readers, as well as throw a little light on the early spread of Christianity in these parts.

The cemetery at Pishpek, extending over eight acres, is situated about seven miles from the present village, and two miles from the mountains, near the road to the Solyan defile, on an eminence sloping to the north-east. No remains have been found of an inclosure or ditch, nor, with the exception of two clay ruins, are there indications of a church or belfry. The

through Tokmak, which seems to have continued a place of importance, since, later on, it gave its name to the Khanate of Kipchak; and both Schuyler and Howorth regard the Sultans of Tokmak, of the fourteenth and fifteenth centuries, as synonymous with the Shahs of Kharezm—that is, Khiva (see Schuyler's *Turkistan*, vol. ii., p. 126, and Howorth's *Mongols*, vol. ii., p. 287). If, then, in the thirteenth century, Old Khiva, having such public erections, was in any way subordinate or inferior to Tokmak, one might naturally expect to find in the leading city of the Khanate such a minaret as this, erected probably by the Muhammadans for worship. A similar tower is mentioned by the Chinese traveller Tch'ang Te in 1259, in the city T'a-la-sze, or Talas (Schuyler, vol. i., p. 399), which Bretschneider, after Schuyler, seems disposed to place on the river of that name somewhere about Aulie-Ata.

greater portion of the cemetery has now been ploughed up, and the part remaining, which consists of small mounds, probably family graves, would most likely have shared the same fate had it not been difficult of access.

Lying about on the surface, but in some cases now buried, are numerous oblong stones (with inscriptions), usually portable and weighing less than 40 lbs.—uncut cobblestones of hard rock, evidently waterworn. A few have been artificially polished previous to their being engraved. Most are of grey granite, but a few of grey sandstone, and two of breccia, these last being the only large stones discovered in the cemetery, and measuring about a yard long and three-quarters of a yard in width and thickness.

On the elevations not yet ploughed the graves are in straight rows, with long mounds, and excavation shows that all the graves were so placed on the level ground. The grave-stones are laid flat in a westerly direction with the inscribed side upwards, whereas on the higher ground they now lie in heaps, slightly embedded in the earth. The number of grave-stones found is 611, but many more are buried.*

* With a view to further examination, a grave was opened under one of the largest stones, seemingly in its original position, and sunk into the earth fully two-thirds of its own thickness. In an easterly direction from this stone, immediately under the turf, lay flat two rows of square burnt bricks, each measuring 150 square inches; and, about three feet lower, under the friable earth with which the cavity had been filled, was a gable roof over a steened vault of sun-dried, straw-made bricks, the roof meeting in the centre at an angle of 45°. This roof was constructed over the lower half only of the vault, whilst over the head was a millstone, or slab, laid flat, and supported on thick pieces of juniper, now rotten.

The grave was 6 feet deep, 3 feet wide at the top, and 21 inches at the bottom. The corpse lay with feet towards the east, and the face towards the north. The bones of the right hand lay on the pelvis; the

Between 30 and 40 miles distant from this Pishpek cemetery, and a mile from the tower on the Burana, another Christian cemetery has been discovered, from which I was shown two of the grave-stones. They resembled those sent by M. Pantusoff to the Imperial Archæological Commission. He gives the measurement of one as 13 inches long by 11 inches wide, and weighing 33 lbs.

Those I saw had each only one Maltese cross incised thereon, without anchor, ornament, or smaller crosses; but in other cases is frequently written an inscription in Syriac characters, which it puzzled M. Pantusoff to find any one in Semirechia to read.

Professor Chvolson, however, has come to the rescue, and the following are specimens of the translations he has made, not, however, without difficulty,
left hand was raised to the head with its bones under the skull. Pieces apparently of fir planks were found in the grave, not seemingly the remains of a coffin, but fragments placed for some purpose above, below, and around the corpse.

In order to secure a better specimen of a skull, a second grave was opened, 14 feet south from the first. As before, the outline of the grave was well marked by burnt bricks under the turf, the cavity was filled with friable earth, and over the head of the vault were found three stones. A steened vault of sun-dried bricks with bones was found at the same depth as before; but the receptacle for the corpse was constructed differently.

Thus the grave, 6 feet 6 inches long, was dug out to a width of 3 feet, and, at the depth of 5 feet, was narrowed on either side by projections, below which, in the centre, was formed a receptacle so narrow that the corpse would seem to have been forced into it, whilst on each side, cut out of the stiff clay, was a ledge or shelf containing the remains of a body. The skeleton in the centre, with hands at the sides and face towards the north, measured 5 feet 6 inches, and the two others 5 feet each in length, these last having the hands apparently over the pelvis and the faces upwards. In one of the side sections of this family grave were two carnelian "false pearls," but no sign of wood, dress, or other ornaments. Nothing has been discovered near the cemetery save square burnt bricks, but near the site where the stones were found are traces of a small artificial cairn.

owing to the impurity of the Syriac affected by Turki words:—

    No. 1. In the year 1169 (858 of the Nestorian era). This is the tomb of Menchitenesh, a believer.*

    2. In the year 1222. The boy Tekin. (Tekin is a Turkish name.)

    3. (At Tokmak.) 1578 (the year of the Hare, 4th year of the Turkish twelve-summer cycle). This is the tomb of Shahmalik Perio-deuta, the son of George Almuts.

    4. In 1600 (the year of the Bull). George, the priest-superior of the church.

    7. 1618. This is the grave of Julia, a graceful girl, betrothed to John, leader of the choir.

    8. 1627 (the year of the Eclipse or Dragon). This is the tomb of Shelikha, the renowned interpreter of Scripture and Preacher, who filled all the monasteries with light, the son of Peter the expounder. He was celebrated for wisdom, and his voice was sonorous as a trumpet. May our Lord unite his enlightened spirit to those of just men and the fathers. May every lustre be his portion!

    11. 1638. This is the tomb of John A . . . . ki Akpasha, son of Tsaliva, archpriest of the church.

    19. (At Tokmak.) The house of rest of Keritlug George.

---

* Chvolson observes that Menchitenesh is a Turkish name, which seems to show that at this date some of the Turks had become Christians. The date is doubtless counted from the era of the Seleucidæ, 311 B.C., as was usual with the Nestorians.

The discovery of these epitaphs in regions where most English people have little idea that Christianity ever penetrated, will interest not a few, if only by way of showing the similarity of human nature and Christian epitaphs all the world over; for how much does the last epitaph, for instance, remind one of that of Dean Alford at Canterbury, *Deversorium viatoris Hierosolymam proficiscentis*—" The way-side resting-place of one travelling to Jerusalem "! *

But I must hasten forward from the Burana Tower, whence this archæological excursus began. Having returned to the village and obtained post-horses, we drove along the valley lowlands, having the Chu on our right, and on either hand in the distance mountain ranges still sprinkled with snow—the Ala-Tau to the left, and the Alexander range to the right. We met on the road, in carts, several Dungans, from the Ili valley, and after driving 18 miles reached Staro- (or Old) Tokmak.

Then crossing the Little Kebin river, near the entrance to the Kastek Pass, we drove south-east to the Chu, which we crossed by a bridge not far from its confluence with the Great Kebin, the banks of both rivers here being rocky and precipitous. Beyond this point the road became hilly, and it looked ominous of hard travel ahead, when at the next station, Djil-Aryk, they gave five horses, though paying for three.

* These epitaphs have a further interest to the linguist and palæographer in showing the old forms of Syriac employed in Central Asia by the Nestorians, who gave an alphabet and instruction, be it remembered, to the Uigurs, or inhabitants of Chinese Turkistan, of whom we shall have to speak hereafter. These discoveries, moreover, may perhaps help us better to fix the sites of some of the ancient cities mentioned by mediæval travellers in Asia, for the identification of which such men as the late Sir Henry Yule, Dr Bretschneider, and Sir Henry Howorth have done so much.

We now entered the celebrated Buam defile, nearly 50 miles long, the name of which, according to some, is derived from a Mongol word *bomo*, signifying "a rift," or, as some prefer, "a pathway over precipitous crags bordering a river." Both are true as regards the facts, and we soon found ourselves toiling up an ascent that needed all the strength of our five horses, and then descending with locked wheels a narrow road, and that sometimes of bare rock over a cornice without rails or safeguards, overhanging one precipice after another, at the foot of which roared the Chu.

Late in the afternoon we approached a fine bridge thrown across this river, where repairs were being superintended by Mr Engineer Kapustin, who was camping close by, and who gave us some tea. Shooting seemed to be his principal pastime, and in his lonely condition it was not unnatural that he should desire us to stay, which the Colonel did, whilst I pressed forward on a fairly level road on the east bank of the Chu, through magnificent scenery, varied by a few trees, such as the wild pistachio, growing amidst what seemed to me a new flora of lilies and irises, to Kok-Mainak, where it was arranged we should stay.

We were now in the very heart of the Buam defile, which bisects the most northerly chain of the huge mass of Central Asian mountains called the Tian Shan. Towards the east stretches the Trans-Ilian Ala-Tau, consisting of two long and lofty parallel chains, known as the northern and southern. The northern ridge presents an uninterrupted mountain chain, rising in its central portion to the limits of perpetual snow, with an average height of 8,600 feet, but its highest peak, Tal-Cheku, attains an elevation of 15,353 feet. The southern range, called Kungei

Ala-Tau, has a mean elevation of 8,825 feet. Towards the west from the Buam defile stretches the Alexander range, at the foot of which we had travelled all along from Aulie-Ata.

The post-station at Kok-Mainak stood quite alone, and on rising next morning and taking a turn outside, the silent solitude was oppressive. The postmaster, too, unless I am mistaken, was living alone as a bachelor, though his guest-room was singularly neat and comfortable, made ready perhaps for the reception of his district chief and the English traveller.

Colonel Pushchin did not accompany me farther, but after early breakfast sped me forward 16 miles to the southern end of the Pass, where was, or ought to have been, the station Kutemaldy; but the earthquake of the previous year had shaken down the post-house, and a tent only was pitched for the accommodation of travellers. We were now fairly out of the Pass into the basin of Lake Issik-Kul, along whose entire northern side for 115 miles we were to have the happiness of driving—a gratification that has fallen to the lot of very few English travellers.

Our road to the next station lay about a mile from the water, which in some places is as much as eight miles from the mountains, and we passed over sometimes meadow-land, sometimes sedge, but rarely through forest growth of any kind. Bushes appeared only at the mouths of mountain torrents, and then consisted for the most part of *oblipikh* covered with narrow silver-coloured leaves, and dwarf trees of hawthorn, barberry, and various kinds of water-willow. We passed a picket of Cossacks, changed horses at Tura-Aigir, and towards evening arrived at Choktal, where the good-natured postmaster gave us a roasted wild duck, and whence we determined to post on through the night.

The shores at first continued flat, or sloped gently towards the water, but in the small hours of the morning I perceived that we had come to a stupendous hill, which caused the horses to jib, nearly backing the tarantass over a break-neck declivity.

This caused me, contrary to my custom, to get out and walk, whereupon the animals again becoming unmanageable, they or the driver turned their heads, and, greatly to our alarm, rushed down from nearly the top of the hill, I following and shouting that the whole concern would be dashed to pieces. Much to our surprise, however, the *yemstchik*, or driver, on reaching the bottom, did not stop, but turned and again charged the hill with perfect fury, my servant Joseph and I following, until at last the animals halted, and I drew breath to give thanks for what I regarded as a merciful deliverance.

From Ui-Tal, a picket post-station, we had a pretty drive, and in the afternoon arrived at our destination, Kara-Kol, seven miles from the lake, and a distance of 251 miles from Pishpek.

CHAPTER IX.

FROM ISSIK-KUL TO VIERNY.

A previous traveller to Issik-Kul; Scenery of Kara-Kol, 117.—Attentions from Colonel Vaouline; Arrangements of Chief of the District on my behalf, 118.—Change of plans, 119.—The Kara-Kirghese; their districts, origin, and costume, 120.—How far Muhammadans; Missions among them of Russian Church, 121.—Kirghese modes of treating disease; Fish, for specimens, 124.—Passing through Pishpek, 125.—The Chu river and the Aral depression; Our wheel fallen to pieces, 126.—Arrival at Otar, and repair of tarantass, 127.—Arrival at Uzun-Agatch, and escort to Vierny, 128.

ON driving into Kara-Kol we were to a certain extent breaking new ground, since Mr Delmar Morgan was the only English writer who had pushed on to this out-of-the-way place, which may be compared in winter to Siberia, and in summer to the Engadine. From November to the close of February the little town is visited by violent storms, and the snow lies more than four feet deep. Spring brings abundant rains and frequent fogs, whilst in summer, from May to July, the heat goes up sometimes to 122°, notwithstanding which the climate is healthy and agreeable.

Kara-Kol lies at an elevation of nearly 6,000 feet, amid charming scenery, at the foot of a magnificent mountain range called the Terskei Ala-Tau, which extends all along the southern shore of Issik-Kul and continues eastward right up to Khan Tengri, the monarch of the region, which may be seen from Kara-Kol towering to a height of 24,000 feet—a virgin peak, awaiting the attentions of some knight of the Alpine Club.

Directly east of Kara-Kol is the Tasma range, over which passes the postal pack-road to the Tekes valley. At the time of our visit these mountains presented a splendid panorama of snow-clad peaks; but I did not hear that mountain-climbing, pure and simple, was much in fashion.

Calling on the *Uyezdi-nachalnik*, I found that he had been kind enough to place a house at my disposal, with a Cossack in attendance; but finding the abode rather out of the way, and foreseeing that my stay would be short, I preferred to put up at the post-house, where I could better get provisions, make sundry repairs, and have my tarantass put in order. Here Colonel Vaouline, whom I fortunately met in the street, kindly came to my assistance, sent to me the battalion smith, and helped in other ways.

In the evening I went to a little party gathered at the house of the *nachalnik*, and met among the guests Colonel Korolkoff, with whose brother, the Governor of Ferghana, I had stayed in 1882 in Samarkand.

I found, moreover, that the *nachalnik* had arranged for horses to take me forward, but learned to my disappointment that my only way of proceeding thence to my destination was by going over the Santash Pass in the snow mountains (where there was no shelter or even tent wherein to spend the night) to Jarkend, and thence doubling back 200 miles to Vierny.

This was a great disappointment, first because I was not equipped for camping out, and next, having been under the impression that I could get down to Vierny by the road somewhat to the east of the lake, which reaches the plains at Chilik in the Ili valley, the idea of going so far out of the way as Jarkend was out of the question. Had we been on horseback matters would have been easier, since there are other bridle-paths, but with a tarantass there was no alternative but to return to Pishpek, which accordingly I determined to do.

Less than 24 hours sufficed for a night's rest, and to replenish our larder, thanks partly to the good people at the post-house, who cooked for us three chickens at the cost of a rouble; whilst a good-natured policeman, told off to guard me and mine, and who, though excused from watching by night, made his reappearance at sunrise, helped us in sundry minor arrangements, so that before the sun was high we were ready to start.

About ten miles from Kara-Kol we crossed the Jergalan river, which runs into Issik-Kul at Jergalan Bay. Here may be seen encamped in summer the Kara-Kol garrison, whilst scattered about are the tents of the nomad Kara-Kirghese.

On my previous visit to Central Asia, a friend in Vierny had been anxious that I should see something of these nomads, but I then succeeded in visiting only the Kirghese of the plains called Kazaks, about whom I afterwards wrote three or four chapters in my *Russian Central Asia*. On the present journey I saw only the Kara-Kirghese, and upon them I have certain comple-mentary observations to make, partly from what I saw and partly on the authority of Dr Sceland, Chief of the Army Medical Department, whom I met at Vierny.

The Kara-Kirghese dwell northward, for the most part in the mountainous districts of Issik-Kul and Tokmak, but many are found also in the southern portion of the Tian Shan on Chinese territory. They spread eastward to the Muzart Pass; westward, among the mountains of Ferghana, to Samarkand; and besides those dwelling on the independent portions of the Pamirs, I met on my way to India a few dwelling as far south as the Kilian Pass.

When or whence the Kara-Kirghese settled in their present homes is unknown. In certain places the Kalmuks preceded them, but it is noteworthy that all about the Issik-Kul valley have been found vestiges, such as hatchets, lamps, spearheads, and sickles, pointing to an ancient people further advanced in civilisation than either Kirghese or Kalmuk. Neither of these works in copper or brass, and their agriculture is only of yesterday, so that seemingly they had formerly no need of the sickle, whilst the bricks and money discovered all point to another stratum of society, an Altaic origin being usually attributed to the Kirghese because of their language.

I had several opportunities of observing their dress, or, I might add, the want of it, for many were very ragged, and the children ran about naked. Next the skin is worn a long shirt of wool or cotton, and stockings of felt; then wide trousers of cotton or leather, over which is put a long *khalat*, like a dressing-gown with long sleeves. They have boots of leather, with goloshes; the shaven head is covered with a *tibeteika*, or skull-cap, which in turn is covered with a fantastically pointed hat of felt, or a busby of sheepskin. When travelling in winter, the busby is replaced by a *malakhai*, or pointed hood lined with sheepskin and furnished with a flap or curtain covering the neck and shoulders.

The costume of the women in many respects resembles that of the men, with one marked difference, however, of head-dress, which in the case of the married woman is an enormous bonnet or series of bandages of white cotton, covering everything—the sides of the face, the neck, the shoulders, and even part of the back. The women's hair is plaited into small braids, from which dangle at the end coins among the rich, but with the poor various metallic ornaments, some of them being exceedingly grotesque, as, for instance, odd keys and a broken brass tap, which I saw suspended from the tresses of a fair one at the western end of Issik-Kul.

The Russian Missionary Monastery at the eastern end of the lake directed one's thoughts, of course, to the religious condition of the Kara-Kirghese, amongst whom it is placed. They call themselves Sunnite Muhammadans, but in general are indifferent and ignorant of doctrine. They pray according to Mussulman fashion, and observe the fasts, but not too exactly. Their mullahs are few and ignorant, knowing only certain prayers learned by heart from the Koran, and their mosques are fewer.

On the other hand, the Kirghese firmly believe in an invisible world. To them the tops of the mountains are peopled with spirits; sickness is the work of the devil, and the intervention of invisible beings in the affairs of men is accepted without question. With a mixture of Pagan and Mussulman beliefs, they venerate here and there objects of extraordinary character. Thus, in the Issygaty defile, near Tokmak, is an enormous stone of unknown origin with a human figure rudely cut on one side ; whereon every Kirghese, in passing, thinks it obligatory to place, as an offering, a piece of tallow.

Their respect for cemeteries and tombs amounts almost to a religion by itself. The corpse is usually placed in the grave, sitting, with the face towards the east; but occasionally there is dug for it a secondary chamber in one of the walls of the principal tomb; and over it is built sometimes a monument of clay or stone. The Kirghese come frequently to say their prayers at these cemeteries, which are well looked after, though without appointed guardians.

On my first visit to Turkistan, Archbishop Alexander at Vierny informed me they were about to begin a mission of the Orthodox Church to the Kara-Kirghese of Issik-Kul; and after seeing the little monastery there in 1888, I turned with interest to the report of the Chief Procurator of the Holy Synod for 1887, to read what had been done. All that could be gathered, however, was that, in consequence of the recent earthquake at Vierny, building operations at the new Mission Monastery had been suspended, and a determination arrived at to rest content for the present with the existing church, which sufficed for the small monastic community.

From a report of the Altai and Kirghese Mission in the eparchy or diocese of Tomsk for 1888, I learn that the Bukonsk station among the neighbouring Kirghese was then five years old, and that 23 individuals had been baptised during the year, including a family of five persons, the good effects of which had appeared in a diminution of drunkenness, though names' days and marriage feasts still gave occasion for excess.

From this young mission had gone out a psalmist, or precentor, Stephen Borisoff, to a small settlement called Great Narim, on the head-waters of the Bukhtarma, in the district of Ust Kamenogorsk, where, whilst acting as teacher at the Cossack School, he also occupied himself as missionary to the surrounding Kirghese. The Cossacks of the settlement are said to be devout, and to have rejoiced greatly when, their church being consecrated in 1888, there were baptised on the same occasion six Kirghese. Since then, on Sundays and Holy Days, the morning service and afternoon devotional readings are said to have kept the church full all day.

From a report of the Orthodox Missionary Society for 1889, it appears that the Russian Church Mission to the Kirghese in the Tomsk eparchy had a teaching staff of two priests, a precentor, and an interpreter under Bishop Macarius, living at Biisk.* The report says also that translation into the Altai languages of liturgies, etc., has been continued, but I find no special reference to the Kirghese.

Some of the missionaries, it appears, practise medicine a little, and even the precentors and teachers in the catechists' school have been taught to vaccinate; whilst to the Dean's house at Biisk is attached a hospital with a *feldscher*,† who goes when needed to

---

* The few particulars given of this Tomsk mission are so mixed up with details of the 12 stations in the Altai Mission that it is not easy to discriminate between the two, but one paragraph says that the members of both missions, numbering 1 bishop, 13 priests, 3 deacons, 9 precentors, 23 male and 4 female teachers, and 3 interpreters, travelled in the course of the year 16,266 miles, and gained as converts 516 heathen and 14 Muhammadans, the latter of which I suppose may be Kirghese.

† Literally a barber, or one who lets blood, but in practice a surgeon's assistant who picks up a certain amount of rudimentary knowledge in attending on a surgeon.

the mission settlements and accompanies the Superintendent on mission journeys.

After driving past the Issik-Kul Monastery, we arrived at Preobajensk, where a man came out to ask medical advice on behalf of his daughter, which I was obliged to decline the honour of giving, though perhaps I could have prescribed as well as some of their Kirghese doctors, who are great believers in "like cures like" and the use of symbolical and sympathetic measures.

Thus, for an obstinate attack of yellow jaundice, they wear on the forehead a piece of gold, or, better, cause the patient to look at it for a whole day, or if a piece of gold be lacking, which is generally the case, they substitute a brass basin.

A singular remedy is adopted against *dyspnœa*, or fainting, which they call "mountain sickness." This they represent to themselves under the form of a young lady, before whom they utter to the patient the most obscene and disgusting expressions, thinking thereby to shock the lady's modesty and drive her away.*

At Preobajensk also, on the outward journey, a number of Kirghese boys and men turned out in force and waded into the stream to catch me specimens of fish, which they brought with great glee to the tarantass.

---

* As illustrative of treatment by symbol, it may be mentioned that if the malady reside in the lungs or liver, they give the patient the corresponding parts of an animal to eat, as, for instance, the roasted eyes of an ox to cure ophthalmia! Again, the treatment of intermittent fever and difficult parturition by fright are still more remarkable.

In the latter case, if the child does not appear with becoming celerity, the sage women press the mother, a strong man being occasionally called in to help. Sometimes, however, they put the patient upon a horse, which they cause to gallop about; or, worse still, they resolve to frighten out the devil (for of course the disorder can be due to no one

And now at Ui-Tul, the neighbouring station, a number of children, remembering my former inquiries for small fish, and hoping no doubt for kopecks, brought me a further collection, and, thus supplied, we posted on all through the day and night, and at an early hour in the morning reached Choktal.

From Choktal we posted to Tura-Aigir, and, towards the western end of the lake, we turned aside from the post-road to a few Kirghese dwellings on the shore. Entering one of these tents, I found a number of lambs and kids taken in for shelter, whilst without were some of their skins stretched in the sun and covered apparently with lime, the whole arrangement indicating great poverty. They seemed to have no objection to my photographic operations, which I finished, and then, having taken a last look at the beautiful lake, we drove to Kutemaldi, posted again over two stages with five horses, and arrived at Pishpek early on the following morning.

I should have greatly preferred to have gone from Tokmak by the old mountain road over the Kastek Pass, followed, I take it, by the travellers of the middle ages; but it was said to be all but unusable for a tarantass, and with no postal accommodation, so that the only alternative was to proceed by the longer road made by the Russians in the plains.

Accordingly, after stopping a few hours at Pishpek,

else) and make him give up his prey. For this purpose the woman is led in front of the tent, supported by the arms, and there suddenly rushes out before her a troop of horsemen brandishing their *nagaikas*, or whips, and uttering screams and noises diabolical.

These items of medical information are given on the authority of Dr Seeland, after which his remarks are not surprising that such remedies sometimes end in the death of both mother and child, though he says the Kirghese women generally bear children with less difficulty than Europeans.

and taking lunch with Colonel Pushchin, we started for Vierny, and made our first halt at Constantinovsk, where a Russian New Testament was shown to me by the *starosta*, or keeper of the post-house, who seemed to remember my coming six years before. At this place, too, we crossed by a bridge for the last time the Chu, one of the important rivers of Central Asia, and frequently mentioned by early travellers.*

From Constantinovsk we continued over a spur of the northern Ala-Tau range, which here, as it sinks into the plain under the appellation of the Koi-Jarligan Mountains, forms a water-parting between the Chu and Ili valleys. We had reached a level road, when soon after midnight our *yemstchik* uttered a cry, and Joseph, on getting out of the tarantass, asked me to do so too, whereupon I saw one of our hind wheels not merely broken, but resolved into its component parts. I suggested, therefore, that the driver should endeavour to borrow a wheel from the station ahead.

---

* The Chu rises south-west of Issik-Kul, and flows within about three miles of the western end of the lake, sending thither at times some of its waters through a small stream, the Kutemaldi; but Ashton Dilke, and Schuyler after him, seem to think that at some period of the world's history, when the level of Issik-Kul was higher, the lake overflowed into the Chu, which continued its course through the steppe to the Syr-daria, and so onwards to the Oxus, and finally into the Caspian. Also both Schuyler and Kostenko speak of the Sea of Aral as having once occupied a far greater area than at present.

I mention this last only to say that it is not confirmed by the recent investigations of Mr Bateson, who in 1886 and 1887 journeyed among the lakes of Western Central Asia for the purpose of making observations on their fauna, and who, in a paper read before the Royal Society, says: "For these reasons it seems that, though the Aral Sea has retired within recent times from such an area as would be covered by it if its level were about 15 feet higher than it now is, yet it cannot be shown that it has continuously receded from an area much larger than this" (*Philosophical Transactions of the Royal Society of London*, vol. 180, pp. 297-330).

It seemed wisest to take matters philosophically, and to turn in and sleep, which I accordingly did. In due time the *yemstchik* came, and by early morning we arrived at Otar.

We had now on the south the Ala-Tau Mountains, whilst northwards, stretching away for about ten miles

THE SOURCE OF THE KOPA.

east and west, was the Kopa valley, through which, when there is water enough, runs the river of the same name, having its head-streams in the Kuldja Bashi Mountains, and flowing into the Kurtu river, and so onwards to the Ili and into Lake Balkash.

There was no resident smith at Otar, but there was

a prison *étape*, where happened to be resting for the day a batch of exiles on their way to Siberia. Amongst them were two Orenburg Cossacks, who for a small price were as well satisfied to mend our wheel as we were thankful to be released from our difficulty.

I much enjoyed the rest by the way, and did not start till evening, when, late in the night, there came on such a storm of wind and dust, with a little rain, that the station-master at Sam-Su almost implored me not to go forward. We stayed accordingly for a few hours, and early next morning arrived at Uzun-Agatch, a village of 113 houses occupied by Russian emigrants.

The majority of the houses were of unburnt brick, and had suffered badly from the recent earthquake at Vierny, 35 miles off. At Uzun-Agatch is a stream, flowing from the Ala-Tau range, whence I secured some specimens of fish, *usman*, *piscari*, and *marinka*, and then posted on to Kiskilensk, our last station for changing horses.

At Kiskilensk the postmaster had received a letter from the authorities about me, in deference to which he mounted his horse and rode before us for 16 miles into Vierny.

CHAPTER X.

VIERNY AFTER AN EARTHQUAKE.

Vierny pleasantly situated, 129.—Eye-witnesses' description of earthquake, 130.—Houses of burnt brick most damaged; Destruction around town; Mud streams from the mountains, 131.—Losses of life, 132.—Removal of inhabitants; Author taken to Governor's temporary abode; Lodged in M. Gourdet's new house, 133.—Money sent to Kashgar, 134.—Anniversary of earthquake, and Memorial Chapel; Seismic record of earthquake shocks, 135.—Baggage delayed; Remissness of Russian Society for Transport, 137.—*Douceur* given and misappropriated, 138.—Arrival of baggage; Luggage forwarded to Jarkend, 139.

WHEN, in 1882, I descended from Western Siberia, through the monotonous steppes of Semipolatinsk, the praises of Vierny had been sung as beautiful for situation and the joy of the land, and not altogether undeservedly. As we drew near, the town was seen lying about a dozen miles only from the foot of the Trans-Ili Ala-Tau Mountains, which lift their summits to the snow-line, whilst two peaks, Almaty and Talgar, attain respectively to 14,000 and 15,000 feet.

Vierny was founded in 1854, by Cossacks, who built their houses of wood, which, with a view to the preservation of the forests, was subsequently forbidden. The later erections were of brick, for the most part sun-dried, and the broad and straight streets, crossing at right angles, were bordered with trees—willows, poplars, elms, and *Robinia pseudacacia*—so that they presently assumed the appearance of park-like avenues, whilst the palaces of the Governor and Archbishop, the Cathedral, the Governor's garden with its pavilion and flowers, the public schools and government offices, together with a population of 25,000 souls, combined to render this capital the pride of Semirechia.

But on June 9th, scarcely a year before my second visit, the city was visited by an earthquake, of which the local effects remaining were only too visible on every hand, and intensified the account given me by my hosts, Monsieur and Madame Gourdet, who were in the town at the time of the disaster.

The first shock, lasting about five seconds, came, by way of warning, at a quarter to five in the morning, and was accompanied by a rumbling noise as of a heavily laden train passing under the town northwards—that is, from the mountains towards the open Steppe. Everybody was aroused, and most persons dressed; but my host going out of doors, and seeing it to be a lovely morning, with things looking as usual, and thinking that, as on former occasions, the shock would not be repeated, returned to bed.

Within another ten minutes, however, there came a second shock, stronger and more lasting than the first, which shook and ruined the whole neighbourhood. Indoors, the plaster of ceilings and walls fell, first in morsels like hail, and soon, to the noise repeated and increased underground, was added that of falling tiles and bricks. For those in bed there was this time no chance of dressing, and my hosts had scarcely reached the exterior in their nightdresses, when the massive Dutch stoves, the ceilings, the arches of doors and windows tumbled in with a crash, and filled the rooms with *débris*.

For some seconds the trembling ceased, but only to be renewed with fresh force, under which the walls began to fall and buildings to crack, whilst on all sides was heard the crash of tumbling houses. The town was covered with a cloud of dust so thick as to prevent any one seeing farther than from 30 to 40 steps, and, to add to the confusion, the frightened animals—oxen, cows, dogs, and horses—rushed pell-mell through the streets, making their way instinctively towards the Steppe.

This violent agitation lasted for about three minutes, almost without ceasing, after which the shocks became weaker and shorter, and by half-past five my host was able to dress and look about the town.

The houses appeared to have suffered in proportion to their solidity. Those least damaged were the buildings of wood, then the houses of sun-dried brick and clay, whilst structures of burnt brick fared worst of all.

It was not, however, in the town alone, but for a radius of 30 miles from it, that the earthquake was felt. In many instances the ground opened in chasms, sometimes hundreds of yards in length and several fathoms in width. Out of these rents burst forth streams of mud and water, whilst on the sides of the neighbouring mountains many and huge landslips took place, the sites of which were plainly visible at the time of my visit.

An idea may be formed of the masses dislodged, when I add that the Ak-Sai defile—which appears to have been about the centre of the disturbance—was choked with mud to a depth of 70 feet, over a breadth as wide as the Thames at London Bridge. Perhaps the most striking landslip of all was that of half a hill, which, with its forest of firs still standing, majestically slid down towards the plain.

It may be readily supposed that these "hydrochemical modifications of the crust of the earth," as Messrs Oshanin and Gramenitsky call them,* caused great damage and loss of life. In Vierny and its neighbourhood were 328 victims, 180 occurring in the town. In the Kiskilensk defile five men, digging chalk, were buried under it; and a Kirghese caught by a landslip was carried by it for about two miles, he springing the while from spot to spot to avoid falling between the disrupted masses. Less happy was the attempt of a Russian in the same neighbourhood. Taking his wife on his back, and two children in his arms, he ascended a slope some distance out of the way of the rolling mass; but, exhausted by the effort, he fell, and all were buried together.

A Cossack was riding in a defile when a landslip occurred and caught his horse by the legs, whereupon the rider jumped off and ran up an adjoining acclivity, but only just in time to see his horse disappear entirely. Too often the people, on coming out of their *izbas* and seeing the advancing mass, set off running towards the plains and were overtaken, whereas one poor woman, with a child in her arms, had the presence of mind to mount the hill above her house, and was saved; only, however, to see her family of five persons buried a few steps below.

Thus the city of Vierny, with its brick houses to

* See translation, by Miss Hay, in *Proceedings of the Royal Geographical Society*, 1888, p. 638.

the number of 1,840, was ruined, and the higher-class people rushed for accommodation to the 840 humbler wooden houses, of which only 30 were two-storied, and whose owners retired in prospect of high temporary rents. Besides this, the Governor requisitioned from the Kirghese nomads of the province scores, if not hundreds, of felt tents, so that a considerable proportion of the population dwelt for a while under curtains, and things were still in a disorganised condition when we arrived on May 29th.

Our outrider from Kiskilensk conducted us first to the house inhabited temporarily by General Ivanoff, the Governor of Semirechia, who had been expecting me some days, and had kindly arranged a dinner-party for the preceding evening, previous to his necessary departure, a few days later, on a tour of inspection. My journey to Issik-Kul, however, had deprived me of this pleasure, and also of staying with his Excellency, who, rather than leave me in his empty house, had asked M. Paul Gourdet, with whom I was already acquainted, to entertain me.

M. Gourdet is a Frenchman by birth, but has lived many years in Russian Turkistan, as well as some time in England. He is on the staff of professors at the local *gymnase*, or government school, and he also holds the appointment of architect of the town. It was natural, therefore, that he should have lost as little time as possible in getting a house again over his own head.

Into this he and Madame Gourdet had just settled, and since he was kind enough to place his study at my disposal, I found myself in excellent company and far better quarters than I could have expected in a city hardly as yet out of ruin. My luggage, however, had not arrived, and therefore I had but to use the delay in making further preparations, in addition to which I set my servant and some of the natives to collect specimens of the local fauna.

I have intimated that I drew my deposit of paper roubles from the last bank we passed at Tashkend, since doing which I had been carrying my fortune, not, indeed, in my face, but at my waist. This, Sir Robert Morier had told me at the capital, would be nothing less than putting a premium on robbery. I might have replied that it was only to gentlemen of approved character like his Excellency to whom I confided such secrets, besides which there was nothing else to be done; and I was getting along with tolerable equanimity.

When, however, news reached me from Miss Hay of the murder of Mr Dalgleish on the very road over which I was to travel, it struck me as highly desirable to send on to Kashgar as much of my money as I could spare, so that if I reached there robbed and spoiled there would be a fund awaiting me. It was possible to send from Vierny to Narin any number of rouble notes by post and insure them to the full amount, but other packets could be insured at the rate of 10s. per cent. to an amount not exceeding 500 roubles each.

Two parcels, therefore, were made up of rupees and one of roubles, and all three insured. Beyond Narin the Governor kindly came to my assistance by promising to arrange with Colonel Larionoff there, to have the packets forwarded six or eight days beyond, by Cossacks, with the monthly letters to M. Petrovsky, the Russian Consul at Kashgar.

During our stay in Vierny occurred the anniversary

of the earthquake, duly inaugurated by another slight shock, and locally observed by the consecration of a small memorial chapel or oratory, built in one of the avenues of the town. The slight shock alluded to was one of a series that had been going on all through the year, recognised only too surely by those who had passed through the great calamity, but unperceived by me. Thus I learned at breakfast on June 9th that about one o'clock in the morning there had been a shock sufficiently severe to rouse the servants out of their beds.*

I did not see much of Russian Church matters or military affairs during my stay, being too busy about my overdue baggage, which had been causing me

* M. Gourdet, who had kept a seismic record for the previous 12 months, told me that after the fatal half-hour on May 28th (old style) there were, from 5 to 9 a.m., continued shocks every 2 or 3 minutes, accompanied by loud subterranean noises; from 9 to 12, shocks about every 5 minutes; and at 1.50, 2.35, and 4.0 tremblings that shook down pieces of walls. At 4.30 came a violent, destructive shaking which lasted 7 or 8 seconds, and caused walls to fall, so that many persons who were getting out their furniture were killed or wounded.

All through the night of the 28-29th shocks were repeated at intervals of 5, 10, and 30 minutes, and on the 29th between 5.0 and 1.0 occurred 10 shocks. On the 30th were recorded 10 shocks; on the 31st, 8; on June 1st, 7; and so on, with the exception of June 7th and 18th, shocks up to 10 daily all the month.

In July the number per day decreased, but there were only 7 days during the month when there was nothing to record. Subsequently, shocks were felt on 15 days in August, 18 days in September, 4 days in October, 7 in November, 14 in December, 18 in January, 3 in February, 7 in March, 3 in April, and so on up to Easter Sunday, after which they seem to have ceased till the anniversary of the earthquake.

According to my latest information from M. Gourdet (February 1891), "The earthquake does not forget us, and from time to time we get splendid shaking. On June 30th, 1889, we had a shock lasting 12 minutes almost as strong as that of 1887. We are now accustomed to these shocks, and do not fear them since the new houses are built of wood. This year we have had two or three shocks that may be called good ones, and about a score of little ones not worth mentioning."

delay all along the road from Bokhara. Nineteen packages, as already stated, were sent from England by sea to Batoum, and when Batoum was a free port merchandise intended for Persia or China passed through, I suppose, easily enough. But now "*nous avons changé tout cela*," and letter and telegram awaiting my arrival at St Petersburg informed me that to get my goods through the Batoum Customhouse, especially in the absence of their owner, without unpacking and the closest scrutiny, required nothing less than the mandate of the Minister of Finance at the capital.

Here M. Sabler was of great use, and took me first to the Minister, M. Vishnegradsky, and then to the Chief of the Customs; with the result that, partly, I think, in deference to the charitable mission I was undertaking, and partly, perhaps, to the good recommendations at my back, an exception was made in my favour, and the Chief telegraphed to his subordinates that 18 of my cases were to be sealed and allowed to pass on their way unopened and without payment of duty; the remaining package, which was my lunch-basket, being examined as usual.

This was a great concession, and I proceeded promptly to arrange in St Petersburg with the Russian Society for Transport that they should forward the 18 cases a distance of 2,300 miles, from Batoum to Vierny, which was their nearest depôt to Kuldja, at the rate of 30*s.* per cwt, with insurance at 13*s.* 4*d.* per cent., and that the time employed in transit should not exceed six weeks.

On two occasions previously my heavy baggage had been taken forward in time by slow transit to the Urals and even Tiumen, the first town in Siberia, by the brothers Kamensky; but they had no office in Vierny, and I was limited to the Russian Society, which I fondly hoped would keep to its engagement, or at all events be not more than a fortnight late, which my arrangements permitted as a margin.

On reaching Batoum I found that Mr Peacock had kindly sent forward the packages. The lunch-basket was still in his care, and when I heard to what treatment it had been subjected I shuddered at the thought of what might have happened to the rest. It appeared that two phlegmatic and precise custom-house officials had inflicted thereon nothing less than a visitation that lasted off and on for about three mortal hours.

There must, of course, be something uncanny about a basket that called for a telegram from St Petersburg, and accuracy was just then the order of the chief of the day. Accordingly, everything was thoroughly searched, weighed, valued, and entered; but, with all their exactitude, fluids were spilled and things not put back properly. And I know not what might have happened to the thousand and one knick-knacks of the larger cases, the scores of bottles of medicine, photographic negatives, and well-nigh innumerable presents for the natives!

Mr Peacock handed me the receipt wherewith to claim the goods and pay for their carriage at Vierny, and upon our arrival at Baku on March 30th the goods were said to have been sent forward on the 3rd of the month. So far all was well, though matters began to look suspicious when, on inquiring next at Charjui on April 9th, it appeared that the packages had reached the end of the railway only on March 18th, and had been sent forward three days later on camels to Bokhara. From Bokhara it was said they would proceed to Tashkend on *arbas*, and thence to Vierny by Russian *telegas*, or waggons.

To my great disgust, however, on reaching Bokhara on April 14th, I found that the goods had been despatched only a week previously on camels, and that they would take 20 days to reach Tashkend; further, that there was no means of communicating with the carriers or spurring them on, since they were not going by the telegraph route, but across the Steppe. It was useless to fret or to hurry forward, so we spent several days in Bokhara and Samarkand, and reached Tashkend to learn that the caravan was expected in three days.

It was disheartening, however, to be told that another 30 days would be needed for transit to Vierny. Could nothing be done to accelerate matters? I asked of the agent, who, by-the-by, had seen me six years previously at Petro-Alexandrovsk, and seemed disposed to be friendly and helpful. He led me to believe that under pressure 15 or 16 days might suffice. Also that, if I would pay a *douceur* of 30s. for the hire of extra horses, he hoped to get the goods to Vierny by May 25th. This I paid, and as soon as the baggage had left Tashkend we quickly followed, made the *détour* to Issik-Kul, and reached Vierny to find, as already said, my baggage not come.

The first news received was that it had left Pishpek on June 4th; then, three days later, that delay had been occasioned by the death of one of the carrier's horses; and presently what seemed to be the truth eked out, that the dishonest Kirghese carrier, having received the extra money, slipped it into his purse, and handed over the job to a brother of the craft, who, hearing nothing of the extra speed required, took his time.

On the 8th four packages were said to have arrived, and a horseman was sent out into the Steppe to expedite the rest, whereupon the agent showed me a letter said to have come from Tashkend, and pretending that I had promised to pay for a messenger into the Steppe if the goods did not arrive in time. I denied having made any such promise, and claimed that the amount of the *douceur* should be refunded, whereupon the agent wrote what he called an "act," setting forth the belated arrival of the goods, and this was countersigned by the agent, M. Gourdet, myself, and the head of police, as an instrument wherewith I was to threaten vengeance, claim damages, etc., etc., the end of the matter being that when the goods reached Vierny they had been thirteen weeks on the road instead of six. Needless to add, I have received back none of the *douceur*.

A local carrier was now found who undertook to transport to the Chinese frontier at Jarkend the 18 packages, and nine others added, in all weighing 60 *poods*, or nearly a ton. For doing this he was to receive 65 kopecks per *pood*, and to be only eight days on the road. He started on the day after the arrival of the goods at Vierny, and we quickly followed.

In many respects our stay in Vierny had been a pleasant one. M. Gourdet was full of information, and Madame of hospitality. Both were helpful in enabling me to make preparations of various kinds, to say nothing of hints and suggestions whereby many hundreds, not to say thousands, of specimens of the fauna were collected, of which last more hereafter.

CHAPTER XI.

FROM VIERNY TO THE CHINESE FRONTIER.

Departure from Vierny, and meeting an Englishman at Ilisk, 140.—A gang of Siberian exiles; False statement as to their chains, 141.—Altitude of Ilisk, 142.—Crossing bridge; Geology of the road; Need of sound wheels; Road to Jarkend, 143.—Hospitality provided, 144.—Introduction to a rich native; Offers of service from Prjevalsky's guides, 145.—Arrangements for money, and modes of conveyance; Purchase of cart and horses, 146.—Kindness of Yuldasheff; Departure from Jarkend, and review of Russian favours, 147.—Driving towards the frontier, and warnings as to being stopped, 148.—Advised to approach from Peking, 149.—Deprived of interpreter, 150.—Cossacks for escort, and "success number one"; Site of ancient Almalik; Martyrdom of mediæval Christians; To and at Suiting; Arrival at Kuldja, 151.

WE left Vierny early on the morning of June 13th, driving across the Steppe about 150 miles, along the course of the Almati, and gradually descending 1,000 feet to the river Ili, which gives its name to the station of Ilisk on its western bank. It was of no use attempting to arrive at Jarkend much in advance of our luggage, because the place was said to be small and without an inn.

At Ilisk, therefore, we stopped for a day to collect specimens, and met a fellow-countryman named John Norman, the first Englishman we had seen, if I remember rightly, east of the Oxus.

Near the Ilisk post-house is an *étape*, where we saw

our last batch of exiles on their way to Siberia. Some had half-shaven heads, signifying that they were criminals of the worst category, including murderers, homicides, etc., and some had chains on their legs; but I do not remember seeing any handcuffed.*

A CONVICT WITH HALF-SHAVEN HEAD.

* The leg-chains reminded me of a passage in the novelette *Called Back*, which roused much anti-Russian feeling in England a few years since, and has often been reproduced on the stage. The author says: "We passed many gangs of convicts plodding along to their fate. Ivan told me that most of them were in chains. This I should not have noticed, as the irons are only on the legs and worn under the trousers" (*Called Back*, by Hugh Conway, pseudonym for the late F. J. Fargus, p. 129).

Now, I have had ample opportunity of examining scores, not to say hundreds, of Russian leg-chains, and at this moment I have an ordinary set, with a prison suit, in my own possession. I once put them on and was photographed, and engravings made therefrom, but with the face altered, have gone over the world in the pages of my own books, as well as those of various periodicals (see *Through Siberia*, p. 155; *Leisure Hour*, March 1881; *Harper's Magazine*, May 1888).

From these pictures it will be seen that the chain, 30 inches long, fastened to each ankle, could not be worn under the trousers. Yet the humane author (who by-the-by had never seen Russia, much less Siberia) adds: "Poor wretched beings, my heart ached for them!" And so, doubtless, has that of many of his readers, but quite needlessly, for these chains worn under the trousers are pure fiction.

Setting out from Ilisk in the evening, we crossed a portion of the Turkistan plains, 500 feet above Lake

CHAINS AND SUMMER COSTUME OF SIBERIAN PRISONER.

Balkash and 1,300 feet above sea-level, to which point I call attention only to observe that we did not again dip to so low an altitude until, after crossing three at least of the very high mountain ranges of the world, we descended six months later to the plains of India.

Our road, after leaving the loess and culturable formations about Vierny, lay across a region of river and lake deposits which continued beyond our first station and some five-and-twenty miles east of the Ili. Then we began to ascend over crystalline limestone and argillaceous schists, as well as porphyries and quartz-felsite, up to a height of 4,000 feet above sea-level, to the post-station of Altyn-Immel.

Here necessity obliged us to stay once more for the repair of the tarantass, the loan of which had been a great accommodation. I had, it will be noticed, to learn over again the lesson taught me in Siberia —namely, the importance of seeing a vehicle put thoroughly in order before starting on a posting journey. This was supposed to have been done in Tashkend at a cost of 30*s.*, but 8*s.* more had to be expended after a three days' run to Pishpek.

The stony road through the Buam Pass enabled one to appreciate to the full the wisdom of M. Bartsch, the Bible Society's Agent in Tashkend, who said that when going to Kara-Kol he took a post telega, and left his tarantass, having regard to its wheels, at Tokmak. This unfortunately I could not do, and, in consequence, we had to stop for repairs at the top of the Pass, again at Kara-Kol, and once more, in returning, at Kutemaldi, where also the shaking was found to have damaged not only the wheels, but to have knocked holes in the bottoms of my spirit cases, jam tins, and fish cylinders.

All this involved, not only expense, but loss of time, and the worst had not yet happened, for on returning to Pishpek the near forewheel was pronounced unsound and was put in dock for five hours, whilst within twelve hours afterwards occurred the incident already recorded, when one of the hind wheels fell to pieces. Six shillings and the Cossack prisoners helped us out of this disaster, and then twenty shillings more were expended at Vierny for the general improvement of the concern, the said improvement lasting less than four-and-twenty hours; for, according to my notes, one of the wheels was pronounced " out of sorts " and we were detained a few more hours at Altyn-Immel.

This, however, I am thankful to say, was the last hindrance of this sort, and we now crossed the Pass, continuing over geological formations similar to the high regions just described, and then descending and crossing for 30 miles over river and lake deposits nearly to the station of Konurolen. Here again towards evening we made our way amongst rugged hills composed of the rocks already mentioned, and others in addition belonging to the Tertiary and Jurassic systems, and including diorite, diabase, and porphyrite. Thus, after posting through the night, on the morning of Saturday, June 16th, we reached Jarkend.

The *Nachalnik* of Jarkend (or Yarkend, as the natives call it) was away on inspection duty, but my coming was anticipated, and two rooms in the posthouse had been placed at my disposal, with a policeman at the door in attendance. There was also told off to be with and to help me a young officer named Dmitrieff who had been degraded to the ranks and sent hither into exile, but the cause of his banishment I did not then inquire into particularly.

Upon calling upon Madame Natalie Paulovna Seletsky, the *Nachalnik's* wife, she asked me to dine at her house daily during my stay, for which purpose she sent her carriage and ponies to fetch me and M. Dmitrieff, who acted as interpreter. I met also at the *Nachalnik's* house the police-master, named Berg, who was attentive and helpful in making arrangements for and sending off to Kuldja my luggage, which, with two men—Redjap and Erbudu—arrived in even less than the time specified.

The chief thing that prevented my pushing forward at once was the temporary absence of a certain Sart merchant, named Vali Akhoun Yuldasheff, to whom I had been warmly commended in writing by M. Gourdet, and who had been described to me as one who during the insurrection supplied corn to the Chinese army, owned a flour-mill in the Kuldja valley, had business houses all along the road to Kashgar, could give me money drafts, procure me horses and guides, change my Russian money, and in fact do everything, so that he seemed a most desirable person to know and to have as a patron in Chinese Turkistan. Moreover, it was said that my official letters, and my recommendation from the Governor-General Kolpakovsky, would be sure to enlist the hearty co-operation of this local potentate and millionaire.

On the day of our arrival there came one Tokhta Akhoun and offered his services to me, saying that he had been one of Prjevalsky's guides. Next day appeared Abdul Abbasid, in the employ of Vali Akhoun, and who said he was receiving 18 roubles a month and all found. He could prepare skins of animals, had acted as Prjevalsky's interpreter, and was willing similarly to accompany me for 30 roubles a month and 50 down. But as his only European language was Russian, I declined his offer, and as the police-master advised me against Tokhta Akhoun, I decided to take neither.

The third day came without the appearance of Yuldasheff, but his brother, as well as the manager of his business, called on me. From them I gathered that they could do far less in the way of money arrangements than I had hoped, but they could in exchange for 1,160 paper roubles give an order on Suiting for a pood of *yambs*, or lumps, of silver, which amount accordingly I purchased. It was not so easy to decide as to what was the best method of conveyance; and opinions varied greatly as to whether I could travel from Kuldja to Kashgar in a tarantass.*

Some advised native *arbas*, or carts with huge wheels, but without springs; and several, out of pity for my bones, suggested that one should be fitted with network stretched across a few inches above the floor, whereon I might sleep comfortably.

Others advised the purchase of horses, which, they said, were cheaper at Jarkend than at Kuldja, a statement afterwards denied at Kuldja. I confess to having been fairly puzzled what to do for the best, especially as the purchase of horses was not at all in my line; but finally I bought an *arba* rigged up with netting, and three big draught horses, a Kirghese cob for Joseph, and a saddle-horse for myself, the whole for £25. Nor must one think lightly of these animals,

* The Talki defile and its numerous bridges was alleged to be the chief difficulty. It was said that M. Balkashin, once Russian Consul at Chuguchak, had travelled that way in his tarantass, but he was escorted by a body of Cossacks, who, if the carriage fell into a ditch, could lift it out. Besides, it was doubted whether the Chinese smiths would be able to repair a vehicle to which they were unaccustomed, and the novelty of the carriage would attract attention. I decided, therefore, that it would be better for the missionary aspect of my work to abandon the tarantass.

for I venture to say that my own, which the policemaster professed to sell me as a great favour, would have fetched in London double the amount I paid for the cart and all the horses put together.

On the fourth day I was informed that Yuldasheff had returned, and calling upon him in his semi-Russian, semi-Chinese furnished house, he seemed disposed to be useful. He even put off on my account a journey he intended to make, promised me letters of introduction to Turfan, Kurla, Kuchar, Aksu, and Kashgar, and engaged to provide me trustworthy men if I telegraphed from Kuldja.

He also urged my stay till the morrow, in which case he would provide for my tarantass a *troika* of horses, send with me his manager, who was going to Suiting, and arrange that my *arba* and horses should be despatched to Kuldja. Next morning, accordingly, the tarantass was re-packed for departure from my last Russian town, at the end of a journey through the Empire of 5,000 miles in 115 days, but 50 days of actual travel.

The many kindnesses everywhere offered me will already have struck the reader. They began at Wirballen in passing me unquestioned through the Custom-house. At St Petersburg the authorities denied me nothing, and allowed my goods to pass through Batoum, as I have said, without examination or payment of duty. Then began steamboat and railway favours—a compartment placed at my convenience to and from Uzun Ada, and a whole carriage from Merv, to say nothing of the little house on wheels with free carriage beyond the Oxus, and lodging in the houses of two of the engineers at Katte Kurgan and Samarkand.

The governors and officials were not less kind in affording me an amount of hospitality quite unexpected and entirely unasked on my part, taking me in sometimes as guest in private houses, as at Charjui, Bokhara, Jizak, Chimkend, and Vierny, and at others accommodating me in guest-houses, as at Tashkend, Kara-Kol, and Jarkend, and this so fully that, with the exception of the little inn at Bokhara station when awaiting trains, I did not go to one hotel between the Caspian and our point of leaving the Russian dominions.

Nor must I forget dinners at Tiflis, Askhabad, Charjui, Samarkand, Tashkend, Vierny, and Jarkend; telegraphic and written communications from the Government at the capital to the authorities along our route, as well as despatches from the Governor-General and Governors in Asia to their subordinates at Merv, the Bokhara customs, Chimkend, Pishpek, Narin, and Vierny; and, finally, horsemen and messengers sent hundreds of miles on my account over the mountains to Kara-Kol and Kashgar.

Indeed, if it is our duty to "speak of people as we find them," I had the most superlative reasons for speaking well of the Russians, and for bowing my thanks as we drove out of the station of Jarkend.

I wished to start at seven in the morning, but delays of one kind and another kept us for six hours. Then we set out with Yuldasheff's manager to drive 24 miles to the river Khorgos, which here forms the boundary between Russia and China. This we did in about three hours without mishap, though a hitch occurred on coming to the last Cossack picket, where Yuldasheff's manager for some reason was detained, and not allowed to proceed.

This was decidedly awkward, for, though I could command a score or two of words in Russian, I knew not one in Chinese, and it seemed no joke to be left to cross the frontier alone, especially as I had been assured in England that I should not be allowed to enter China from the west.

My advisers from the outset, beginning with Mr Ney Elias, had recommended approaching Chinese Turkistan from Peking. The proper way, they said, was to go to the *Tsung-li-Yamen*, or Foreign Office, and ask for a passport to the interior, which passport in my case, Sir Thomas Wade thought, they would not give; whilst for an Englishman to enter from the west was a thing unheard-of, and, he thought, would not be allowed.

In keeping with this was a note received by a friend from an under-official at the Chinese Legation in London, who said there was but one way the thing could be done. He advised that I should go to Peking, and call upon the British Minister there, begging him to send a despatch to the *Tsung-li-Yamen*, acquainting them with all my wishes, explaining and stating fully what places and districts I should like to visit; and then the *Tsung-li-Yamen* would grant the necessary passport, and the local authorities in the different places through which I might pass would be responsible for my protection, but otherwise it would not be safe to go far into the interior.

This was not encouraging, and Mr Hudson Taylor, notwithstanding all his faith and hope, wrote : " The more I think of your present plans, the more I fear their failure. The absence of such a passport as you could only procure personally at Peking will, I fear, keep you back."

Again, a member of the British Embassy at Peking, who happened to be in London, said that the correspondence for procuring such passports passed through his own hands, and he urged the absolute necessity of my having the document from Peking, because without it I should be turned back; and when I showed him, perhaps a little triumphantly, the passport I had received, he recognised it as valid in form, but shook his head, saying, "I am horribly afraid that when you get to the frontier they will ignore it, and refuse to let you pass."

After all these monitions I had thought it desirable to strengthen my position, as advised, by asking another letter from the Chinese Minister at Berlin. I had accepted also at Jarkend, as a second string to my bow, a Russian document or passport enabling me to travel in China, and I had, besides, my British passport and London letters; but, even thus furnished, to go and knock at a remote back door of the Empire, kept by a few ignorant Chinese soldiers, to whom none of my party could speak a word of their language, looked rather formidable.

I accordingly produced my Russian letters, and asked the officer to lend me a couple of Cossacks for an escort to Kuldja. A few minutes sufficed for their preparations, and with these in advance I charged the *p'ai fang*, or gateway, built on or near the bridge spanning the Khorgos.

What the Cossacks said or did I know not; but the great doors, with "warders," or painted dragons, flew open, my tarantass rolled majestically through, without my being stopped, or, so far as I remember, asked for my passport, and in five minutes we were calmly driving through the fields of the Flowery Land and among the Celestials, quizzing their pigtails and feeling on excellent terms with ourselves and the world in general. This was success " number one " in China.

Passing over a flat, cultivated country, lit up by the declining sun, we passed, at ten miles from Khorgos, a place called Alimptu, the modern representative, as some say, of the ancient Almalik, so often mentioned by mediæval travellers. This agrees with what Dr Bretschneider has written; and M. Pantusoff told me at Vierny that he thought the ruins existing near the modern Chinese town of Lao-tsao-ghoo to be those of Almalik.

It would be highly interesting if another cemetery could be discovered here, as at Pishpek and Tokmak, for we know that once there were Christians at Almalik, both of the Nestorian and Roman Churches.

I myself, at the moment, expected to pass the spot again on my way to the Talki defile, and it was my intention to have stayed, if possible, to investigate the ruins; but for the present we sped forward past the town of Chimpanzee to Suiting.

Suiting (pronounced Soo-ee-ting, and spelt also Suitsing, and meaning, I was told, "a spring of water") is called by the Russians Suidun. The Russian capital was at Kuldja, where their Consul still resides; a superior post-house only, with large garden attached, being kept up at Suiting. At this post-house, where lived the only Europeans in the place, we arrived at midnight. Here we slept till morning, and then pushed on with our Cossacks the remaining 26 miles through a thickly populated country, and arrived on the afternoon of June 21st at Kuldja.

CHAPTER XII.

MANCHURIA, MONGOLIA, SUNGARIA.

China within and beyond the Wall; Outer China girdled by mountains; Former extent of China's dominion; Character of surface, 153.—Political divisions of Outer China, 154.—Manchuria; its boundaries, dimensions, mountains,. and rivers; its provinces, government, and population, 155.—Our knowledge of Manchuria, and whence acquired; Nomad tribes, their Shamanism, and partial conversion, 156.—Manchuria colonised by Chinese; Manchu, the court and official language of China; Efforts to Christianise Manchuria, 158.—Mongolia; its dimensions and climate, 160.—Divisions and towns of Mongolia; Kiakhta, and tea route; Inhabitants of Mongolia, 161.—The Mongols, lamaists, 162.—Missionaries' translation of Bible still in use; Baptisms by Russian missionaries; Missions to southern Mongols, 163.—A difficult but open field, 164.—Sungaria; its depressions a highway to and from the Turkistan plains; Three districts of Sungaria, 165.—Chuguchak; its troops and trade, 166.—District of Kara-kur-usu; its lakes and towns; The imperial high road to Hami, 168.—History of the Sungars, and their approximate extermination; Sungaria repeopled by various nationalities, 169.—Translation of Scriptures into Kalmuk; Another field for missionary effort, 170.

ARRIVED at Kuldja, we were really in China, though only midway between Moscow and Peking. So little, however, is this generally realised that more than one friend, pointing to Kuldja on the map, has asked me, "Do you mean to say that China extends all out there?" Let me, then, observe that the Chinese Empire may be divided into China within, and China beyond, the Wall. China within the Wall, or China proper, is known more or less to every one, and of its 18 provinces I need say little here.

China beyond the Wall is girdled by mountains. Thus, beginning northwards at the Sea of Okhotsk with the Yablonoi Mountains, and continuing westwards in a semicircle, we have a succession of ranges —the Saian, the Altai, Tian Shan, Tsung-ling, and Himalayas—which bring us by a fairly continuous frontier line of 6,000 miles to Yunnan, the south-west province of China proper.

In her palmy days, and at various other times, the power of China extended not only to the ridges of all these mountains, but overflowed in some cases, as in the south, to Nepal and Butan, and westward down into the plains as far as the Caspian. In Bokhara I found traces of this remote dominion, for, on asking who built the city walls, they were traditionally ascribed to the Chinese; whilst another statement, in praise of the melons of Khiva, informs us that they used to form part of the tribute taken all across Asia to the Emperor at Peking.

The rule of China long ago retired from the Trans-Caspian plains, and the dividing line between Iran and Turan, or Turks and Chinese, has been shifted from time to time; but China appears for many centuries to have considered as her own, whether the whole was enjoyed for the moment or not, all the territory within the above-named mountains.

The general slope of this vast region, as indicated by the course of its rivers, is towards the Pacific, though many streams are confined to land-locked basins and do not reach the ocean. The surface of the region consists, for the most part, of enormous deserts, and a number of lofty tablelands, such as are possessed by no other empire in the world, whilst here and there only, and chiefly on the skirts of the mountains, are tracts of arable land.

It is a noteworthy circumstance that the southern side of the mountains is always bare and scarped, presenting to the eye a chaos of overturned rocks, heaped one upon another. Only the side facing the north is covered with bushes, or presents gentle slopes of soil that may be cultivated. Near the valleys are seen, here and there, crooked and stunted poplars and willows, whilst the majority of the inhabitants spend their lives in dire poverty, the like to which is unknown in civilised countries. Even where the soil is good, the harvest is always uncertain, because rain seldom falls before the end of June, and then only for three weeks. At all other times a shower is a welcome exception.

The Chinese themselves, according to Wells Williams, divide their empire beyond the Wall into Manchuria and the Colonies; understanding by the Colonies, Mongolia, Ili (now Sin-Kiang, or New Province, comprising Sungaria and Chinese Turkistan), Koko-Nor, and Tibet. Accordingly, I proceed to speak briefly here of Manchuria, Mongolia, and Sungaria. The remaining colonies will be noticed hereafter.

Manchuria comprises the most easterly portion of the high tableland that runs across the centre of Asia. Its northern limits, first defined at the Treaty of Nertchinsk in 1688, extended to the Sea of Okhotsk, and continued along a line westwards, which embraced what are now the Siberian provinces of the Amur and part of the Trans-Baikal; whilst on the east Manchuria extended to the Pacific.

Later, in 1858, the Russians managed to wrest from the Chinese, during their trouble with England and France, all Manchuria north of the Amur—a territory larger than the whole of France—together with the seaboard east of the Ussuri; so that now the province of Manchuria is bounded on the north and east by the Amur and its affluent the Ussuri, on the southeast by Korea, and on the south by the Yellow Sea. On the west, towards Mongolia, it has no such prominently defined natural boundaries; but beginning from the north, the west frontier follows the course of the Argun, and then takes a south-easterly direction, along the rivers Nonni and Sungari, to what was once the Palisade, or barrier of stakes.

Chinese Manchuria measures approximately 800 by 500 miles. The province includes three principal mountain chains, which serve to give variety to its surface of sandy wastes, rich arable lands, grassy steppes, and extensive forests. Of its two rivers, the Shara-muren, flowing into the Yellow Sea, is of little use for navigation; but the Sungari, flowing into the Amur, forms a highway by which numerous fleets of junks make their way from town to town.

Manchuria is divided into three provinces, Shinking, Kirin, and Tsitsihar, the capitals respectively being Mukden, Kirin-ula-hotun, and Tsitsihar-hotun. The country is ruled by military boards and generals at the garrisons. Every male above the age of 18 is enrolled, according to his birth, under one of eight standards. The population of Shinking has been estimated, according to Williams, at twelve millions, of Kirin at less than three millions, whilst Tsitsihar is to a large extent an uninhabited mountainous wilderness.

Of a large part of Manchuria we know almost

nothing, and before the advent of the Russians we knew less. When, at the time of the Crimean War, these first descended the Amur in numbers, their troops were accompanied by men of science, to whom we owe our first glimpses of this part of Manchuria. Some of their information reached the English public in the volumes of Atkinson, who described, but never saw, *The Upper and Lower Amoor*.

Later, there appeared in the United States two volumes on the Amur by the Americans Collins and Knox, after which it fell to my lot to be the first English traveller to describe from personal observation the entire length of the river, as also the Ussuri. Since my voyage the reverse journey has been made in winter, on the ice, by Mr L. F. Gowing, as detailed in *Five Thousand Miles in a Sledge across Siberia*.

Certain parts of Southern Manchuria adjacent to China were described by Fleming and Williamson. In 1882 two French travellers—M. de Mailly-Chalon and the Baron Benoist-Méchin—made a remarkable journey through Southern Manchuria to Vladivostock, and the latest book on the region is that of Mr James, called *The Long White Mountain*.

The Manchus, or Mandjoors, after whom the country is named, were originally nomads who, in 1644, conquered the " middle kingdom " and placed the present dynasty on the Chinese throne. When ascending the Upper and Middle Amur I saw certain tribes—for instance, the Solons, Manyargs, and Orochons—who still wander along the river banks; but the majority of the Manchus are now settled, and are rapidly becoming absorbed by the nation they conquered.

The nomad tribes most distant from China proper

GROUP OF GOLDI CHRISTIANS.

are still Shamanists, who believe in evil spirits and in the necessity of averting their malign influence by spells and magic rites, as I found to be the case with the Gilyaks and Goldi, on the Lower Amur and Ussuri; but I met a Russian missionary on the Amur who in 23 years had baptised 2,000 natives, of whom 403 were Orochons and 1,501 were Goldi.

He thought that all the Gilyaks in his district were baptised, which might well be the case, seeing that formerly natives were baptised by Russian missionaries in crowds without their understanding much of what was being done, though this missionary said in his own case he had required them first to know certain prayers.

In Chinese Manchuria the Government commenced its colonisation of the country by establishing military stations, and banishing thither convicts, as well as criminals and political exiles. A great many Chinese Muhammadans also are expatriated thither, and have their own mosques and schools, all assisting to make the population of Manchuria of a very mixed character as to origin, language, and religion.

So largely are the Chinese colonists taking possession of the land that the Manchu language might have been extinct before this, but for its being that of the reigning family. This has caused it to become one of the classic languages of the empire, so that all high functionaries need to acquire it, since it is the language of the court, and of state documents in some parts, for my passports and official papers at Kuldja were written in Turki, Chinese, and Manchu.*

As for efforts to Christianise Manchuria, they were

* This, however, I am told by M. de Deken is exceptional, for that in China, as at Liang-chow, where there is a strong Manchu garrison,

begun, according to Mr Ravenstein,* in 1838, by Roman missionaries, one of whom, M. de la Brunière, in 1845 descended the Amur, alone, to the Gilyaks. He went on shore, and at the White Village was murdered.

When passing the spot more than 30 years afterwards, the bay was pointed out to me where he met his death. I came across a man whose father, he said, had told him about the missionary, and an elderly Russian officer who affirmed that, going to the place in the early years of Russian occupation, the people still had in their possession the missionary's crucifix, watch, and spoons, which the Russians bought.

After my distribution of Scriptures along the Amur in 1879, I heard of a colporteur being subsequently sent over the same ground by the American Bible Society, but I suspect that both he and I touched only the Russian population.

In the south of Manchuria, the British and Foreign Bible Society have a depôt at Newchwang, under the direction of Mr Robert Turley, who, with his colporteurs, has circumambulated a large portion of the country, his sales being chiefly, I think, among Chinese.

At Hsi-wan-tze, eight days north of Peking, there are, M. de Deken tells me, a bishop and sixteen Belgian missionaries, with nine Chinese priests; and, farther east, north of the barrier of stakes, at Gehol, Hei-hsui, etc., there is another bishop with eleven Belgian missionaries and seven Chinese priests.

There are also Scotch and Irish Presbyterian

---

all the state papers are in Chinese, and the Manchu military chiefs stationed there no longer know their national language, but speak Chinese only.

* *Through Siberia*, p. 612.

missionaries at Newchwang, Mukden, Kirin, and some few other stations, but none of the Church of England. There still exists, therefore, an extensive field for missionary effort in this little-known country.

We now pass westwards to Mongolia, which is first in order of the Chinese colonies, and covers an area nearly as large as China proper.

It consists of an elevated plain, at an altitude of 4,000 feet above the sea. The climate is excessively cold and dry, and the soil, except in the acclivities of the mountains, unfit for agriculture, though there are sufficient grass-lands, especially in the north, to support the flocks of the nomad inhabitants, who number, it is estimated, about two millions.

The character of the inhabitants of Mongolia, M. de Deken tells me, is made up of excellent qualities and abominable defects. Advancing westwards, the people become more warm-hearted, until among the Mongol nomads is attained the height of simplicity.

More noteworthy still is the difference between east and west as to temperature, soil, and vegetation. At the barrier of stakes the mean temperature of summer attains 77°, and they harvest indigo, cotton, poppy, rice, and superior tobacco, renowned as of Kuangtong; whereas in Central Mongolia the soil barely produces a little wheat, oats, buckwheat, and millet. Winter lasts in Central Mongolia for eight months, with a thermometer in December and January at 31° below zero.*

* This last remark is confirmed by a table of isothermal lines drawn up by M. Fritsche, director of the Russian Observatory at Peking, wherein the line falls in proportion as it advances towards Central Mongolia, and rises at the frontiers, this table being drawn up from daily observations taken from 25 observatories between the latitudes of Yakutsk and Bangkok.

The principal divisions of Mongolia, according to Williams, are four:—1. Inner Mongolia, lying between the south of the Gobi and the Wall, having no common capital. Each tribe is governed by its chief, and the whole by the Foreign Office in Peking. 2. Outer Mongolia, between the north of the Gobi and the Altai Mountains. This is subdivided into four *khanates*, and governed by four Khalkhas Khans under two Manchu residents seated at the common capital, Urga. 3. The country about Koko-Nor—that is, north-east of Tibet—administered under a Manchu resident, and having for its capital Sining, in Kansu. 4. The dependencies of Uliassutai, lying north-westward of the Khalkhas Khanates, consisting of Kobdo and Ulianghai, ruled by an Amban and chieftains, and having Uliassutai as the capital.

Towns in Mongolia are few and far between. I have mentioned nearly all of them, but may add Kiakhta on the Russian frontier.*

As for the inhabitants of Mongolia, they may be

* Kiakhta is about 200 miles north of Urga, whither most of the Mongolian trade routes converge. It is the chief station on what was, and to some extent still is, the great tea highway between Kiakhta and Kalgan, the latter at one of the gates in the Great Wall. This route was opened by the Treaty of Argun in 1858, soon after which it was travelled by Mr Wylie, of the British and Foreign Bible Society. My neighbour at Blackheath, Mr Howell, in 1863, crossed from Shanghai to Kiakhta in company with Mr Michie, who wrote the *Siberian Overland Route from Peking to St Petersburg*.

Mr Michie was followed by three English writers—in 1869 by Mr Athenry Whyte, in 1875-6 by Professor John Milne, and in 1877 by Captain W. Sheppard—after whom came the late Mr Gilmour, of the London Missionary Society, whose journey to Kiakhta was spoken of as recent when I was there in 1879. Since this date the journey has been made by Mr Harry de Windt, who crossed Mongolia in August 1887 and published *From Peking to Calais by Land*, and by Mr Julius Price, who travelled in 1891 *From the Arctic Ocean to the Yellow Sea.*

roughly divided into—1. The Buriats in the north-east, through a portion of whose country I drove from Kiakhta, when traversing the Trans-Baikal; 2. The Kalmuks in the west—that is to say, of Sungaria and the Ili and Tekes valleys—with whom I came in daily contact during a portion of the present journey, and to whom may be added the Ulianghai tribes of the Upper Yenesei basin, a race somewhat akin to the Samoyedes; 3. The Khalkhas of the centre, which in the north are the most numerous and widely spread; whilst south of the Gobi, towards the east, are the eight tribes of the Tsakhars, governed by a *tutung*, or lieutenant-general, residing at Kalgan; and west of them, in the fluvial peninsula formed by the Yellow River outside the Wall, are the Ordos, or Ortus.

The Mongols are usually spoken of as Buddhists, but they have so far departed from the teaching of the founder of that faith, and are so unlike the Buddhists of south-eastern Asia and Ceylon, that I prefer to call the Mongols Lamaists. Their sovereign is the Grand Lama of Tibet, to whose capital at Lassa they make frequent pilgrimages.

At Urga dwells another high priest and inferior incarnation called the Kutuktu, to whom the tribes of that region owe religious fealty, and by whom they are kept in subjection. For this assistance in the government of the country the Chinese pay the ecclesiastics and ruling princes (whom it reserves the right of deposing) yearly subventions, varying, according to Réclus, from £30 to £800, according to their rank; and thus the natives are said to be not a little lama-ridden and oppressed.

At the time of Jinghiz Khan the Mongols were

Shamanists, as are still some of the Buriat tribes remote from Tibet in the Trans-Baikal. Early in the present century the London Missionary Society was allowed to send to the neighbourhood of Kiakhta, to the Buriats under Russian rule, English missionaries, who translated the whole of the Bible into Mongolian, and established a small school at Selenginsk.

They were compelled, however, to retire in 1840 by an *ukase* dismissing all foreign missionaries from the Russian dominions, under the pretext that the Synod wished to do all the mission work for the pagans of the Empire. Some of the scholars trained by the English were subsequently baptised by Russian missionaries; and when calling (as I crossed the Trans-Baikal) upon one of these, who was working among the Buriats, I found in his possession many of these Buriat Scriptures.

I learned that, with the Buddhist Buriats, the Russian missionaries found work difficult; but with the Shamanist Buriats it was more promising. The missionary was able to tell of 300 Buriats baptised during 1878, east of the Baikal, and more than 1,000 to the west. All this is on Russian territory.

The late Mr Gilmour, of the London Missionary Society, and author of *Among the Mongols*, for some years made summer tours from Peking among the tribes in the south-east, where he was followed by a Mr Parker, a missionary of the same Society; and at Kuldja I met Belgian missionaries, who had come from the stations whence work was being carried on among the Ortus Mongols. In the Ortus the Roman missionaries devote themselves almost entirely to the tribes of the Alachains. The staff included, M. de Deken informed me (in 1892), a bishop, who is Vicar

Apostolic, with fifteen Belgian missionaries and two Chinese priests. With these exceptions, however, I know of no other missionaries of any denomination working in Mongolia proper.

The nomadic habits of the people present great obstacles to the establishment of schools or getting the people together, as I learned from the aged Mr Stallybrass, who was one of the pioneers to the Trans-Baikal in 1817.

The Belgian missionaries have met with the same difficulty, M. de Deken informs me, among the Ortus nomads, for whom they have tried, and partially succeeded, in forming exclusively Christian centres, and even entire towns, such as the walled town of Porrobalgason, which contains 160 Mongol families.

Accordingly, one would suppose that a strong mission might be profitably established at Urga, whence its members could itinerate, and smaller missions of a similar character at Uliassutai and Kobdo, in all of which it would be most desirable that physic should go hand in hand with divinity.

Passing farther west, we come now to Sungaria, which one writes with hesitation because the name is not strictly scientific. It lingers only as a geographical expression, indicating the region that was once the centre of the kingdom of the Sungarians, or Mongol "tribes of the left wing"—that is, the Kalmuks. Towards the north-east it is divided from the province of Kobdo by the Great Altai Mountains, but directly east it possesses no natural boundaries to divide it from the Khalkhas of Mongolia. To the north-west lie the Russian provinces of Semipolatinsk and Semirechia, and on the south lies the easternmost extension of the Tian Shan. The region calls for separate mention by reason of the configuration of its surface and its history ; and in reference to the former, Réclus very well puts it that " Sungaria is the broad gateway leading from the Chinese to the Western World." Here it is that the three depressions in the mountains which environ Western Mongolia occur, and by means of which access is gained from the Turkistan plains to the Mongolian tableland.

The northern opening lies through the valley of the Black Irtish, and presents an easy route over the Steppe at an elevation of scarcely 2,500 feet above the sea. Through the southern opening passes a road from Lepsinsk to Urumtsi; whilst between these two openings is a third passage, narrower, but more frequented. It goes by the town of Chuguchak.

Through these depressions the devastating hosts of the Mongols advanced westwards, and should a railroad ever be laid from Moscow to Central China, it will probably pass from the lowlands of Russia to the highlands of Mongolia through Sungaria. The imperial road of the Chinese coming in this direction from Kansu, after skirting the north of the easternmost branch of the Tian Shan, descends to the Ili, through the Talki Pass, farther south than Chuguchak.

Wells Williams divides Sungaria into the three districts of the Ili valley in the south, Kara-kur-usu in the middle, and Tarbagatai in the north. In Northern Sungaria there are no towns of any considerable size. Réclus mentions the two military stations Bulun Tokoi and Tulta, but the busiest mart in this part of the country is Chuguchak, or Tarbagatai.

Here was stationed a Russian Consul in 1882. There are also two Chinese residents, with high powers, to oversee the trade across the frontier ; but their duties are of inferior importance to those of the officials at Urga, where is maintained, it is said, a force of 2,500 Manchu and Chinese troops.

Chuguchak is one of nine fortified places under the control of a commandant at Kuldja; and not far distant is Durbuljin, where the Chinese have Kalmuk mercenary troops, some of whom, to judge from a photograph in my possession, are armed with modern rifles and bayonets; whilst in another are seen Chinese or Manchus, at the same place, at sword exercise and bearing huge shields, a yard or more in diameter. Chuguchak is said to contain about 600 houses. Its trade consists chiefly of domestic animals and cloths.

MANCHU SOLDIERS AT S\

South of the Tarbagatai district is that of Kara-kur-usu, remarkable for its system of lakes extending eastwards, of which the largest are named Sairam, Ebi, and Ayar. Of towns in this district there are certain military stations, such as Jinho (or Djin-ho), Shiho (or Hsihou), Kara-kur-usu, and Manas, peopled to a large extent by exiles, and situated for the most part along the imperial high road.

The traveller who would pass this way to North-west China from the Ili valley, which he can do on wheels, ascends the Borokhoro range by the zig-zag tracks and 48 bridges of the Talki Pass, to the eastern shore of Sairam-Nor, the beauties of which have been described

AT DURBULJIN, NEAR CHUGUCHAK.

by Mr Delmar Morgan, as also previously by Mr Ashton Dilke. Of this Pass I was able to procure several photographs characteristic of this most picturesque portion of Sungaria, Lake Sairam, for example, presenting the appearance of a vast crater surrounded by wooded hills.

After skirting the shores of the lake at an altitude of 5,900 feet, the road descends and passes Jinho and Kara-kur-usu, leaving to the left Shiho with its gold washings, coal-fields, salt-beds, and naphtha lake, and continues to Manas, a fertile district in which colonisation is said to be advancing. From Manas the road bifurcates, one branch continuing north of the Bogdo Tian Shan range, through the towns of Guchen (Ku-cheng, or old city) and Barkul, the other continuing to Urumtsi, situated in a depression of the range, and then crossing and running south of it. Both roads unite again at Hami.

Of the Ili valley, or southernmost district of what we are calling Sungaria, I need write little here, since I have devoted five chapters to it in my *Russian Central Asia*. Something must be said, however, of the inhabitants who gave their name to the region generally, and whose history is remarkable.

Early in the eighteenth century the Sungars suddenly acquired great power, and established themselves over nearly all the elevated region of what is now Russian and Chinese Central Asia, but more especially from Hami to Lake Balkash. They captured even the sacred city of Lassa, and exacted tribute from Yarkand and Kashgar, with Tashkend and other places in Western Turkistan.

Against this people the Chinese sent two armies, both of which were defeated. Afterwards they sent a third and victorious army, whose leader, determined to make short work and guard against further trouble, slew every inhabitant of the country, to the number, some say, of 600,000, and others, a million ; thus leaving Sungaria in 1756 an uninhabited waste.

However, about half a century before this a tribe of the Sungars, more definitely known as the Torgout Kalmuks, had migrated, owing to tribal quarrels, to the region of the Volga, where they had lived under Russian sway, but were now invited by the Emperor of China to return to the lands of their forefathers. They did so in 1771, and were settled in Tarbagatai and Kobdo, in Karashar, in Chinese Turkistan, and in the Ili valley.

Also Chinese and Manchu troops, emigrants, and exiles, as well as the neighbouring nomad tribes and Turkish agriculturists, were sent and encouraged to come into the vacant territory. Thus Sungaria became quite an *olla podrida* of races, languages, and religions.

The Kalmuks are Lamaists, the Turkish peoples are Muhammadans, and the Chinese probably Confucians, or perhaps Buddhists, but not generally, I think, of the same way of thinking as the Kalmuks. The only attempt that is now being made, so far as I am aware, to Christianise the two millions of people, as estimated, of Sungaria, is by a small Roman mission in Kuldja, to which I shall presently refer in connection with my sojourn in that town.

Some attempt was made towards the evangelisation of the Kalmuks of the Volga, and a portion of the Scriptures was translated into their language, but I am not aware that any results from this have extended to their present camping grounds.

In 1882 I had the privilege of distributing the first

Chinese and Kirghese Scriptures in the Ili valley, and the Bible Society's agent in Tashkend has since visited Kuldja; but as regards permanent work, I would point out that here again, in Sungaria, are extensive and unoccupied fields awaiting the missionary.

And now, having attempted to give some idea of Manchuria, Mongolia, and Sungaria, which may be regarded as making up the northern portion of China beyond the Wall, I shall return to my narrative, which has brought us just within the Chinese frontier.

CHAPTER XIII.

CHINESE OFFICIAL PRELIMINARIES.

Lodgings at Kuldja, 171.—Book-post parcels not opened by Censor, 172.—Packages from Russian Consul; Visit to M. Uspensky, 173.—Changed appearance of Kuldja under Chinese, 175.—Arrival of horses, 176.—Paucity of public buildings; Call from Lutheran postmaster, 177.—Letter from the *Tsian-Tsiun*; Excursion to Suiting, 178.—Appearance of Suiting, 179.— Chinese inn; Intruding natives and distracting noises, 181.—Called to breakfast with Kah; A score of dishes, 182.—Chinese table etiquette and conversation, 184.—Return call from Kah; his Manchu agility; Audience with the *Tsian-Tsiun*, 185.—Presents to *Tsian-Tsiun* and Kah; Calls from and upon Mattie, a former acquaintance, 186.—Presents from *Tsian-Tsiun*, including a sucking-pig; Disgust of Muhammadan innkeeper; Return to Kuldja, 187.

MY coming to Kuldja had not only been expected, but provided for, and a lodging hired in what was pronounced the best quarter in the town. Let no one suppose, however, that this signifies apartments palatial, but rather an empty room in a native house—large indeed, and airy, with glazed windows, and walls recently whitewashed in my honour, but without flooring, and the bare earth only partially covered with matting of rushes.

Here, then, was a clear case for spreading of felts, and erecting for the first time my camp chair, table, and bedstead, on the last of which were extended an air-bed and pair of sheets. Some trunks and boxes placed here and there served for sideboards and divans whereon to place provisions and seat guests; whilst for meals our host lent a large round table, about six inches high, around which we might squat or lie on the ground.

Having on the way called at the Russian post office, I received handfuls of letters and armfuls of book-packages; for it had been ascertained before leaving England that to carry extra luggage from the English to the Russian capitals, a distance of 1,600 miles, would cost 8*d*. per lb., whilst book packages could be sent by post to Kuldja, a distance of 4,600 miles, at the rate of 4*d*. per lb. I had felt, therefore, in conscience bound to patronise largely the postal arrangements of his Imperial Majesty.

The only drawback seemed to be, that as the Censor is supposed to read all foreign books coming to Russia, with the power of rejecting those he disapproves, I might find on arrival certain volumes to be wanting. They could not tell me, strange to say, at the General Post Office in London, what became of books disallowed by the Censor; for though they had in their office any number of newspapers sent back as "*Refusé*," they had not a single instance of a book thus treated.

When calling, therefore, in St Petersburg on General Besac, the Postmaster-General, for an open letter, such as I had been provided with on previous journeys, and with which I was once more kindly favoured, I asked also whether my printed matter had safely passed the ordeal, and was informed that books posted from London to Kuldja, which is beyond the Russian frontier, would not be opened in passing through St Petersburg. Those addressed to the capital I had already received ; and to this may be added that now, on my arrival, not one of my two score of books and book-packages was missing.

Another economy in the cost and trouble of carriage had been discovered in St Petersburg in the Parcels Post, established many years before ours in England, whereby boxes or parcels of books, examined by the postal authorities before closing, and not exceeding 1 cwt each, could be sent from the capital to Kuldja for $5d.$, and other articles for $6\frac{1}{2}d.$, a Russian lb.

Accordingly, I had purchased at the depôt of the British and Foreign Bible Society such Scriptures as I needed in Persian, Kalmuk, and some few other languages, which the Rev. W. Nicholson, their agent, always so kind and helpful, had just forwarded, together with certain provisions, medicaments, etc., to Kuldja, the six cases wherein the foregoing were contained weighing about 5 cwt.

These were consigned to the care of the Russian Consul, to whom my arrival quickly became known. The six cases were soon sent, also the 27 boxes and parcels which had been delivered on the previous evening from Jarkend, and the whole stacked in my room, giving the establishment very much the appearance of a warehouse at one end, and a compound dining, drawing, dressing, and reading room at the other.

With the baggage came also a message from the Consul that he had been summoned to meet his Governor-General at Jarkend, and, having to depart next day, begged that I would visit him in the morning.

Consequently, I called betimes to pay my official visit to M. Victor Romanovitch Uspensky, whom I found surrounded by his staff, M. Nicholas Bornemann,

Dragoman-Secretary to the Consulate, and several interpreters. Fortunately for me, M. Bornemann spoke both French and English.

Having presented the letter from the Foreign Minister at St Petersburg, and shown my other Russian credentials, I stated what I wished to do and where I wanted to go, and intimated that I had a letter from the Chinese Legation in London to present to the principal Chinese authority in the Ili valley.

This official, called the *Tsian-Tsiun*, it was replied, was living in Suiting, where we had touched on our way; but a letter, written in Manchu, should be sent, stating that I was in Kuldja, and asking for an audience. Meanwhile everything that was possible to further my wishes should be done speedily. Nothing could have been more kind or helpful, and glasses of refreshing tea were then brought in, over which to discuss affairs. After this I returned to my lodging to breathe and look about me.

Since my visit in 1882 Kuldja had been retroceded to the Chinese, who had transferred the seat of government to Suiting; and, the Russian *tchinovniks* and troops having been withdrawn, the consequence was that the town was too large for its inhabitants. The former place of encampment for the Russian soldiers was left desolate, and numbers of houses, which before were full to overflowing, were now empty and crumbling to decay.

Of course I went to revisit the Taranchi, or native Turkish quarter, the flat, earthen roofs of which afford so uninteresting a prospect when seen from a height, though the dulness is relieved here and there by trees and verdure. The Taranchi market looked less crowded than of old, though one saw numerous donkeys and oxen laden with straw and fodder, or saddled for riding; sheep exposed for sale; and their owners, clad in *khalats* and sheepskin or *tibetcika* headgear, lounging about to talk, or idly lying on the carpeted housetop to smoke and contemplate the bustle below.

It is perhaps hardly fair to compare Kuldja under

TARANCHI MARKET AT KULDJA.

the Russians with Kuldja under the Chinese, since it is no longer the capital. Certainly the town has unmistakably deteriorated. The Russian Governors in Turkistan appear to take more or less interest in the education and development of the natives, whereas the remarks made to me, on the spot, of Chinese mandarins in general, were to the effect that their one object is to enrich themselves as speedily as possible, and, provided this is done, all else may go "to the dogs." At the same time I ought to add that I saw examples, and was told, of public testimonials being presented to certain mandarins whose administration seemed to have been acceptable to the people.

On the next day, Saturday, arrived our five horses and new cart, which necessitated the addition to my staff of a groom, one Amin Agha, who tendered his services in that capacity, and offered also to act as postillion in driving a cart to Kashgar. Amin was not a handsome man, and had lost the greater part of his nose. Nevertheless, Joseph prophesied that he would make a good servant, as he had been employed by the great Vali Akhoun Yuldasheff, and was known to the Russian Consul's servant. Besides Taranchi he spoke Persian, which no doubt endeared him to Joseph, and a little Russian, by means of which I could exchange with him a word or two. It was said, moreover, that he knew something of Chinese, having been born in Kashgar; and, since Joseph would have the man under his command, I judged it better to take my factotum's advice, and give him a trial.

The purchase of my horse, and my lack of technical knowledge of such matters, have been mentioned; also I paid amply at Jarkend for barley and fodder for the route. Nevertheless, the horses arrived in poor condition; of corn, I suspect, they had had little enough. One of the men, however, was so good as to advise that the animals should be fed at once, and it looked very much as if they had been left to pick up what grass they could by the roadside.

Joseph ordered them to be immediately given as much fodder as they could eat, which they did ravenously, but not at great expense, for clover cost only a halfpenny a bundle, of which four sufficed a horse for a day, together with 10 lb. of barley, at a further outlay of $3\frac{1}{2}d$. To this $5\frac{1}{2}d$. must be added $2\frac{1}{2}d$. a day for each horse for standing room, which amount the landlord further increased on the arrival of my team by raising my rent. One of the horses was speedily condemned as not being strong enough for the journey I contemplated, and I was advised to sell him; whilst a second turned out to be so vicious as to allow no one to go near him.

The rest, on being brought out for an afternoon canter, answered well as saddle-horses, and we visited the town suburbs, and, among other places, the native cemetery, where most of the tombs were crumbling to pieces. It was, in fact, very hard to find, in or about Kuldja, anything of a monumental character worth looking at. The tombs of the Khans are merely oblong structures of brick, with a little carving or moulding on the exterior, the interior being filled with earth. Even the entrance to the Taranchi Mosque is only mud-built, and is very poor in comparison with similar buildings farther west.

On Saturday M. Bornemann paid me a formal call, as did also M. Immanuel Romanadt, the director of the Postal Telegraph Office. The latter was a Lutheran, and had heard from friends at Tashkend of my holding a service there. At Kuldja they had neither Lutheran minister nor Russian priest, and he asked that on the morrow I would hold service and administer the Lord's Supper to himself and his wife, as well as baptise, during my stay, their baby—all which I did, saying the Communion Service as best I could in German and French. The baptism was performed a few days later, according to the English rite, and the child's name sent to be registered at the English Church in Moscow.

On Monday two visitors came from the Consulate, the Manchu secretary in the morning bringing me some visiting cards, or slips of crimson paper, about eight inches by three, bearing my name in Chinese— the equivalent of Lansdell in the language of the Celestials being, I was told, "*Lahn-sse-dur-rhe.*"

In the evening came a letter from Dzunli Djun Wo Dzui Kar-chun Yi, President Commissioner of Russo-Chinese affairs at Suiting, saying that the *Tsian-Tsiun* would receive me at my convenience. This meant a little excursion of 50 miles there and back, and a sojourn of a few days at the Chinese capital.

Taking my own cart and saddle-horses, as well as provisions, we set out on Thursday for Suiting. Travelling by *arba* was new to me, and, though dreadfully slow, was not so uncomfortable as might have been anticipated. I was glad, however, to exchange it occasionally for the saddle.

On leaving Kuldja we passed by the old Russian telegraph station, adjoining which were other houses built by Europeans, but now falling to pieces, and presenting typical instances of the ruin and decay visible over a large part of the town. Here and there the Chinese had erected new houses, in their own fashion, and we passed by one of them in the suburbs.

There were also two or three tea-houses that served for halting-places, but, for the most part, the journey was through an uninhabited district; whilst, as a proof that travelling by night was a trifle dangerous, there were stuck up on poles, at various places along the road, small cages, each containing the head of a brigand.

Not long before we reached our destination, there was visible down in the valley, a few miles distant from the low hill we were crossing, a large rectangular area surrounded by a lofty and well-built wall. This, I was told, was the work of the Chinese, who, mindful of the slaughter of their fellow-countrymen during the Dungan rebellion, had taken the precaution of fortifying a position before inhabiting it. I have a suspicion, however, that the walls indicated the " New Kuldja " of the maps, which was destroyed about 1867, when the insurrectionists fell to killing each other.

Arrived at the capital, Suiting was found to be a much larger and more thoroughly Chinese town than the present Kuldja. It is surrounded by a high wall, which I remember they were strengthening in 1882, and has brick-built gates, a fortress, and many streets, also some few buildings and shops outside the walls. Under Russian rule in 1878 it contained 1,260 houses, with a population of 2,700 males and 1,300 females.

Since that date I should say the population has increased considerably, especially the Chinese portion and the official class. The bazaars are numerous and well stocked with merchandise, as were also the markets with vegetables and fruit; and there were said to be plenty of inns, to one of which—a new one, and therefore supposed to be preferable—I and my party were taken.

This was my first experience of a Chinese inn, and it made the flesh creep. Passing through a wide doorway, we entered a square courtyard with rooms on two sides, and occupied in the centre and on a third side by horses, carts, and drivers. The removal of such trifles as foul straw and manure was deemed superfluous, and through this I had to wade towards the door of a room, and there wait till the coal in it

THE DISCOMFORTS OF A CHINESE INN AT SUITING—PREPARING A ROOM FOR THE AUTHOR.

was swept into a corner and what looked like a brewing apparatus removed.

There was no flooring, not even of bricks, and no furniture, but at the end of the room was a *kang*, or platform of loose boards, over what appeared to be an ash-pit, though the cinders no doubt represented the remains of fires for winter heating. Over this receptacle for rubbish of various kinds I was to sleep and eat.

The servants and fellow-guests of the inn came, of course, to look at the foreigner, and if I presumed to close the door, it simply meant to shut out the light and send the crowd to the window, through the paper panes of which they could poke their fingers and so make spy-holes. One man insisted upon entering, whereupon one of my party asked him what he wanted.

"Cannot I come into a room," said he, " in my own country?"—a question my attendant did not argue, but again asked him what he wanted, and so got rid of the intruder; but on sitting down to read and write I was again surrounded.

Added to these little annoyances there was continued through the night the tinkling of horse and mule bells, whilst at early dawn began the incessant hammering of a flour-mill working next to my room. This went on all day, and what with the stench of manure, distracting noises, windows unglazed, and inquisitive visitors, my lodging proved to be the worst I had ever had.

Yet I was assured, and subsequent experience confirmed it, that not only was this inn the best in the town, but above the average of Chinese inns elsewhere. It gave me a taste, therefore, of what itinerating missionaries and travellers in the interior have to put up with.

My card was speedily sent to the proper office to announce our arrival, whereupon there came a request that I would call next morning on Kah-lee-ooin-ee (or, according to a later version, Kah-i-chang), the Commissary of Russo-Chinese affairs, with an invitation that I would not eat my breakfast beforehand, but take it with him. This general invitation was brought by a messenger overnight, and on the morrow another messenger came to say it was nine o'clock, and bidding me to come forthwith.*

I did so in a rough Chinese cart, answering to our cab, and was met by servants at the outer gate, through which we passed and crossed a court, to be received at the door of the apartments by our host. He appeared to be of Manchu, or Mongol, or perhaps mongrel origin, but was hearty in manner.

After leading me into an ante-room and placing me in a position of honour, the ante-repast began with yellow tea and fruit. Then we adjourned to the next room for a more serious gastronomic encounter, four persons being seated at a small table, perhaps a yard square, with about half a dozen saucers thereon.

These were added to up to the number of 20 save one, arranged in 5 rows of 3, 4, 5, 4, 3, after which 4 more were brought and placed in order on the top of the others. Now, as I had been on doctor's diet, and had not been allowed a decent meal for some time, and meat only once for nearly a week, I was of ready appetite, and am bound to say I thoroughly enjoyed the feast.

Some of the dishes were extremely nice, notably the

* Reminding me of a certain man who made a great supper and invited many, and sent his servant at supper-time to say to them that were bidden, "Come." (Luke xiv. 16, 17.)

little shreds of roast mutton, excellently seasoned, such as I learned ever after to call for with confidence at Chinese inns. On the other hand, the chicken was

BREAKFAST WITH THE COMMISSARY OF RUSSO-CHINESE AFFAIRS AT SUITING.

made uneatable, and the eggs on this occasion I am bound to say were inexpressibly nasty. The taste for them as eaten in China had need to be acquired, no doubt, for I had been told at Vierny of the wonderful pains and expense at which Chinese gourmands preserve their eggs till they are black and putrid, and of which they are as proud, when many, many years old, as an English squire of his crusted port.

I have, moreover, a vague impression, which for the moment I cannot verify, that I somewhere tasted these ancient delicacies, and found them good, but on the present occasion my note-book condemns them utterly. The rissoles of pork sausage were tasty, and so were the French beans, peas, the hearts of cabbage stalk cut in slices, and the Mandarin oranges preserved in syrup.

We helped ourselves to these delicacies as we pleased, but our host every now and then, with his chopsticks, placed on the plate of one or other of his three guests a choice morsel, which, mercifully, it was not a matter of unbending etiquette that one should eat. It was polite, of course, occasionally to return the compliment, and help him to tid-bits with one's knife and fork.

The conversation did not dwell too exclusively on my journey, for this was regarded as a preliminary meeting only—to such an extent indeed that when at the close I offered presents, my host said he could not accept them at the first visit. He added, however, that the *Tsian-Tsiun* was ready to do for me all he could, and would give me audience to-morrow.

In China it would seem that they like to do their politeness early, and, to return my visit, Kah came next day at six in the morning. His cart, or carriage perhaps I ought to say, was driven through the dirty yard close to my door, in leaving which I saw him perform an athletic feat that fairly surprised me. Kah was no longer young—fifty and eight he said was the tale of his years—and he had attained to a rotundity which, though in China held to be synonymous with happiness, is hardly conducive to agility.

When, therefore, he had to surmount the three feet or so between the ground and the floor of his vehicle, I expected to see a footstool brought, on which he might gravely step. Instead of that he approached the vehicle, and without ado sprang from the ground into his seat, and tucked his legs under with a gracefulness that left nothing to be desired. This feat was equalled by a Manchu afterwards sent with me, who, standing one day at his horse's shoulder and talking, turned round and, without touching mane or bridle, leaped from the ground clean into the saddle.

Shortly after this visit I went to Kah's house. He took me into the fortress for an audience with Seh-Tsian-Tsiun—the first word being his name (which in full was Sse-teng-nge) and the remaining two his title, which I was told is a high one and equivalent to Governor.

His civil jurisdiction extended over the Ili valley, whilst the local military affairs were then directed, if I mistake not, by Chang-tu-ting, or the General. I recognised the dwelling as that in which I visited a former *Tsian-Tsiun* in 1882 ; but I found the present officer more genial and intelligent, and not so ignorant of Western ideas.

He received me with much ceremony and asking of formal questions, after which I showed my passport and presented my letter from the Chinese Legation in London. That letter, he said, invited him to give me further documents. I next intimated my desire to travel by the imperial high road to Urumtsi, and thence westwards and round Chinese Turkistan, through Aksu, Kashgar, and Yarkand to Khotan. This, he kindly said, should be arranged, and the necessary papers got ready in four or five days, by which time I should have to revisit Suiting, on the way to the Talki Pass.

I then offered several presents, meaning that he should take them all, but was told afterwards that it was customary to display one's offerings in order that a selection might be made, there being a sort of tacit understanding that the recipient returns the value of what he takes. In the present instance, the *Tsian-Tsiun* seemed by no means greedy of gifts. He appeared pleased with a plume for his horse's martingale, which I had intended for the Emir of Bokhara; and I pressed upon him also a telescope, a pair of coloured spectacles, and some oleograph pictures.

Some light refreshment followed, and we returned to the house of Kah, who, after his chief had led the way, was now ready to receive as presents a field-glass, a set of oleograph pictures, watch-chain, and compass, and for his family a flageolet, pocket microscope, and needle-case.

Later in the day came an interpreter, one Mattie, the secretary or adjutant of the *Tsian-Tsiun*, bringing his master's card. He remembered my coming six years before, still possessed my photograph which he then received, and now seemed disposed to be helpful.

On the next morning I visited Mattie in his own house, and learned more of his influence, for whereas nine of his fellow-assistants after serving five days were allowed to go home for ten, he was too important to be spared by the *Tsian-Tsiun* for a single day. He had, he said, a cousin, or brother, Foo-Shan, an interpreter to the Russian Consul at Kashgar, for whom he would give me a letter; and he also knew Jun-Wang, a great personage among the Torgout Kalmuks at Karashar.

On the same morning the *Tsian-Tsiun* sent Mattie again, saying that as my stay was to be so short he could not prepare me a banquet, but sent, nevertheless, some provision for the way—namely, a sheep and four live chickens, a couple of ducks, and a sucking-pig roast, two dishes of pastry, and two sacks of rice and fine flour, all of which he desired me to accept.

The bringing of these presents by the *Tsian-Tsiun's* servants, and repeated visits of government officials, increased my consequence at the inn; but the landlord, who was a Dungan or Chinese Muhammadan, was reported as greatly disgusted at the pig being brought upon his premises. Our Chinese servant, who had inadvertently put the unclean animal upon a tray, was afraid I should have to replace it with a new one.

Fortunately, the landlord took a business view of the matter, and subsequently evinced a great desire when I called for my flour and rice to have the honour of entertaining so great a man again. Meanwhile the ducks were eaten, the pastry, I fancy, given away, and poor piggie, since none of my party wished to taste him, was sold at the nearest Chinese eating-house. The innkeeper was requested to sell the sheep, and to keep the flour and rice till called for.

On Monday morning we set out for Kuldja, feeling that progress had been made; but we were glad to get back to our Turkish lodging and baggage.

CHAPTER XIV.

PREPARATIONS AT KULDJA.

My impedimenta, 188.—Food, physic, and clothing, 189.—Furniture, books, and instruments, 190.—Presents; Visit from a blind native, 192.—Call on Roman missionaries, 193.—Their assistance sought by Chinese; Ill effects of child-marriage, 194.—Shelter given to the girl by missionaries; Names added to roll of adherents; Chinese quarter of Kuldja and magistrate's procession, 195.—Instruments of punishment, 196.—Intended route changed, 197.—Interpreter into Chinese unwilling to proceed, 198.—Withdrawal of interpreter into Turki; Perplexing, but subsequently proving well; Objections to route *viâ* Urumtsi; Consideration as to mountain roads, 199.—The Muzart Pass, 200.—A caravan leader willing to attempt it; How affecting main object of journey; Where to find interpreter? 201.—Another excursion to Suiting, 202.—Chinese temple and theatre, 203.—Change of route sanctioned and arranged for, 204.—Return to Kuldja; Interpreter sent for to Kashgar, 205.—My Tatar hostess, 206.—Farewell visit to Suiting and Chinese officials, 207.

THE number of my packages in Kuldja now amounted to about 50, and their weight to nearly two tons. Perhaps the reader might like to peep at these impedimenta, which for convenience shall be classified under the heads of Food, Physic, Clothing, Furniture, Books, Maps and Stationery, Instruments and Arms, and Presents, the last including publications for distribution.

Of Food not much was taken from England save essence of coffee, which I rarely used, compressed tea,

Liebig's extract, meat lozenges, anchovy paste, marmalade (to render palatable indifferent bread-and-butter), and biscuits. In addition to these were purchased in Russia condensed coffee and cocoa with milk, compressed vegetables, extract of Russian berries called *klukva*, recommended to me by Prjevalsky for drinking in tea, and essence of lemon for the same purpose; also effervescing drinks for the teetotal Muhammadans, a few sweetmeats for children, curry powder and jam as adjuncts to rice; and lastly, flour, baking powder, sugar, butter, and cheese.

Under the head of Physic were included the drugs said to be needful for stocking a small medical mission for upwards of a year. These were contained in five cases, and Messrs Allen and Hanbury's invoice alone numbered 80 items. Another case contained about a dozen medical appliances, the gift of Messrs Newberry Brothers, of King Edward Street. To these must be added 14 dozen spectacles, a set of ophthalmic instruments, kindly given by the late Dr Grimke, four or five small cases of surgical instruments, and a magnetic machine, together with the medicaments obtained at St Petersburg.

As for Clothing, I had to provide against every degree of temperature between the Arctic cold of mountains 20,000 feet high and the heat of the plains of India—from a fur-lined ulster, that is, to a vest of gauze—whilst in quality my wardrobe had to range from a peasant's sheepskin jacket for the road, to court dress for St Petersburg or the Viceroy's palace at Calcutta.

Added to this, it was desirable to have for my companions a small reserve in case of emergency, and as presents a few articles of English underclothing, such as woollen vests, said to be much valued by Chinese mandarins. The items in my journal under the head of clothing number 90.

By Furniture is meant various requisites for camp-life, or dwelling in an unfurnished room. This included a tent, bedstead, air-bed and bellows (presented by Canon Erskine Clarke), bath, metal and india-rubber pails, a hammock (kindly given by Madame Rosenbach), waterproof sheet and air-pillows, table, chair, and toilet necessaries, canteen, frying-pan, fire-shovel, and spirit cooking apparatus.

To the culinary portion of this outfit the servants did not take kindly, but preferred a huge copper kettle and an open saucepan, with tripod, large enough to boil a sheep. To the foregoing must be added a lantern, and half a hundredweight of candles and soap. My personal effects were packed in four bullock trunks, portmanteau and fitted bag, waterproof linen bag, and a hold-all. Besides these must be mentioned two saddles with fittings, and all the horse requisites from fodder and nosebags down to spare shoes and nails—the items under the head of furniture being 82.

Books for reading was a serious question in the face of a contemplated absence of two years amongst people to whom one could not speak, and in regions beyond the range of travellers' guide-books. I took, therefore, the best topographical works available, whether from Russian, Chinese, or Indian sources, a few books for the Tibetan and Turki languages, and some technical treatises on anthropology, medicine, surveying, and photography.

The only book I allowed myself, not bearing in some way on my work, was a small Chandos edition of Shakespeare (which, by-the-bye, I never once found time to open), notwithstanding which the number of my reading books stood at little short of a hundred volumes, and they weighed, I suppose, nearly twice as many pounds.

As for Maps, I had a copy made on six sheets of canvas of a large MS. of Mr Carey's route round Chinese Turkistan; also Walker's Turkistan in four sheets, A.K.'s route in Tibet in three sheets, a large geological map of Turkistan by Romanovsky and Mushketoff, another of Khorasan made and presented by Colonel Stewart, some large-scale maps of the Trans-Caspian region as well as of the Upper Oxus and Sungaria, procured in Russia, and others by Stanford and Stieler of India, China, and the Inland Missions; to say nothing of smaller maps in periodicals, and for occasional presents. The entries under this head numbered 39, and of stationery only two less.

In connection with Stationery I could not get out of my head the fate of two travellers who preceded me to Chinese Turkistan—Schlagintweit, who was put to death, and Shaw, who was kept virtually a prisoner for many weeks. It seemed probable that I should in any case be stationary for several months in the winter, and therefore I provided many manuscript books, diaries, note-books, and journals, that, whether in prison or out of it, I might busy myself in writing, most of this material being forwarded to Kuldja by the fourpence-a-pound arrangement.

As for Instruments and Arms, they will be alluded to more fully when speaking of collecting specimens of fauna, and of photography. Here it may suffice to indicate the possession of a few surveying and meteorological instruments, binoculars, and telescopes, with some carpenter's tools, bringing up the number of items to 108.

The list of Presents was of 109 varieties, but these must be regarded as a form of exchange. It is of little use to offer a nomad a shilling if he has nowhere to spend it, and the reading of Mr Carey's wanderings had shown me that he failed sometimes to get provisions from the nomads for money, whereas broadcloth or tea would have effected his purpose.

I was fortunate enough before starting to make the acquaintance of Mr Carey's brother, who showed me the list of articles he had sent out for presents. Thus guided, and on the introduction of my friend Mr Stapley, of London Wall, to a wholesale house in the City, I was able to get a considerable store of useful articles in cutlery, cheap jewellery and watches, optical instruments, fancy stationery, photographs, flageolets and musical boxes, and toys.

The publications for distribution shall be mentioned hereafter, but it may be readily believed that the unpacking and re-arrangement of the foregoing in Kuldja gave me plenty of occupation, besides which I had sundry visits to receive and calls to make. One ancient inhabitant, a blind native, having heard of the coming of the English traveller, brought something to show me which he evidently deemed mysterious and almost priceless. It was borne by a young man in a box wrapped in a handkerchief.

On being opened, the box was found to contain a wooden figure, the remaining space being filled with rice to prevent breakage. The said wooden figure, 11 inches long, was a fair representation of a man with a flat Mongol face, and this the owner would have us believe had grown in the ground in its present shape.

He would like to be favoured with an explanation by the learned traveller. The learned traveller suggested carving, and opened his knife to examine the image.

The old man, hearing this, was horrified, and begged him to desist. Whether he really wanted explanation, or expected to be offered thousands of roubles for his treasure, I am uncertain; but on the matter being mentioned to a Chinese servant on the premises, he said that similar objects were sometimes discovered in Kansu, and were looked upon as presaging great misfortune to the persons by whom they were found. I am afraid the old man thought me lacking in appreciation of his treasure, for which I did not even make him an offer.

On my previous visit to Kuldja I had found 65 Chinese Roman Catholics, who had been deprived of their missionary and his priestly functions for 17 years. They were still holding on, however, and asked me for a service, which I gave. My visit was still remembered, and since then missionaries from the Ortus country had arrived, to whom I was taken to be introduced. I found two priests only—M. de Deken, a Belgian, and M. Steenemann, a Hollander—their superior being expected to arrive shortly from Europe with more missionaries as recruits.*

I did not gather that the number of adherents had much increased, being still less than a hundred; but their chapel was so enlarged that I should not have recognised it. A photograph of the congregation was given me, with M. de Deken seated in the centre. I

---

* The staff, M. de Deken informed me in 1892, consisted of a superior with the authority of a Vicar Apostolic, and four missionaries, having also a station and permanent residence among the Kalmuks on the banks of the river Kash.

dined with the missionaries, and received much kindness at their hands, in the way of interpretation, and help in making local purchases. I was, therefore, the more glad to ask their acceptance of some copies of the Gospels in Kalmuk for a small mission I understood they had in the upper part of the Ili valley, as well as to help the expected recruits in the study of the language. I added also some maps, fancy biscuits, and quinine.

They found it very desirable, it seemed, to know a little of medicine, since they were not infrequently applied to in cases of Chinese women who had attempted suicide by an over-dose of opium. In such cases they invariably administered a dose of strong coffee, and with success in most cases. Nor were these the only cases in which their interference was sometimes sought, since during our stay they were sheltering one of their female adherents from a man who claimed her as his wife.

It was an instance of child-marriage. The woman was the daughter of a most respectable Chinese Christian, who was acting as secretary at the Russian Consulate. This man, who remembered my first coming, and now did some Chinese writing for me, had betrothed his child to a boy who was then a professing Christian, but had since lapsed and become a disreputable character. Her parents did not now wish to give him their daughter. Unfortunately, however, in China the law of child-marriage obtains, and, provided the agreement be duly registered, the contract holds when the parties come of age.

In the present instance the affianced husband threatened to come with a rabble, worthless as himself, and take the girl by force, in anticipation whereof, and with the sanction of another odious law in China, he had sold his wife to a mandarin. The missionaries, therefore, had been asked to interfere, and were giving the girl asylum, so that the mission-house was in a minor state of siege. It was hoped the girl might be smuggled away; and the case perhaps throws light upon the charge I have heard brought against Roman missionaries in China generally, that they interfere in politics. If so, one cannot but sympathise with their efforts to avert from their adherents the effects of such legislation.

I cannot, however, extenuate another practice among Roman missionaries that has come under my notice, who, when mothers bring to them sick children for medicine, ask whether the parent would not also like a good prayer said over the child. Consent, of course, is given without knowing what is to be done, the child is baptised, and an additional name entered on the register, which, even if in keeping with the *opus-operatum* view of the sacrament, is hardly consistent with Christian straightforwardness.

The Roman mission-house is situated on the outskirts of the town. The road to it goes through the Chinese quarter, in which is a Buddhist temple with an entrance of brick, through an arched gateway carved at the top and ornamented with dragons. There is also a Chinese bazaar, with abundance of running water near and numbers of ducks, with which the Chinese are delighted. In this quarter I made acquaintance with several features of Chinese life and manners that were new to me.

On my second day in the town there passed through the streets the local magistrate, preceded by his retinue, the foremost of whom carried gongs or musical instruments. Next came lictors with whips to clear the way, and executioners carrying their instruments of punishment. Then came several secretaries and attendants, one of them carrying a sort of umbrella which had been presented as a mark of appreciation by the people; and, lastly, the great man himself, in a little bird-cage sort of cart, the procession being closed by one or two mounted guards. The instruments of punishment attracted my attention, and set me longing for additions to my prison curiosities.

Upon communicating my wishes to M. Bornemann, and requesting that he would ask for a set on my behalf, he replied, "Oh, no, no; that is not the way here! If you merely ask, you may wait long enough: the better way is to command." Whichever he did, in a day or two there were ready for me three Chinese batons or staves and a whip, facsimiles of those in local use. The largest of the staves was about the length of a broom-handle, but rather thicker, and spatulated at one end.

It is used for administering from 60 to 100 blows on the thighs of soldiers and the worst of criminals. The smallest instrument is perhaps half the length of the foregoing, and lighter, and is used for spatting men on the hands, or beating women (on the abdomen when not pregnant) with from 10 to 50 blows. The weight of these staves was prescribed, it was said, with great nicety by Chinese law; and, in addition to beating with these large or small rods, three other kinds of punishment were mentioned—namely, temporary and permanent exile, and execution. Temporary exile was said to last from one to four-and-a-half years, whilst permanent exile implied moving the offender from 2,000 to 4,000 *li* or more from home.

In this matter of the staves and similar local matters M. Bornemann was very serviceable; and not many days after our return from Suiting I had to ask his assistance again with the Chinese authorities, in prospect of a change of route, brought about as follows.

I have intimated that from the outset Mr Hudson Taylor was kind enough to offer that one of the China Inland Mission agents should accompany me as interpreter, and the first meeting-place thought of was Hami. When, however, a letter was given me from the Chinese Legation in London to the Governor-General at Urumtsi, it seemed better for purposes of translation to make that place the point of meeting, which was accordingly done, and plans laid for me to arrive there by June 1st.

I have explained how delay of baggage made me a month behind, in consequence of which my interpreter, not finding me at Urumtsi, had come forward to Kuldja, arriving a day or two before me. Circumstances, however, with him had altered, so that within a few hours of our meeting he told me that he had given up all hope of getting into Tibet, and intimated that he would like to return to Kansu, instead of going to Kashgar.

He said that a little war had broken out between British India and the Tibetans, and that to attempt to enter the country now was to fly in the face of Providence; which seemed, I confess, not altogether unreasonable. Next, as he came along, he had been inquiring as to the number and character of the Chinese inhabitants of Kashgar and the neighbouring towns : had learned that they were comparatively few, and chiefly soldiers, who were not of a reading class, and therefore not likely to profit much by our distribution of the Scriptures. He had accordingly made up his mind at Urumtsi, before meeting me, that it was inexpedient for him to go, as he thought my Turki interpreter would suffice.

This information concerning the military character of the Chinese population afterwards proved correct; but, as a third reason, he went on to state that, since he originally expressed his willingness to go, his family circumstances had changed, and that he did not wish to be absent another winter. If, therefore, after this, I still determined to go to Kashgar, he would accompany me to Urumtsi, and thence continue his way homewards, leaving me to turn westwards.

This I determined at first to do, and had asked letters of the authorities at Suiting; but before they arrived a fresh obstacle had arisen. I have said in my introduction that I had a correspondent who, I hoped, might accompany me as Turki interpreter, giving the mission the benefit of his medical skill. He was at that time in Tashkend without employment, being unqualified to practise for lack of a Russian diploma; and in answer to my letter proposing terms, etc., he promptly telegraphed "Yes."

But between this and the date of our meeting the circumstances of both of us had altered. He had migrated to Kuldja, and was established in what he considered a good practice; whilst I, after an interview with Prjevalsky in St Petersburg, and a letter from Mr Carey, to which I shall allude presently, foresaw that I should not need to winter in Chinese Turkistan, and that my journey round the valley must be too rapid to allow of working a medical mission. When, therefore, after what passed between me and my Chinese interpreter, to which I need not refer in detail, my expected Turki interpreter asked to be released from his engagement, I consented.

This step subsequently proved a right one, and not to be regretted ; but there is no hiding the fact that for the moment I was in a corner, and that an anxious one. Apparently circumstances were against me ; in reality they were in my favour. I had now to consider very carefully and prayerfully what was to be done. To go back could not be thought of. By what route, then, forward ?

The possibilities of proceeding by one of the mountain roads had already crossed my mind soon after reaching Kuldja, first on hearing that the high road was infested by robbers—a not very serious hindrance, since the authorities had promised me an escort. Worse, however, was the rumour that, owing to the lateness of the season, the melting snows on the mountains had swollen the rivers and rendered some of them impassable, so that we might be detained for days, and even weeks ; and this was a very serious consideration for one already a month behind, who foresaw that he must hurry round Kashgaria if he was to escape over the mountains before the passes were blocked. The resignation, however, of my Turki interpreter put a quietus on the route *viâ* Urumtsi, for to try and make my way during a three months' journey thence to Kashgar without an efficient interpreter either into Chinese or Turki was out of the question.

The remaining routes from Kuldja to Chinese Turkistan were three : first, that by which Prjevalsky proceeded, up the Ili valley and over the mountains to Karashar. Another way was to return to Jarkend and proceed to Issik-Kul, and thence over the Bedal Pass to Ush-Turfan ; or the more frequented path farther west by Narin to Kashgar. But this meant leaving unvisited nearly all the towns of Northern Kashgaria.

The third and shortest route was up the Tekes valley, and over the Muzart, or Ice Pass, to Aksu, and of this I knew only the statement of Kostenko that no European had ever gone its entire length; and that, according to native statements and a Chinese geographer of the last century, the Pass was depicted as something frightful.

No Asiatic of note, that I am aware of, had crossed it since Hiuen Tsiang, the Buddhist monk of the seventh century, who described the mountains as steep, dangerous, and reaching to heaven, with snows piled up since the creation; where the eyes were blinded with glare, and even fur garments penetrated by icy coldness, the pot being cooked as well as the sleeping mat spread on the very ice itself, and by reason thereof 12 or 14 of his company, besides cattle, were starved and frozen to death.

Hence it seemed to me doubtful whether, supposing I decided on the Ice Pass, I should find any one to accompany me; but when, at a christening feast in the house of M. Romanadt, M. Uspensky told me he thought he knew a man who would go, I replied, half defiantly, that I should like to see him.

Accordingly, on the same day, one of the Consul's interpreters brought to me a certain Osman Bai Yusup Ali, or the last two words Russianised into Yusupayeff, a native of Marghilan, in Khokand, a fine, handsome man of perhaps 40, who, during the rebellion under Yakub Khan, had been commander of 100 men.

He, in answer to my question whether he had crossed the Muzart, said he had done so more than 20 times. Upon my speaking of the difficulties of the ice, he replied that the only thing he feared just then was the swollen rivers during June, July, and August, but he was willing to make the attempt.

It was, of course, an important consideration with me, how this change of plan would affect the main object of my mission, and careful consideration seemed to show that it need do so less than at first sight might appear. The American Bible Society had sent from Shanghai, to my intended Chinese interpreter, three boxes of Scriptures for me, or, in case we failed to meet, to be distributed by himself. One box was left at his house for lack of room in his cart, another was left at Urumtsi to be called for on the return journey, and the third brought forward and partially distributed during my first visit to Suiting.

Of the Scriptures brought from the East, about nineteen-twentieths were Chinese, and therefore suitable for Urumtsi and the towns on the northern road where the Chinese populations predominate, whilst of Scriptures brought by me, four-fifths were in Western languages, and therefore needed for the Turkish inhabitants of Chinese Turkistan.

Accordingly, I suggested to the interpreter that if in returning he would distribute his books along the towns north of the Tian Shan, and perhaps make a *détour* southwards to Karashar to distribute some among the Kalmuks (for which purpose I had copies to spare), whilst I, beginning at Aksu, with my Turkish and Chinese books, went all round the valley to Khotan, then we should separately cover almost all the ground we had thought to go over in company.

But what was I to do for an interpreter? To find a man who spoke Turki, or even Chinese and Russian, might not be so difficult—M. de Deken knew a

Kalmuk who spoke Taranchi, Chinese, and Russian—but to get, at Kuldja, a Turki or Chinese who spoke English or even French was a very hard matter.

I would fain have persuaded M. Bornemann to accompany me to Kashgar, or, say, to Aksu, on the assumption that he needed a holiday; and he would gladly have come, but he had buried in the grounds of the Consulate his first child, and now another was shortly expected, and he could not leave home. I knew of a European, last heard of at Kashgar, who spoke the necessary languages, but how to communicate with him quickly enough was a puzzle.

In fact, the whole affair taxed my faith and ingenuity not a little. I should not have dreamed of penetrating Chinese Turkistan unless, before leaving England, or, at farthest, European Russia, I had seen my way to efficient interpreters. But Gideon's army had to be lessened, and so had my forces to be reduced. I had a secret confidence that, my interpreters being taken away, another would be provided, and it presently appeared that all had been wisely predestined, though the interval of uncertainty was to me a painful trial of faith, and for three days made me ill.

Thinking over the matter very carefully on the morning after seeing Osman Bai, I remembered three persons to whom I might telegraph—namely, M. Oshanin of Tashkend and M. Gourdet of Vierny, both of whom would about this time be free from their scholastic duties; and, thirdly, the young soldier who had interpreted for me at Jarkend. To each of these I sent a telegram, and once more started for Suiting, to lay my change of plans before the authorities.

I was lodged on this occasion at the Russian post-house, which had a fine large garden with first-ripe apricots, and a running stream delightful for bathing. Some Chinese Roman Catholics of the place called on us, which involved a return visit to some of their houses. I saw likewise what seemed to be the principal religious building of the town, and, on asking its purpose, was variously answered that it was a temple and a theatre. Perhaps it was both, for the heathen Chinese are great believers in the alliance of Church and Stage, build them close together, and frequently turn from one to the other.

Before the *p'ai fang*, or roofed gateway, were erected two masts, usually seen before *yamens* or mandarins' offices, with something like bird-cages towards the top—emblems, I believe, of authority—but within these gates the temple itself was rather insignificant. The only noteworthy features about it were the yellow tiling, such as one sees in abundance in Peking, and the carved ridges and eaves of the roof.

Calling upon Mattie on the evening of our arrival, I presented him with a watch and chain, which seemed to stimulate his interest in my affairs, and next morning he brought the paper now ready for my route *viâ* Urumtsi. Notice, he said, had been sent all along the road to have soldiers ready for my escort, and it would cause some difficulty, he implied, to reverse this, but he hoped that a change of route might be arranged for; and I offered, if necessary, to pay for messengers to countermand orders.

We heard no more on that day, or the next; but the day after we breakfasted again with Kah, Mattie also being a guest. On this occasion Kah mixed a dish of macaroni for me, and helped his guests generally with his fingers. Another instance of Chinese manners was the calling for a large swan's quill—his toothpick—after which he rinsed his mouth, and told me that he gave me such a good reception because I was so well and worthily recommended.

Whether my change of route excited suspicion I do not know, but I was closely questioned on the subject. Kah's astonishment had been a good deal excited, I perceived, on our present visit, at two men being able to come from the opposite ends of the earth and meet at a given time at Kuldja. Moreover, the Chinese authorities are not very fond of foreigners prying about in the interior, as Mr Carey had frequently found when wishing to diverge from the highway in Chinese Turkistan.

I feared, therefore, at first that difficulties might be raised. The *Tsian-Tsiun* seemed to know little about the newly proposed route, and professed to be doubtful of my safety. But here my good friend Kah came to the rescue, saying he would be responsible for that, seeing the nomad Kalmuks were under his jurisdiction as far as the glacier, up to which point should be provided for me at seven stations a tent, brick tea, and mutton daily; whilst, beyond, he would despatch one Tch'ai Kuan, a controller, to ask the authorities there to send men to meet me, and he added that I should perhaps meet him coming back.

In addition to this kindness, he volunteered a favour of which I thought not lightly, to send a letter to Kashgar for me to the Russian Consul to aid in getting an interpreter, saying that I was a stranger, and must be helped as far as possible. There was, in fact, but one drawback to all these kindnesses, and that only one of delay. I was informed that, when in about five days my papers were ready, I must again come to Suiting formally to thank the *Tsian-Tsiun*, and to be escorted out of the town with drums beating and banners flying.

We therefore returned to Kuldja, where, in answer to my telegrams, I found that my interpreter at Jarkend was willing to go, and suggested my asking permission of Governor-General Kolpakovsky. When at Jarkend this young soldier had told me he was exiled thither "*pour une petite faute*"; but when at Kuldja I learnt that this *petite faute* was Nihilism, it seemed so extremely improbable that he would be allowed over the frontier, whence he might invite the authorities to catch him again if they knew how, that I thought it useless to trouble General Kolpakovsky in the matter, but wrote at once a full letter to M. Petrovsky at Kashgar, asking him to send the man I wanted, or if not him, then if possible another, to meet me at Aksu, or, better still, on the southern side of the Muzart Pass.

Final arrangements were now taken in hand. Wheel traffic on the Muzart route was out of the question, and my native cart was therefore sold, with the vicious horse—both at a loss, of course—to Abu Kadair, the Russian *Aksakal*, whose house, as that of a rich native, I visited outside the town. There we saw two *birkuts*, or eagles, trained for hunting, one of which had cost him £10. My tarantass was handed over to the postal authorities, who, in deference to my letter from the Postmaster-General, undertook to forward the vehicle free of cost to Samarkand, putting the post-bags inside and using it as a mail-cart.

I despatched also by post some of my books no longer needed and more specimens to Batoum, to be forwarded to England, and was helped not a little in the packing of boxes by my landlord's son, who was in weakly health, fond of carpentering, and was greatly delighted at a present of tools.

A TATAR WOMAN.

My landlord was a Nogai Tatar, whose wife could read. I talked from time to time with her, and saw something of her son's wife, also an inmate of our premises, but without children. I gave several pieces of jewellery to the two women, and the elder, on leaving home for a visit before my departure, as she bade me farewell, expressed great satisfaction at having entertained an Englishman.

On the Sunday following came a message from Mattie that my passport was ready, written in Chinese, Manchu, and Taranchi, as also two soldiers and two Kalmuk and Manchu interpreters, and I was desired to come to Suiting at once. We started, therefore, at five o'clock next morning, taking some quinine I had promised Mattie, who, next day, breakfasting again with Kah, gave me a letter of introduction to his relative at Kashgar.

I asked Mattie's and Kah's acceptance of some Kalmuk Scriptures, and I had before offered to the latter some hosiery and jewellery, in return for which, I suppose, he now gave me two tins of tea and two boxes of sweets. After this it transpired that I was to be excused the drum-and-flag arrangement, and I left with four men attendants for Kuldja.

This was not quite the last I saw of the Chinese officials, for, on the next day, Mattie came to Kuldja with the *Tchyan*, or adjutant, from the General Chang, about whom more anon. He now sent me a present of two pieces of satin, two tins of tea, and a fan. I was then free to start again.

CHAPTER XV.

FROM KULDJA TO THE PASS OF CHAPCHAL.

Caravan travel by horses; M. Bornemann and his linguistic abilities, 208.—Caravan leader and negotiations; Text of contract, 210.—Departure from Kuldja, 212.—Swollen condition of river; Escort of four, 213.—Jing's pretensions: Whipping the ferryman, 214.—The Ili, and how crossed; Bivouac, and departure next morning, 215.—*Personnel* of caravan, 216.—A Sibo village; Solon colonists, 217.—Reception at Kalmuk encampment, 218.—Shooting grouse, and ride to Damarchi; Taranchi inhabitants, 219.—Hospitality at Damarchi; Ride along the Uzun-Tau Mountains, 220.—Arrival at gorge of Chapchal, 221.

CARAVAN travelling by horses was new to me, and in making arrangements I was obliged to throw myself once more on the kindness of M. Bornemann, to whose house Osman Bai, my caravan *bashi*, or leader, was summoned. Osman spoke Turki, Persian, and, it was said, a little Chinese.

How many languages more M. Bornemann spoke I have never discovered; but, when paying him a visit one morning, he called my attention, by way of illustrating the polyglot character of the place, to the fact that the seven persons there chanced to be in his room at that moment each represented a different nationality and spoke in a different language—namely, English, Belgian, Russian, Chinese, Manchu, Nogai Tatar, and

Kalmuk—all residents in Kuldja, I suppose, except myself and the Kalmuk, who was a Torgout Khan, come in from a remote part of the district. He was well dressed, but not so superbly arrayed as another Kalmuk Khan whose photograph I possess, and named Van, in Baratola, north of Sairam-Nor. I fancy M.

VAN, A KALMUK KHAN, WITH HIS SUITE, AT BARATOLA.

Bornemann could converse with them all; and, in fact, he seemed to be a thoroughly capable man, working as hard as if the welfare of the whole Consular establishment depended upon him.

He helped me to question Osman Bai, according to whom it seemed that the journey from Kuldja to Aksu was a matter of 12 days, travelling light; but with baggage it was about 18 days. If each horse carried only 2 cwt. it might be done in 15 days; but with the maximum of 2½ cwt each, then 20 days would be required. His first price was 20s. for each horse. He would be responsible for keeping the baggage dry from rain, but not from being wetted in crossing rivers, nor for loss if washed away.

Upon being asked whether, if I wished it, he would continue the journey to Kashgar, he assented, but desired to put in a clause to the effect that he should not be required personally to enter the town of Aksu. This aroused suspicion, and M. Bornemann, after a good deal of cross-questioning, elicited that Osman owed many debts, and feared to show himself in the town, lest his horses should be seized for payment.

In such an event what would become of my baggage? M. Bornemann, however, anticipated no danger on that score, and said that for such men to be in debt was quite usual; and, having discovered that one of Osman's principal creditors was the Russian *Aksakal* at Aksu, added that a letter should be written to this man to protect me from annoyance. M. Bornemann then wrote the letter, which he delivered to me, and drew up an excellently framed contract, in Russian and Turki, for the caravan *bashi* and me to sign.*

* This 7th day of July, 1888, I, the undersigned Sart of Andijan, Osman Bai Yusupayeff, have made this contract with the English traveller Doctor Lansdell, as follows:—

1. I, Osman Bai, engage to convey Dr Lansdell, with his servants and baggage, from Kuldja to Aksu in 15 days, exclusive of those days on which Dr Lansdell may wish not to travel.

2. I engage to provide 15 horses required for the baggage, which weighs 1½ ton.

3. On the journey I engage, at my own cost, to provide what is necessary for myself, three assistants, and my horses.

4. I further engage, during the journey, to protect from injury, rain, or other accidents the said baggage.

Osman promised to be ready in three days, and thought that a convoy of two or three Kalmuks from the Chinese authorities, if not absolutely needful, was, at any rate, desirable, for the sake of prestige. He also readily agreed to my resting on Sundays, or, in fact, when I liked, and said there was so much pasture on the way that it would be unnecessary to take corn for the horses.

Joseph, however, did not approve of my animals being thus treated, and purchased 3½ cwt of barley, and for himself and fellow-servant 200 loaves or cakes of native bread; also for me ten chickens at 3¾d. each, and a quantity of fresh white bread, from the one man in the town who could make it—the last of its kind I was destined to see for many a day. To these were added some onions, and, thanks to an official in the Post Office, some potatoes.

At last, on Thursday, July 26th, came the day of departure. I called to say good-bye at the Post

5. In case of the death of any of my horses, I engage to replace the same immediately.
6. For custody and transport of the baggage, I have agreed to accept for each horse, from Kuldja to Aksu, 18s.—that is, £13 10s. in all.
7. If Dr Lansdell should be satisfied with me during this journey, I will engage to convey him, his servants and baggage, from Aksu to Kashgar, in 16 days, for payment at the rate of four *liang* silver for each horse.
8. Dr Lansdell is bound to give me his final decision not later than a day and a half's journey on this side of Aksu.
9. If I should undertake to convey Dr Lansdell from Aksu to Kashgar, this agreement is to be binding for that journey also.
10. On signing this agreement I have received 75 roubles; 25 roubles more are to be paid to me on arriving within a day and a half's journey from Aksu, and the remaining 35 roubles on arriving there.

The Andijan Sart Osman Bai Yusupayeff being unable to write, I, Diamatin Tadjitovitch, have signed for him at his personal request.

This 8th July, 1888, the Imperial Russian Consulate certifies the above, etc.—(*Signed and sealed*) V. USPENSKY.

Office and the Consulate, and also bade farewell to my intended Chinese interpreter, who was on the point of starting for Kansu, and to my other intended interpreter, whom the European inhabitants were well pleased should remain behind.

Indeed, they had looked upon me all along as somewhat of a sheepstealer for wishing to take away the only medical man they had within 80 miles, and their appreciation of the doctor was shared by his Chinese and Turkish patients. My landlord was amiable in settling up, not exacting in his charges, and in return for my European presents gave me a Chinese body-girdle or purse, together with his dog " Kara Beg," or " Black Prince," which had become attached to us, and might, I thought, be useful to sleep in my tent.

The landlord's son evinced kindly feelings on my departure, and mounted his horse to make one of a cavalcade to conduct me out of the town, as did also several of the native inhabitants, including, I think, some of the interpreters at the Consulate. The cavalcade was joined also by M. Steenemann and M. de Deken, the latter mounted on a war-horse which formerly belonged to General Kaufmann, and could still, for not too long a spurt, go splendidly.

M. de Deken would fain have made a holiday of it, he said, and accompanied me as far as the glacier, but in the absence of his ecclesiastical superior did not like to leave M. Steenemann alone.*

It was about noon when I " placed my foot in the stirrup," as Tamerlane used to say, and went forth to

---

* M. de Deken has since made a more famous journey through Karashar, and past Lob-Nor, into Tibet towards Lassa, and thence through Western China to Tongking, in company with M. Bonvalot and Prince Henry of Orleans.

encounter the difficulties of an unpremeditated route into Chinese Turkistan. Osman Bai's horses were at grass on the other side of the river, to which the baggage was to be taken in carts, whilst our cavalcade took a roundabout way of some two hours.

I cannot speak, as we made our way across the grassy valley, of gilded domes flashing in the sunlight, or of cathedral spires or minarets growing dim in the rear, unless it be the minaret of the Dungan Mosque, which, Muhammadan though it be, is built in purely Chinese style, and for a photograph is the finest building in the town.

The waters of the river being swollen by the melting snow of the neighbouring mountains, the usual place of crossing was not available, nor, when we arrived, was the ferry-boat visible. We had, therefore, to scramble down a bank, perhaps 40 feet high, and patiently wait in the shade.

I may now introduce to the reader my escort of four. Two of them, Koo-Kah (Chief) and Tcho-gah, were guards, and armed, the former being reputed a mighty hunter, and therefore of prospective use in procuring game. A third, Tor-jee, was a tall, stout, good-natured, broad-faced, ethnological nondescript, at home in Chinese, Taranchi, Solon, Sibo, and Kirghese; whilst the fourth, though the smallest in stature, was, in his own opinion certainly, the greatest of all. This Jing-jee-tai spoke Manchu, Chinese, Kalmuk, Sibo, Solon, Taranchi, and Kirghese—in fact, "a man of seven tongues."

The first two were servants of Kah, the last two hailed from the *Tsian-Tsinn*, Jing being on his personal staff, and of such importance, he would have me to understand, that he rarely left his master's presence.

For ordinary travellers, he said, two or three Kalmuks were told off, and there was an end of it; but in the present instance the *Tsian-Tsiun* had said that this English traveller was a very great man, and that Jing accordingly should accompany him!

In keeping with his pretensions Jing soon began to show his authority, and after we had been waiting about three hours, I heard a great shouting from the top of the cliff above. Presently the ferry-boat arrived, out of which they dragged the ferryman near to where I was sitting, Jing the while vociferating loudly and making a great to-do. Next the boatman was ordered to lie down and be beaten, which the lubberly fellow immediately did. One man sat on his head and another on his feet. Then Jing told off one of his men as lictor, and to kindle his enthusiasm administered one or two cuts across his back, after which the delinquent boatman received the allotted number of stripes.

All this was "Greek" to me, until it appeared that the boatman had not come so quickly as he ought when called by Jing. But he was not killed, within a great many inches, for the lash of the whip fell well beyond the culprit's back on to the ground. He seemed, moreover, on getting up to be little hurt, and my impression is that the whole thing was got up by Jing as a demonstration of his zeal on my behalf. The ferryman at all events seemed to have regained his equanimity when I gave him a present on reaching the other side of the river.

The width of the Ili at Kuldja is variously stated at 500 and 700 feet, the latter being the width of the Thames at low-water at London Bridge. But the breadth evidently varies greatly according to the season, and crossing the stream now was a very different matter from doing so in September 1882; so that I doubt whether London Bridge, if placed at our disposal, would have taken us more than halfway over. Kostenko gives the depth of the river at Kuldja from 3 to 30 feet, and its velocity from 2 to 4 miles per hour.

All these conditions were now, I suppose, at their highest, the summer heat having set in, and we prepared for crossing as for a voyage. The baggage and the saddle-horses were brought on board, whilst the sumpters swam across attached to the boat. There was, first of all, a certain amount of towing up-stream, the tow-ropes being fastened to the stumps of the horses' tails, which the men of the place did not seem to think cruel. Then we rowed into mid-stream, and were carried by the torrent a long way down-stream to the opposite bank.

What with waiting for the ferry and embarking and disembarking baggage and horses, the day was now far spent, and Osman Bai proposed that we should bivouac in the grassy meadows alongside the river, he always having an eye, as I afterwards found, to food for the horses.

The escort declared themselves bound to go forward a few miles distant to their appointed station, though they agreed, if I wished to go no farther, to come again early in the morning. I elected, therefore, to stick to the baggage and spend the first night on the bank of the Ili within sound of its waters, a small tent being improvised just large enough to shelter me; the rest slept in the open.

Before sunrise next morning—that is, soon after three o'clock—the men were astir, and so was I at 4.15, to observe the temperature in my tent to be 70°.

By seven o'clock they had finished shoeing 17 horses, after which packing and loading 65 parcels took up two hours more, and then we made a start.

Seeing a man going off in the opposite direction, I learned that he had accompanied Osman Bai thus far to help him gratuitously in shoeing the horses, and was now returning to Kuldja. This I thought a neighbourly act, gave him a present, and then, all outsiders having departed, turned to look at the *personnel* of my caravan.

"Your humble servant" was dressed in a drab drill suit, leathern leggings, and black felt hat. His saddle, new from Long Acre and made to order, had holsters,—left, for a small biscuit-box and enamelled bottle for cold tea ; right, a revolver and space to spare for small etceteras. Behind my right leg was suspended, in a case made by Joseph, a double-barrelled gun, and behind the left leg a saddle-bag with waterproof coat and a book to read ; whilst behind the saddle was a valise, in which could be carried telescope, field-glasses, clinometer, and sundry other instruments and necessaries.

Next in rank came Joseph, dressed in European costume, with rifle on shoulder and revolver in belt, of both of which he was proud. Stowed away on and about his saddle were numerous travelling requisites and little comforts for me, which he knew well how to pack and carry.

Third came Amin Agha as groom. He had signed, or rather put his mark (something like a cross-bow), to an agreement to accompany me to Kashgar at the rate of 30*s.* a month and his food, which was about three times the amount he would receive whilst stationary in Kuldja, without subsistence. Amin was

dressed like a Taranchi, save that he wore a new and rather Chinese-looking hat. He was mounted on his own horse, fairly laden with etceteras before and behind.

We three for a long distance kept in the rear. Osman Bai, with his brother and two assistants, Tokhta and Ismail, were dressed as Sarts, and had two extra horses beyond the 15 agreed upon, so that they could take turns in riding.

Then came the four men of my escort, and, lastly, an old man, a shoemaker, who, hearing that I was going to Kashgar, had some days previously offered his services for the road, which had been declined. He was now said to be going on his own responsibility, and, for safety, to have joined my caravan. Now I had been warned against such hangers-on as not being always quite honest, and was at first disposed to dismiss him ; but Joseph pleaded that the man had on the previous evening made himself useful at little odd jobs, whereupon it was agreed that " the mullah," as he was called, should be hewer of wood and drawer of water to my men, in return for which he would have the benefit of protection and sundry scraps of the servants' food.

Thus we numbered in all 12 men and 27 horses.

After fording a branch of the Ili sufficiently deep to bring the luggage on some of the horses to within an inch of the water, and advancing for perhaps an hour away from the river, we marched through what I took to be Khair-Sumun of the Russian maps, eight miles south of Kuldja, a walled Sibo village, perhaps the same—at least very like—that I visited in 1882.

The Sibos and Solons were military colonists from Manchuria and Daouria, the Sibos being settled south of the river and the Solons on the north. My friend Mattie was a Solon.*

This walled village was the station I presume we were expected to occupy on the previous evening. There was nothing in it to stop for now, so we merely passed through it by the straight road from wall to wall, and arrived about two o'clock, after a five hours' march, at a valley, the name of which (if it had one) was given me as Ghaljat.

Here there was a small Kalmuk encampment, with an empty tent set apart for me. Two chiefs, with buttons above their hats, came to pay their respects, and presented a sheep for a feast in my honour. In return they received two bricks of tea, or about double value. Subsequently I went the round of the tents, and distributed sweets to the children, a knife, key-ring, beads, and needles.

Before leaving I also gave away copies of the four Gospels in Kalmuk. I was not sure any of the people

* M. de Deken informs me that the Chinese Government, always fearing a revolt of the Manchus combined with the Mongols, have exiled from the plains of Manchuria the Manchus, Solons, and Sibos (Si-po or Hsi-po) to the Ili valley, whilst the Chinese Muhammadans of Ili, after their last revolt, were transported to Manchuria.

The Manchus in Ili are divided into two classes. South of the river they inhabit eight small towns, and are called Sibos. The Sibos speak Manchu and the Sibo dialect, which is not understood by the other class, the Solons, who live north of the river, and whose language stands by itself, though possessing certain affinities to Mongol and Manchu.

All are labourers, but bound to military service at the call of a general from Peking. Many of their ancestors, when they arrived in Ili, were Christians. "We know still," says M. de Deken, "two families, of which the fathers, who had been baptised at Peking, made their children promise to worship none but the true God."

As for the Manchus of the north—sometimes called Manchu Tatars——they are unapproachable, proud, and arrogant, and all claim to belong to the Imperial family. It is from among them the great mandarins are chosen.

could read, but I hoped the books might find their way into the hands of some of their lamas. A few of Mrs Grimke's illuminated text-cards in Kalmuk received only scanty respect, and were in some cases speedily crumpled and soiled.

All of the tents looked squalid and miserable, to be accounted for perhaps by a rude spirit-still which we got a glimpse of in one habitation. The *koumiss* bag standing near suggested the raw material. In another tent were two sick men, one having a deformed knee, for which we could do nothing. A little before seven next morning we departed.

We had scarcely mounted when, within a few yards of the encampment, I shot a leash of grouse, as fine, I venture to think, as ever came from a Scotch moor. Then we marched on in a south-westerly direction, passing the tomb of a Mussulman saint, and in an hour came to Kainuk, a village of 90 houses and 600 inhabitants, but formerly, under the Russians, more populous.

Then, turning in an easterly direction, we were passing through another village, Damarchi, when our men asked me to turn aside into the house of the chief man. This we did, and learned that in the village were 55 houses and 300 inhabitants, the people, as in the last village, being Taranchis.

The Taranchis are of Turkish origin, and were brought by the Chinese to the Ili valley from Kashgaria. They are Muhammadans, but differ from their co-religionists farther west in not keeping their women so secluded. The Taranchi women wear Turkish *khalats* opening down the centre of the front like a dressing-gown, whilst the Dungan women—their sisters in creed, though not in race—wrap themselves in robes of Chinese pattern that fold all across and button at the side.

Both, if I mistake not, wear low, stiff cylindrical hats with conical tops; but these, I think, are for summer or home wear, whilst others I saw were perhaps for travelling or winter wear, of huge proportions and made of fur. The women go about unveiled; but now and then I noticed, when my Kuldja hostesses were receiving visits from their female friends, that some arrived in the yard with their skirts or *khalats* thrown over their heads.

The head-man of the village at Damarchi gave us a kind reception and tea, and when I presented him with a ring he offered a *chowry*, or fly-brush, that had attracted my attention, together with some unripe apples. We stayed less than an hour, and then continued our easterly march along the plain till nearly one o'clock. Damarchi was the last village we entered, though there was another to the south, not far distant, called Kan.

Meanwhile we had on our right one of the numerous ramifications of the Tian Shan, running parallel to and south of the Ili, and filling the space between that river and the Tekes. This range bears the general name of Uzun-Tau, or "Long Mountains." The upper valleys of the Charin (which flows northward into the Ili) separate this range from the Trans-Ili Ala-Tau; and the western portion of the range is called in turn, looking eastwards, the Temurlik, Ketmen, Ak-Bur-Tash, and where it approaches the Lower Tekes, the Kara-Tag.

Over this portion we were to pass, and although, as Kostenko says, the Kara-Tag does not reach the snow-line, still its system is sufficiently high to make progress difficult over those passes which have not been improved by art. The most noticeable of these are the Ketmen, Suashu, Khanakai, Chapchal, and Sharbo-Guchi. The last, at the eastern end of the range, is the easiest, and practicable even for carts ; but it is circuitous, and we were to be taken by the most direct road through the Chapchal gorge and over the pass of that name.

The northern slope of the Uzun-Tau range descends in three terraces to the Ili, whilst the southern slope separates into several branches, which lose themselves in a flat plateau to form the south side of the Tekes valley.

At one o'clock we turned abruptly at a right angle into the hills, and in half an hour were wending our way through a pretty defile by the side of a stream with maple, willow, sycamore, mulberry, apple, and, above all, apricot trees, at which last a general rush was made. Here I picked my first wild apricots, whilst Joseph prudently brought away a supply for the morrow's dessert.

The hills on either side were bare, on the left precipitous, and it took the horsemen three hours of steady climbing before we reached, at four o'clock and after nine hours in the saddle, the gorge of Chapchal. Here was another Kalmuk encampment, larger than the one we had left in the morning. On the arrival of the baggage, two hours later, with Osman Bai, who had not been this way before, we prepared for spending the next day, Sunday, amidst novel surroundings.

CHAPTER XVI.

THE TEKES VALLEY.

First Sunday in camp, 222.—Lodging in Kalmuk tent, 223.—Breakfast *menu*, 224.—Review of month, 225.—My servant Joseph, 226.—Lack of efficient interpreter, 227.—Altitude and temperature of Chapchal; Visit to Kalmuk tents, 228.—Pass of Chapchal; Defile of Sua-Chow; Geology of Uzun-Tau, 229.—Altitude of Pass, 230.—Descent to Booghru; Cattle of the Kalmuks, and dogs, 231.—March from Booghru and butterfly hunt, 233.—Manchu larking on horseback; Caution against spirit-drinking, 234.—Arrival at Khanakai, 235.—Taking photographs; Departure to the Tekes; its rise and course, 236.—Impracticable ford at Geelan and *détour* to Narin-Kol; Welcome at Russian picket, and help of Cossacks, 238.—Fording the Tekes, 239.—Another night on river bank; Awakened by Lama's prayers; Departure for Muzart defile, 240.

OUR first Sunday in camp was in many ways interesting. A messenger had been sent in advance to announce our coming, and at Chapchal, as elsewhere, we found a tent erected. The Kalmuk tents resemble those of the Kirghese, already spoken of, except that I do not remember at any station occupying one of which the felt was not torn, and that not because they gave the visitor of their worst, since none of them appeared to be housed any better.

Usually my tent was found pitched in a clean place on grass at some little distance from, though within hail of, the encampment, and there was sometimes a rug or piece of felt within. Joseph began furnishing by covering the floor with two large pieces of felt; next, four bullock trunks were brought in, and when placed side by side made a platform just large enough for the air-bed and pillow. Thus bestowed it was less easy at night for personal effects to be stolen. Close to my head, and sometimes partly under it, was placed my fitted bag containing papers and valuables, and near at hand the fire-arms.

When making a stay (but not for a single night) it was more comfortable to open my bedstead, a capital one for lightness, and adaptable as a lounge by day. Mr St George Littledale, whose experience of tent life is greater than mine, feared that I should find this camp bedstead too fragile for rough wear or uneven ground; and perhaps he was right, but I found it useful when occupying a room, and the same remark holds good, to a certain extent, of a folding chair and table.

They were of "Paragon" make, the legs doubling up after the fashion of a camp stool, and the table-top rolling up like a sheet of thick cardboard. Though frail, with care they travelled with me safely for thousands of miles, but were not in very frequent use. The saddles were also usually brought into the tent, and that most necessary article of commissariat, the lunch-basket.

I gave so good a report to Messrs Langton & Son of the behaviour of their lunch-basket which accompanied me, almost uninjured, through Siberia and round the world, that on the present occasion, and in sympathy with my expedition, they fitted up and presented me with a new basket for three persons, valued for the Custom-house at £5.

This proved a great comfort, and could the reader

have peeped in at the door of our tent in the Chapchal Gorge at breakfast-time, he would have seen the little table covered with a white damask cloth with red edges, enamelled plates and dishes filled with white bread, butter, eggs, the remains of last night's mutton, grouse, Peak & Frean's biscuits, apples, and wild apricots; whilst in the lunch-basket on the ground were condiments of various sorts, jam and marmalade, —a breakfast, in fact, than which many a Londoner had not a better. Truth compels me to add, however, that this luxurious level was not maintained, and things were very different before the end of the journey.

Some have asked me how we managed for bread. So far back as Vierny it had been said that we should be unable, over the frontier, to procure either white bread or flour, European candles, sugar or cheese, to say nothing of butter fit to eat. It seemed desirable, therefore, to think betimes what should be done for these things during a period of several months, should those prognostications prove true. Orders were accordingly given for the purchase of 120 lbs. (Russian) of flour for 9s. 9d.; 52 lbs. sugar for 26s.; 40 lbs. of candles for 24s.; and 100 lbs. of bread and rusks for 22s. 6d.

Into the bread my Siberian experience suggested the putting a small quantity of butter, and making the loaves about the size of halfpenny buns.* Though the loaves became hard as bricks, yet when six months old, and after enduring all the degrees of temperature between the plains of Russia and of India, they were still, if not delicious, at least eatable.

* These were packed in two tea-chests covered with cowhide, that had served for bringing caravan tea across Mongolia, and now made strong, light, and cheap cases for carriage by pack animals.

But this was not my real reserve, for Joseph fortunately could make bread. Putting a spoonful of carbonate of soda into a cup of water and stirring it, he added two spoonfuls of kali-bitartaric. With this home-made baking-powder he worked up the flour and put it quickly into the oven, the said oven being a frying-pan with an iron cover. The product was a species of scone, quite eatable for a couple of days, though not so nice when dry.

As for butter, it was to be had in Vierny both cheap and good—31 lbs. for 19s. 6d.—and we thought to preserve it in tin boxes made and soldered down by the local whitesmith. But here my 'prentice hand did not succeed, for the soldering seemed to impart an ill savour to the butter, so that it could be used only for cooking. But Joseph again came to the rescue, and by shaking up cream, which he could usually procure, always managed to keep my table supplied.

Hence, on rising from breakfast in Chapchal Gorge, I felt on improved terms with mankind in general, and my present surroundings in particular. I was able calmly to review the anxieties and worries of the past month, and was thankful to feel that they were in the rear.

I have said that they were all wisely predestined. What I meant was this. At an early stage of my preparations in London I happened to be calling on Colonel Stewart, who, hearing of my possible departure for Central Asia, said that he could recommend me a servant, a Persian from the Strangers' Home for Asiatics in East London, where the Colonel was charitably keeping him. I had thought, however, for economy's sake, I could manage without a servant as far as Kuldja; and to take a man 5,000 miles before his services were absolutely needed seemed doubtful policy, so that I did not jump at the proposal.

A short time afterwards, on my way to hear Mr Carey's paper at the Royal Geographical Society, as I left the train at Charing Cross, Colonel Stewart was on the platform.

"Have you thought any more of that servant?" he asked, whereupon I mentioned the drawback of taking him so far before he was wanted.

"Very well," replied the Colonel, "I am anxious to get him back to Persia, and am willing to pay his passage to Constantinople, if you will take him."

"Send him down, then, to Blackheath," I replied, "and let me see him."

Joseph shortly appeared on a dark muddy day in December, and I suppose his swarthy skin rather alarmed the Rhoda of my establishment, for it was afterwards reported that she murmured to her mistress, "I hope master isn't going to take *that* man along with him."

But Joseph had some good antecedents On the Afghan Frontier Commission he had served Sir West Ridgeway, whose testimony in brief was, "Not brilliant, but trustworthy." The Chaplain at the Home gave him a good character; and so in due time Joseph and my baggage were shipped to Batoum, at a reduced fare and free freight, thanks to the good offices of my friend Mr Pembroke, of the firm of Galbraith, Pembroke, & Co.

When I reached Batoum, the first person to meet me was Joseph. He had been receiving pay since the beginning of the year, and now expressed concern that he had thus far been able to give me so little in return. "But now," said he, "you shall see how well I will serve you "—a promise which, Oriental though he was, he nobly redeemed.

His capabilities developed and his value increased in proportion as we got away from civilisation. In the hotels at Tiflis and Baku he was not required; but, the Caspian crossed, he began to be handy in Bokhara, still more so in Tashkend, and when the baggage was reached, and horses added to the expedition, he adapted himself to the situation admirably.

Mr St George Littledale, whom Joseph afterwards accompanied across the Pamirs, wrote in his testimonial, " He can mend anything, from a pocket-handkerchief to a piece of saddlery." True to this, on opening my saddlery bag, it was found that the packers in Long Acre had omitted the crupper, whereupon Joseph either made a new one, or adapted one locally bought, and then slung to my saddle a capital leather case, which he judged necessary and had made for my gun.

I cannot pretend, however fluent may have been his Persian, that his English was other than feeble—several degrees, in fact, below that of a second-class interpreter—yet this was the provision made for me, and the only instrument I had to depend on, in making the plunge into Chinese Turkistan. Had he fallen ill or left me, I must have run aground, and in writing to England a statement of affairs up to date, I confided to no one but Mr Hudson Taylor how precarious was my situation. Having penned that epistle, and held with Joseph something like a Sunday morning service, I proceeded after lunch to take a turn round the camp.

We were now probably from 5,000 to 6,000 feet above sea-level. After the heat of the valley, which

Prjevalsky had specially decried to me, and which certainly exceeded anything I had been accustomed to, the rest and slightly cooler air of the mountains were refreshing.

The temperature in my little tent on the bank of the Ili at eight in the evening had stood at 78, and by the next morning at four had come down only 8; also during the first night at Chapchal there was a difference of only 12° between the maximum and minimum temperature, whilst on the Sunday night the mercury did not rise above 73°, and it fell to 57°. In Kuldja I had slept in a room under a sheet only; by the river side and partially undressed, under one fold of a shawl; but at Chapchal, after undressing completely, I lay in the tent between sheets, under a double shawl and my fur-lined ulster, and was not too warm.

Our surroundings too at Chapchal were exceedingly pretty. On either side were lofty hills, and on the slope below us 22 Kalmuk tents. I went the round of these, and found a box of sweetmeats efficacious in paving the way to the affections of the children, and through them, of course, to their mothers, so that I was allowed to examine their trinkets and jewellery, and such objects of ethnographical interest as attracted attention. To one woman I gave a fashionable London hair-pin in exchange for an instrument of primitive make, which she used instead of a comb for parting the hair.

Speaking generally, all things looked squalid and poor, there being no signs visible of nomad affluence. The chief man of the encampment, to whom I gave a brick of tea and a knife, was called On-Bashi (the Turki title of an officer commanding ten soldiers), and when, on my arrival, he came to salute me, he went down on all fours to make the Chinese *kotow*, putting his head to the ground. There was also a lama in the camp, to whom I gave a book.

On leaving the Gorge of Chapchal, we had two hours of steep climbing to the Pass of that name; and from one of the turns in the defile, where it joins that of the river Sua-Chow, a fine view is to be had on a clear day of the Ili valley, framed on the north by the Borokhoro Mountains, and spread out below with a sharpness of detail resembling that of a map in relief, and deeply furrowed in two directions by the course of the Ili and that of the Kash tributary, somewhat east of Kuldja.

The banks of the Ili are diversified with villages, as if floating amid waving verdure, and animating the landscape when brilliantly lit up by the sun. The valley has an obvious slope from north to south, and here we took our leave of the Ili proper, the second of whose head waters is the Kunges, running parallel to the Kash, and receiving on its western bank first the Tsagma, and then, about 70 miles above Kuldja, the Tekes. Into the Tekes valley we were in a few minutes to look down.

The defile of Sua-Chow, whence the above-mentioned view is seen, wears a strange and fantastic garb, the soil being coloured with shades of red, blue, violet, green, and orange.

Looking at the geology of this district by the aid of Romanovsky and Mushketoff's map, it would appear that we passed, between Kuldja and the spot whence we turned into the mountains, over formations capable of cultivation, and loess. After this the road rises gently for about ten miles over river and lake deposits, and then on to rocks, first of the Tertiary series, and then of the Jurassic and Triassic systems. Among the Jurassic are indicated three deposits of black and brown coal, two of them, one on each side of the road, being worked.

Still ascending, we passed over a narrow band, there about three miles wide, but running the whole length of the range, of palæozoic rocks (mountain limestone, etc.). In the vicinity of the Chapchal gorge one crosses also a band, extending uninterruptedly along the whole length of the Uzun-Tau, of massive crystalline rocks, with outcrops, near the summit, of dolerite. The foregoing strata include a band of rocks of the azoic group.

This band crops out at the summit all along the range, and consists of crystalline limestone, phyllite, etc., over which we rode at the top of the Pass, and then descended over a similar series, but of course in reverse order, into the fluvial and lacustrine deposits of the Tekes valley.

Mention should also be made, as occurring in the Uzun-Tau, besides coal, of gold, silver, lead, copper, iron, manganese, rock-salt, and mineral oil, the last being found in the lower formations of the Ili and Tekes valleys.

As we approached the summit of the defile there was abundance of grass and numerous fir-trees, and from the absence of these at the actual top, Kostenko infers that the Pass may be 9,000 feet high, but it appears in my Russian map as 6,500.

Here at the summit of the Pass, which it took us two hours from the camp to reach, was raised an *obo*, consisting of five heaps of stones with poles, whence might dangle and flutter tails of *yaks* or horses, and pieces of calico inscribed with Tibetan or Mongolian writing. In the country of the Buriats I have seen on similar spots sweetmeats and copper coins scattered about, but not so here; though on arriving at the place my Chinese attendants all dismounted, each to add a few stones more to the heaps, and to make their obeisance in Chinese fashion ; perhaps also to say a prayer, but of this I am not sure. It was not easy to get from them information on the subject, though they told me that these were graves of two celebrated lamas, " who lived 30,000 years ago!"

The descent from the Pass on the south is more convenient than the ascent on the north, owing to the ground falling gently, as well as to the absence of large stones. The verdure and beauty of the defile increased rather than diminished, being enhanced by various specimens of fir-trees, their lower branches resting on the ground as on an English lawn, and their spires rising to a considerable height.

After six hours' marching we reached, about two o'clock, our stopping-place called Booghru, a small sheltered valley by the side of a clear and swift stream. Here was a camp of eight tents and many cattle, some of the owners of which had come out to meet us, bringing *koumiss* and spirit. These they invited us to quaff reclining on the grassy pile. But south of the Pass a drizzling rain had come on, and we preferred to hasten onwards to cover, where we arrived slightly wet ; my waterproof overcoat being here first called into requisition since leaving London, five months previously.

The cattle in this camp consisted of horses, cows, and sheep, the last being of the fat-tail breed, and affording excellent mutton. The Kalmuks of the Volga keep camels also, of which we saw none in the

Tekes valley, nor, so far as I remember, of asses. The excellent condition of the cattle was accounted for by the abundant pasture, and it was not at all difficult to believe that worn and battered horses of the inhabitants of the Kuldja valley, on being sent to the mountains after winter work, soon became so fat and sleek as to be unrecognisable. Most of the Kalmuks kept dogs to guard their tents, but of very poor breed, and, like most Asiatic dogs I have met, seemingly devoid of affection.

At the previous station we had been obliged to part with our " Kara-Beg." So long as the princely animal was lording it in his own yard at Kuldja, barking at strangers and not unfrequently biting them, he appeared to be a brave fellow. But when tied to the cart and made to walk to the Ili, he was very much crestfallen, and apparently exhausted. On the morrow we had to cross an arm of the river, and he stood on the bank, cried like a baby, and had to be dragged or carried across. Again, on his third day out he became so wearied and footsore, that he arrived at Chapchal Gorge with swollen feet on horseback.

It became plain, therefore, that he was not the dog for a long march. Nor was he a "carpet knight," albeit his name of "Black Prince." At Kuldja he used to present himself at my open door, and wag his tail for scraps, but never presumed to pass the threshold ; and if, with a view to closer friendship, I once or twice dragged him in to eat a morsel, he seemed frightened at treading on felt, and speedily retired to the yard, which he evidently regarded as his proper domain.

Accordingly, Kara-Beg did not promise to be of much use in my tent as a bodyguard, and the question arose as to what to do with him. When starting from Chapchal, Joseph made for him a pannier arrangement in which to ride; but to this the beast so strongly objected that we gave him away in exchange to a Kalmuk woman, with a rouble as a *douceur*, for another dog less daintily fed, without superabundance of fat, and accustomed to wander in the mountains.

Our old friend was something like a long-haired sheep-dog. The new one, whom we named "Kuldja," more nearly resembled a Scotch collie, and when led off by a string speedily showed himself capable of doing his 20 miles a day. He arrived at Booghru without a sign of fatigue.

Next morning at eight, on the last day of July, we left our pleasant dell and the flowing stream (which I take to have been one of the head waters of the river Khanakai, flowing down to the Tekes), and under the direction of a guide made our way over what was said to be a march of 70 *li* to Khanakai. Our route took us in a south-westerly direction over a secondary chain of low hills called Altyn-Tau (or in some maps Alt-Tau), covered with splendid vegetation and profusely strewed with flowers, among which butterflies were flitting in all directions.

Some of these lepidoptera were large and beautiful, and I thought rare; so we improvised a butterfly hunt, and the Chinese attendants, who handled the nets like new toys, entered into the chase with zeal. In their Chinese top-boots and queerly cut trousers they rushed hither and thither, as if for dear life, with hats blown off and pigtails flying, now toppling over, and next lying down to pant for breath. Their prey I at once killed and enclosed in envelopes, with due record of date and locality. In this way we secured specimens enough to fill all the envelopes just then at hand, and to the satisfaction of all parties concerned. This variation from the tedium of the march was relished by the men.

Afterwards we had a gallop to overtake the baggage, in the course of which Jing and his fellow-interpreter took to racing and larking on horseback in a fashion that showed them to be excellent horsemen. I was glad, of course, to see them in such high spirits, and desirous also to keep them on good terms with one another; but it was plain that in their case, as with children, playing and quarrelling were near neighbours. I had begun also by this time to get an insight into their characters. Jing's countenance reminded me strongly of the hypothetical descent of man from the ape, and I mentally christened him " Monkey-face."

Only that morning he had been to me to complain that one of his comrades, who had been drinking spirits, had struck him, and, what was highly derogatory to a gentleman of his degree, had kicked over his tea. This was a matter too serious to be passed over. The delinquent was summoned to appear before me. He turned out to be none other than his portly, good-natured fellow-interpreter Tor-jee, who appeared, looking very sheepish.

That worthy's love of strong water was evident more than once in the course of the journey. When asked whether the charges were true he pleaded guilty, but said they were playing, whereupon I lectured him upon the evils of spirit-drinking, and told him to do so no more, lest I should have to report him to the *Tsian-Tsiun* for punishment. Upon this he meekly promised obedience, and " Monkey-face " seemed satisfied.

After starting from Booghru, our guide regaled us, after 20 *li* of travel, with *koumiss* which was innocent enough; but when there came out four men to meet us from Khanakai bringing spirits also, I not only declined to drink, but warned my men against doing so, and Tor-jee in particular, who contented himself with a sip.

On reaching Khanakai, after a march of eight hours, we found an encampment of 21 tents in the midst of a wide plateau, being that, I presume, called by Kostenko the "Altyn hollow," with the long snow-capped Muz-Tag range on the south, and on the north the bold lofty mountain tops, not snow-capped, over which we had passed. In the lofty regions of Central Asia, the moisture is precipitated nearly every summer day, and as it came on to rain in the afternoon I had to reprove Osman Bai for allowing the baggage to arrive rather wet, and threatened him with liability for damage to the goods.

This was the only occasion I had of complaint, and on the morrow he and the others suggested, there having been during the night much rain and tempest, that we should not start till the sun came out. The waters of the Tekes, it was alleged, would be too much swollen to allow of our fording the stream, and I therefore listened to their advice, which subsequently expanded into stopping the whole of the day.

It was well that we did so, since violent thunderstorms occurred, with very large hailstones, so numerous as to whiten the ground, whilst the rain poured in torrents. The effect of these storms amidst this mountain scenery was extremely grand, and served to account for the uneducated natives connecting such phenomena with the spirits of the mountains.

Our stoppage at Khanakai gave opportunity to take a few photographs and to see more of the customs of the Kalmuks, in going the round of the tents, and purchasing of one woman a head-covering something like, but smaller than, the biretta-shaped hats worn by the Volga Kalmuks. The Kalmuks of the Volga appear also to use as ornament for their head-dresses the Astrakhan lambskin, of which, however, I saw no representatives among their sisters of the Ili valley.

The rain brought with it comparative cold, so that, at Booghru, sleeping in a fur coat, I was none too warm, and on the second night at Khanakai the maximum temperature did not rise above 55°, and the minimum was 43°. Next day we were delighted with lovely weather, and rose at three, so as to have plenty of time for crossing the Tekes.

So fully, however, did the horses appreciate the excellence of the pasture that five of them took a long time to catch, and we did not start till six. The cool air of the mountains was invigorating, and we had not gone far before the abundance of butterflies, flitting among the flowers on every hand, invited another hunt, which relieved our march of eight hours. At two o'clock we reached the river Tekes at a place called Geelan.

The Tekes emerges from the main mass of the Tian Shan at the high group of Khan Tengri, within 50 miles of Issik-Kul, and flows at first through a deep rocky gorge, which separates the principal mountains from their spurs. These spurs are called by the natives Kara-Tau.

The river, after piercing these mountains and winding round the high and stony Tash-Tube, or Tekes-Bash (about 10,000 feet), flows more quietly, though still rapidly, eastward to Uch-Karkak, about 30 miles west of the Russian frontier, where it passes into a wide valley. There it receives on its southern bank at least a dozen streams—named on the Russian map—flowing down from the Muz-Tag range, whilst northwards of the 16 streams marked on the Uzun-Tau, the Khanakai is the only one whose waters are not absorbed before reaching the Tekes.

The Tekes, in its course north-easterly to the Kunges, flows through Chinese territory for about 130 miles, or the length of the Thames, its entire length from the Khan Tengri being about 200 miles, and its width where it joins the Kunges 350 feet, as mentioned by Prjevalsky in August 1876. It is fordable in several places, and Kostenko gives the "point of passage" as 700 feet wide and 3 feet deep, with low and firm banks, the bottom being also firm shingle.

This corresponds (speaking from memory) with what we found on arriving at Geelan, save that the stream, swollen by snow and rain, was deepened to nearly a fathom. As a precautionary measure I had suggested sending on a messenger to ask that a tent should be erected on the northern bank, in case we should not be able to cross. This was done, and ten Kalmuks were in waiting to carry the baggage over.

So far, well; but when I perceived that they found it necessary to undress completely, and that, in crossing, the water covered the backs of their horses, I was alarmed for the baggage, and, when Osman Bai came up, asked what he proposed to do. Each package was to be placed, it seemed, on a man's head—which, in the case of the larger ones, would need his two hands to keep it steady—and in that fashion he was to ride through the swift stream; a suggestion being made that, in the case of the heaviest parcels, their contents should be lessened.

"Thank you," said I, "that won't do for me! Is there no other plan?" The only alternative was to ascend the stream to another ford, but that was in Russian territory, whither my Chinese escort was unwilling to go, and where it was said papers would be needed for crossing the frontier.

I was not afraid of coming to grief for lack of Russian passports, and on my promising to go to Kalmuk stations, two of my men, who, in prospect of entering Russian territory, had talked of going back, consented to proceed. I slept, therefore, that night in the tent, and left Geelan next morning about seven in a westerly direction towards the Russian frontier in the neighbourhood of Narin-Kol.

Immediately on the banks of the river the soil was alluvial, with two deposits of oil, but to our right as we rode along were hills with rocks of the Tertiary system. Butterflies again were captured, though not in such numbers as on the higher ground. We also saw partridges and other birds.

The ride, however, seemed very long and trying to the temper, whilst, to make matters worse, none of the party appeared to know exactly where we were going. At last, after a march of some six hours, there was observed on a cliff above the river, with habitations and stables below and the Russian village of Narin-Kol in the distance, a tent, said to be the Russian Tekes picket, to which I at once rode forward.

The tent was found to be inhabited by a few Cossacks, commanded by a corporal, who, on reading my papers, at once received me cordially. I was getting tired and a little out of spirits, and lay down in their sleeping-place, whilst they entertained me hospitably with black bread and soup, and such things as were prepared for their midday meal. The corporal, with a view to correct behaviour, asked my *tchin*, or rank, and by what titles he should address me; and then, after refreshing us with tea, and giving me half a loaf of bread that was newer, though coarser, than my own, he sent two Cossacks to show us the ford and help us over.

On our way to the river a thunderstorm came on, and it rained in torrents. No shelter was to be had, and we were obliged to stand on the river bank and take our chance. A waterproof protected me pretty well, but most of the others must have been wet to the skin, the Cossacks included, who, when I commiserated them, laughed good-humouredly and said, "*Nichevo*" —"It is nothing."

The storm past, and everything sopping with wet, we had to get the baggage across. The river here was not quite so deep as at the other ford, but reached even now half-way up the horses' barrels, and I had much fear lest the packages should dip in the water, which in some cases would have spoiled their contents.

Osman Bai promised to be careful, and as an extra incentive I promised him and each of his men a special present if they got everything across dry and undamaged. Neither they, the Cossacks, nor the convoy spared themselves. Packing the baggage high on the saddle, the men stripped and walked through the stream again and again on each side of the horses, and so brought everything over.

At last they had to get me across, and to accomplish this they put two thick pack-saddles on a big horse, so that I was seated about a foot above the animal's back, and then with Cossacks on each side to keep the *barin**** steady or catch him if he fell, the party waded across and safely reached the other bank.

Whether we were now on Russian or Chinese soil I am uncertain—I think Chinese—but there was no friendly Kalmuk tent erected, and the nearest camp being some miles distant, and the day far advanced, it was proposed to bivouac once more on the banks of the Tekes. Accordingly, Joseph rigged up, for the first time, my *palatka*, or summer tent, and the men apparently soon forgot their troubles round a fire.

Our party had been reinforced at Chapchal by a merry and communicative lama, who wanted to go a few days' journey with us. He put himself *en évidence* next morning at sunrise by shouting aloud a number of long Buddhist exclamations or prayers. This man had evidently imbibed the sentiment which I think I have met somewhere, connected with monastic early rising in writings on Buddhism, that "prayer is better than sleep." At all events he did his best to make us think so by rendering it impossible to continue our slumbers.

After breakfast, I dismissed the Cossacks with thanks and presents, and let them return to the Tekes picket, whilst we set our faces in the direction of the Muzart defile.

* Russian for " squire."

CHAPTER XVII.

UP THE MUZ-TAG MOUNTAINS.

Orography of Tian Shan system, 241.—Abundance of glaciers, but few rivers, 242.—Sources of our knowledge of the Tian Shan; the Muz-Tag range, 243.—Fording the Urten Muzart, 244.—Absence of Kirghese; Entrance to Muzart defile; A quiet Sunday, 245.—Remains of stone fort; Starting-point of Shepeleff; Kostenko's route, 246.—Departure from Shattoo; Inscription on granite rock; Forest zone of birch, fir, etc., 247.—Beauty of path, 248.- Butterfly-hunting on horseback, 249.—Arrival at Udungei; Chinese picket, and Kalmuk tents; Kalmuk food, 250.—Osman Bai's orthodoxy as to food, 251.—Departure to Khan-Yailak, 252.—Visit to last Kalmuk tent; Comparison of *koumiss* of Orenburg and farther east, 253.—Kalmuk photographs and anthropological remarks, 254.—Dress, numbers, and administration, 256.—Russian education of Kalmuks; their intellectual capacities, 257.—Buddhist objects of worship; Kalmuk women, marriage customs, and morals, 258.—Features of nomad life; Chinese picket, 259.—Willingness of Jing and Tor-jee to proceed; other two attendants sent back, 260.

BEFORE describing our journey up the Muzart defile of the famous Muz-Tag range, a few words may appropriately be said of the vast orographical system of which it forms a part, and to which reference has already been made under the name of the Tian Shan Mountains. This system is 1,500 miles long, or the distance from London to St Petersburg, and is the largest of those in Asia sloping towards the north.

The chain begins eastwards, in a rocky crest, and running south-westwards is joined by a second, a third, and many other ranges, which, as they advance westwards, open out more or less fanwise, the several ranges being connected by intervening plateaux, and continuing to preserve somewhat of a parallel direction. Towards the centre the plateau is 250 miles wide, whilst to the westwards the ridges or folds become reduced in number, and sink into the plains about Tashkend and Samarkand.

The area covered by this mass is estimated by Réclus at 400,000 square miles—as large, that is, as the whole of France and the Spanish peninsula—and it covers, therefore, considerably more ground than all the mountains of Europe put together. And whereas the Englishman who ascends Mont Blanc takes pride in procuring a certificate of his exploit, let those who aspire to higher things know that greater distinction awaits the climber of one of the peaks of the Tian Shan, which is more than half as high again as the Franco-Italian monarch; whilst for smaller climbers there would be no difficulty in finding in the Muz-Tag alone half a dozen peaks overtopping by at least 3,000 feet the apex of the Alps.

Again, the number of glaciers in the Tian Shan is remarkable, for they are estimated at not less than 8,000, and of course the extent of the snowfields is proportionately large. But though so amply covered with glaciers and snow, the Tian Shan gives rise to fewer rivers of importance than does the secondary range of the Altai, farther north, whence flow the Obi, Yenesei, and Lena. Moreover, of the rivers flowing from the Tian Shan, not one reaches the ocean. The Syr and Amu run into the Sea of Aral, the Ili into Lake Balkash, the Tarim into Lob-Nor, and numberless others are lost in, or dried up with, the small lakes of the steppes.

Down to the middle of the present century we knew little of the Tian Shan, and of that little much was wrong. M. Semenof, in 1855-6, led the way into the Ala-Tau range north of Issik-Kul, and he has since been followed by Russian explorers and surveyors, who have mapped the whole country and extended their triangulations southwards to the Pamirs, to meet those of the Indian surveyors working northwards. General Kostenko, in his admirable work on Turkistan, has brought together the varied information gathered by Russian explorers of the Tian Shan, which he describes so fully as to give a detailed though brief account of nearly 40 of its mountain ranges.

Of these ranges one of the finest and most lofty, with vast glaciers, is the Muz-Tag, signifying in Turki the "ice range." Of this we first caught sight after crossing the Chapchal Pass, the huge mass rising up like a wall beyond the valley of the Tekes, and extending from as far eastwards as the eye could reach towards the enormous Khan Tengri group, 26 miles west of which the range is broken by the Muzart gorge. It is through this difficult gorge that Asiatics have passed southwards from time to time between the Ili valley and the basin of the Tarim.

The appearance of the range struck me as particularly beautiful on the lovely morning we descended from Khanakai; and on our way up the valley one never tired of the snow-crested horizon on the left. On the morning we struck camp on the bank of the Tekes I tried, during the four hours they were getting ready, to photograph the view, but had no success.

Then, starting at eight o'clock, we first made our way across a bog—one of the few I saw in Central Asia; two of my convoy, with Tor-jee and the lama, having gone off to an encampment to procure, I suspected, a few drops of refreshment.

They reappeared bringing a Kalmuk to pilot us across the wide but shallow stream of the Urten

BAGGAGE TENT AND "PALATKA" AT KHANAKAI.

Muzart, near its junction with the Tekes. The passage was so easy, the water not reaching the stirrup, that I suspected the volunteer guide had an eye to his own advantage rather than ours.* He seemed much delighted with the present of a two-penny whistle.

* I notice, however, that Kostenko speaks of the Aksu (another affluent joining the Tekes, a little farther east) and the Muzart as

Before remounting, on the west bank of the river we had another butterfly hunt, and quickly caught 50. After this we rode for some hours through magnificent meadow-lands towards the foot of the mountains, and in the afternoon turned into the hills to a place Osman called Shattoo, at the entrance of the Muzart defile.

Here, on a lofty terrace, perhaps 100 feet or more above the river, was pitched for me a solitary Kalmuk tent, whilst on the opposite bank, in meadows at a lower level, were the encampment and the cattle. Why the river, there unfordable, was thus placed between us did not appear. The usual sheep was presented and killed; but my convoy, instead of staying with us to eat it, went higher up the stream and crossed to their camp, there to visit, it was said, some of their lady friends, and, in any case, leaving me and my party to spend a quiet Sunday.

Accordingly, I rose next morning, after a long and restful sleep, to take in our surroundings. To the south were visible abundant pastures and enormous forests of fir, clothing the sides of the mountains about half-way to the summits, which were bare, and not yet clear of snow. Alongside the Kalmuk tent provided for me Joseph had erected the *palatka* as shade for the servants, whilst farther to the left was the modest shanty of Osman Bai and his assistants, who delighted to be so situated that they could lie under canvas and watch their horses grazing.

A few minutes' walk behind our tents rose a terrace,

difficult to ford. He mentions also that the valley of the Upper Tekes is deserted except in July, when it is enlivened by a tribe of Kara-Kirghese called Bogins, and along the central Tekes, he says, Kirghese of the Atbanof tribe wander. Whether this continues in those parts of the valley now handed back to China I am doubtful. We neither heard nor saw anything of Kirghese in the Tekes valley.

on the top of which I found the somewhat dilapidated remains of a stone-built fort or barrack, supposed at first to be a Chinese picket, but too well built for that. I subsequently came to the conclusion that it had been the site of a Russian military post. It was now used as a dwelling-place by the neighbouring Kalmuks in winter.

At the time of Yakub Khan's insurrection, he ordered that all caravans proceeding from Kashgaria to the Ili valley should go by the Muzart Pass. He also sent a force of men to improve it, and established a picket on the southern side. The Russians, therefore, fearing that the object of Yakub was the conquest of the province of Kuldja, kept a watch on his movements, and when, in May 1870, the Taranchis who guarded the Pass had attacked five Russian Kirghese, the Governor-General of Russian Turkistan directed the Pass to be occupied.

I suppose this Shattoo was the position of the Tian Shan detachment, whence Shepeleff set out in the autumn of 1871 (after the Russian annexation, during the previous spring, of the Ili valley) to explore, chain in hand, the gorge to the summit.*

* Kostenko appears to call it "Muzart Picket," giving its distance 134 miles from Kuldja. His route seems to have varied from mine, and to have crossed the Ili at a different point, passing through the village of Kan, and, by crossing the Tekes at the lower ford, to have avoided the angle we made by going to the Tekes picket. We took 54 hours of caravan travel, which gives, reckoning at three miles an hour, a distance of 162 miles; but probably Kostenko's reckoning is more accurate.

By way of illustrating the difficulty of getting accurate figures from the Chinese, I may add that the convoy gave Joseph the distance as 680 *li*, or 235 miles. Williams says: "The *li* is usually reckoned at 1825·55 feet English, which gives 2·89 *li* to an English mile. This is based on the estimate of 200 *li* to a degree, but there were only 180 *li* to a degree before Europeans came. Thus its length is increased to 2028·39 feet, or 2·6 *li* to a mile, which is nearer the common estimate."

Leaving our camp on Monday morning, and riding in a south-easterly direction, in a few minutes we were joined by our truant convoy, and came to a large stream called the Lesser Muzart, flowing from the south into the Urten Muzart.* Near the junction of the two streams are said, by Kostenko, to be traces of a Chinese redoubt.

Here also stands a vertical granite rock, apparently *in situ*, about six feet high and as many broad, having on one side an inscription, the letters of which are about six inches high. Kostenko speaks of the letters as unknown forms, and therefore of great antiquity; whilst Schuyler, alluding, I presume, to this stone, says he was informed it had upon it a human face roughly drawn, and a long inscription supposed by his informant to be Tibetan.

I have no recollection of seeing either the face or the Tibetan characters. Joseph pronounced the inscription to be Arabic, the initial words reading, "There is but one God," etc. He thought he could make out the date 573 A.H. (1176 A.D.), but the letters were too weathered to allow of his discerning more.

After examining this stone we speedily entered the forest zone of the gorge. On a low bank near the junction of the two streams is a small birch grove. Kostenko points out that its trees do not resemble the Russian birch, but are more slender and pliant, though very tall, having cinnamon-coloured bark, with fine leaves but few branches.

Throughout the whole extent of the forest belt of

* This stream I take to be that mentioned by Shepeleff as rising in a group of mountains separated from the rocks bordering on the gorge by a considerable ravine, out of the middle of which rise the three lofty rounded bosses, rather than peaks, of the Saikal.

the gorge, the birch-tree is seldom met with, but as we passed along I noticed the mountain ash very much like the Russian species, though the tree most frequently met with was the silver fir, sometimes growing out almost at a right angle from the steepest of slopes, yet raising its head vertically and gracefully, the bend in the trunk being noticeable only at the root. The leaves of the Muzart fir, like those of the Central Asian species, are generally soft and short. They grow thickly on the twig, and this hangs downwards with the weight. Downwards, too, hang the violet-coloured cones on their long stems.

I do not know of other trees in the Muzart forest, but of the larger shrubs and flowers (*e.g.*, meadow-sweet, etc.) my journal records the barberry and wild currant, hawthorn-trees of considerable height, the common juniper, and the *tuya-kuiruk*, or "camel's-tail" —which is widely distributed and abundant in the higher forests, especially towards the limit of trees. At a lower level this *tuya-kuiruk* is found with a stem 14 feet high and 2 inches thick, its upper part being thickly covered with leaves and thorns.

Our road from Shattoo was the prettiest of any we had seen since leaving Kuldja, and, after wading through the Lesser Muzart, we entered a narrower passage of the defile, the path meandering now along terraces, and then passing through natural meadows bounded by forest or hill, and bright with a great variety of flowers.

Here we saw some very large butterflies. Upon receiving the nets the Kalmuks initiated a new departure, and, true to their equestrian instincts, hastened to the chase on horseback. This gave opportunity for some very fine riding, in comparison with which polo on a level sward is child's play. The ground was not only very rough with rocky *débris* from the mountains, but also the many trees and bushes in all directions had to be carefully dodged, as the butterflies flitted here and there.

Monkey-face and Tor-jee greatly distinguished themselves on this occasion, bringing me again and again their nets to be emptied, and grinning with delight when I cast into the net a few biscuits by way of reward. In this way 50 lepidoptera were added to my collection, and henceforward Jing and Tor-jee usually did their butterfly-hunting on horseback.

Continuing our route, the path lay for a considerable distance along the left bank of the Urten Muzart, winding picturesquely, now along narrow cornices, on slopes of the mountains not as yet very high, occasionally through clumps of firs resounding with the chirping of birds, and from time to time over plateaux, whence we gained transitory glimpses of the fine panorama that awaited us.

The beauty of the route was unmistakable, and the only drawback worth mentioning was the number of large and small stones which now and then obstructed the road. But even these were of interest, since among the various kinds of rocks fallen from the mountains there stood erect here and there huge blocks of marble, like monuments and memorials of nature's workmanship.

Sometimes we forded narrow streams such as the Mai-boulak, running down to the bed of the Muzart, and occasionally crossed crazy bridges—notably two, about four miles from the entrance of the gorge, thrown across projections in the cliffs and hanging over a yawning precipice, at the foot of which roared the

Muzart. Another of the streams thus entering the Muzart is the Tosti. At the confluence the valley widens to more than half a mile, and is dominated by the gigantic snow-clad peaks of the Tian Shan, a noble range.

After six hours' riding we came to a fine open valley, where we camped for the night at a place called Udungei, near to a tumble-down Chinese picket, built of logs like a Russian *izba*, and capable of accommodating about 50 men. It is these *urten*, or pickets, or huts, that give their name to the stream, along which they were built and maintained formerly by the Chinese for the supply of horses and the convenience of messengers between Aksu and Ili. Now they seem to be of little account.

We found, however, at Udungei a camp of Kalmuks, again at some distance from the tent pitched for me on the open sward. The view around us became increasingly beautiful. Looking westwards, we had mountains on either side, with trees below those on the left; whilst nearer and below the hills, on the right, ran the silver stream of the Muzart, with the Kalmuk tents on its bank. Before we started next morning I took photographs, and looking eastwards had in the foreground the horses being laden, a forest of firs beyond, and the head of the valley bounded by some of the higher mountains, towards which we were to proceed in the course of the day.

At Udungei they brought us, in addition to the usual sheep, abundance of butter and milk in various forms, as well as, if I remember rightly, some attempts at bakemeats, which were interesting as varieties of Kalmuk food. The remarks of Dr Seeland on the food of the Kirghese of Semirechia would, I presume, apply pretty nearly to the Kalmuks of Sungaria, since both are nomads and neighbours, but with the difference, so far as my observation went, that the Kalmuks are the poorer.*

Among drinks both Kirghese and Kalmuks have tea, which reaches them in the form of twigs, coarse leaves, and dust, pressed into the shape of bricks, or thick tiles rather, measuring perhaps 8 by 5 by 1 inches. This they boil in a large saucepan with milk and flour, salt, millet, and a piece or two of fat, making a decoction which at my first attempt, near Kiakhta, was anything but to my taste, though I acknowledge that when subsequently favoured with a cup by the Rani of Sikkim, near Darjeeling, it was fairly palatable.

To my own servants I gave Russian tea, which, with sugar, was highly appreciated; and as they had likewise plenty of bread and mutton, to say nothing of occasional tid-bits from my tent, they fared sumptuously every day. This helped to make things go smoothly.

Osman Bai put on a show of great orthodoxy at the first Kalmuk camp by declining to eat any of the offered sheep, because he said it had been killed by an infidel Kalmuk. When assured that it was slaughtered

---

* "As for meat," he says, "the Kirghese eat little. Oxen and horses are not superabundant, and a rumpsteak of horseflesh, though the delight of a gourmand, is a rarity. The meat ordinarily consumed is mutton. Since, however, the Kirghese of Semirechia possess on an average only six sheep per man, of which three must be spared for breeding, it follows that there is left only eight ounces of mutton per man per day, whereas such is the appetite of these nomads that one of them will easily eat four pounds at a meal! Only the rich, therefore, can have meat daily; and of the masses the base of their food is millet and other cereals, and various forms of milk diet, notably, in summer, *aïran*, or soured milk, and *koumiss*, or milk of mares; whilst in winter, when these cannot be had, their place is taken by gruel and cakes of flour."

by a Muhammadan Taranchi, he still declined, saying that he had not seen it done. Afterwards, therefore, in deference to his prejudices, I directed that the daily sheep should be slain by a Muhammadan, so that Osman might partake of the feast.

This somewhat mollified him, and when, later on, I gave him half a pound of tea, his scruples so far gave way as not only to permit him to accept it with thanks, but to add, "May God love you!" My servant asked him why he made such a fuss about the mutton, and yet could drink an infidel's tea and sugar. He replied that Joseph argued like a mullah! and when, in the course of conversation, something was said as to the possibility of our shooting a deer on the journey, he wished me to be informed that in such a case he would eat a portion, if it were killed by me.

At four miles from Udungei, which we left at eight o'clock, the Muzart receives two streams from the south and west called Maralty, and at 20 miles from the entrance of the gorge we had to cross the Muzart and follow the right bank of the river through a valley which expanded to more than a mile in width.

There the river divides into several channels, and the road follows for about five miles a flat foreland of the eastern slope, bearing the name of Khan-Yailak, or "the summer pasturage of the Khan." It reminded me of a saying of the Kalmuks, about the upper valleys of the Yulduz, "A fine place for gentlemen and cattle."

It would be difficult to find a spot with more abundant pasture, whether for the horses of the Kalmuk Khan, who, according to one story, was obliged to keep animals here for official messengers, or for Chinese cattle, which, according to another story, were sent here for the summer. The view, moreover, was the most imposing I had thus far seen in the gorge, for above and beyond the valley arose three majestic peaks of the Tian Shan, their snowy whiteness set off by the blue sky above and the verdure below.*

As we rode along we presently saw some Kalmuk children catching butterflies, which was certainly unusual; but, on reaching their tent, it was explained that they had heard at the previous station of the English traveller, and were catching them for him. Into this tent, which was the last belonging to the Kalmuks that we saw, we turned aside to rest, and to study further this little-known people.

The wife brought forth *koumiss*, and spirit said to be made from it. What the latter was like I cannot say, but the *koumiss* I came to like on occasion, though I tasted none among the Kalmuks or Kirghese comparable with that produced from the Bashkir mares near Samara and Orenburg.†

I am afraid that I was not so diligent as I ought to

* In this locality, in October, Shepeleff's party noticed smoke coming out of the ground at a spot where they had no reason to suppose a fire had been lighted. "The clods of dark-brown earth," he says, "we took up smoked, and continued to smoulder even when we stamped them under foot in the snow. Specimens having been subsequently submitted to analysis at St Petersburg, they were said to be composed of a mixture of clay, sand, and carbonate of lime, impregnated with organic substances such as are found in 'humus,' and minute crystals of pyrites—in other words, alum-bearing earth."

† Near Orenburg Dr Carrick has a large establishment for condensing mares' milk for infants' food, where the mares are kept and milked with the regularity and precision of a well-appointed English dairy. At Samara are establishments for the *koumiss* cure, where corks fly out of "magnums" with the report of a cannon, and one drinks the beverage foaming like champagne, and almost envies the poor invalids whose lot it is to drink a dozen bottles a day.

But, farther east, where the milk is collected in vessels of doubtful have been in taking photographs of the Kalmuks; but my remissness has to some extent been remedied by the kindness of Prince Roland Buonaparte. He has been good enough to give me a set of photographs, taken for his anthropological series, of Kalmuks of the Volga and Astrakhan steppes.

These are stated on his photographs to be of "pure race," but if so, and speaking from memory, the portraits of the Volga Kalmuks before me look more European in feature than most of the people I saw in the Tekes valley. The average Mongol has a flat face, with prominent cheek-bones and small slit-like eyes obliquely placed.

M. Ujfalvy, whose anthropological description of the Ili Kalmuks is the best I know, speaks of their "lips as colourless, set in a strange, almost idiotic, and sad smile." The hair is straight, coarse, and invariably black, and, on the Tekes, is worn by the men in a queue, and by the women in two long thick plaits, whereas the Kalmuks of the Volga, both men and women, appear to wear the hair much as do the Russians.

So also with regard to the women's dresses. In the west these are somewhat Europeanised, whilst their sisters eastwards wear garments, not indeed quite Chinese, but such as give their outer dress the appearance neither of the Turki *khalat* nor of the

cleanliness and put into a leather bottle that from one season to another is never washed out—a little of the sour milk of yesterday being left at the bottom to turn the new milk of to-day—it is not difficult to imagine that either fancy or fact sometimes adds a rancid taste to the noble liquor, which the Kalmuk deems to be fit alike for gods and men. The spirit made from it is, of course, intoxicating, but ordinary *koumiss* appears to contain only about as much alcohol as ginger-beer made with yeast.

A GROUP OF MONGOLS IN CHINESE TURKISTAN.

lady's garb of China proper; whilst the women's hats of felt worn about Kuldja resemble a Mongol hat I bought in Kiakhta, and are not very unlike the turban-shaped felts worn in England about 30 years ago.

When writing about the Kalmuks of the Ili valley in *Russian Central Asia* I obtained much information, seemingly original, from a pamphlet by M. Ostroumoff, who states their numbers in 1876 as 9,600 males and 6,400 females. To these must be added, I presume, the Kalmuks about Chuguchak, Kobdo, and Karashar.

For administrative purposes they are divided into *sumuls*, or squadrons (each of 200 tents), which are supposed to constitute Chinese irregular cavalry. Each *sumul* is under the direction of a lama, called a *gelem*, who is priest, doctor, and sorcerer; and a laic, called a *zang*, who is concerned with the military and judicial affairs of the community.

I am not aware that anything is done, now that Kuldja is Chinese once more, for the education of the Kalmuks. In 1871 a school was opened in Vierny for the children of recently baptised Kalmuks, and, at a public examination in 1875, the progress of the pupils not only gave satisfaction to their benefactors, but surpassed expectation.

The school, however, had been discontinued at the time of my first visit to Vierny, and though on my second visit I heard of Kalmuks still living there, to whom I sent subsequently from Kashgar through the Governor some copies of the Gospels in their vernacular, I heard nothing of any schools on either the Russian or Chinese side of the frontier.

During the last century the Kalmuks would appear to have lived along the whole course of the Tekes, to judge by the ruins of *sumbes*, or monasteries, still remaining in several places. One of these is marked on my Russian map on the river Sumbe, near the Russian picket we visited. Another, called Akburkhan, is near the spot where we struck the Tekes, and a third ruin about 15 miles farther west; but we heard of only one monastery now existing, which lay too far out of my way, in the lower part of the valley.

As for the intellectual capacities of the Kalmuks, I would refer again to what Dr Seeland says of their neighbours the Kirghese. Their memory for persons, places, and things that immediately strike the attention, is more powerful than that of persons more civilised; whilst recollection of sounds and forms of language is weaker, and abstract conceptions are to them extremely difficult.

Young scholars learn quickly, needing but three months to be taught how to read and write Kirghese, and to learn enough Russian to enter the gymnase requires but a year only. They learn mathematics better than languages; other branches of education are difficult; only ten per cent. show any aptitude for drawing. Later on, education does not progress so rapidly. As they advance towards their teens, they become idle and inattentive.

It sometimes happens that scholars at the gymnase of Vierny, or cadets in Orenburg, finish their course with distinction; but to imagine that the Kirghese only need education to raise them to the level of civilised nations, Dr Seeland thinks, would be a mistake. The experiment has now been tried for half a century at Omsk and Orenburg with only moderate results. The scholars manifest no enthusiasm to continue their studies at the universities or academies. Once become officers or translators, they do not continue their reading, and a great many forget the Russian they have learned and go back to their primitive manner of living.

The foregoing is still more true, I think, of the Kalmuks, for whom the little Buddhism they possess does less intellectually even than a meagre Muhammadanism does for the Kirghese. As I entered the tents of the various encampments we visited, I usually asked to be shown the *burkhans*, or objects connected with religious worship, such as images, prayer-wheels, amulets, etc., which they would let me see, but would not allow me to purchase. I do not remember seeing religious objects of intrinsic worth. It may be that they feared to produce anything valuable, lest it should be pounced upon by the officers with me; but I am disposed to attribute their absence to the real poverty of the Kalmuks with whom we came in contact.

The women appeared to have a hard time of it, though much freer to come and go than their Muhammadan sisters. A Kalmuk girl on the Tekes is a shepherdess, and soon becomes bronzed by exposure; whilst even those farther west at 15 and 18 look as old as English women of 30. They are married early, by arrangement between the parents, who for the nonce turn their backs upon the girl, pretending not to see, and the form is gone through by the bridegroom of stealing his bride and carrying her off by force.

The knot thus tied is not tied very tightly, for she is at liberty to leave her husband and return to her relations; and, if a widow, she may marry again after a month's mourning. The morals of the people are spoken of disparagingly, though I have nothing original to add one way or the other; but the disparagement may well be true, seeing that a very large proportion of the males are lamas, and therefore celibates, so-called, which results in immorality on the one hand and polygamy on the other.

In the last tent we visited they gave us a warm reception, and exhibited, it seemed to me, a favourable example of nomad life. I saw no hay stored for winter use. In autumn, probably, the people descend to the lowlands—perhaps to cultivate a little land— though I came across no fields. There are, however, traces of old irrigation canals in the Tekes valley; and Prjevalsky, on his way up the Ili valley, mentions, near the Kash, lands temporarily tilled by the Kalmuks.

I observed no cats or poultry at any of the encampments we stopped at, and few traces of foreign merchandise. The jewels were of silver, and those I obtained were of home make, and showed little taste or skill in design. The people seemed not quite to understand the use of some of the finery which I gave them, but were always pleased with cutlery; large tent and packing needles proved acceptable; and bricks of tea at once met with approval.

Starting once more, we continued to ascend, the valley of the Muzart getting narrower as we approached the principal chain; also on the last terraces of the Khan-Yailak the soil became rugged and swampy. As we were approaching the upward limit of trees, firs appeared less frequently, and the bushes of "camel's-tail" were only from two to three feet high. Presently we came to a black, tumble-down, smoky timber shed—the last Chinese picket on the northern slope of the range.

The place was little better than a ruin, but there

was standing room for horses and accommodation of similar quality for human beings; whilst we found there, I suppose awaiting us, two men, one of whom was a post messenger on foot, the difficulties of travel over the next stage being usually considered too great for horses.

We had now arrived at the limit of our friend Kah's jurisdiction. His two servants, Koo-Kah and Tcho-gah, had talked of going back even at Geelan, but Jing and Tor-jee had informed me that the *Tsian-Tsiun* told them they might accompany me to Aksu if I wished it. Jing had also made me a present of a Manchu pocket-razor, lancet, and tweezers combined, and volunteered his readiness to go with me all the way.

I wrote, therefore, to the *Tsian-Tsiun*, saying that I should probably avail myself of his permission to take his two interpreters with me to Aksu, unless we found on the way that the Aksu authorities had made such arrangements as to render this unnecessary. This letter I inclosed to the Russian Consul at Kuldja with two letters for England, asking him to be good enough to translate the one and post the others, and handed the packet that morning to Koo-Kah, with presents for himself and his fellow. They were then free to return.

Subsequently Jing and Tor-jee seemed a little disposed to wish not to go forward. Tor-jee had crossed the Pass before, and knew its hardships, and in the light of subsequent events I was not surprised at his hesitation; whilst Jing had raised the difficulty of procuring a mount on his way back, since the document by virtue of which, as I suppose, he had received horses from the Kalmuks would have no force on the other side of the mountains.

I said something about hiring one for him, whereupon, in a roundabout way, he gave me to understand his doubts whether it would be becoming in a gentleman of his dignity to ride a horse that was only hired, though the gift of such an animal, he intimated, would solve the difficulty. Osman Bai undertook to send two horses, if no one else would, for £1 from Aksu to the first Kalmuk station; and as each interpreter said he could not go without the other, I undertook to be responsible, if necessary, for their carriage back, and said that I wished them to go forward.

They seemed also to be somewhat afraid, not knowing what I should write about them to their master, but were pleased when I told them that thus far they had given ample satisfaction, and that I intended so to testify.

Hereupon it happened that Osman Bai had the offer of a horse from a Kalmuk, which he asked me to advance money to purchase; so that with this increase of cattle and a spare horse or two of my own, we continued our way to a favourable halting-place, whence to attack early next morning the Muz-davan, or ice pass.

CHAPTER XVIII.

OVER THE MUZ-DAVAN, OR ICE PASS.

From Khan-Yailak to bed of Muzart, 262.—View of Archali-Karachat glacier; Camp at Toghri-su, 263.—Stir at daybreak, 264.—Basin receiving five glaciers, 265.—Photograph of the "White Mountain," 266.—Kaulbars' remarks on Jalyn-Khatsyr glacier, 268.—Ice-tables and stony roads; View of *mer-de-glace*, 272.—Ice-hummocks, crevasses, grottoes, and pinnacles; Difficulties of pack animals, 274.—Fall over precipice of horse and baggage; Mazar-bash; former hermitage, and fort, 275.—Soldiers' provisions and horses hauled up an ice-cliff, 276.—Scrambling down the Muz-davan, 277.—Road over rocks and stones, 278.—From Mazar-bash to Tamgha-tash; End of glacier, and superb ice-cavern; Hiuen Tsiang's description, 279.—Frequent loss of horses; Good fortune of first European in completely crossing the Pass, 281.

THE picket station at Khan-Yailak, reached on August 7th, would have been the proper place to sleep at; but Osman Bai wished to push on to the very edge of our difficulties, in view of the severe exertions which he knew awaited him on the morrow.

We descended, therefore, into the bed of the Muzart, and presently made our way round the slope of a moraine on a foot-wide pathway, along which my horse had to pick his way very carefully. It seemed to me at the time the most dangerous thing I had attempted on horseback, the loose stones threatening a slip of horse and rider into the stream below.

Presently we came to an affluent of the Muzart, called the Archali-Karachat, and looking up to our left, whence the stream rises, we saw a magnificent glacier shattered by crevasses—very like the Rhone glacier. When Shepeleff reached this spot in October 1871, he found the snow five feet deep, but sufficiently firm on the surface to bear his weight. The glacier is mentioned also by Poltaratsky, who reached this spot in 1867, as did Kaulbars in 1870. I have not seen either of their accounts; but, according to Shepeleff, they think this glacier the largest on the northern slope of the Muz-Tag range, and that it is connected with the *mer-de-glace*, to be mentioned hereafter, on the southern slope. Shepeleff gives its distance from the entrance of the defile as 27 miles.*

Where the Archali-Karachat falls into the Urten Muzart the gorge penetrates the main mass of the range, and the forest region gives place to that of glaciers. Here we clambered to a little patch of grass, called by Osman Toghri-su, arriving at one o'clock, to spend the night. We had no longer a friendly Kalmuk tent, and my *palatka* was therefore erected. Matters were not improved by its coming on to rain.

Kostenko remarks concerning the Tian Shan in general that during the summer months, on heights from 4,000 to 5,000 feet, rain falls almost daily from 4 to 7 p.m., and seldom in the morning or at night. On heights from 5,000 to 8,000 feet rain is said to

---

* In writing this chapter I have before me the accounts of both Shepeleff and Kostenko; and as they spent much more time in the Pass than I, and examined it with professional eyes, I have frequently used their descriptions, as better than anything I could give of my own.

alternate with snow, which quickly melts. Above 9,000 feet, he adds, there is no rain, and the snow which falls instead quickly disappears.

According to this we might have expected a fall of snow, instead of which we were pelted with rain, which came into my tent, and the men had to erect a shanty for shelter at its side. Things were a little gloomy, therefore, as night came on, and Osman Bai seemed excited—old soldier though he was—as if on the eve of a battle.

Usually my men were in no particular hurry to stir in the morning, and sometimes it was I who had to rouse Joseph and set things going again ; but on the present occasion Osman was about before daylight, and, shouting to his men, wanted me to hurry up with the rest. The rain had passed, but not all the clouds, and as I peeped out in the cold grey of dawn I saw we were approaching some splendid mountains.

The view to the south-west was too tempting not to be photographed, even at half-past four, whilst the valleys were still in shadow, and the sunlight lit up only the highest peaks. The central mountain on my camera screen was snow-capped, and rose up thousands of feet, whilst at the foot of the picture ran the Muzart, through which we waded about five o'clock. Then we climbed over a steep ascent of bare rock, higher and higher, the road up to the top of the gorge following now the right and now the left bank of the Urten Muzart.

Presently we arrived at a bend in the gorge towards the west, where it presents the appearance (as Kostenko observes) of an elevated valley or oblong basin, about three miles long and nearly a mile wide, bounded on the north by a steep and rocky declivity of the snowy range, whilst the main chain shuts in the basin on the south.

Into, or towards this basin, five glaciers descend. The first and largest of these comes from the east, and is fed from several sources. The second glacier lies

SUNRISE ON A PEAK IN THE MUZART PASS, LOOKING SOUTH-WEST FROM TUGHRI-SU.

north and south. Its area is comparatively small, for it descends only to about the middle of the slope. The *débris* which has been brought down by it reaches, however, to the edge of the basin.

The third glacier likewise moves from north to

south, but it descends much lower than the second one, and the moraine material narrows the basin by several feet. The western portion of the steep slopes of the mountains in this locality has been formed, says Kostenko, by broken rocks brought down by the glacier. These, in the course of ages, have been covered with soil, from which have sprung small clumps of firs.

These represent the advanced point of forest growth on the northern slope in the Muzart gorge; for, beyond it, neither trees nor even bushes are to be seen, though, during the short summer, vegetation appears in the form of rank grass and a few kinds of flowers, amongst which violets are plentiful.

Here too, Kostenko adds, at the very hottest time of the year the nights are cold and the mornings frosty, though I observed that at three in the morning of our leaving Toghri-su, my thermometer in the tent registered a maximum during the previous night of 52° and a minimum no lower than 42°.

The fourth glacier descends into the valley we are describing by a narrow cleft, along which there is a road. This, however, suddenly changes its direction towards the south; whilst the fifth glacier, moving from the west, shuts in the valley on that side, close to where the Tura-su falls into the Urten Muzart. Shepeleff climbed to the lower moraine of this glacier, which he places at 30 miles from the entrance of the gorge, the snowfield being not much elevated above the valley of the Muzart.

We reached the above valley in about an hour and a half, and I could not resist setting up my camera, though in the shadow and with only a feeble sun, whereby was obtained, however, a capital view, looking east, of a grand mountain, partially snow-covered, and called by my men the White Mountain, with darker peaks below, between two of which descended a glacier, whose foot almost reached to the central expanse of water at the bottom of the basin.

THE "WHITE MOUNTAIN" IN THE MUZART PASS, AS SEEN WHEN APPROACHING FROM THE NORTH.

After crossing this valley, our road, as already intimated, turned sharply as in an elbow to the south, threading a pass of the main range. From this bend up to the highest point the distance is given by Shepeleff as three miles. The road now becomes difficult and lies over precipitous crags, and is choked with stones, between which the horse must pick his way with caution—now across glaciers, below which streams descend with deafening noise; or perhaps no track at all exists, and progress has to be made over the almost perpendicular sides of the moraine.

For my own part I managed to keep the saddle, but hereabouts, says Kostenko, "it is necessary to advance on foot, or rather to creep along and cling with hands and feet to the sharply projecting stones, pieces of which become detached and clatter down into the raging Muzart. On both sides of this gorge tower gigantic cliffs—sharp-pointed, vertical peaks, or majestic bluffs—over which cascades fall into the depths below. Cornices of snow hang overhead, threatening to give way and fill up the entire gorge. From time to time fragments of the cliffs detach themselves and come down with a crash, rebounding from the crags in their descent into the abyss."

Kostenko's journey was in summer. Shepeleff's description is a winter one. "Turning," he says, "at a right angle towards the south, our view was extended over a grand and magnificent picture. Before us was, as it were, an immense cascade suddenly congealed, and descending nearly to the spot where the Tura-su flows into the Muzart. It was the grandest and most beautiful of the glaciers we had thus far seen. It was 350 feet wide, taking up nearly all the opening of the defile, and, proceeding from the east, turned abruptly to the north. . . .

"Baron Kaulbars called it Jalyn-Khatsyr. It appeared about a mile and a half in length, formed of blocks of dark grey ice, heaped successively one upon the other, and of boulders buried beneath the snow.

The surface of the glacier presents clearly defined and generally pointed outlines; the ice of the higher beds being of a lighter tint than that of the lateral and lower, which are intermingled with sand and earth. Seen in profile, the glacier presents the appearance of an immense train, the piling up of the ice being most considerable at the lower end, where it attains the height of from 70 to 100 feet."

After riding for an hour from the spot whence I took the photograph last mentioned, I attempted another looking south, and bringing in the same White Mountain and glacier as before, but with a dark mass in the foreground to the left.

From the foot of the last pass on the northern slope begins the reign of chaos, and the road is strewed with the bleached skeletons of horses which have succumbed. In summer, animals make their way a little better than in autumn or winter, when the snow fills up the interstices between the stones. At such a time a horse is likely to fall and wrench off his hoofs.

Shepeleff speaks of his animals as suffering cruelly, both as regards their bruises and also from the rarefaction of the air. Of this latter, however, I have not the least recollection at any part of the Muz-Tag range, nor did I know what rarefied air meant until reaching the higher passes of the Kuen Lun.

The route leading up to the crest of the Muzart skirts the east of the Jalyn-Khatsyr glacier, and, blocked more or less with large stones, winds along the flanks of the lateral rocks. On the east is seen the Urten Muzart, issuing from beneath the ice like a slender thread, and forming the source of the river, 31 miles from the spot where it issues from the defile into the Tekes valley.

The crest of the Pass is saddle-shaped, and about a third of a mile in length, presenting the appearance of a little plateau sloping slightly towards the south, and affording a superb view right and left of the magnificent peaks of the Tian Shan. None of my predecessors appear to have had in their possession a barometer, whilst as for my own—an excellent aneroid graduated up to 20,000 feet, and lent me by my friend and former fellow-traveller the Rev. J. P. Hobson—the rough travel, I suppose, of the tarantass had put it out of order. Hence the exact height of the Muzart Pass remains undetermined.*

Kostenko, arguing chiefly from the cessation of vegetation, speaks of 11,000 feet as the altitude of the Pass, whilst Shepeleff, taking the Tekes valley at 5,500 feet, adds 5,000 to the glacier before coming to the last ascent, for which he further adds upwards of 1,000 feet, giving a total estimate of 12,000 feet above the level of the sea. The measurement by chain from the northernmost spurs of the Muz-Tag to the top of the Pass he gives as 49 *versts* 420 *sajens*, or about 33 miles.

My last photograph on the northern side of the crest was taken at eight o'clock, and was successful in portraying clearly the outlines of one of the grandest peaks we saw; whilst in the foreground there lay a huge mass of rocks, something like a fallen mountain broken into a thousand pieces.

* Réclus quotes Regel as giving the height at 11,600 feet, but if Dr Regel has written thus, it has escaped me. Réclus also mentions Dilke as having crossed the Pass; but neither in conversation with Mr Dilke, nor in reading what he wrote upon his journey to Kuldja and Issik-Kul, have I ever understood that he went over the Muzart Pass, and I am inclined to think the names of Regel and Dilke are mentioned in error.

Taking these pictures of course delayed us (though not the baggage), and involved the stoppage of Joseph, who carried my camera on horseback, and another who carried the tripod, together with the interpreters and guides, who became a little impatient of this study of the artistic under circumstances they could only feebly appreciate.

Moreover, they did not know the way too well, and probably desired not to be lost in this region of chaos and horror and many skeletons of horses, where the only beings at their ease, apparently, were the ravens and kites, which saluted us with their ominous cries, and longed, no doubt, for the pleasure of picking our bones.

On finishing the photograph just mentioned, I perceived that a stranger, one Mullah-Khoja, had joined our party, as if dropped from the clouds. He had, he said, been in the mountains hunting, and soon showed that he knew his way about better than the rest of us, so that before long he proved a valuable acquisition.

From the crest the road proceeds southwards, the cliffs sometimes on the right and sometimes on the left, whilst between them lies a hollow with a flat bed, along which, in summer, streams trickle towards the south. At half-past ten we came to what looked like the lower part of a long attenuated glacier, which did not occupy the whole breadth of the valley. The surface was extremely uneven, and stood up like a miniature range of ice-mountains, gradually melting, and causing thereby a stream to run at their base.

In a sketch by a Russian named Kludoff, of which I possess a photograph, this miniature ice-range is called the Dorga glacier, and near it the artist has sketched what looks like an exaggerated mushroom, or a table of rock supported on a pedestal of ice.

These ice-tables are well known to Alpine climbers, and are formed by the surface of the glacier thawing more slowly under a fallen rock than in uncovered parts. Hence the "leg" is left, but only to thaw flankwise till the stone falls and begins again to form

THE DORGA GLACIER IN THE MUZART PASS.

another table. I took a photograph of this miniature ice-range, looking north, and then another in the opposite direction, where the ice is less prominent, but, from the multiplicity of rocks and stones, presents a difficult country for horses, though less difficult than some portions of the northern slope.

From a slight eminence, about two miles from the highest point of the Pass, there is a view of a *mer-de-*

glace, across which the route lies. The ice, stretching towards the south, is confined between the main peaks of the range and its branches. The upper portion of this sea lies east and west to the length of about four miles. It then turns at almost a right angle towards the south, and stretches in that direction for five miles, its width throughout being upwards of a mile. Enormous ice-waves and piles of *débris* and broken rocks, lying in the most varied positions, present a picture of terrible disorder.

In one part these waves and heaps are strewed with rubbish of a smaller kind, and are overgrown by grass, which swarms with myriads of black and grey spiders, as well as small ants. But I was much struck with the paucity of animal life seen on the day of crossing the glacier, the only quadruped being a small rodent, I think a souslik, to which Tor-jee immediately gave chase, but to no purpose.

Continuing our journey, on either side are cliffs rising like mountain walls, usually bare, and here and there of reddish hue, as of granite. Scattered over this sea of ice are innumerable specimens of coloured marbles—of jasper, of agate, and a mass of other stones with coloured veins of beautiful pattern. In places the heaps of ice are free from fallen stones, and their tops then glitter in the sun. Deep down in the layers of ice flow streams which are heard but not seen. Here and there the ice is cracked and broken up into crevasses or ice-wells, into some of which I would fain have peeped; but to approach them was perilous, since a false step might entail a fall into an abyss.

The farther we advanced, the less we found of *débris* and rocks, and the cleaner and clearer was the ice; but at the same time the road became more difficult. We kept for a long time to the right of the ice, and close to the mountains, where at first sight there seemed to be soil for the horses to tread upon, until, having occasion to dismount, I discovered that the supposed soil was only a thin coating of dust over ice.

To judge from Shepeleff's description, the picture presented by this locality in autumn and winter is still more striking and effective. He speaks of glacial pinnacles from 500 to 600 feet in height (meaning, I suppose, on the Dorga glacier), and of corridors of ice with overhanging walls. The channels and the lakes are frozen, and the newly-formed crystals of ice take the most fantastic shapes. The ice-grottoes, crevasses, and pits are veiled with snow as with a fringe. Inside are roofs of icicles, and from below ice-pillars, built as if for ornament and intended to receive statues.

The surface of the waters in these places is frozen so hard that it is impossible to break the icy covering, and each blow yields only a metallic but musical ring. At times beneath this glacial sea deep sounds are heard, proceeding from internal rupture of the ice. Such sounds alternate with the crash of falling rocks, or the dull roar of avalanches of snow which fall to pieces like scattering shells.

My photographic efforts had so far delayed us that we had seen nothing for some time of the baggage. At last, after about a couple of hours' ride from the Dorga glacier, we saw the animals ahead, with Osman Bai and his helpers painfully picking their way and toiling among ice-hummocks and over crevasses, the animals being helped over special difficulties one by one. The party appeared on the left of the glacier, whither by a roundabout way we had to follow, crossing the uneven ice.

Nothing looked easier than for one's horse to slip, and pitch his rider headforemost into a crevasse or against an ice-hummock, so I dismounted. But this was for the worse, since the horse proved the surer footed. I had to remount, and ride with loose rein, dangling my feet so that at the first sign of a slip I might spring from the saddle.

In this fashion I was doing my best to cross the glacier, following the lead of the old huntsman, when, along with a great shouting, Joseph called out to me to look at the baggage-horses filing along an ice-cliff, over which one of them had fallen, baggage and all. This seemed exciting enough to make one look up, but so difficult was the portion of the way I was just then creeping over that I dared not allow my attention to be diverted, and in due time we came to the scene of the accident.

The horse had gone too close to the edge of a precipice, fortunately not very deep, and without water at the bottom, so that, wonderful to say, it was not killed, nor seriously hurt; and as its load happened to be only the two chests of bread and a sack, no damage was sustained. Osman Bai, as we came up, was soundly rating his men for carelessness, after which we got ahead of the baggage-horses, and by one o'clock reached a spot called Mazar-bash, five miles from the crest of the Pass.

Here awaited us the most trying ordeal of the whole route. Mazar-bash is situated on the eastern side of the *mer-de-glace*, where, for a portion of the width, the ice was broken off almost vertically, leaving a cliff from 40 to 50 feet high, down the face of which we had by some means to descend.

Mazar-bash signifies the "head of the tomb"; in memory, I gathered, of a saint—I suppose a Buddhist monk—who, possessed probably with the crazy idea that he was to heap up merit by freezing himself to death, had pitched upon this horrible spot for his habitation. He had, however, left enough of the odour of sanctity about the place to afford an occasion to my Buddhist attendants to offer their devotions.

The first European, if I mistake not, to reach this spot was Shepeleff, who found here a small square fort which had been constructed three years previously on a little plateau upon one of the mountain slopes. It had a terraced roof defended by loopholes and battlements, and was built of very hard Chinese baked bricks, without a door, and entered through a hole in the roof, to which one mounted through a loophole by means of a ladder.

He found here 30 soldiers armed with matchlocks and *yatagans*, and rejoicing in an allowance of two *khalats* and a pelisse per annum, with a monthly pay of eight shillings, usually six months in arrear. Scant wages this, for the pleasure of living on a glacier! The soldiers, needless to say, were all infantry, since there was no food for horses, to say nothing of the difficulty of getting them there.

Notches were cut into the cliff of ice by which men from below could mount, but provisions and fuel brought from Tamgha-tash, the nearest picket southwards, were hauled up with ropes, and in this fashion the horses of caravans were let down when proceeding to Aksu.*

* Kostenko says that caravans never returned in the opposite direction, because of the difficulty of pulling up the horses. I was a little

Shepeleff mentions as behind the fort several tombs, which, if now existing, escaped my observation. They are said to be alluded to in an itinerary by Ritter. What had become of the fort at the time of my visit I am not sure. I am under the impression they told me that the Chinese, on regaining possession of the country, had demolished it; and as for getting down the face of the cliff, we found two or three men who said they had received orders to smooth my way, and had been some hours at work.

Just then they were laying boughs of trees across a crevasse, covering them with blocks of ice, and over these, if you please, not only I but the horses were to pass! Small wonder that one of the beasts fell in; but Osman Bai was again successful in recovering his horse without serious damage.

Needless to say I dismounted, and presently came to the top of the cliff, down the face of which we were invited to scramble.

It looked as if blocks of ice and *débris* had been hurled from above, and perhaps the face of the cliff to some extent broken away, and steps cut here and there; but how to get down whilst maintaining the perpendicular looked well-nigh impossible.

One man, however, took hold of my hand on either side, and after sliding, stepping, slipping, jumping, and all but falling half a dozen times, we alighted at last on a spot a little less uneven than the rest, whence we could survey the route whereby we had descended.

" Do you mean to say," I asked, " that the horses have to come down there?" to which reply was given

surprised, therefore, to meet, a few hundred yards north of this obstacle, a trader who had managed to pull up his baggage and a few animals, wherewith he was proceeding to Kuldja.

in the affirmative, and I watched curiously to see how the feat would be accomplished.

I do not remember seeing ropes attached, but my own horse was taken by one man at his head, whilst another held him back by the tail, and, thus steadied, he was made to scramble and slide on legs or haunches as he chose, till something like *terra firma* was reached at the bottom of the glacier.

The whole proceeding struck me as the most horribly dangerous piece of progression I had ever witnessed, or probably ever shall witness again ; and as Joseph had succeeded in safely bringing my camera down, I celebrated the occasion by taking a view of the Muzdavan with our horses descending. Why it does not figure in my book will presently appear.

There was no need for me to stay to see all the horses and baggage descend ; so, after agreeing as to the spot for spending the night, which Osman expected to attain before dark, my suite and I rode forward, our route hugging the mountains on our left, and having the gradually contracting glacier on the right, whilst beneath our horses' feet were rocks and stones, some of them a yard thick, over and around which we had to proceed.

Sometimes stepping-stones had to be placed against elevations that the horses might ascend, which mine on one occasion disdaining to use, took a standing jump, to the surprise, though happily not the unseating, of his rider.

Joseph came off less fortunately, for perceiving that he was to be thrown by, I think, his horse falling, and remembering what store I set on the apparatus he was carrying, he generously thought of my camera first and his own bones afterwards, and allowed himself to be

thrown, camera upwards, on to a rock that bruised him a good deal, so that he felt the effects for some days, though happily no bones were broken.

Shepeleff was rightly informed that from Mazar-bash to Tamgha-tash the route continued to present serious difficulties. It is encumbered by a mass of gigantic stones and fragments of rock fallen from the neighbouring mountains, and deposited by the *mer-de-glace*. Over these we had to make our way as best we could for about two miles, which took fully three hours, till we came to the southern end of the glacier.

Late in the afternoon we passed a superb ice-cavern, out of which a torrent issued. I judged the cave to be from 50 to 100 feet high, with roof and walls broken into a thousand curious shapes, and its weird splendour was a fitting close to a day full of scenic marvels.

I am reminded, however, that it would be but the beginning of wonders in the case of Hiuen Tsiang, my worthy and only predecessor of note in this portion of the Pass, since Kostenko says, " No European has ever gone beyond the Mazar-bash picket." I am not in the least surprised, therefore, that coming from the south and filing past this cavern and scaling the ice-cliff, suggested to Hiuen's imagination the need for some very strong superlatives.

Accordingly he says, as translated by Beale, " The mountain is steep and dangerous, and reaches to heaven. From the creation the perpetual snow which has collected here in piles has been changed into glaciers which melt neither in winter nor summer; the hard-frozen and cold sheets of water rise mingling with the clouds; looking at them the eye is blinded with the glare, so that it cannot gaze for long. . . .

"The icy peaks fall down sometimes and lie athwart the road, some of them 100 feet high, and others several tens of feet wide. On this account there is extreme difficulty in climbing over the first, and danger in crossing the others. Moreover, the wind and the snow, driven in confused masses, make it difficult to escape an icy coldness of body, though wrapped in heavy folds of fur-bound garments. When desirous of food or sleep, there is no dry place to be found for a halt; the only way is to hang the pot for cooking, and to spread the mat for sleeping, on the ice."

Hiuen Tsiang has been called the "Asiatic Marco Polo," and has been suspected of telling "Travellers' Tales." Thus far, however, his words are true, after which he or his Chinese editor, in the *Records of Western Countries,* adds:—

"Frequently fierce dragons impede and molest travellers with their inflictions. Those who travel this road should not wear red garments nor carry loud-sounding calabashes. The least forgetfulness of these precautions entails certain misfortune. A violent wind suddenly rises, with storms of flying sand and gravel; those who encounter them, sinking through exhaustion, are almost sure to die."

Now, if my honourable predecessor in Muzart literature instead of "dragons" had employed the word ghosts or hobgoblins, then, though I would not risk my reputation by going quite so far as to say that I actually saw any of these supernatural appearances, yet I would venture to add, if there were none in the vast, mysterious cavern whereon we last set eyes, then I can only say there ought to have been, so appropriate a dwelling-place did it appear, according to all the traditions of childhood, for a whole tribe of ogres, demons, and genii of the mountains!

To return, however, to sober criticism, Beale suggests that the dragons and their inflictions may allude to the sand and gravel storms, whilst as an alternative rendering of the next sentence he would substitute "ought not to carry calabashes nor shout loudly," as if water freezing in and bursting the calabashes might with the sound so caused, or by shouting, cause the "snow piles" to fall. "Why red garments," he adds, "should be interdicted is not so plain, unless dragons are enraged by that colour."

It took the Buddhist pilgrim seven days to get clear of the mountains. Twelve or fourteen of his party were starved and frozen to death, whilst the number of oxen, or *yaks*, and horses that perished was still greater.

They told me at Mazar-bash, if I remember rightly, that as many as 30 horses are sometimes killed there in a month. It was, therefore, no small mercy to have got off the glacier with a sound skin, and without loss of cattle, and thus have been permitted to be the first European to completely cross the Pass of the Muz-davan.

Beyond it we were still to continue over undescribed ground as far as Aksu.

CHAPTER XIX.

DOWN THE MUZART VALLEY.

Tamgha-tash station unapproachable; Waiting for baggage, and supperless to bed in the open, 283.—A remarkable day, 284.—Arrival next morning of Osman Bai; Military insignificance of Tamgha-tash, 285.—Departure southwards; A marble monument, 286.—Fine view from Balguluk; Professor Bonney's note on Romanovsky's geological map; Kungei Ala-Tau range; Rocks east, south, and west of Issik-Kul, 287.—Shaping of mountains, and suggested periods of earth movements, 288.—Alexander chain compared with Swiss Oberland; Complicated orographical structure at Kara-Kol watershed, 289.—The Ferghana mountains and their characteristic rocks extending to Pamirs; Geology of route southwards, 290.—Three lines of orographical folding; Continuation of author's route, 291.—Accident in fording river; Camera washed away; Attendants' pursuit, and success in recovering baggage, 292.—Arrival at Kailek, 294.—Breaking into a post-station, 295.—To Tuprak; An afternoon's shooting, 296.—Purchase of an eagle, 297.—Joseph's taxidermical masterpiece, 298.—Departure from Tuprak, and pursuit of partridges; Narrow escape from homicide; Arrival at Muzart-Kurgan, 299.

WHEN we had quite descended from the glacier and moraine we found ourselves within hail of the picket of Tamgha-tash, or "stone seal," and could see the building on the western side of the river. This river came dashing out from under the ice in a stream perhaps a hundred feet wide, and extremely swift. It bears the name of Muzart, but is called Muzart-nin-su, or southern, in contradistinction to the Picket Muzart flowing northwards.

Tor-jee boldly plunged his horse in to cross, but found the water too deep, so that he was obliged to shout his communications to a man on the opposite bank. By dismounting we could, no doubt, have approached the station by the end of the glacier and moraine; but it was already late in the afternoon, and we had to proceed nearly a mile farther to Tamgha-tash, the spot predetermined by Osman Bai.

It looked as if we might ride along the eastern bank of the stream under a cliff about 50 feet high, but the old huntsman pronounced this impracticable, by reason of water farther on. He then led the way on his little horse, which scrambled like a cat up to the top of the cliff, whither we had to follow. Then, after travelling above the flooded banks, we descended to a sheltered nook beneath the bluff, with the river a few yards in front of us, there to wait for tent and baggage.

Waiting soon became monotonous. Sunshine had ceased after midday, and, as twilight came on, rain came with it, but not the longed-for Osman Bai. "What could have happened?" we all asked; and I sent back a man to reconnoitre, but he brought no tidings, and it looked as if we should have to spend the night as we were. If he had not descended from the glacier before dusk, clearly he could not do so with his horses in the dark.

There was nothing, therefore, to be done but to bivouac supperless. Nor was there a stick of fuel at hand, though much to be desired in the proximity of glaciers, and with rain descending. Happily, a man at the picket, knowing our necessity, by a long and roundabout way brought us an armful of wood, and Joseph found for me a narrow ledge under the bluff, partly sheltered by the overhanging cliff from the rain.

Here he spread the felt from under his saddle, and proceeded to do his best for my comfort. Rummaging among his saddle-bags, he found a few spoonfuls of tea; but though we had fire, and water more than enough, there was to hand neither saucepan nor kettle. Suddenly I remembered that the maker of my enamelled tea-bottle (of the pattern supplied to the British troops in the Egyptian campaign) had said to me casually, "You know you can put this bottle in the fire without harming it"—whereupon we extemporised a kettle, and Joseph produced an enamelled cup.

Next, I bethought me of the few biscuits left in my holster, and, lastly, of a box of meat lozenges. These provisions had, of course, to be shared with our fellows in tribulation, and, knowing how far imagination goes, even in matters of meat and drink, I proceeded to descant upon the wonderful properties of the little brown lozenges, seen now by my attendants for the first time. I was not able to tell them the exact number of pounds of beef condensed into the lozenges, but they were to suck, and suck, and suck again, till the whole was melted, and then to believe that they had swallowed the efficacy of an undefined quantity of meat without the trouble of cookery, of serving, and of mastication.

Then, our too scanty supper over, I lay down for the first time I could remember wanting a meal but unable to get it. I could write no diary, but my note-book reminded me that it was the only date in my life that could be written by five out of six figures alike—namely, 8/8/1888—and I thought it had been verily a day much to be remembered.

The wonder to me was that on any one of 20 occasions I had not broken my neck, so dangerous was the journey we had just been permitted to accomplish ; whilst to spend a night in the open without proper wraps was likewise to me a new experience.

When tempted to grumble I recalled an episode in the life of one who spent a night and a day in the deep, in comparison with which my situation I thought enviable ; and then, putting on my waterproof for what little warmth it could afford, and hoisting an umbrella against wind and rain, and with Joseph sitting at my feet with his back to the bluff, wearied I fell asleep.

Sunrise brought light, and gladness too, when at six o'clock Osman appeared, and to my great relief reported the loss neither of beast nor burden. Darkness had overtaken him on the moraine, and finding a little spot tolerably clear of stones, he had bivouacked there, and was now ready to continue his march without stopping.

A tall black horse of mine, which carried the kitchen necessaries and sundry provisions, was detached to remain with us whilst a breakfast was hastily prepared, pieces of meat, I remember, being cooked in native fashion on skewers. After our meal we were to follow and overtake Osman Bai. Meanwhile I thought the spot should be delineated, so I took a photograph of it, including an inscription I could not read on the rock above where we slept.

At Tamgha-tash are, or were, two stations; one built by the Chinese, and the other by Yakub Khan, who was so bent upon getting his little fortress erected that they told me he came there in person, and encouraged his followers by working with his own hands.*

* Shepeleff thought that his placing soldiers here and at Mazar-bash could be due only to fear and suspicion, though, it might be, the Khan

From Tamgha-tash, at eight o'clock, we set out in a south-easterly direction, continuing on the western bank of the river through a grand valley with bare mountains rising on each side. They gave me the name of one on our left as Kalpak-tash, and it had on its face, half-way up, the remnant of a glacier, whilst farther on we saw another glacier and two arches, like huge bridges thrown across a chasm, and connecting the two mountains.*

In front of us was a mountain named Go-gil-ga, with its head in the clouds. Behind was another known as Kara-davan, blocking up the north end of the valley; whilst all around were bare peaks, and little verdure anywhere, except a few bushes bearing red berries.

The route was most difficult by reason of the large stones, over which our horses had to pick their way. This opinion seemed to have been shared by some of our predecessors, who, towards the southern end of the valley in the locality we are speaking of, had erected a block of white marble, and cut upon it a Turki inscription to the following effect, as translated by Joseph:—

"He who comes this way once may be pardoned, as not knowing what he is doing;
He who comes twice is a fool; whilst
He who comes a third time is hopeless as a kafir" (or infidel).

wished thus to afford assistance to caravans and travellers in this inhospitable region. From a military point of view Shepeleff considered Mazar-bash as of no real value, and that the better place for a military post to guard the Pass was in the narrow part of the defile leading to the picket of Tamgha-tash.

* Snow bridges in the Tian Shan, Kostenko says, are often met with much below the glaciers—namely, at 5,000 feet or lower. They sometimes attain more than a mile in length and 100 feet in thickness. They are formed out of the masses of spring avalanches, and therefore the snow in them is mixed with rubble and pebbles brought down from the surrounding crags.

Presently we came to a spot which the men called Balguluk, whence, looking northwards, the valley presented a magnificent appearance, the river meandering along its comparatively flat bottom, and a huge mountain mass lying at right angles thereto, whilst at the southern end was Mount Upga-tash rising to the left, and Tugh-balshi in front.

But what struck me most of all in this locality was the clearly defined and fantastic conformation of the rocks, the principal varieties of which are indicated on Romanovsky and Mushketoff's map * as granite, syenite, and gneiss.

Riding for another hour brought us to a part of the

* This valuable geological map of Russian Turkistan seems to be little known in England, and is not in the possession, I am told, even of the Geological Society of London. Professor Bonney (who had not seen the map until I showed it to him) has favoured me with the following remarks, which scientists will appreciate, on the geology of the Tian Shan, especially those portions of it over which I passed. With the map lying before him he writes:—

"The mountain chain, Kungei Ala-Tau, which separates the basin of Issik-Kul from the head of the great lowland (covered by post-Tertiary deposits), evidently consists of two or three roughly parallel ranges forming a series of folds. The basement rocks are crystalline, chiefly granitoid and gneissoid, together with masses of "porphyries" and felsites, and occasional dioritic rocks.

"This is very probably a group similar to that which in several places forms the core of the Alpine ranges—namely, granites and other rocks of igneous origin, but of great antiquity, to which a foliated structure has been imparted by pressure.

"On this group rests, obviously with a great interval between them, a group of not very highly altered rocks—crystalline limestones, phyllites, quartzites, and conglomerates. These are indicated as older than Silurian, and they are not improbably rather anterior to the Cambrian system. On them, towards the eastern end of the chain, Devonian rocks are resting, evidently unconformably, and these are followed by Carboniferous, which are either unconformable to or overlap the Devonian.

"Until we have travelled some distance east of the lake, where Jurassic rocks set in, we find nothing between the Carboniferous system and the Tertiary series (which is not subdivided into systems); even the valley called Coombell, the rocks being light-coloured on our right and dark on the left. In sheltered spots

last being absent over the greater part of the chain. They occur, however, on both sides of the basin of Issik-Kul, where they are frequently overlain by post-Tertiary deposits.

"It is evident that the whole region has been affected by earth movements of more than one date. As we carry our eyes westward along the general strike of the rock masses, we are brought insensibly into the vast mountain *massif* west of Issik-Kul (the basin of which appears to be only a trough, broader than usual, in a series of folds), and we see that the southern part, at least, of the Kungei Ala-Tau is inseparable from the *massif* of which the Alexander range forms also a part.

"In this range we find that crystalline schists (mica, chlorite, talc, etc.) set in between the phyllite-marble group and the fundamental gneissoid group. They are not, however, invariably present, for the former sometimes rests directly on the latter.

"It is therefore probable that, as a rule, the phyllite-marble group is separated from anything below it by a considerable break, and was formed at an age much nearer to Palæozoic times than either of the others. When it was being deposited, probably old land surfaces of granite, gneisses, and schists already existed, and supplied the materials of the conglomerates, quartzites, and phyllites. We may expect to find that, as earth movements of pre-Carboniferous age have left their mark in the Alps (where the chain, as a whole, is much more recent), so they have here; only in this case we may date them as pre-Devonian.

"But the shaping of the existing mountain chains must certainly be post-Carboniferous. If we may assume that the evidence obtained from the eastern end of the chain holds good for the rest, we may affirm this shaping to be post-Jurassic. Cretaceous rocks do not appear to occur, but, so far as I can form an opinion, I think that the mountain chain was developed before the Tertiary rocks were deposited, though it is probable that some of these have been affected by important movements.

"In short, so far as I can interpret the map, I should say that, as in the case of the Alps, the mountain system of the Tian Shan was due to more than one process of movement. Whether there is any connection in time between the disturbances which have affected the European and the Asiatic systems depends on the date assigned to the Tertiary deposits on the latter, on which question the map gives no information. In this region, however, it is probable that there was no such continuous depression from the beginning of the Trias to the end of the Eocene as there was in the Alps. But just east of the east end of Issik-Kul there were a few trees, but vegetation was scanty everywhere—a striking contrast to the luxuriant ver-

Jurassic rocks occur, forming an elongated mass, and covered directly by Tertiary deposits.

"As the map is not coloured for more than a comparatively short distance south of Issik-Kul, we must shift our position to the west of the lake, *i.e.* to somewhere in the neighbourhood of Tokmak, which is at the head of a great inland basin lying north of the Alexander Mountains. From here, by following a line rather to the west of south, we can keep on the geologically coloured part of the map.

"The Alexander chain is obviously a prolongation of the Kungei Ala-Tau, immediately north of Issik-Kul: the Chu valley, traversed by the post-road from Tokmak, not indicating any real orographical boundary. It is therefore probable that, as in the case of the Swiss Oberland range, the complete elevation of this Alexander and Kungei Ala-Tau range is a more recent event than the definition of the mountain range forming the watershed to the south.

"These Alexander Mountains consist, as already said, of a central gneissic axis, fringed on each side with crystalline schists, which are overlain by the phyllite group. Farther west, Devonian and Carboniferous rocks set in on the northern face, and above all comes a continuous border of Tertiaries. There is, however, a strip of Jurassic rock, probably a minor infold, extending from a point south-west of Tokmak to the longitude, approximately, of the west end of Issik-Kul.

"South of the Alexander Mountains the orographical structure is extremely complicated. From the Kara-Kol Pass (on the longitude of Pishpek), which crosses a southern offshoot from the Alexander Mountains, the streams on the eastern flank flow eastwards, and ultimately, after being joined by rivers that rise much farther south, form the Chu and run northward past the west end of Issik-Kul to Tokmak; whilst from the west side of the Pass the streams all find their way in a southerly direction, joining the Kara-Kol river (one of the upper streams of the Syr-daria), the basin of which seems to encroach in a northerly direction, and produces a marked flexure in the general line of the watershed.

"The geology of this region is correspondingly complicated. The broad trough of the Issik-Kul basin can be traced for some distance west of the longitude of Tokmak, but the trough itself seems to consist of a group of folds which are composed of phyllites and older rocks, with some Carboniferous deposits and considerable masses of Triassic, Jurassic, and even Tertiary rocks. Hence it would seem to have been an area of deposition up to a comparatively late date. The folds have a general east to west direction, but the river courses are remarkably complicated, as if, after they had first been defined, they had been

dure of Khan-Yailak, and other pastures on the northern slope of the range.

We were thus making our way, all going well, until affected by movements in new directions. The watershed for a short distance from the Kara-Kol Pass runs due south, then sweeps off to the east, passing south of Issik-Kul, and inosculates with the main range of the Tian Shan, which follows a south-west direction.

"The foregoing complication is increased by a long range, the Ferghana Mountains, which runs off from the southern Tian Shan (from near the Terek Pass) in a general north-westerly direction, and consists of members of the phyllite group, flanked locally with Carboniferous rocks, and everywhere by Triassic or Jurassic rocks, with which Tertiary strata seem to be infolded. Presumably this area was one of deposit up to a comparatively late period, and has been since disturbed by flexures in more than one direction.

"Rather to the south of the junction of the above-named Ferghana range with the main Tian Shan chain (which takes place a little west of the lofty lake Chadir-Kul), lines of flexure, running east and west, become again more conspicuous, as we come to the ranges south of the Ferghana basin, which is drained by the upper waters of the Syr-daria.

"These ranges, forming the northern part of the Pamir, consist of the gneissic and the phyllite groups, infolding, at first, Carboniferous, with some Tertiary rocks. Then some Devonian beds appear below the Carboniferous; and some Jurassic are seen locally beneath Cretaceous (these last rocks appear to be limited in a north-easterly direction by the line of the Ferghana range). Tertiary rocks still occur as before. East and west folds continue towards the south till we reach the great Kara-Kol lake in the Kargosh Pamir, and they affect the drainage of the head-waters of the Amu-daria. The folds consist mainly of the gneissic and the phyllite groups, with or without crystalline schists; but as strips of Cretaceous and Tertiary rocks are involved, there must have been great earth movements since the date of the latter.

"From near the Kara-Kol lake, the main watershed of Asia strikes off over the Pamir plateau, dividing the drainage of Chinese Turkistan, first, from the tributaries of the Amu-daria, and then, from those of the Indus.

"The route from Kuldja southwards crosses the Uzun-Tau (a prolongation of the chain north of Issik-Kul), which range is a complicated wrinkling of the gneissic and phyllite groups with some crystalline schists, flanked by Carboniferous, Triassic, Jurassic, and Tertiary rocks. Kashgar appears to be situated on a post-Tertiary deposit overlying Tertiary rocks, beneath which are rocks assigned to the Trias.

"In the foregoing description I have not taken note of the dioritic about two o'clock, when it became necessary to ford the Muzart-nin-su, here as wide perhaps as the Thames at London Bridge, but divided into several streams, and rushing rapidly. We had successfully forded streams on so many occasions, that it seemed unnecessary to take special precautions now; and, our old Nimrod having stayed behind to chat, probably with Osman Bai, Joseph, Amin, and I prepared to follow Tor-jee.

I suppose our dog did not like the look of the rocks, which are probably subordinate members of the gneissic series, or of occasional masses of gabbro, serpentine, etc., and but little of the "porphyries," felsites, etc., these being all orographically of minor importance; and as they must be, in many cases at least, intrusive in the rocks with which they are associated, there are no means of ascertaining their age. Also I have left unnoticed the occasional patches of dolerites, andesites, etc., which, even if they may occasionally form elevated peaks, as in the Caucasus, are probably very late in date and of little structural significance.

"Looking at the map as a whole, the mountain *massifs* of these parts of Asia appear to be due to three leading lines of folding, the axes of which run respectively north-west (or a little to the south of it), west-south-west (or a little to the south of it), and nearly west. Possibly the last may be due to the combination of the first and second, but I believe all three to be distinct. All seem to be post-Jurassic.

"I cannot decide from the map whether the Tertiary rocks form flanking ranges like the *nagelfluh* and *molasse* in the Alps, or whether they enter into the composition of the main ranges, like the earlier Tertiaries of those mountains. Although the information before me is not sufficient to enable me to venture upon any suggestion as to the relative age of these disturbances, yet they point strongly to the comparative newness of this great mountain system. As the folds which run from west-south-west to east-north-east and from west to east seem to be especially effective in complicating the drainage systems, I am disposed to think that both these, at any rate in part, are due to movements of very late date.

"The peculiarly irregular paths followed by some of the rivers suggest that, after their courses had been roughly determined by an early set of movements, others took place, along different lines, so that the rivers had to escape from the rocky labyrinth thus produced as best they could. But upon this question, in the absence of detailed information, one can do no more than offer a surmise.—(*Signed*) T. G. BONNEY."

current, nor perhaps the icy water, and was hanging back, whereupon Tor-jee kindly dragged him up to his pommel, and thus found occupation for one hand, whilst with the other he was leading the black horse laden with the saucepans, and, on the top, what was far more valuable—my precious camera.

And now began a scene. The rough stones of yesterday's route had made the black horse footsore, so that on getting into the middle of the stream he stumbled, and Tor-jee, unable to attend to so many things at once—his own horse, the dog, and his own safety—let the sumpter go.

This was exciting enough, to see the animal lying in mid-stream, with part of his baggage under water; but matters grew worse when, trying to rise, he only partially recovered himself, and was washed by the force of the current into deeper water, where the baggage kept going down and down, till at last the whole of it, camera and all, was completely under water, and the only thing above the surface was the horse's black head, he struggling for dear life. On and on he swam, and farther and farther receded from my vision my camera, with its roll of 48 views completed only an hour or two since, and including the wonderful "Muz-davan with our horses descending."

Of course I shouted and bellowed directions with all my might, and in turn Joseph had to shout to me in mid-stream that I was exposing myself to danger, and should be carried away too if not careful. So swift was the current that to look down, even when my horse was standing still, made me quite dizzy, and I was glad with Joseph and Amin to reach a shoal in the middle of the river, whence we could see the horse floating farther and farther away, until presently we saw him washed on to a bank, where he managed to loosen the baggage ropes and break himself free.

Meanwhile Tor-jee had not been idle, but had descended along the stream, and, knowing the value I set on the camera, left the horse to look after itself and made for the baggage, of which only a small portion was visible above the surface. What he was doing with it we could not, owing to the distance, make out, and I sent to his assistance Amin, who quickly stripped himself and ran off in nature's robes by the nearest way.

We saw him come up to the spot, but were puzzled to observe both now stooping and apparently unable to do what they wanted. This, of course, was highly exciting, nor were we greatly helped on getting out my telescope to view the proceedings.

At this juncture the old huntsman came up, and galloped his little horse over the stony bed of the river and through its streams in truly workmanlike style. The black horse had made his way out of the water, and was standing sheepishly on a shoal far down the river. Nimrod brought him back to his fellows, and also approached to the help of Tor-jee, whilst Amin came back to his clothes, his teeth chattering, and his whole frame shivering.

I never in my life saw a man shiver so, and was fearful as to what might be the result; so I helped him to get at once into his sheepskin coat, after which, but not before, he could give us a little information. As for Osman Bai, he came up when the excitement was beginning to abate, and, taking things very coolly, chose a different place for his horses to cross, and quietly went on his way.

Amin being dressed, we prepared to follow, and crossed the remainder of the river, to be met by Tor-jee, who brought me my camera with a smile of triumph, as if aware that he was doing something that would please me highly.

He said that on stooping to detach from the other baggage the felt wherein for protection the camera was wrapped, so icy cold was the water that his hands were numbed, and he was obliged to hold all down till assistance came, to prevent the whole being washed away. This explained his apparent inaction as seen from a distance, and I forthwith concluded that Tor-jee, Amin, and the old huntsman had exerted themselves nobly, and promised each a special reward.

The pots and kettles suffered nothing by the ducking; but the flour was prematurely made into paste, the bread was reduced to a similar condition, and one of the component parts of the baking powder had fizzed away. The wreckage, however, with my camera case emptied of water, was placed again on the back of the horse, whose temper was not improved by the episode, for he kicked Tor-jee when urged forwards after his fellows.

We then made our way along the western bank of the river, and in about an hour came to a small pasture with sheep feeding. Here Osman Bai wished to encamp, saying that if we went on to the station a mile or two farther, he would have to bring back his horses to this spot for pasture. This he was told he must do, and about six o'clock, after a ten hours' ride, we arrived at the station of Kailek.

Kailek was found to be a Chinese picket, large and well built compared with any of the pickets we had seen north of the Pass, and situated in a little grove of poplars. Its courtyard was surrounded by stables and rooms, but the officer supposed to be in charge had gone away on a visit, and had locked the door.

Since necessity knows no law, we took French leave, forced the door, and obtained possession; the room appropriated by me having a *kang*, or sleeping platform, and a fireplace, but nothing more. A few chickens wandering about helped to afford us a welcome back to settled life, after sleeping in nomad tents, and my first care was to look after affairs photographic.

My camera, selected and arranged by Dr Lindsay Johnson, was a half-plate expanding apparatus made by Perken, Son, & Rayment, measuring, when folded, only 8 × 8 × 3 inches, wherewith, if needful, ordinary glass negatives could be used. It had been fitted with one of the box roller slides of the Eastman Company, containing a sensitised paper roll for 48 exposures, the whole, with a double back and everything except the tripod legs, fitting into a leather case 10 × 10 × 7 inches.

This case was usually wrapped in a sheet of felt, which served for protection during conveyance on horseback, and was spread on the ground when taking views, Amin carrying for me that and the tripod bag.

I think it says a great deal for the excellence of the cabinet-making and workmanship of this box, that, notwithstanding the thorough ducking I have described, little if any water got inside the roller box, and I lost only the last two of the 48 views, that of Mazar-bash and Tamgha-tash, the last being unrolled and having nothing but the vulcanite slide between it and the water in the outer camera case. The glue fixing the leathern portion of the camera had been here and there dissolved by the water, and I greatly feared my picture-taking was at an end; but things were not so bad as they looked, and, though stopped for the next few days, I managed afterwards to repair the damage.

Next morning we left Kailek at half-past nine, starting thus late partly because, after the rugged route of the previous two days, some of the horses needed to be re-shod. Three hours sufficed to bring us to Tuprak, where was a station, inhabited and in somewhat better order than at Kailek.

Here I challenged old Nimrod in the afternoon to go out with me shooting, and was amused to watch his proceedings. He carried a curious old gun, to the muzzle of which was affixed a pronged rest to place on the ground and steady his aim, whilst the trigger brought down, not a hammer, not even a flint, but a piece of lighted string into a little pan of gunpowder communicating with the charge, loaded with ball.

Near the station was a leafy dell of small trees and long grass, wherein we very soon saw a hare, sitting on her haunches with ears erect, making a reconnaissance. I nodded to Nimrod to take the first shot; off went his hat, and, advancing a step or two, his prong descended in a moment to earth, aim was taken, and down came the clumsy trigger, but all too fatal for Bunny, for she was hit clean in the shoulder, and immediately fell.

The old huntsman threw down his gun and rushed immediately to stick a knife into his prey, to ease, I suppose, his Muhammadan conscience, according to the dictates of which he would, I fancy, be forbidden to eat a creature not killed by the letting of blood.

I managed to get an azure Titmouse (*Parus cyanus*), one of three specimens of small birds secured, of which there appeared to be very few, in the locality. On the day following I was more fortunate, and secured about eight specimens, including two red-legged Partridges (*Caccabis var. pallescens*), a Masked Wagtail (*Motacilla personata*), a Brambling (*Montifringilla Brandti*), a Bullfinch (*Carpodacus erythrinus*), a Magpie (*Pica leucoptera*), and a red-legged Crow or Chough (*Pyrrhocorax graculus*), the last of which, stuffed, now appears in a glass case before me.

But my greatest ornithological "find" in this neighbourhood was a Golden Eagle (*Aquila chrysaëtos*), locally known as a *Birkut*, the most powerful of birds trained for hawking, and one that will attack a wolf or kill a deer. The old huntsman told me that he possessed three of these, trained, or partly so, and at the next station brought them for my selection.

One was just then without a tail, and therefore not so good for my purpose; a second, trained, was three years old, and comparatively costly; whilst the youngest, though the handsomest bird, was not yet trained, and therefore to the owner was less valuable. He had obtained it at Kailek-davan, near the station of that name, during the previous Ramazan (about the middle of May). Letting a boy down by a rope, the young eagle, not then fully fledged, had been taken from the nest—the only occupant in this instance, though there are sometimes two, but never more, the old man said.

Hence the bird was approximately only six months old. It weighed, nevertheless, 7 lbs., measured a yard from beak to tail, whilst its outstretched pinions extended to seven feet. Not a feather appeared to be wanting or out of place, and as I looked into its cold, drabbish-grey eyes, it seemed nothing short of a shame to think of killing so noble a creature.

But how else was it to be conveyed from the Tian Shan to South Kensington? and how was the foul deed to be done? To shoot it in cold blood was too dreadful, and, besides, would partly damage the skin and plumage.

So I bethought me of the injunction of my naturalist to beware of letting anything eatable come near his arsenical soap, because it was "deadly poison." Surely, then, thought I, a nice little morsel of meat seasoned with a pinch of arsenical soap will be just what is wanted.

A tender morsel accordingly was prepared, which Joseph flavoured under directions, after eating which I expected to see my beauty ready for *post-mortem* honours; whereas, to our amazement, she stretched out her neck, and asked for another helping of the same sort! A second was given her, and, I think, a third; but, as with the Jackdaw of Rheims,

> "That which gave rise to no little surprise,
> Nobody seemed one penny the worse!"

After this Mullah Khoja was requested to take his bird to the roof and there kill her, which he did by strangulation.

The preparation of the skin of this bird was Joseph's masterpiece, and it reached the Museum in such good condition as to receive "honourable mention" from Mr Bowdler Sharpe, in the ornithological department, which to me was the more gratifying because, on looking at the skin a few days after preparation, it appeared to betray signs of decay under the pinions, whence it had been necessary in so large a bird to remove portions of flesh that in a smaller bird are usually left to shrivel up.

We quitted Tuprak at six on a Saturday morning, and continued on the west of the river in a southerly direction, coming in one spot to a little verdure, where my men reported red-legged partridges.

Of course I was glad, for we had no longer the regal allowance of a slaughtered sheep per day, but were dependent upon what the road afforded, and that was not much; besides, we were looking forward to making the morrow a feast day. The men were all alive and keen to pursue the game.

The only creature who did not seem to share these sentiments was my horse, who, though he cheerfully carried my gun, objected to my firing it from his back. The first time I did so, in the Tekes valley, I expected to be unseated; but the sensation was so novel to him that I think he did not know what to make of it.

Later on he manifested a decided fear of explosions, and on the present occasion, after I had taken aim, wheeled round and nearly caused a serious accident; for, my finger being on the trigger, the gun went off painfully close to Joseph's head, who declared, indeed, that the smoke came in his face. It was not till after I had dismounted and secured a brace of birds that I learned what cause I had for thankfulness for so narrow an escape from homicide.

As we continued south the valley became narrower, and after a ride of five hours and a half we came along a level plateau to the end of it, where the entire width of the gorge was closed by a wall and a fortified Custom-house station called Muzart-Kurgan. Here we determined to stay over Sunday.

CHAPTER XX.

FROM MUZART-KURGAN TO AKSU.

Lodging at Muzart-Kurgan, 300.—Objections to Customs examination ; Advice concerning Chinese officials, 301.—Standing on one's rights, 302.—Visit of Customs official, 303.—Inspection of Muzart-Kurgan : Nimrod's cunning, 304.—Route continued over undulating tableland ; Dust columns, 305.—Kizil-Bulak ; Route southwards over curious geological formation, 306.—Messenger from Aksu ; Stay at Auvat, and ride to Jam, 307.—Southern view of Tian Shan, 308.—Khan Tengri, visible 100 miles off, 309.—Glaciers and crests westwards ; From Jam to Tash-Lianger, 310.—Death of a horse and dog, 311.—Thermometrical observations between Kuldja and Aksu ; Arrival of Madamin Bai from Russian Consul, 312.—A minatory letter. 314.—Escorted into Aksu, 316.

ON arriving at the Custom-house of Muzart-Kurgan, my party was not all together, and when the leading detachment was stopped at the gate, the men said their master had a special letter. Thereupon all were permitted to enter, and I was conducted at first to what was supposed to be a travellers' room in an inner court.

It was, however, so dark and dirty and dismal that I preferred going to the outer yard, on the north side of which was a number of rooms for serving-men and cattle, especially the latter, but airy and light, and affording something to look at from the door. I directed one of these rooms to be cleaned out, and determined to lodge there among my men and baggage.

Soon after our arrival and the handing in of my letter from the *Tsian-Tsiun*, an official came to say that my baggage must be searched, for that there was nothing in the letter to the contrary. To this I objected, saying that I had been given clearly to understand that my luggage would be exempt from examination.

I had learned this so far back as St Petersburg, where in M. Tching Tchang, the *Chargé d'affaires* at the Chinese Embassy, I found a gentleman speaking excellent English and better French, who had spent some years in Paris, and was more Europeanised than most of his countrymen I have met. He entered with zest into my proposed travels, and upon my asking him what I should do, supposing the petty Chinese officials should be vexatious, he advised me to threaten complaints to the great men I knew in Europe.

This was not vain counsel, for I afterwards met an Englishman who told me that, when travelling in the Chinese interior, an inferior official told him his baggage must be searched, to which he replied, "Very well, then I shall complain to the authorities in Peking"; whereupon the trouble vanished.

Very different advice was given me by the Russians in Asia, who to a man said, "Ask nothing; but demand everything. With small officials, send for them to call upon you, and not *vice versâ*. Do everything by force, and never allow a Chinaman to take the least liberty with you." This was the counsel given me by General Prjevalsky, and another General in Kuldja. Also I have heard it said by Englishmen living in

China, and even by the son of a Chinese woman, that "the Chinese respect nothing but force."

Let me not fail to record, on the other hand, a beautiful reply that came well from my heathen friend Mattie at Suiting. Seeing him disposed to be friendly, I asked for any hints he could give me for dealing with the Mandarins in the new country I was about to visit, whereupon he said, "There is one rule that is useful all the world over. The fussy, bubbling, noisy brook is always shallow. Still waters run deep. In short, be humble; and apologise to the officials for not knowing their ceremonies as you should, asking that your shortcomings may be attributed to ignorance, not to lack of good intention."

Here, then, was a bundle of modes of address, each of them, I doubt not, expedient on occasion and in measure, and the difficulty was at Muzart-Kurgan to know which to adopt, and how far.

At the first encounter I contented myself with claiming that my baggage should not be examined; and the young official caved in, saying, as he walked off, that he would copy the *Tsian-Tsiun's* letter, which having done he returned it, and we were left awhile in peace.

Presently Joseph came to say that "one greater man" had arrived, and wished to see my letter, which Joseph having taken, the official invited him in and offered tea, asking sundry questions about his master, and then sent me a pass to show at another Custom-house farther on.

This was quite a change in the wind, partly attributable perhaps to a talking-to given them, Joseph afterwards informed me, by Monkey-face and Tor-jee. "Don't you know," they said, "that this Englishman is a very great man, one who has dined with the *Tsian-Tsiun*? What do you mean, then, by troubling him about his baggage? Evidently you don't know Chinese good manners and proper behaviour to a foreigner!"

This lecture was given behind my back, and when, later in the afternoon, I went to call on the "one greater man," he showed me into his opium den, and, with an evident intention to be polite, offered me a whiff of the detestable pipe which he had seemingly been smoking—anyway he seemed to be somewhat excited.

Next morning the head of the station, Chian-da-loya, called on me, looking ghastly and emaciated from the use of opium, and slightly hilarious, as if with his morning pipe. He excused himself for not asking me to dinner by saying that he did not know how to prepare a meal to my taste. This was a fortunate deliverance. He sent, however, a present of four fowls, one of them an old rooster, as tough as cow-hide.*

* He gave me the following estimate of distances:—

Udungei to Khan-Yailak	60 *li* or	21 miles.
Khan-Yailak to Tamgha-tash	100 ,,	35 ,,
Tamgha-tash to Kailek	80 ,,	28 ,,
Kailek to Tuprak	40 ,,	14 ,,
Tuprak to Muzart-Kurgan	60 ,,	21 ,,
Muzart-Kurgan to Aksu	300 ,,	105 ,,

Kostenko's distances from Muzart Picket (our Shattoo) to Mazar-bash are:—

Muzart Picket to entrance of Muzart defile	5	*versts*.
Entrance of defile to summit of Pass	50	,,
Summit of Pass to Mazar-bash	12	,,
Mazar-bash to Tamgha-tash	20	,,
Total	87 ,,	or 58 miles.

And this must be accepted as nearly correct because based, I presume, on Shepeleff's measurement by chain from Muzart Picket to Mazar-bash. We took 23 hours from Shattoo to Tamgha-tash, which in my

After breakfast I mounted to the roof, which was indescribably filthy, and had a good look round the station. It was in reality a fortress, and the residence of the chief of all the pickets up to the glacier. Shepeleff was informed that there were in garrison here under Yakub Khan 500 soldiers, 30 at Kailek, 25 at Tamgha-tash, and 30 at Mazar-bash, whilst farther south there were said to be 20 at Kizil-Bulak, 100 each at Jam, Kent-Shlentchi, and Tash-Lianger, and 600 at Aksu.

Judging from the size of the station at Muzart-Kurgan, I should think 500 soldiers would have been squeezed therein with difficulty; but it had two, if not more, quadrangular courts, with many rooms, though nearly all were now empty, and the military character of the place, as with all the pickets, appeared quite departed. But I was less struck with the buildings of the fort than with the remarkable walls continued from it (on one side across the Muzart, if I remember rightly), and, after the fashion of the Great Wall of China, right up the mountains to the most inaccessible places for builders to approach.

The authorities were evidently minded that no one should get by unobserved. Yet I noticed that old Nimrod managed to elude their demands. So grasping were they, we were told, that they would make him pay for bringing in the skin of the hare he had shot. Accordingly, the old man had entered with my party, and remained with us an hour or two, as if belonging to the caravan.

Presently I observed him looking over the parapet to see whether the coast was clear. His brother

itinerary gives 68 miles; but here the average of three[3] miles an hour, over the glacier, is manifestly too high a calculation,

Turkis willingly connived at what was going on, but I was quite innocent of the ruse. Mounting his horse, he slipped out of the gate and made off to his not distant home. Later he returned, bringing an eagle, and on the morrow two more, one of which I purchased, besides giving him an enamelled tea-bottle like my own but better, as well as other presents I had promised, and which were richly deserved, for various services.

On Monday morning at eight, after bidding farewell to Chian-da-loya, to whom and his underlings I gave several presents—including the New Testament in Chinese—we left Muzart-Kurgan, and with it the Muzart-nin-su, which continues thence in a south-easterly direction till it joins the Tarim on its way to Lob-Nor.

Our route to Aksu lay to the south or a little west of south, across a tableland, unlike anything I have seen elsewhere, in that its surface was of bare earth in parallel ridges undulating with the regularity of low waves of the ocean, presenting, in fact, the appearance of an earthen sea.

I have sometimes heard the spiral dust columns raised by wind called "sand devils"; and if there is any truth in Dr Beale's suggestion that these, or something of this character, are what Hiuen Tsiang intended by "dragons," then the Buddhist pilgrim might well have noticed them among the terrors of the locality, for I counted no less than 15 of these spouts whirling about at the same time, and that on a not very windy day. It may well be, therefore, that the passage of this plateau, which took us five hours, is very trying in windy weather.

At ten o'clock we came to Kizil-Bulak, a small

hamlet of half-a-dozen mud huts, on the first of two small streams that unite to form the Auvat, and flow southward for about 90 miles from their confluence, to be absorbed in a sandy desert north of the Tarim.

Kizil-Bulak was surrounded with cultivation—of bearded wheat among other crops, but not yet ripe. Tor-jee, after galloping about with his butterfly net, brought me a few *lepidoptera*; but animal life was here scarce, and I fear that he got little refreshment for the inner man by visits to the people, who looked exceedingly poor.

Our horizon on the south was bounded by low, pointed hills, at which we arrived at one o'clock; and before descending out of sight of the spot whence we emerged from the mountains, I turned and took a magnetic bearing of the defile, and found it 358°, or about due north, after allowing 2 easterly variation. On mounting these pointed hills, we had before us, on the other side, another extraordinary geological formation, such as I do not remember to have seen elsewhere.

It consisted of comparatively lofty hills bounding the horizon on the south, whilst between us and them were hundreds of miniature mountains on a level below us, each of these little mountains being perfectly devoid of verdure and formed of highly-coloured clay, also furrowed from the top, presumably by the action of water, to such a degree that there was hardly a square yard of smooth surface visible. We were reminded at once of the Muzart glacier, only that the hummocks and inequalities were now of clay instead of ice.

Among this mass of hillocks we descended, following the bed of a wide but shallow stream, which, after much meandering, at last had to cut its way through the final counterfort of the Muz-Tag range, and in so doing laid bare a quantity of coppery earth and honeycombed rock.

We were picking our way somewhat gingerly, now by the side of, now across, this stream, as it emerged from a little gorge to join, if I remember rightly, the second and wide branch of the Auvat, when, on turning a corner, we met a Turki horseman, who addressed my people, and turned out to be a messenger, sent three days since from Aksu, by the native Russian *Aksakal*, to meet me with a present of fruit. This was deposited at the station a few hundred yards distant, called Awat, as pronounced, or, as it appears on the Russian map, Auvat.

Now I had feasted the previous day on partridges and the tough rooster of Chian-da-loya, but the wild apricots of Chapchal had never recurred. Imagine, then, our delight when, on reaching the station at four o'clock, we there found a whole sieveful of the most luscious nectarines, two sieves of apples, and a sackful of melons, to say nothing of a sieve of peaches spoiled through keeping.

As in the case of Tuprak, Auvat does not appear to have had a garrison in the time of Yakub Khan, but the two places served as residences for men attending to the administration of the picket postal service, and to caravans. The stations at both places were of similar construction.

We left Auvat at seven next morning. A few minutes after starting we emerged from the mountains at what might be called the end of the Muzart break or defile, which we had entered at Shattoo. The entire length Kostenko reckons at about 100 miles, and since the northern slope measures only 33 miles, he naturally argues that the southern is less steep, which is precisely what we found it. From Auvat, beyond the plain to the south, we could see a clump of trees, towards which we rode across another bare flat and stony expanse, but not furrowed in this instance with waves.

After crossing this desert, or *chul*, for four hours, we approached the oasis of Jam, a village of 130 houses, and surrounded with cultivation; where, on what would be with us "the village green," and beneath shady trees, we rested for an hour. We were now nearly 30 miles from the spot whence we emerged from the mountains, and had here perhaps our grandest distant view of the southern range of the Tian Shan. Beginning as far east as the town of Kurla, and running west, the range is first known, south of the Yulduz basin, as Kok-Teke; then as the Eshikbashi; beyond which follow the Khalik-Tau and the Muzart Mountains, the last of which we had just crossed.

A little west of Muzart rises the dominant mass of the whole Tian Shan system, known as the Khan Tengri group, which, though exceeded in height, as Réclus remarks, by some of the Trans-Alai peaks, yet contains a greater number of snowy crests, glaciers, and streams flowing to the four points of the compass.

Here the monarch of the mountains, known as Khan Tengri, raises his head in lofty grandeur, far above the surrounding peaks, to an altitude, according to my Russian map, of 24,000 feet, though Walker's map (probably in error, since his information on this part of the country is presumably taken from Russian sources) gives only 21,000 feet.*

Our distance at Jam from the peak being, according to my Russian map, about 80 miles, we could, of course, distinguish very little. I say "of course" in reference to an individual peak; for not only could we see the outline of the range from Jam, but a few days afterwards we did so from Sai-Aryk, where on a clear morning my attention was called to the appearance of the Tian Shan, and a suggestion made as to why they were called "The Heavenly Mountains."

Above the range was the deep blue sky, and an azure mist hid its base, so that its snowy peaks floated like clouds in mid-air. I could scarcely believe that the unaided eye could have seen so far, and I tried to obtain a photograph, but in vain, for though the picture gives well enough the details of the foreground, nothing can be seen of the celestial mountains, which the map shows to have been 110 miles off.†

The only souvenirs that I possess of the Khan Tengri Mountains are photographs of two sketches by a Russian artist of two gorges through which flow the upper waters of the rivers Kokjar and Karkara. These streams, which appear to be very rapid, push their way through extremely rugged rocks, indicated by

* According to Shepeleff's calculation, made by compass from one of the northern elevations of the Muz-Tag range, about four miles from the entrance to the Muzart defile, he found the position of Khan Tengri to be about 15 miles south and 26 west of the Muzart Pass.

† The snow-line in this portion of the Tian Shan is 15,000 feet above the sea. In the northern ramifications of the system, as the Jungar Ala-Tau, it is about 10,000 feet; on the 43rd parallel of latitude generally, 11,000 feet; and in the Alai, Turkistan, and Zarafshan groups, more than 14,000 on the northern slopes; whilst still farther south, in the Hissar groups and the Mountains of the Pamir, it is found at a height of upwards of 15,000 feet.

Mushketoff's map to be of the Tertiary system, and so make their way over, one or both of them, into the Charin.

West of the Muzart is a world of crests and glaciers. Some of the latter, especially that of the source of the Sary-jassy, a tributary of the Tarim, are comparable, Réclus says, in length to the Aletsch glacier in the Valais Alps, and this I am told is about 15 miles long.

From the Muzart to the western extremity of the Sary-jassy Mountains the snowy range for 60 miles has a mean elevation of upwards of 16,500 feet, all the peaks overtopping Mont Blanc by at least 3,000 feet.

Still farther west the range, under the name of Kok-shaal, maintains a mean altitude of more than 15,000 feet, with summits rising 2,000 feet higher, and so continues in a south-westerly direction till it joins the Pamirs.

After reposing at Jam we continued our journey, crossing the river Jai-tugrak-ustang, which after a course of nearly 100 miles runs into the sandy waste alluded to on the north bank of the Tarim. Other streams which we crossed do not run so far even as that, but are quickly exhausted by irrigation or evaporation near the localities where they rise. Several aquatic birds were flying about the river at Jam, and my gun brought me specimens which Tor-jee was ready to go through fire and water to pick up.

The next inhabited point arrived at was Tash-Lianger, to the suburbs of which, southwards, we were brought to spend the night in a house in a garden of melons. My room was small, but comfortably furnished with carpets and quilts, the spare number of which appeared to indicate an owner in easy circumstances; but the room had the drawback of being lighted only through a hole in the roof.

The caravan arrived at two o'clock, after a march of seven hours, and had to report a death in the family. Joseph had come to me at Jam to say that the horse I have already alluded to at Kuldja as being weak was ill, and would eat no barley. A consultation of horse-doctors was held, whereupon both Osman and Monkey-face pronounced that the sick animal's nose must be cut to let blood, which was accordingly done, but not to much purpose; for after crossing a long stretch of desert in the stifling plain north of Jam the poor creature dropped.

The old mullah was left by its side to see if it would recover, and if not to hear its dying speech and confession, which were, I believe, to the effect that the heat of the plains, following on the toils of the glacier, had proved too much for it—a result reminding one of Shepeleff's experience on the glacier with his horses, or rather mares, which all prematurely cast their young.

Nor was this our only loss. Our dog "Kuldja," purchased at Chapchal, was led by a string up the Tekes valley, lest he should go back to his Kalmuk home, and he ran well at first. By the time we reached the Muzart stream he had discovered that his new owner could feed him quite as well, to say the least, as his old one, and he followed without being led.

He was, however, very timid, and appeared to consider no one as a friend but Joseph and myself. When, therefore, at Toghri-su, where he arrived tired, he was suddenly roused out of a snooze by a horrid cry some of the men made in playing, he jumped up, and, seeing neither of his friends, bolted off to such a distance in the mountains that we feared he was lost.

Allured back by Joseph, he got across the glacier

pretty well, though he had to be carried, as I have said, over the Southern Muzart. But when we exchanged the cool air of the mountains for the heat of the plains, where the maximum temperature at night was 99°,* he too, like the horse, succumbed.

Meanwhile the messenger who had brought me the fruit went back from Jam to herald my approach to his master, Madamin Bai, Russianised into Madamin Alim Baieff, who during the night came out from Aksu, bringing delicious grapes and other fruit.

He had received a letter, he said, from M. Petrovosky, the Russian Consul at Kashgar, asking him to help me, and he was come out to do us honour. Accordingly, he and his attendants set out with our

* RECORD OF THERMOMETRICAL OBSERVATIONS BETWEEN KULDJA AND AKSU.

Date.	Locality.	Hour.	At time of Reading.	Maximum during Night.	& Minimum during Night.
1888					
July 27	Kuldja, in tent	4.15 a.m.	70	—	—
,, 28	Ghaljat ,,	4.0 ,,	—	80	68
,, 29	Chapchal gorge, in tent	9.0 ,,	—	73	57
,, ,,	,, ,, ,,	6.30 p.m.	73	—	—
,, 30	,, ,, ,,	4.30 a.m.	—	65	58
,, ,,	Booghru ,,	6.0 p.m.	65	—	—
,, 31	,, ,,	5.0 a.m.	—	65	48
Aug. 1	Khanakai ,,	6.0 ,,	—	64	53
,, 2	,, ,,	4.0 ,,	—	55	43
,, 3	Geelan ,,	4.30 ,,	—	62	52
,, 4	Tekes Picket ,,	5.0 ,,	—	57	44
,, 5	Shattoo ,,	9.0 ,,	—	70	49
,, ,,	,, ,,	5.0 p.m.	—	80 (during the day)	—
,, 6	,, ,,	5.0 a.m.	—	63	49
,, 7	Udungei ,,	4.30 ,,	—	59	43
,, 8	Toghri-su ,,	3.0 ,,	—	52	42
,, 9	Tamgha-tash ,,	—	—	—	—
,, 10	Kailek, window-sill	—	—	65	61
,, 11	Tuprak, verandah	5.0 a.m.	—	65	55
,, 12	Muzart-Kurgan, window-sill	8.0 ,,	—	71	60
,, 13	,, ,, ,,	5.30 ,,	—	73	58
,, 14	Auval ,,	5.30 ,,	—	99	69
,, 15	Tash-Lianger, door-sill	—	—	—	77
,, 16	Aksu, verandah	—	—	—	74

caravan at seven o'clock, and in two hours we approached some houses at a place they called Shlengir, where, to my surprise, was awaiting me a deputation of a dozen white-turbaned Afghans and Andijanis, all of them mounted and ready to escort us into Aksu.*
But before proceeding we had to turn aside for a

---

* Of distances between Muzart-Kurgan and Aksu I have four estimates.
  1. Chian-da-loya gave it as 300 *li*, or 104 miles.
  2. The Russian *Aksakal*, Madamin Bai, gave it:—
     Muzart-Kurgan to Auvat . . . . 5 *tash* or *farsang*.
     Auvat to Jam . . . 4 ,,   ,,
     Jam to Lianger . . 1 ,,   ,,
     Lianger to Shlengir . 1 ,,   ,,
     Shlengir to Aksu . 2 ,,   ,,

     13 *tash*, or (at 20 *li* to the *tash*) 260 *li*, or 90 miles.

  3. Kostenko's (or rather Shepeleff's) distances, supplied from native information, are:—
     Tamgha-tash to Kailek . . 12 *versts*.
     Kailek to Tuprak . . . 15 ,,
     Tuprak to Muzart-Kurgan . . 32 ,,

     59 *versts*, or 29 miles.

(We took from Tamgha-tash to Muzart-Kurgan 21 hours, or, at three miles an hour, 63 miles, which I think to be nearer the mark.)

     Muzart-Kurgan to Kizil-Bulak 14 *versts*.
     Kizil-Bulak to Auvat . . . 12 ,,
     Auvat to Jam . . . . . 35 ,,
     Jam to Kent-Shlentchi . . . 20 ,,
     Kent-Shlentchi to Tash-Lianger Serai . 18 ,,
     Tash-Lianger to Aksu . . . 22 ,,

     121 *versts*, or 81 miles.

  4. We took from Muzart-Kurgan to Aksu 19 hours, or 57 miles. Thus Kostenko's distance from Muzart Picket (Shattoo) to Aksu is 177 miles, and ours 63 hours, or 189 miles.
  Finally, Kostenko's distance from Kuldja to Aksu is 311 miles, and ours 117 hours of travel, or 351 miles.

feast they had prepared of a slaughtered sheep, under shady trees, near sparkling rills, with further abundance of the fruit of the land. Here we quaffed tea as we lay on carpets, and those who had not breakfasted early, as I had already done, did ample justice to the viands. Conversation also flowed apace, and if any one was not at his ease, perhaps it was Osman Bai, for Madamin Bai was one of his chief creditors, and my caravan *bashi* was walking like a lamb into the mouth of the lion.

I had a letter, however, to Madamin Bai containing some very straight hints on this subject from the Consulate at Kuldja. He was "to give full assistance to the bearer of this letter, to find for him a suitable lodging in the town, or perhaps in his own house" (the Sarts, I heard, had inns at Aksu, but not the Chinese or Russians), "also to seek for Dr Lansdell a trustworthy *arbakesh* or carter at moderate cost, and on no account, under pain of expulsion, or perhaps exile, to hinder Osman Bai, the bearer's caravan *bashi*, since the Russian Government had given to Dr Lansdell full protection."

I thought Osman Bai looked rather sheepish when he went up to shake hands with a crowd of his old acquaintances from Aksu, where, I suppose, he had long been "wanted," but for the present all was peace.

I was considerably at a loss to know what could be the meaning of all this unexpected fuss made about me by the Afghan traders of the town, and on broaching the subject they said they had similarly gone out, not long before, to meet two others of my countrymen—namely, Mr Carey and Lieutenant Younghusband—each of whom they said had stayed in Aksu for three days, Colonel Bell also having stayed there.

NEARING AKSU—TEA BY THE WAY.

The action of the Turkis, who were Russian subjects, was not so hard to understand, and they informed me that for a traveller to come, heralded by two Russian Consuls, from Kashgar and Kuldja, was an event that did not happen twice in a century, and they therefore felt bound to do for me all they could.

Accordingly, after the feast, they all formed, or wished to form, in procession before me, which had the not trifling inconvenience of covering me with a cloud of dust, from which I insisted upon escaping, and riding at the head of the force. In this fashion we continued for two hours, Joseph talking hard with the column of horsemen, who had fifty questions to ask concerning his master, and all he intended to do.

Thus we approached the enormous cemeteries on the top of the bluff that overhangs Aksu. Having descended this bluff, our company was conducted through the streets between astonished and gaping crowds to the house of Madamin Bai.

CHAPTER XXI.

CHINESE TURKISTAN.

Chinese Turkistan; its boundaries and varying names, 318.—The Sin Kiang, or New Frontier; its eastern boundary and latest cartography, 319.—Its dimensions, mountains, rivers, and lakes, 320.—Surface and communications, 322.—The country described as approached from Peking by northern route, and by southern route, to Hami, 323.—Hami; its history, European visitors, and present condition, 326.—Roads from Hami to Kobdo, Barkul, and Guchen, 329.—Urumtsi; its history and situation as headquarters town of the Sin Kiang, 330.—Route *via* Toksun to Pishan and Turfan, 333.—History of Turfan; its sacred mountain and latest European visitors, 334.—Karashar and its Kalmuks, 337.—Kurla, Kuchar, and Bai, 338.

I HAVE glanced already at those portions of extramural China known as Manchuria, Mongolia, and Sungaria. I purpose now to treat of that portion of Chinese Central Asia which consists of a horseshoe depression bounded by the Tian Shan, Kuen Lun, and Pamir Mountains on the north, south, and west respectively, but lying open to the Gobi desert on the east.

The name of this region has varied much and often among Europeans, Mongols, Turks, and Chinese. Along the south of the valley ran the great "silk route" 2,000 years ago, but without bequeathing to us any particular name for this portion of the "land of the Seres." In the first map of the region, made by Rénat, the word "Cottoner" figures conspicuously, with the information that the people of Khotan were then subject to the Kalmuks; but Réclus observes that "the kingdom of Khotan" fell into disuse after the city of that name had ceased to be the capital. A century ago the territory was thought to be a part of the vast "plateau of Tartary," then supposed to occupy the interior of the continent, whilst in some maps of that period it figured as "Little Bokhara." Twenty years ago, during the insurrection of Yakub Khan, it was called "Kashgaria," which was for a time its current name in Europe; but the Turki natives spoke of the country as Alti-shahr (or six cities), an expression afterwards replaced by Jiti-shahr (or seven cities). Other two names, still in vogue and applicable, are Eastern Turkistan—to distinguish it from the land of the Turks west of the Tian Shan—and Chinese Turkistan, which I prefer, as differentiating it from Russian Turkistan, and what some writers have called Afghan Turkistan.

The Chinese appear to have formerly spoken of the country in general as part of Ili in its widest sense, and more particularly under the appellation of Tian Shan Nan-lu, or Southern Tian Shan route, as opposed to the Tian Shan Pe-lu, or Northern Tian Shan route of Sungaria; but on the recovery of the country from Yakub Khan, a new name was given to the territory, including Sungaria and Chinese Turkistan. Accordingly, when, in 1882, I received from the Chinese Legation a letter of commendation, it was said to be to the Governor-General of Sin Kiang, or the New Province, or Frontier.

It is not easy to get authorised information of the exact limits of Sin Kiang eastwards. Old maps represent Kansu, the north-west province of China proper, as projecting like a tongue across the Gobi, and continuing north of the Tian Shan to the frontier. The last edition of Stanford's map of Asia, recently published, does away with this "tongue" altogether, and draws the eastern boundary of the Sin Kiang, beginning at the Altyn Tagh Mountains, midway between Lob-Nor and Sachu, to the Kuruk Tagh hills, about 100 miles north of that town, and then running eastwards along a continuation of these hills, called Chukum Shan, to the meridian of Kan-chow. Further, it follows the old border of Kansu without-the-wall, proceeding north-westwards to the hills north of Barkul; then it strikes northwards to the Great Altai chain, which forms the northern watershed of the Black Irtish, and runs along that chain to the Russian frontier. Mr Littledale tells me, however, that, when he was camping in Sungaria, a Chinese official, from Chuguchak, on his way to Peking, told him that the Black Irtish is the frontier between the Chuguchak and Kobdo divisions. Accordingly, the dividing line in this region should probably be drawn along the Upper Irtish and Urungu rivers, instead of along the crest of the Great Altai chain.

I happen to know that this new piece of map-making is based on information given by a recent traveller, and that the frontier thus indicated must be regarded as delimited by the plenipotentiaries of the map-room, rather than by the Chinese Government, from whose representatives in London I could get no detailed information. I believe Stanford's map, however, to be accurate, the south-eastern border of Chinese Turkistan having the Gobi on the east, and on the south a portion of Kansu beyond-the-wall. Thus it appears that the new province of Sin Kiang takes in the whole of what

I have called Sungaria, the Ili valley, the part of Kansu formerly north of the Gobi, and the depression we are now speaking of, which last I shall continue to call Chinese Turkistan. Mr Bolton (geographer to Mr Stanford), after careful calculation, gives me the area of the Sin Kiang as 611,840, or, say, 612,000 square miles—the size, that is, of France, Austria, and the British possessions in Europe.

Taking the extreme length of Chinese Turkistan on the 40th parallel as lying between the 74th and 100th meridians, it stretches about 1,500 miles from west to east; whilst from the Muzart Pass to the 36th parallel—the widest part from north to south—the 81st meridian measures 400 miles. Réclus estimates the area of Chinese Turkistan at 480,000, the *Encyclopædia Britannica* at 465,000 square miles—that is, about the size of France and Austria together.

There is probably no other valley in the world of equal extent possessing such an environment of lofty mountains of the first rank. Nevertheless, the depression itself is everywhere flat, unless account be taken of a ridge of hills called Mazar Tagh, north of Khotan, and an offshoot of the southern range of the Tian Shan, called, near Karashar, Kuruk Tagh, which continues east to Kansu. But, though flat, the valley is not low, but rather a high plain or plateau, varying from 3,250 feet above the sea-level at Lob-Nor to about 4,500 feet west and east at Kashgar and Ngansi.

Into this valley the encircling mountains pour numerous streams, not all of which reach the open plain. Enough, however, are gathered together to develop a considerable water system, the end of which is Lake Lob. The principal river is the Tarim, and hence the depression is sometimes called the Tarim valley or basin. This river is made up westward by the confluence of the Kashgar-daria and Yarkand-daria, and these give their names to towns through which they pass. After this, flowing east, the Tarim is joined by the Khotan river from the south, and a smaller stream, the Aksu, from the north, and flows onwards to Lob-Nor. Just before reaching that lake it receives another affluent from the south, called the Cherchen-daria, the only one of the Kuen Lun torrents, east of Khotan, that reaches the central depression. One more stream that tries to do so from farther east is the Bulundzir, the head-waters of which rise in the Nan Shan, or continuation of the Altyn Tagh eastwards, and after a total course of 300 miles, 200 of which is westwards towards Lob, the river is lost in the desert lake of Khala-chi. Besides these lakes may be mentioned three more to the north-west of Lob, near the skirts of the Tian Shan—namely, Bagratsh-Kul, Sari-Kamish, and Baba-Kul—as well as a salt lake or marsh near Barkul; whilst away towards Kansu are Lakes Khua-khaitsi (spotted lake) and Alak-chi, into which run small streams from the Nan Shan.

From the foregoing sketch of the hydrography of the country it will be readily understood that oases of verdure and fertility are found only along the skirts of the mountains, and even then in such places alone as are watered by descending streams. Hence the greater part of Chinese Turkistan is barren desert. Between Lob-Nor and the river Khotan stretches the vast Tarim desert, and between that and the Kuen Lun lies the desert—nearly as large as Great Britain —of Takla Makan. East of Lob-Nor are the sands of Kum Tagh, sometimes regarded as part of the Gobi, by which name, however, Réclus says the desert is unknown in Chinese Turkistan. The Gobi may therefore with greater propriety be said to begin somewhat farther east.

The lofty mountains shutting in the valley on three sides suggest its inaccessibility by ordinary roads from the north, west, or south; but from the east there is a road, practicable for carts, which leaves the western end of the Great Wall near Su-chow, and crosses the desert to the eastern extremity of the Tian Shan Mountains at Hami. Here the road bifurcates. The northern branch continues through Barkul, Urumtsi, and the towns on the northern slope of the mountains to Sungaria and Kuldja; the southern continues entirely round the Tarim valley, passing successively through the towns of Pishan, Turfan, Karashar, Kuchar, Aksu, Kashgar, Yengi Hissar, Yarkand, Khotan, and Keria. Beyond this point there was in ancient times a route passing south of Lob-Nor, probably over an easy pass of the Altyn Tagh, to Su-chow, but this route is now disused.

Besides the cart-road from the east, there are several bridle-paths whereby the valley can be approached from the other points of the compass. On the north Kuropatkin enumerates no less than 13 passes used by the traders crossing the Tian Shan and the Alai, all except one practicable in summer, whilst that over the Terek-davan, or "Poplar Pass," is open throughout the year. South of this, over the Pamirs, is a path connecting Badakshan with Yengi Hissar; whilst the Kuen Lun is crossed by paths converging on Yarkand; by others approaching Khotan and Keria (the last through Polu); and, finally, a little-known track northward from Lassa, after crossing the Kuen Lun and Altyn Tagh, descends to Lob-Nor.

I have mentioned already the advice given me before leaving England, that I should approach Chinese Turkistan from Peking; and for purposes of description I shall now do so. Regarding Hami as the first town to be approached, the traveller from the Chinese capital has a choice between two routes,—one called the Alashan route outside the Great Wall, occupying 12 days, to Kwei-hwa-cheng, and then by camels across the desert; the other route by a cart-road through Shansi, Shensi, and Kansu to the end of the Wall at Su-chow, and then across to Hami—a journey of 2,162 miles in 68 days.

By the Ala-shan route the traveller from Peking passes on the second day through the inner branch of the Great Wall at the Nankow Pass, and on the fourth day reaches the mountain frontier at Kalgan (whence start the caravans to Urga and Kiakhta), where is a station of American missionaries. Turning west from this route, he passes through the outer wall to a district of grassy steppes and Mongol tents, and in eight days reaches Kuei-hwa-cheng, or Kuku-Khoto. Here is a station of the China Inland Mission, where the traveller will receive a welcome.

From Kuei-hwa-cheng is a route to Uliassutai in the north-west, and another of 67 days to Barkul. By this second route our traveller passes, west of the former, along the skirts of the Hurka Hills to the farthest offshoots of the Great Altai Mountains, and then turns southwards, and circumvents the eastern end of the Tian Shan spurs, to Hami. The only Englishman who has travelled by this route to Hami is Captain Younghusband, who rode the distance of 1,255 miles from Kuei-hwa-cheng in 70 days.

The cart-road or southern route is easier, though

somewhat longer. The first 12 stages from Peking take the traveller through Pau-ting (Pao-ting-fu), the capital of Chi-li, across its alluvial plains, and over the hills separating it from the next province, before descending to Tai-yuen, the capital of Shansi. This is a town of some 50,000 inhabitants, where are stations of the China Inland Mission, a Baptist Mission, and a Roman bishop and cathedral, the last claiming to have 600 adherents in the city and 18,000 in Shansi.

The next 13 stages bring the traveller to Singan, the capital of Shensi, founded B.C. 1122, and for 2,000 years the capital of China. Its population is stated to be 1,000,000, including 50,000 Muhammadans. It is the most populous of Chinese cities after Peking and Canton. Another 12 stages cover the journey from Singan to Lan-chow, over a hilly road at from 6,000 to 7,000 feet in altitude, through a depopulated country, with villages destroyed during the 17 years of Muhammadan rebellion. Lan-chow is said to have 40,000 houses. The Roman Catholics in the city number 80, in the neighbourhood 200, and in the province of Kansu 2,400. The China Inland Mission also maintains a station here.

From Lan-chow extends, in a north-westerly direction, for some hundreds of miles, but sometimes no more than a few miles wide, a remarkable depression or channel, between the Kuen Lun Mountains on the west, and the sandy plain of the Gobi on the east. This lengthy portion of country throughout is level and has much fertile ground, its western end being the outlet whence to cross Mongolia to Central Asia. Along this channel from Lan-chow are 16 stages through Liang-chow and Kan-chow to Su-chow.

Liang-chow is a walled town of from 20,000 to 30,000 inhabitants, and it is the advanced post in this direction of the China Inland Mission. Here, too, is a Lazarite bishopric, established in 1879, with adherents round the city, it is said, of 600 persons, and with stations at Kan-chow and along the Yellow River, in addition to the Mission I have previously referred to at Kuldja.

Formerly the administration of the Kansu province extended a variable distance along the Pe-lu and Nan-lu routes, with the towns settled on them; but now the traveller passes out of Kansu about 70 miles north of Ansi-fan at Shing-shing-she, and comes to the first halting-place in the Sin Kiang province at Iswa Chenza.

The journey from Su-chow to Hami is accomplished in 15 stages. At 18 miles from Su-chow is Kia-yu-kuan, a walled town and fortress standing in the channel referred to on a neck of land, and guarding the north-west entrance into the Empire, in much the same fashion, to judge from a sketch I have seen, that the Muzart-Kurgan, with its walls, stretches across the valley leading to the Ice Pass. The Great Wall circles round Kia-yu-kuan across the neck, and ends about ten miles distant. Six stages from Su-chow bring the traveller to Ansi-fan, or Ngansi, the residence of a *Tautai*, but a poor place of 400 or 500 houses, where stores are laid in for crossing the Shamo, or Gobi, which for 200 miles along the trade route is almost wholly desert. There are, however, all along the way stations consisting of a few huts and inns kept by Chinese; and water, though sometimes brackish, is plentiful everywhere. The road is of two cart-ruts six inches deep, generally over sandy gravel and sometimes over rock. The desert ceases on the last stage but one ; and the last stage, over a reedy grass prairie, brings the traveller to Hami.

Hami enjoys the respectable distinction of dating back to the first century, when, in A.D. 73, the Chinese took I-wu-lu, as it is first called, from the Hiung-nu, the ancient inhabitants of Mongolia, and established there military colonies. Some centuries later the oasis was occupied by Turkish tribes, but was again subjected by China, and under the T'ang dynasty of the seventh and eighth centuries its name was changed to I-chow. In the eleventh and twelfth centuries it belonged to the Uigurs, to whom probably Marco Polo alludes when he speaks of the inhabitants as idolaters " with a peculiar language." He calls the place by the Turkish name of Camul, or Kamul, changed by the Mongols to Khamil, or Khami. The Chinese annals mention that in 1289 the people of Ko-mi-li were afflicted with famine, and the Chinese Emperor ordered corn to be sent to them from Kansu.

The first European, probably, to come here was Marignolli in 1342, who stayed some time, and baptised a number of the natives. In 1420, when Shah Rukh's embassy passed through, they found a fine mosque and convent of dervishes side by side with a Buddhist temple. Before this the Ming Emperor Hung-wu had obtained the allegiance of the Uigurs, and received from the ruler of Hami, in 1403, a tribute of 190 horses ; and, in addition, the Chinese Government bought from the same source 4,710 horses. In 1406 a Chinese military station was established in the place. About 1472 Sultan Ali of Turfan captured and plundered the city, which for the next 40 years was alternately in the possession of the Chinese and Turfanese, till in 1513 the Sultan established his rule.

Hami depended on Turfan down to 1696, when the chief of Hami, Beg Abdullah, acknowledged the supremacy of the Emperor Kang-hi, of the present dynasty. In 1757 Hami was again administered from Kansu.

The next European traveller at Hami after Marignolli was Benedict Goes, in 1605. About a century later Jesuit missionaries, by order of the Emperor Kang-hi, determined by astronomical observations the position of the place. From this date for a century and a half these regions were closed against Europeans. In 1873 appeared in the Proceedings of the Russian Geographical Society an account of Hami, compiled by M. Uspensky from little-known Chinese sources. The expedition of Sosnovsky travelled through Hami in 1875, as also did Potanin in 1877, and Prjevalsky, who spent five days there in 1879. No Englishman, however, seems to have visited Hami till Mr Carey's caravan arrived in 1886, to be followed next year by Colonel Bell and Captain Younghusband.

Prjevalsky gives the oasis as from eight to ten miles from east to west, and a little more from north to south. He describes the fertile soil as of clay and sand, producing wheat, millet, barley, maize, watermelons, pumpkins, grapes, and melons—the last being famous, and sent sometimes so far as Peking. The poppy also is grown. The present Hami is described as consisting of three quarters, two being Chinese and one Muhammadan, the last called Khamil. Khamil was founded 300 years ago. Of the Chinese quarters, Low-chen (Lao-cheng, old town) is only about 180 years old, and Sin-cheng (new town) is quite modern.

Coming from the south, Sin-cheng is first approached. It has walls of mud 20 feet high, a top width or *terre-plein* of 20 feet, with a loopholed parapet, and is regarded by the Chinese as a fortress. The deep moat is ten feet broad, and at the east and south gateways are ramps leading to the ramparts, the interior being taken up chiefly by Government offices, *yamens*, and barracks. There are said to be 1,000 Hunan soldiers in garrison. In Low-chen are 1,000 Chinese families, and in the Muhammadan town a fourth of that number. The shops in Low-chen are well stocked with goods, mostly Russian.

The Muhammadan city Khamil lies one mile to the south-west of Sin-cheng, the intervening space being occupied with gardens. It is surrounded by a dilapidated mud wall about 25 feet high, and inside are a number of huts built round inclosed yards. The kings of Hami lie under a mausoleum, the dome of which is covered with green-coloured tiles, but of poor quality and appearance. The tombs are elevated oblong structures. In addition to these, there are many buildings half-destroyed by war. Nevertheless, the town, shaded by large trees, is said to have a clean and comfortable appearance.

In the bazaar everything is dear except flour, which costs 4s. 6d. for 133 lbs. A sheep costs about the same; a draught pony from 30s. to 45s.; a cow 50s.; and a camel from £4 to £5; whilst beans or split peas for horses cost 3s. 6d. per cwt. The town is well supplied with coal; also firewood from the Tian Shan, 30 miles distant. Russian merchants established themselves here in 1881. They receive their goods from Moscow, Nijni-Novgorod, Omsk, and Tomsk two or three times a year, *via* Biisk and Kobdo, employing their own camels to bring cottons, hardware, sugar, soaps, candles, lamps, clocks, matches, vodka, and wines. All the outlying stations of China in this direction are said to be supplied by the Russians, there being three Russian shops at Kobdo, and at Uliassutai four; but nothing is exported from Hami to Russia.

The Chinese soldiers at Hami are reported to be unbearably impertinent and oppressive, sometimes taking what they want from the stores at their own price. Colonel Bell says the Chinese are behaving most foolishly in this respect, giving no protection or justice even to the Russian merchants. He himself met with great incivility here from the mandarins.

From Hami to Kobdo and Uliassutai there are camel tracks of 22 and 23 stages respectively, the route to Kuldja being 800 miles, and passing through Barkul, Guchen, and Urumtsi. Barkul is reached in three days, crossing the Tian Shan by its most easterly pass—an easy one, with an altitude of 9,000 feet. The road leads up a stony ravine, 150 yards wide, over indurated shales, the highest slopes of which are clothed with pine, larch, and juniper. The descent is steep, amidst clay hills, to an exceedingly rich valley, and so onwards to the Chinese lake Pa-li-kul, or Barkul, which is 5,300 feet above sea-level.

Barkul comprises both a Manchu and a Chinese city, the former occupied by 1,000 Manchu and 1,000 Chebing soldiers, or local militia. This is the garrison on paper; what it may be in reality is quite another matter. In the city are 1,100 Chinese families; 70 Dungans, or Chinese Muhammadans; but no Chentu, or Turks. The soldiers are under a Chen-shi-ting. The climate differs from that of Hami because on the north of the mountains rain frequently falls. The extent of cultivated land about Barkul is small, but must once have been much greater, to judge from the size of the ruined villages. The soil is very rich.

Cart-roads lead from Barkul northward to Uliassutai, and over the hills southward to Pishan and Turfan, whilst westward the road continues across the Lake Pa-li-kul basin and over hills branching out from the Tian Shan, with pasture and occasional ruined hamlets. At the ninth stage, and distant 240 miles from Hami, is Guchen, razed to the ground during the last rebellion. It is now a small place of trade occupied by 1,000 Chinese, 25 Manchu, and 40 Turki families, with a garrison of 500 Hunan braves and 500 local militia. The bullocks of the country are fine and numerous. In Guchen there are 100 shops. English cottons penetrate here from Tientsin, *via* Kwei-hwa-cheng and Han-kow, and, though dearer than Russian goods, are preferred by the Chinese as of superior quality. American cottons are also in good repute.

Four stages farther—408 miles from Hami—is Urumtsi. According to Klaproth, this place is the same as Pei-t'ing of the T'ang period. Thus it carries us back to the seventh century, when this district, with that of Barkul, became dependent (according to one Chinese source) on the Government of Kansu, till the Uigurs, forsaking their homes on the banks of the Orkhan, Tola, and Selenga, settled here, and called the place Bishbalik, which signifies, in Turkish, the "Pentapolis," or five cities; whence the country round was sometimes called Bishbali.

Thus, from the Si-pei-ti, or Mongol-Chinese mediæval map, we find that in 1278 Ba-sa-cha-li received a tiger tablet, investing him with authority to direct the military post-stations in Bie-shi-ba-li. In 1280 a commander of 10,000 was sent to guard the frontier at Bie-shi-ba-li. In the next year Prince A-dji-ghi requested that 30 new post-stations might be established between the town and the mountains ; and in 1284 he asked that two cities, lapsed to Khotan, might be restored to Bishbalik. In 1287 a Chinese military colony was established in the place.

The Ming Shi speaks of Bie-shi-ba-li as a great empire, bordered on the south by Khotan, north by the Oirati, west by Samarkand, and east by Karakhojo, near Turfan. This empire was that of the Jetes or Getes of Muhammadan authors, and the country was known in the west also as Moghulistan (not to be confounded with the country of the true Mongols, eastward). Moghulistan was ravaged by Timur in 1389. In 1418 the name of the kingdom was changed to I-li-ba-li, and its rulers sent tribute to China for some years afterwards. The Ming Geography describes the people of I-li-ba-li as nomads, living in tents, of fierce appearance, subsisting on flesh and *koumiss*, and dressed like the Oirats.

Bretschneider says that the Sungarian name of Urumtsi first appears in Chinese annals in 1717. After the Emperor K'ien-lung had conquered Sungaria, in the middle of the last century, the Chinese built, in 1765, a new city on eight hills, at a distance of three miles from Urumtsi. Here 3,000 Manchu were settled under the command of a Chinese general. In the days of Jinghiz, the great highway from Mongolia to Western Asia passed through Bishbalik. It is mentioned by Ye-lü Ch'u-ts'ai, who accompanied Jinghiz. King Hayton's route led also through it. In 1756 the Jesuit Father d'Arocha determined the astronomical position of the place ; and, in November 1879, Dr. A. Regel penetrated to it from Karakhojo. In 1887 the first Englishman, Mr Carey, arrived, and the year following came Colonel Bell, who gives the present Chinese appellation of the place, which I heard also in Kuldja, as Umiotza or Hung-miotza.

The present Urumtsi is a town rising from ruins. The district is poor and sparsely populated, and has no nomadic inhabitants. It contains a population of 20 Chinese and 1,000 Turki families, besides 1,000 Chinamen without their families. Its shops number 500, many of them kept by men from Hunan. Excellent coal and natural coke is brought from the hills, and fetches from 6s. 9d. to 11s. 3d. per 1,333 lbs., or about 11s. to 18s. a ton. Iron costs 43s. 6d. per cwt. It is not found here, but is brought from Kwei-hwa-cheng. M. Grum-Grjimailo speaks of Urumtsi as producing nothing but corn and the poppy. Nearly every kind of food has to be imported, including rice, grapes, and other fruit. The people of Urumtsi have not even cattle of their own. The animals are all driven hither by Kirghese. Kalmuks, he says, are not allowed to trade, and Kirghese are suffered to pasture their cattle only on the way to market, Russian subjects being under like disabilities. There are said to be in Urumtsi and the neighbouring nine or ten small towns 20,000 soldiers, but some think this probably includes the total number from Hami to Kuldja. I heard at Kuldja of much discontent among the troops in Sungaria, and I have since learned from M. de Deken that, their pay being six months in arrear, they revolted and completely destroyed Chuguchak, nor did he know in 1892 whether the barracks had been rebuilt.

Urumtsi is the headquarters town of Sin Kiang, or New Province. The Governor-General lives there. Under his authority are the *Tautais* of Aksu and Kashgar, as well as the *Tsian-Tsiun* of Suiting and the *Tutung* of Chuguchak. Hence, M. de Deken told me, in 1892, there had been recently placed in Suiting and Chuguchak Chinese generals, who command the Chinese troops, leaving it to the Manchu authorities to command the Manchu, Solon, Sibo, and Kalmuk forces. The Chinese generals are from Yunnan, and recognise no authority but that of Urumtsi. The late Liu Joshive, as Mr Carey called him (or Lu-ko-sai, according to Bell), enjoyed the *prestige* of having regained the province for the Chinese in 1878. If I am not mistaken, he had charge of the province for the rest of his life, and Carey speaks of him as popular with all classes. With him lived two *Miah-tai*, four *Tautai* (or generals), and three *Tutung* mandarins. M. Grum-Grjimailo in 1890 speaks of the Governor-General as Fan-tek.

The town, with a side of 1,000 yards, has been remodelled. Old walls have been thrown down and new ones built, or the old, where retained, thickened to a top-width of 24 feet. They are of well-rammed mud, 15 feet high, the gates being of wood, six inches thick, faced with thin iron. The town is situated in an undulating valley from five to seven miles broad, and, as it is commanded by hills approaching to within 1,500 yards, would be at the mercy of artillery.

The valley runs up into the Tian Shan, the foot hills of which form a minor watershed on the south, whilst a broad river-bed skirts the downs westward. Urumtsi, being situated on the northern road from Sungaria to China, and commanding the southern road to Kashgar, must always be an important post. To join this southern road, the Tian Shan is crossed to Toksun, 103 miles distant, on the way from Hami, *via* Pishan and Turfan.

Pishan is on the ninth stage from Hami, situated in a rich oasis ten miles long by three broad, with numerous hamlets, the town itself being inclosed within mud walls 25 feet high and 400 yards in length on each side. The one street has a few good shops in it. There are only 100 men in the garrison, but there are an additional 200 men in a fort at Shigatai, 30 miles eastward. Between Hami and Pishan the first three stages are over level country at the base of the Tian Shan, which for the most part is desert, but with oases at every ten or fifteen miles. These are covered with ruins of houses built by the Chinese army under General Tso-tsung-tang, who, on their way to meet the forces of Yakub Khan, settled down quietly for a season, cultivated the land, grew some corn, and then, reinforced, went forward to conquer. Remains of forts of this period are still to be seen, and occasionally a monument to a fallen Chinese officer. Pishan was claimed as the first frontier town of Kashgaria, under Yakub Khan. Fifty-five miles westward is Turfan.

Turfan is another of the towns of this region which has existed for many centuries. The Ming Shi mentions it, under the name of Kiao-ho-ch'eng (or "the city surrounded by a river"), as the capital of Ch'e-shi, a kingdom of the time of the Han dynasty, before the Christian era. For a while the name was changed, but it was restored under the Sung 960—1127. The country was then occupied by the Uigurs, who used to send tribute to China, and in 981 Wang Yen-te was sent by the Chinese emperor to Kao-ch'ang. The Mongol dynasty established here the headquarters of a corps of 10,000.

The name Tu-lu-fan appears first in Chinese annals under 1377, when the imperial troops are said to have ravaged the country to punish the ruler for plundering foreign embassies on their way to China. In 1406, the emperor having sent an embassy far westwards, the envoy on his way made a present of silk stuffs to the ruler of Tu-lu-fan, after which there followed return offerings from Turfan in subsequent years of jade, horses, and gyrfalcons. In the middle of the fifteenth century the ruler of Tu-lu-fan, becoming powerful, assumed the title of Wang, then that of Sultan, and seized Hami.

Turfan, since the fifteenth century, has been repeatedly visited by Muhammadan and Christian travellers. We hear of it in connection with Shah Rukh (whose embassy found there a Buddhist temple) and Haji Muhammad. Benedict Goes stayed in it for a month, and Father d'Espinha went there for surveying purposes, after which Chinese Turkistan was closed to Europeans. Dr A. Regel visited Turfan in 1879, and Carey, Bell, and Younghusband in 1887-8. The latest European travellers are the brothers Grum-Grjimailo, who, in 1890, explored the Bogdo Mountains, visited the sites of former Uigur towns, and penetrated the desert south of Turfan.

The Bogdo Mountains north-west of Turfan are mentioned very far back in Chinese literature. In the Ming Geography the rocks of Ling Shan, or the mysterious mountain, are said to show veins like hair, and the Sung History says that the interior of the mountain contains sal-ammoniac. "Inside there is a perpetual fire, and the smoke sent out of it never ceases. In the evening the flames issuing from it resemble torch-light. The bats also appear red." M. Grum-Grjimailo states that Bogdo-ola may be ascended by a fair road from Urumtsi.

The mountain is reckoned by the Mongols to be God's throne. The whole locality is sacred, and around it numerous temples have been erected. A notice, too, has been put up near the lake forbidding any one, under penalty of instant death, to violate the tranquillity of this holy land. There must be no shooting nor tree-cutting, nor any depasturing of cattle.*

At the present day, the oasis round Turfan is about eight miles long and four broad, to a considerable extent under cotton and wheat. Water is procured from wells, but irrigation is carried on chiefly by underground canals from springs at the foot of the hills. On nearing the place from the east the traveller passes through the ruins of an ancient town (destroyed, according to Regel, 400 years ago), with a large mosque or tomb and a minaret 200 feet high. There are two distinct towns about a mile apart, and both walled; the eastern one, 150 years old, being occupied by Chinese, the western by Turkis. The Chinese town has a population of 3,000 or 4,000, including perhaps from 800 to 1,000 soldiers. The four gateways of its square walls are defended by semicircular bastions. There are a few shops in the Chinese town, but most of the trade is carried on in the one street, a mile and a half long, of the Turki town. Younghusband describes the heat in July as intense, and says that the people, to avoid it, live by day in underground rooms. Around the town for miles are hundreds, if

---

* Compare with this the directions concerning Mount Sinai: "And thou shalt set bounds unto the people round about, saying, Take heed to yourselves, that ye go not up into the mount, or touch the border of it: whosoever toucheth the mount shall be surely put to death. There shall not a hand touch it, but he shall surely be stoned or shot through; whether it be beast or man, it shall not live" (Exod. xix. 12, 13).

not thousands, of open wells, some of them 100 feet deep, dug by the Chinese army when besieging Turfan during the late rebellion.

Ten miles distant from Turfan is Mazar, or a tomb locally noted as a place of Muhammadan pilgrimage, its houses and galleries being fastened apparently to the rock, and having a crypt. Dr Regel was shown there sundry banners, with Sart and Dungan inscriptions, and other curiosities.

Travelling westward, the next place of importance is Toksun, near which are located 200 Kalmuk families. The population of the town consists of 400 Turki, 200 Dungan, and about 15 Chinese families, besides a garrison of 250 cavalry and a like number of infantry. Yakub Khan held nothing securely east of Toksun, and Toksun may be regarded as the outpost of Karashar. It was also at one time the limit of the province of Kansu.

From Toksun to Karashar is about 145 miles, over country generally barren. For a great part of the distance the road runs through low hills. In winter there is considerable traffic in frozen fish, which are brought from Lake Bagratsh and carried to Urumtsi.

In the time of Timur, Karashar was called Jalish, and it was here that he divided among his troops the booty taken in ravaging Moghulistan. The ruins of the old town are still visible. The present town consists of 460 Dungan, 250 Turki, 100 Chinese, and 400 Kalmuk families, but there are in the vicinity from 1,000 to 2,000 Mongols, all Kalmuks. The town would seem to exist to supply their requirements, and as a strategic position. The country between it and Urumtsi—a heavy ten days' journey for carts—produces but little. Lob-Nor is ten days' journey distant in a south-easterly direction. Grass is found on the road, but water is scarce. The Karashar river near the town is about 200 yards wide in winter, and is crossed on the ice; but increases to 500 yards in summer, when a ferry-boat is poled across in half-an-hour. From Karashar there is a road leading over the Tian Shan by the Yulduz valley to Kuldja, 280 miles distant.

About 32 miles south-west from Karashar is Kurla, with a population of 2,000 Turki, 50 Dungan, and 10 Chinese families, ruled by a mandarin of low grade—a Wang. Beyond Kurla the road still runs through a country generally barren, though somewhat less so than farther east. At several of the halting-places are small patches of cultivation and a tiny bazaar. From Kurla, at a distance of 85 miles, is reached the large walled village of Yengi Hissar, of 800 Turki and 5 Chinese families. Bell computes the population of this oasis at 200 persons to the square mile, and considers that a fair estimate for the oases hereabouts. Twenty-one miles westward bring the traveller, through a barren country and little grass, to Bugur—a large oasis occupied by 1,500 Turki, 15 Dungan, and 8 Chinese families. It is locally famous for its manufacture of rugs. From this point, through Yaka-Arak, the road passes to Kuchar over small oases for the most part unoccupied.

Kuchar was anciently an important little principality and a flourishing seat of Buddhism. On a hill to the north are ruins of an ancient temple and monastery, where are found fragments of sculpture. Forsyth states that in certain rock-cut galleries are paintings of men and animals, still fresh and bright. A large figure also is said to exist here on the face of a rock overlooking the road to Kurla. It is described as having the tongue lolled out and the right shoulder depressed, with extended arms, as is the fashion of Kalmuk salutation, but neither Carey, Bell, nor Younghusband mentions it.

Kuchar is now a walled town in a rich oasis, occupied by 3,050 Turki, 1,200 Dungan, and 30 Chinese families, with 450 shops. This district is occupied by 7,000 Turki families. In the neighbouring hills copper ore in nodules is found in sand or sandy clay. Coal also is reported to be found in the hills. The town is garrisoned by 500 soldiers, who get 22*s*. 6*d*. a month and beans for their ponies, which are Government property. The soldiers find grass.

The only place of importance between Kuchar and Aksu is Bai, famous for the excellence of its dairy produce. In the district are 40,000 families, and in the town 1,100 Turki and 140 Dungan and Chinese families. Proceeding south-west from Bai, the road passes over sand-hills, and several streams are crossed before the traveller reaches our old acquaintance the Muzart-nin-su, which at the point of fording is 400 feet wide, rapid, and from two to three feet deep.

The road then passes through Jam (not the place of that name on the road from the Muzart), and onward to Aksu, where, as I have said, my party arrived on August 15th. Having thus given a general idea of the geography of Chinese Turkistan, and some account of the north-eastern portion of the country, which was not visited by me, I shall now proceed to speak of those portions through which I travelled.

CHAPTER XXII.

OUR STAY AT AKSU.

Aksu; its history and area, 340.—Our arrival and lodging, 341.—Intricacies of Chinese money; shoes, tengas, and cash, 343.—Visits from merchants; distribution of Scriptures, 345.—Reward offered for Dalgleish's murderer, 346.—Aksu bazaar, 347.—Riding round the town; its buildings, cemetery, and mode of burial, 348.—Repair of camera, 349.—Visit to Chinese Aksu; Reception of official visits, 351.—Inspection of prison, 352.—Preparations for departure, and payment to Osman Bai; Presents to Monkey-face and Tor-jee; Letters despatched to Kuldja, 354.—Cart-driver taken before the magistrate, 355.

AKSU is a place of considerable antiquity. According to Deguignes, it appears in the Chinese annals under the Han dynasty as early as the second century B.C. Sir Henry Yule thinks it to be the "Auxacia" mentioned in the second century A.D. in the geography of Ptolemy. Hiuen Tsiang, before crossing the Muzart Pass, stopped one night in the kingdom of Poh-luh-kia, as the eastern portion of Aksu in his day was called.

About the date of Timur's conquest of Moghulistan we read of Mirza Eskender besieging Aksu, which in 1399 is described as consisting of three castles, having communication one with another, and deemed by the inhabitants of the neighbouring provinces to be an asylum in time of war. Nevertheless, after several assaults in the course of 40 days, the defenders had to yield to the cogent arguments of the sapper and the battering-ram, and several rich Chinese came out of the place and offered presents.

At the beginning of the sixteenth century Aksu was ruled over by Sultan Ahmed Khan, whom his son Mansur succeeded and died A.D. 1545. Haji Muhammad (about 1550) mentions Aksu on the high road from China to Samarkand, and in 1604 Benedict Goes passed through Aksu from Yarkand, probably by the route recently followed in the reverse direction by Mr Carey, and later by Major Cumberland—that is, along the Yarkand river.

The Aksu district now extends east to within two marches of Bai, and west to within three of Maralbashi. It contains about a dozen villages, and is said to have a population of 180,000 souls. Our party approached Aksu, as I have said, from the north along the top of a cliff, from the edge of which the town below came suddenly into view. We descended into the town by a ten-foot gully, on a gradient of one in ten, and passed through narrow streets barred by four gates and shut off by palisades into quarters, as at Kuldja—a precautionary arrangement, I was told, in view of possible insurrection.

On reaching the premises of Madamin Bai, they were found to be large and commodious, with plenty of stable accommodation, or rather standing room, for my horses. My host's reception room, too, was large and lofty, whilst to me was given his wife's apartments, that lady having taken her departure for a season. I was thankful indeed to have once more a tolerably comfortable dwelling, and celebrated the occasion on the first night by taking a whole 12 hours in bed. After this I rose refreshed, and, breakfast over, proceeded to master the intricacies of Chinese money-changing.

I have said that I purchased at Jarkend for 1,160 roubles a *pood*, or 36 lbs avoirdupois, of *yamb*-silver. This was given me at Suiting in several large " shoes," or lumps bigger than a closed fist, commonly spoken of as 50 *liang* each, and still smaller " shoes," the rest being made up of half-shoes, quarter-shoes, and odd pieces (I suppose "toes," "heels," and "uppers"!), of various shapes and sizes.

Furthermore, at Kuldja a miniature balance or steel-yard of wood was obtained, about 12 inches long, with a pan slung from one end, and at the other a scale indicated by dots, whence to suspend a piece of brass according to the weight required. One *liang*, it was said, was equal to ten *chian*, and each *chian* to ten *ping*, but all differing according to whether small, medium, or large scales were used. The custom on this point varied from place to place, whilst, by way of nicely mixing up Russian, Chinese, and English ideas, it was explained that in a Russian *pood* were 27 Chinese *jing*, which latter was about an English pound, the *jing* being divided into 16 *ser*, or the approximate equivalent of an English ounce.*

So long as payments were of large amount, as when I paid Osman Bai 35 *liang* of silver, all was tolerably simple. A few pieces were found of the right weight, which he received without question, and there ended

* Thus provided and instructed, I was to go to market, as did, I suppose, the patriarch Abraham, when he went shopping in Damascus, or when he " weighed to Ephron the silver which he had named in the audience of the children of Heth, four hundred shekels of silver, current money with the merchant " (Gen. xxiii. 16).

the matter. But when payment for small purchases was required, then commenced such a complicated business as I had never before experienced.*

The people of Aksu do not, in the case of small purchases, speak of fractions of a *liang*, but of *tengas* (a Turkish silver coin) and of Chinese *chakra* or *dah-chan*, better known in China proper as " cash," 25 cash being equal in reckoning to a *tenga*.†

The *chakra, dah-chan, sapek*, or cash is a round coin supposed to be of copper, but heavily alloyed, about the size of a farthing, and with a square hole in the centre to allow of its being threaded on a string. Five hundred of these coins were at Aksu equivalent to a *liang* at par. On the day of my arrival the *Aksakal* said he could give me 488 (or for each paper rouble 178), but a day or two later the price had fallen to

* The *pood* of silver was said at Jarkend to contain 440 *ser* or *liang*, the same, I presume, as the *tael* of Peking; but at Aksu they said that now the *pood* was reckoned at only 432. I was further informed, with delightful lack of precision, that in a *liang* were about two *soom*, that each *soom* was equivalent to 250 *chakra*, and each *chakra* to two *puls*, the last an obsolete coin, of which I remember seeing a specimen, I think, in Khiva.

† I say in reckoning, because the *tenga* is now only a coin of account. Yakub Khan minted a number of these coins, resembling those of Khokand and Bokhara, with a fixed value in Kashgaria, and passing in Russian territory for 20 *kopecks* each. However, on the arrival of a new Chinese Governor at Kashgar, he upset the market (and everybody in it) by proscribing the *tenga* and annulling its fixed value. Hence my "white *tengas*," of which I had purchased a small stock in Kuldja, I found at Aksu to be worth only their weight as silver, and that not pure silver, since alloy had been added, and a great many of the coins, it was said, were counterfeit. To make matters still more complicated, the Kashgar merchants having melted down their *tengas* into *yambs*, which not being of pure metal like the old, there was thrown on the market more than one quality of *yamb*, thus affording ample room for higgling as to how many *chakra* should be given for a *liang* of "old" or "new" silver. Of all this I knew nothing when receiving my *pood* of *yambs*, but accepted what was offered, supposing each fragment to be alike good.

475, and subsequently in a different locality to as little as 350.

Now, as I started with English money, and my accounts would have to be translated, roughly at all events, back into English, the reader will perceive that matters stood thus:—With English pounds were purchased roubles in London, St Petersburg, and Tiflis at a different price in each. At Jarkend roubles were turned into lumps of silver, of value differing according to their standard of purity. This silver purchased "cash" at prices varying from 475 to 350 to the ounce, after which what mathematician would undertake to state exactly in £ s. d. the price of an article purchased?

To me, who love exactness in accounts, and enter every penny spent, the puzzle fairly made my head swim, and the only way seemed to be to keep separate the accounts paid in silver, the small expenses in two columns of *tengas* and cash, and then envy the auditor who had to subscribe "Examined and found correct."

Nor was keeping accounts the only difficulty, for on sending to the bazaar for small change to the value of 10 *liang* (or about £2) there were brought 4,750 coins on the back of a donkey! Subsequently, in Peking, this *embarras de richesses* was still worse, where 10 *taels* brought nearly 30,000 cash; but at Aksu copper was scarce, and warning was given that at Kashgar the *liang* would bring less than 475 *chakra*.

"Better, then," I said, "to buy some more here?"

But that raised two other questions: first, would any one in the bazaar have so much change? and, next, would the taking so much money to Kashgar affect the rate of exchange there? Were I a native merchant, they said, I certainly should not be allowed to do it; but since I was a foreigner, and my baggage not subject to examination at the intervening Custom-houses, I might smuggle the money through; and this I believe was done surreptitiously by one of the party who travelled under my shadow.

For my own part, fearing that we should not have sufficient small money for the road, I sent, on the morning of our departure, for the value of ten *liang* of cash more, but was told, rightly or wrongly, that inquiry had been made in all directions, but that no one in the bazaar possessed so much!

As may be surmised, these transactions did not inspire me with lofty ideas of the wealth of the merchant princes of Aksu, who, nevertheless, did not delay to cultivate my further acquaintance. Not content with having escorted us into the town, the Afghans and other traders came next morning, early —I think before I was up—to pay me a formal call.

There are said to be about 100 foreign traders in Aksu, most of them Andijanis or Russian subjects, and some no doubt were killing two birds with one stone when calling first on their *Aksakal*, and then asking for his guest. I received and regaled them with sherbet, and, on casting about for their business with me, learned that it was the feast of Kurban-Bairam, when everybody called on everybody, and so I had been included.

They appeared extremely desirous to impress me favourably—why, I could not for a long time make out; but it occurred to me to make capital out of a return call on the Afghans, by seeking information as to the possibility of crossing the Baroghil Pass into Chitral, and trying to dispose of some of my Scriptures amongst them. And this I did successfully.

As for the Baroghil Pass, Gufur Khan, the Afghan *Aksakal*, informed us that the road was free from robbers, practicable in autumn or winter, but that a Wakhan tent would be needed. The Chief of Chitral, we were told, was Aman-el-Mulk, who could speak and read Persian.

Gufur Khan subsequently asked me for a letter of recommendation to all and sundry, thinking it might serve him, I suppose, on his journeys to India. I was uncharitable enough to suspect that this might explain in part the assiduity of his attentions, though he appears to have been attentive to Colonel Bell also.

Others suggested that since Mr Dalgleish had been murdered by an Afghan, the traders of that race here were afraid that they might lose the British favour and protection they had enjoyed in passing through Kashmir, and so were anxious to ingratiate themselves with me, seeking my protection in the form of a letter. But just then I was not in a very good humour with the Afghans, and Gufur Khan had served me in no recognised capacity; so that, although I did not think it politic to refuse his request, yet, not knowing what use he might make of the letter, I took care not to make it too laudatory.

During our stay notice came from the Russian Consul at Kashgar to the Russian *Aksakal* at Aksu that the Indian Government had offered a reward of 5,000 rupees for the arrest of Daud Muhammad Khan, the murderer of Dalgleish, and 3,000 more for a certain dervish supposed to be implicated in the murder. This notice the *Aksakal* received instructions to publish throughout the bazaar, and not to depend upon what the Chinese authorities might do; but he came to me first with the letter, and took counsel how he should act.

Daud Muhammad Khan, he said, had been in Aksu not many days previously—a fact known to the Afghan *Aksakal* and a few others. He had brought four horse-loads of what I understood to be indigo or blue, which was left in the care of certain traders, who, he thought, might afford a clue to the owner's whereabouts. Subsequent inquiry only elicited that he left for Ush-Turfan, and was now said to be in the mountains among the Kirghese.

On looking round the bazaar we saw exhibited for sale both English and Russian goods,—the English of fine muslin, though I do not remember much else ; and the Russian of cotton and chintzes, but everything looking poor.*

For ourselves we were able to secure a few objects of local make, such as ear- and finger-rings, and a sheep-skin-lined head-dress something like the shape of the pope's hat, or that seen in old pictures of the early Russian Czars. This was worn far and wide through Chinese Turkistan, but I do not remember to have seen it in Russian Turkistan.

We also obtained a woman's veil and bonnet, or rather hat, of a shape new to me, bulging out towards the top, and possibly the remote ancestor of some of the stiff crowns worn by European monarchs. To these must be added some specimens of local pottery and earthenware, and children's curiosities. Fruit was

---

* Twenty years ago Aksu was said to be celebrated for its manufactures of saddlery and harness, its pottery, raw hide, jars called *dabba*, for oil, butter, etc. Its tobacco also was considered the best in the country. All these, with cattle and the shawl-wool of Ush-Turfan, were exported to the neighbouring towns. Also, at a still earlier date, lead, copper, and sulphur mines were worked in the neighbouring mountains ; and coal, found in the hills (near Karabagh, where there are hot sulphur springs), was brought into the town.

plentiful and cheap everywhere. Nectarines, as luscious as one need desire, cost 2*d*. for 75, and grapes in proportion. Flour, ground by donkey- or water-power, cost five cash and three cash the catty, or, say, ½*d*. and ¼*d*. per lb.; rice, five cash the catty.

The bazaar was full of men and women, the latter not being in all cases veiled. Our foreign appearance attracted attention and collected a crowd, amongst which the Turkish element was respectful or timid. They rose to their feet; not so, however, the few Chinese we saw in the Turkish quarter.

Later on we took a ride round the town. It is said to contain 4,010 houses, some of them mounting up the sides of the surrounding cliffs. All were flat-roofed and low, presenting a poverty-stricken appearance. There are in the town 500 Chinese and 500 Dungan, or Chinese Muhammadan, families; the rest are Turkish.

Mounting to what was the fort, built by Yakub Khan in place of an old Chinese citadel, we obtained a good view of the place, with the river and adjacent gardens and rice-fields, the verdure of which was in striking contrast to the parched appearance of other portions of the landscape. The houses looked crowded together, one or two mosques only rising above the dull level of the earthen roofs.

In this place Yakub Beg had a small-arms workshop, manned chiefly by natives of the Panjab; but now all munitions of war come from China. The only buildings that invited attention were the tombs with domes, in the vast cemetery on top of the cliff. Some of them had inclosures entered by gateways. Besides these there was one good-looking mosque, and several mausoleums of considerable size.

We saw a body being borne to burial. Unlike the staid procession of the West, this is done at Aksu with a rush. At death the chin of the corpse is tied with a cloth, and the thumbs of the hands are tied together as well as the big toes. Then the body, after being washed and laid out, is buried within 24 hours, mullahs at the cemetery reading the Koran.*

After the rough experiences which my camera had gone through, as already recorded, I examined it with some anxiety. It had suffered little, and some glue quickly repaired the leather where it had been loosened by damp. This done, I secured a capital view of my host at home, seated beside his pots of flowers, and his *mirza* or clerk with my Chinese interpreter standing near the principal door, over the top of which was a window-lattice, covered as usual with paper, there being little or no window-glass in the country.†

I took early opportunity to send my card to the Chinese *Tautai*, or General, named Chen, whom I had heard of at Kuldja as Ji-li-ju, or *Commandant de district*. Of this, at first, no notice was taken, nor was it until the fifth day after my arrival, and

---

* No cooking is done in the house for three days, food being supplied by friends, and on the fourth day a feast is prepared for the mullahs who praise the dead. The women remain in the house for seven days. A widow mourns her husband 40 days, using his name in her prayers daily, and wears a black cloth over her shoulders. A widower wears a white waist cloth. A woman indicates her mourning for father or mother by covering the upper part of her head-dress with white cloth.

† Also I attempted a view of my host's gateway, which was a covered porch with an earthen bench, and on this, sitting with his haunches drawn up and head between his knees, was a poor little idiot boy, who, when fruit was offered, took it and grinned. Deserted alike by father and mother, the *Aksakal* allowed him by day to take refuge here " at his gate," where he was fed with crumbs that fell from the rich man's table, whilst at night he was locked up, generally in tears, in a shed near at hand.

after two subsequent messages, that this dignitary summoned me to an audience at the "Yengi Shahr," or New City, seven miles off.

The proper thing was to go in a Chinese cab or springless cart, which I did, taking with me Joseph and the interpreter into Chinese sent me by M. Petrovsky from Kashgar. This man wished to be nameless. Monkey-face and Tor-jee said that he spoke "English" Chinese, which they could not understand, but I hoped that between us all we should be able to manage.

On arriving, the *Tautai* sent to say that he had "lost his father," which I heard was sometimes a polite way of excusing oneself from a personal interview, and we saw his secretary instead, one perhaps of the three or more mandarins under the *Tautai*, whose jurisdiction extends from Karashar to Chilian.

Our reception was conducted with some ceremony. My name being announced, the great gates of the *yamen* were promptly thrown open, and we were conducted through a crowd, assembled *en fête* to witness a theatrical display. Passing by and beyond the canopied stage, where the players were acting, we were taken to an inner audience chamber, and regaled with tea and pudding, with variations.

I then opened business by asking that the two men who had accompanied me from the *Tsian-Tsiun* might be sent back to Kuldja; next, that two Chinese might be given me as an escort to Kashgar; and, lastly, that I might be allowed to visit the local prison. All these requests were granted, after which I asked acceptance by the *Tautai* of a Chinese New Testament and other Scriptures, and some large oleograph wall-pictures.

I also gave much the same to the secretary, and

proceeded to distribute to the people standing around some of my large illuminated text-cards, and smaller ones to the playgoers outside; the result of which was that, in the eagerness of the people to get them, we were speedily mobbed. The secretary, however, did the honours by accompanying me to my carriage, and bowing me away.

There is an old Chinese town, now deserted, near the Turkish quarter, but the present Chinese city of Aksu was only five years old at the time of my visit—built, it was said, by forced Turkish labour, on a subsistence allowance of six cash, or a halfpenny a day! During its construction several hundred men were reported to have died from accidental causes.*

On the morning after my audience a Chinese official called and confirmed yesterday's arrangements. He brought me from the *Tautai* a present of two sheep, two fowls, and a donkey-load of clover; but not, as one Englishman was treated to, a thousand of cash.

My pictures had evidently made an impression, for this envoy alluded to them very tenderly, asking whether some could be bought. I therefore gave him two, and also a Chinese New Testament. On the next day the *Tautai's* secretary called; but as he was so very polite as to come before I was up—that is, between four and five in the morning—I excused myself from receiving him.

* The town is about 1,000 yards square; the walls 20 feet thick and about 16 in height, with a musketry parapet 6 feet high and 3 thick. The projectures at the angles are from 40 to 50 feet long, those at the gates more than 150 feet. The ditch is from 30 to 40 feet wide, and shallow, but can be easily filled with water. On the east side is a suburb, but on the other sides the land was under cultivation. Within are large granaries, offices, and shops, kept for the most part by Chinese. The whole is intended as a place of refuge should there be another Turkish uprising.

On the afternoon of that day we went to visit the prison—"one of the most horrible I have ever entered," says my diary. The room that called forth this remark was a small one, into which 23 men were crowded, the only furniture in it being long wooden stocks, like those of Bokhara, to hold the prisoners' feet at night. The ventilation was by a hole in the roof, and the atmosphere was so close and hot that one could hardly breathe.

Several prisoners wore the *cangue*, or wooden frame about the neck, which Williams says "is considered rather a censure or reprimand than a punishment, and is supposed to carry no disgrace with it. The frame weighs between 20 and 30 lbs." (I think I have seen one heavier at Kiakhta), "and is made to rest upon the shoulders without chafing the neck, but is so broad as to prevent the person feeding himself" (unless provided, like my man at Kiakhta, with a long-handled wooden spoon). "The name, residence, and offence of the delinquent are written upon the *cangue* for the information of passers-by, and the culprit is usually exposed in a public place."

Besides the *cangue*, I saw at Aksu two instances in which a wooden post, 6 feet high and perhaps 18 inches round, was chained to a man's neck and ankle, so that, wherever he moved, this undesirable companion had to be carried with him. I distributed some *tengas* among the prisoners, and asked that they might be brought outside into the yard. I was then allowed to take several photographs, some of the poor wretches being almost without clothing, and all very miserable in appearance.

The feast of Kurban-Bairam kept me well supplied with visitors, three parties of Muhammadans calling

IN THE PRISON AT AKSU—METHODS OF PUNISHING THE PRISONERS.

upon us in one day, so that time did not hang on my hands, especially as preparations had to be made for starting afresh. After paying Osman Bai the balance due to him, it was arranged that he was to take us to Kashgar for 60 *liang* of silver, of which 35 were to be payable in advance; our transport expenses thus standing at about £12 from Kuldja to Aksu, and £13 from Aksu to Kashgar. He was to start on Tuesday, August 21st.

To Monkey-face and Tor-jee I gave sundry presents, both for men and womenkind, including needle-cases, buckles, hair-pins, besides Scriptures in all the languages they could command (and some they could not), photographs, flour for the way, two cups, an enamelled bottle, chain and compasses, pencils, and, finally, a watch and medal to each.

These medals were a happy thought when laying in suitable presents. They consisted of half-crowns, double florins, and crowns, all of them new Jubilee coins, with a hole (contrary to law, I fear), through which was passed a riband of imperial yellow. They were a great success, and enabled me to score off my friends the Russians.

"See," said Amin, the groom, "what excellent people the English are. You may serve the Russians a very long time before you get a medal, and here, after a few days' travel, is a man decorated for life!"

Nevertheless, Monkey-face did not seem perfectly happy, and, on parting, spoke fearfully as to whether and how the *Tautai*, who was not his master, would send him back. The face of Tor-jee, who had sold his watch for several roubles, was radiant.

The *Aksakal* was despatching a letter to the Russian Consul at Kuldja, so I took the opportunity to send one too, and put in a good word for my host at Aksu, who spared no pains to make us comfortable. I wrote also to the *Tsian-Tsiun* and Kah, saying how well their men had behaved.

We had then only one more difficulty to surmount. There was now to be added to our caravan an *arba* in which my interpreter had travelled from Kashgar, with a *mirza*, or writer, as servant. The *arbakesh*, or driver, had agreed at Kashgar to go to Aksu and back. The return journey was to cost 20 roubles, all of which he asked now in advance, pretending that he wanted to buy a new horse, but wishing, if I remember rightly, to hand over his job to some one else.

To this we objected, being willing to advance only half the money and to pay the rest on the man's return home. As he continued obstinate, my interpreter took him before the Chinese magistrate, who put the interpreter upon oath, by making him say his prayers, and then, having heard his statements, ordered the *arbakesh* to fulfil his engagement.

CHAPTER XXIII.

THE SOURCES OF OUR KNOWLEDGE OF CHINESE CENTRAL ASIA.

Meaning of "Chinese Central Asia," anciently "Cathay," 356.—How regarded by Greeks and Romans; Ptolemy's "Serica"; Chinese historians, 357.—The Buddhist pilgrims, 359.—Arabian knowledge of the "Seres"; Armenian and Persian intercourse with China, 360.—Nestorian and Roman missionaries, 361.—Marco Polo, 362.—Benedict Goes; Translations from Chinese records and from Tchuen-yuen, 364.—Russian contact with Mongols; Missions to Peking and Yarkand, 368.—Advances to Sungaria and Kashgar, 370.—Prjevalsky's journeys in Mongolia, 371.—Renat's map of Sungaria, 372.—English explorers in Sungaria, and in Tarim basin, 374.—Forsyth's missions to Kashgar, 375.—Later travellers in Chinese Turkistan, 376.

HAVING now reached the northern capital of Chinese Turkistan, and indicated the geographical features of the country generally, I proceed to give some account of the sources of our information about this and other parts of Chinese Central Asia, by which is meant here the western portion of extra-mural China.

What we now understand by the Chinese empire was known to the ancients of the West, when approached by sea, as Sin, Chin, Sinæ, and China; but when approached across Asia, as "the land of the Seres," and, later, "Cathay" or "Kitai," none recognising that the country indicated was one and the same. But with China as approached by sea, or what we now call China proper, we are not here concerned.

From Yule's *Cathay*, and the extracts from classical authors in Cordier's *Bibliotheca Sinica*, we learn that the Greeks and Romans regarded the region of the Seres as a vast and populous country, touching on the east the ocean and the limits of the habitable world, and extending westwards nearly to the Himalayas and the confines of Bactriana. And this we now know from other sources to have been about the width of the Chinese empire for a century before and after the Christian era.

In the geography of Ptolemy (about 150 A.D.) we read: " Serica is girdled round by the mountains named Annibi, by the easternmost part of the Auxacian Mountains, by the mountains called Asmiræi, the easternmost part of the Casian Mountains, by Mount Thagurus, by the most easterly part of the ranges called Emodus-Sericus, and by the chain of Ottorocorras. Two rivers of special note flow through the greater part of Serica ; the river Œchardes is one . . . and the other is the river called Bautes." This Serica is judged to describe mainly the basin of the Tarim (*Œchardes*), and Colonel Yule suggests that in Auxacia we probably trace the name of Aksu, in Casia perhaps Kashgar, whilst the Oikhardai on the river of that name (probably the Tarim) may represent the Uigurs.

Turning now to early Chinese historians, they tell us that certain " inventors of arts and sciences arrived in China as far back as 2698 B.C. from the western kingdoms in the neighbourhood of the Kuen Lun Mountains," which is not very definite. We learn more clearly, under the Han dynasty (B.C. 140—86), that the Yuechi had been driven by the Turkish race of Hiongnu from their seats (somewhere between China and Khotan, Yule thinks) westwards over the Pamirs, first to Ferghana and then onwards to Bactriana, where they destroyed the Greek dynasty and settled themselves.

The Chinese Emperor, desiring to secure co-operation against the Hiongnu (who also disturbed his border), about 135 B.C., sent for this purpose a party under Chang-kian, who were caught on their way by the Hiongnu and kept prisoners ten years. Chang-kian then escaped, and continued on his way to Ferghana, whose people had heard of, but had not come in contact with, the power and riches of China.

Journeying forward to Bactriana, he found the Yuechi unwilling to leave lands on the Oxus to return to their eastern deserts and battle with the Hiongnu. Thus unsuccessful, he tried to return to China by way of Tibet, and was again taken by the Hiongnu, but at length reached China again after 13 years' absence.

Subsequently, the Chinese subdued the Hiongnu, and by B.C. 59 extended their power all over the Tarim valley, so that, about the beginning of our era, 55 states of Western Tatary acknowledged themselves vassals of the empire, as did the provinces of Trans-Oxiana and Bactriana. During the first century, the Hiongnu emancipated themselves, but in A.D. 83 were subdued afresh by the Chinese General Panchao, who, in A.D. 94, reconquered Kashgar, crossed the mountains and killed the king of the Yuechi in Bactriana, and then pushed his conquests to the Caspian.

For our next source of information concerning Chinese Central Asia we are indebted to Buddhism, which at an early date reached Western China from Northern India, probably by way of Kashmir. In A.D. 65 the Emperor Ming-te sent ambassadors to India to obtain instruction in the new religion, and to bring back images of Buddha. Twenty years later Indian sovereigns are mentioned as sending presents to the court of China, and in 405 arrived the first embassy from Ceylon—probably by land, since it was ten years on the road—and bringing a jade image of Buddha.

Meanwhile, Chinese devotees began to go on pilgrimage to India to study Buddhism in the land of its birth; and it is from the record of their travels that we get information of the countries through which they passed.

The first whose travels we have was Shih Fa-hian, who journeyed from 399 to 414. Leaving Chang'an in Shensi, he passed through the province of Kansu, and then by the desert south of Lob-Nor to Cherchen, whence he seems to have gone north to Karashar, where he found companions who had come thither from China by the northern route through Hami. The party then proceeded south to Khotan, westwards to the Pamirs, and so to the Indus and India. Another pilgrim, Sung Yun, set out in 518, and from China proper seems to have travelled by the route south of Lob-Nor to Khotan, and thence by the same route as Fa-hian.

The most noted, however, of Buddhist pilgrims from our point of view was Hiuen Tsiang, who travelled between 628 and 645. Proceeding from the end of the Great Wall to Hami, he continued by the Nan-lu route to Aksu, thence over the Muzart, and past Issik-Kul to Tashkend, Samarkand, and across the Oxus into India. Thence he returned by way of the Pamirs to Kashgar, Khotan, and across the Takla Makan desert to Su-chow, his record furnishing more information than any of his predecessors.

Turning now to the Arabs, we find them acquainted with the Seres early in the eighth century. One Muhammadan author reports the defeat in 709 of 200,000 Tatars, who had broken into the Muhammadan conquests under command of the Chinese Emperor's nephew.

About 713 the victorious General Kutaiba, after overrunning Bokhara, Samarkand, Khiva, and Ferghana, crossed the mountains to Kashgar, and sent to the Chinese Emperor an embassy of 12 Muhammadans, who experienced a friendly reception.

Perhaps it was they who brought notes of the country traversed, for Abu Said, in 916, shows himself acquainted with the general character of the overland communication between Sogdiana and China proper, saying that the frontier of the empire was not far from Khorasan, but that the frontier of China proper was two months' journey beyond, over an almost waterless desert, the difficulty of passing which, he says, had alone prevented the Mussulman warriors of Khorasan from attempting the invasion of China proper.

Inquiring next of Armenia and Persia, we find Moses of Khoren (about 440) speaking of China as a great plain country east of Scythia, at the extremity of the known world, comprising 29 nations, and furnishing silk, musk, saffron, cotton, and peacocks. The country of the Sinæ, he said, adjoined China, which embraced seven nations, and extended likewise to the unknown land. Moses of Khoren states likewise that, between 142 and 178, several bodies of settlers, including Chinese, were placed in Kurdish Armenia for the defence of the country.

In the Chinese annals, the first record of Persia is that of an embassy sent there in 461, and another in the reign of Naoshirwan, who, in 567, sent an embassy from the Persian court to China. Under Tai-tsung of the Thang (627—650) Chinese authority, which west of the mountains had previously lapsed, was fully re-established, and carried to the borders of Persia; but when, in 638, Yezdijerd III. of Persia was pressed by the Muhammadans, and asked aid of Tai-tsung, it was refused, though asylum seems to have been granted to Firuz, the king's son, who established himself in Tokharistan, near Balkh.

Thus far, nothing has been said about Christianity. Yet we know, in addition to legendary accounts, that it was introduced to China at an early date. Arnobius (of the third century) speaks of the " Seres," with the Persians and Medes, as having been reached by the Word, and the celebrated monument of Singanfu bears testimony that, in 635, the Nestorian missionary Olopan arrived in China from Syria, after which, in 745, was issued an edict by the Emperor Yiun-tsong concerning Christian temples.

In the time of the Patriarch Timothy (778—820) we hear of Nestorian missions east of the Caspian, and of the conversion of a Khakan of the Turks, as also, later on, of the Kerait Tatars at the beginning of the eleventh century. In the thirteenth century Marco Polo speaks of Christians as numerous at Yarkand, Urumtsi, Su-chow, Kan-chow, and all over the kingdom of Tangut; in Tenduc (the land of " Prester John," north-east of the Ortus), and cities eastward; as well as in Manchuria, and the countries bordering on Korea.

This brings us to the era of the Mongol supremacy, under which Jinghiz Khan and his successors conquered everything and everybody from the Pacific almost to the Baltic. Western Europe was quaking in its shoes, when it occurred to the Pope and some others to send messengers and missions to the Mongol conquerors, inviting them to become Christians. These messengers were the first Europeans to bring news to the West of what we are now calling Chinese Central Asia. The localities about which they brought information will be indicated by the mention of some of the routes they followed; thus :—

In 1245 John de Plano Carpini proceeded by the Syr-daria and seemingly by the shores of Lake Alakul up the Irtish valley, and so through Sungaria to Karakoram, the Mongol capital.

In 1253 Rubruquis started on a similar journey, of which we have somewhat fuller details. From Alakul he appears to have gone north-eastward towards the Black Irtish, then to have ascended the river Urungu towards Karakoram, where he remained six months.

In 1254 another traveller, King Hayton, or Hethum, of Armenia, went to give in his allegiance to the Mongol, Manghu Khan; but he proceeded from the Volga by a route north of that followed by the above travellers, across the Ural river to the Irtish, and up the valley of its head-waters. He returned from Karakoram through Urumtsi and Sungaria to Almalik, Talas, Otrar, Jizak, Samarkand, and Bokhara.

In 1271, however, set out the most celebrated traveller of his century, the merchant Marco Polo, who from Badakshan crossed the Pamir plateau, and continued by way of Kashgar, Yarkand, Khotan, and south of Lob-Nor to Tangut, and arrived in 1275 at

Kubilai's court in China proper. He remained 17 years in China, and returned homewards by sea to the Persian Gulf, bringing to Europe more information about China than had been known in the West before.

In the century following we have other merchants making their way overland to China, as well as missionaries proper; for, in 1339, William of Modena, a merchant, and certain friars were put to death at Almalik. This we learn from a letter by Pascal, a young Spanish Franciscan on a mission to Tatary, and it is confirmed by Marignolli, who was one of an embassy from the Pope to the Khan. The embassy set out in 1338, and proceeded by the usual route through Old Khiva to Almalik, where it arrived a year after the martyrdom just mentioned, and where it stayed some time, not arriving at Peking till 1342.

From a handbook of the fourteenth century (1330—1340), written by Pegolotti for traders to China, we find it stated that from Otrar, on the Syr-daria, to Almalik was 45 days' journey with pack-asses, and from Almalik to Kan-chow 70 days.

In 1419 we hear of a new route followed by an embassy sent by Shah Rukh, or Rokh, son of Timur, from Herat, through Samarkand to Tashkend, and up the Ili and Yulduz valleys to Turfan and Hami, whence they crossed to Su-chow.

It is more than 100 years after this (about 1550) that we get the next notice, from a Persian merchant, Haji Muhammad, who, in an after-dinner conversation at Venice, indicates the return route from Kan-chow to Kaotai as 6 days' journey; thence to Su-chow 5 days, and Hami 15 more; from Hami to Turfan 13, and from Turfan to Aksu 20; thence to Kashgar 20 days of wildest desert; from Kashgar to Samarkand 25 days, and Bokhara 5 more.

We now come to the last of this series of authorities in the person of Benedict Goes, who, in 1602, hoping to discover by a land-journey whether China was one and the same as Cathay, left Agra, and, proceeding through Cabul and Badakshan, followed Marco Polo's route over the Pamirs. He then descended upon Yengi Hissar, and went on to Yarkand, whence he made an excursion to Khotan, and, after his return, proceeded to Aksu, thence to Hami, and in nine days to the Great Wall, having discovered before reaching it that China and Cathay were identical.

For the material of the foregoing sources of information we are largely indebted to Sir Henry Yule, who, in his *Cathay* and *Marco Polo*, brought together with much labour the testimony of early authors, chiefly Western, on China; but since Yule wrote much additional light on the geography of Chinese Central Asia during the Mongol supremacy has been given by Dr Bretschneider in translations from Chinese records, whence we learn that various Chinese travellers have left narratives of what they saw in the "Western Country," as they call the region we are speaking of.

Thus Ye-lü Ch'u-ts'ai, who accompanied Jinghiz Khan as Minister to Persia, left behind an "account of a journey to the West," called *Si-yu-lu*, from an abstract of which it appears that in 1219 this Minister left Northern Shansi, and crossed the deserts of Mongolia to the camp of Jinghiz Khan (probably at Karakoram). Hence the army of Jinghiz crossed the Great Altai Mountains for several hundred *li* to Hanhai, thought by some to be a dried-up inland sea. Urumtsi is mentioned to the south, and south of

Urumtsi occurs Hami, and, as distant from Hami 3,000 or 4,000 *li*, Khotan.

After crossing the Han-hai, they arrived at Bu-la, or Pulad (not far from Lake Sairam, and probably in the valley of the Borotola, south of which are named the Borokhoro or Talki Mountains), and after leaving these they arrived at Almalik. West of Almalik is a large river named "Ili," and several hundred *li* westward is Talas.

The abstract then speaks of Khodjend and other towns of Ferghana, as well as Otrar, Samarkand, Bokhara, and Urgenj—that is, Khiva. Southward are mentioned Balkh and India, "where it is so hot that a vessel of tin put in the sand melts immediately." Mention is made of the realm to the north-west of K'o-pu-ch'u (probably Russia). "In that country the days [in summer] are long and the nights short. In little more than the time necessary to cook a mutton chop the sun rises again."

Another account, *Pei-shi-ki*, contains the narrative of the envoy Wu-ku-sun, sent by the Chinese Emperor in 1220 to sue for peace of Jinghiz Khan, who had gone westwards. Wu-ku-sun, on passing the northern frontier of China proper, proceeded along the Lin-shan deserts of moving sand (south of Lob-Nor?), passed over the Tsung-ling, and was presented to Jinghiz.

His narrative mentions several tribes which can be identified as then living in Central Asia, and he notices several points about the region—such as lack of rain, the roofs of the houses, and the yellow-dyed beards of men—which appeared to him strange. However, the geographical yield of his memoirs is not great.

In the *Si-yu-ki*, or *Travels to the West*, of K'iu-ch'ang-ch'un—a Taoist monk summoned to the court of Jinghiz

Khan—we are more fortunate. "The Master" started in 1220 from Shan-tung with 19 disciples, one of whom kept a diary. Leaving Peking, they crossed the Mongolian desert to the upper waters of the Kerulun, and, finding Jinghiz gone, were obliged to follow.

The monk seems then to have passed through Uliassutai, across a horrible desert in Sungaria, to Urumsti, to the south of which the party saw "three rugged mountain peaks supporting the heavens" (probably Bogdo-ola), not far beyond which Buddhists cease and Muhammadans begin. Lake Sairam the Master named "The Lake of Heaven," and descended the Talki defile to Almalik.

The monk continued in pursuit of Jinghiz through Talas, Samarkand, and the Iron Gates to the Oxus, being at last presented to the monarch in the mountains of the Hindu Kush. The Master also visited Balkh, and afterwards returned by the way he came to the Altai Mountains, where he had left some of his disciples in an extemporised monastery. They then proceeded by a sandy road to the northern frontier of Tangut, and entered China proper at Su-chow, reaching home after an absence of three years.

The next Chinese traveller whose route westwards we are to glance at is Ch'ang-te, who in 1259 was despatched as envoy by Manghu Khan to his brother Hulagu, who had just taken Baghdad. The narrative of Ch'ang-te, called *Si-shi-ki*, relates his leaving Karakoram, crossing Han-hai, and coming to the Uliungur and the lake now known by that name. Then he comes to Emil in the region of Alakul, "where a furious wind comes out from the hill and blows people passing there into the lake." He then proceeds through the Talki Pass to Almalik, Talas, Tashkend,

Samarkand, and over the Oxus to Tabriz, where Hulagu had fixed his residence.

The speciality of Ch'ang-te's narrative is that he says more than his predecessors about the animals, products, and customs of the Western countries; whilst his remarks take high rank as "travellers' tales."

Thus, of the lion of the West he says that "by a blow with its tail it can seriously hurt men. When it roars the sound comes out from the belly, and so frightens horses that they pass blood instead of water." "Dragon-horses," he adds, "exist in the Caspian, provided with scales and horns. Hence they allow no mares with colts to graze near the shore, since the colts are drawn into the sea and do not return."

Most wonderful of all are the "sheep planted upon hillocks," also a product of the Western countries. "The people take the navel of a sheep, plant it in the ground, and water it. When it hears thunder it grows, the navel retaining connection with the ground. After the beast has become full grown, they take a stick and frighten it. Then the navel breaks off, and the sheep begins to walk and eat grass."

Another of these "travellers' tales" states: "There is a woman in those Western countries who understands the language of horses, and can by this means predict good or evil"; after which Ch'ang-te concludes with the observation that "Many other marvellous things are seen there, but all cannot be reported!"

The last of the Chinese translations given by Dr Bretschneider is from the peregrinations of Ye-Lü-Hi-liang, 1260-3. His wanderings, so far as they concern us, begin at Su-chow, whence he walks over the Tian Shan through winter snow to Urumtsi, and in the summer crosses the river Manas to Emil and Pulad.

Then, seemingly, he goes fighting to Kashgar, whence he is recalled by Kubilai Khan as courier, and posts through Kucha and Hami, across the desert, to the Emperor's summer residence at Shang-tu.

Another Chinese authority to be mentioned here is Tchuen-yuen, a Mandarin, who, living in the districts of Barkul and Urumtsi, in 1778, in the 71st year of his age, wrote *Memoirs of the Western Countries*, which have recently been translated by M. Gueluy, a Belgian missionary. References to his work will be made hereafter.

Thus far, it will be observed, the sources of our information concerning Chinese Central Asia have come from west, east, and south. Now we have to notice Russian sources from the north. It was in 1579 that Yermak and his handful of Cossacks crossed the Urals and defeated Kuchum Khan, prince of one of several small khanates, into which the main horde of Jinghiz Khan had been broken up. Tobolsk was founded as a capital, whence in 70 years the Cossacks pushed eastwards, partly conquering in 1620 the Buriat Mongols, east of the Baikal.

Westwards, as early as 1594, a fortress was built at Tara on the Irtish, which brought the Russians into military and commercial relations with the Kalmuks, then masters of Sungaria. Some of their princes asked the help of Russia, and it was through the Kalmuk country, in 1655, that the Russians sent their first embassy to Peking.

This was with a view to arrange a commercial treaty, but the envoy refused to fall down and perform the *kotow* before the Emperor, and was sent away empty. In 1665 Baikoff, on a similar mission, left Tobolsk, and spent the winter among the Kalmuks.

Thence he proceeded to Lake Zaisan and up the Black Irtish to China, but was no more successful in negotiating a treaty than his predecessor.

In 1684 Russia and China came to blows on the Amur, and some of the Russians were taken prisoners to Peking, which they liked so well that, on peace being proclaimed, they did not care to return, but asked for priests to be sent to minister to them there. This led to priests being sent at intervals of ten years, and thus the Russians learned more of the country through which these ecclesiastics travelled, and added to their scholars several illustrious sinologues.

Soon after, we find Prince Gagarine, in 1713, sending a gentleman of Tobolsk, named Trouchnikoff, to China across Little Bokhara, as it was then called, to gather information about gold dust. He visited Koko-Nor; the Altingol, or river of gold, which forms the source of the Hoang-ho; the Chinese towns of Sining and Daba; and in 1716 returned, by way of Kalgan, to Tobolsk.

He brought about 20 lbs. of gold dust, which so excited the cupidity of Peter the Great that he ordered a line of forts to be built from the Irtish to Yarkand, whence the gold was said to come. Accordingly, in 1718, as a first step, the fortress of Semipolatinsk was built, and Urasof and Somof surveyed the shores of Lake Zaisan and the banks of the Upper and Lower Irtish. The death of Peter the Great stayed the building of forts, but Semipolatinsk grew into a place of trade, and in 1811 the Russians obtained facilities to trade also at Chuguchak and Kuldja, where in 1851 Russian factories and consuls were established.

Meanwhile, rays of scientific light had been thrown on the mysterious Sungarian country. In 1793 the

Russian botanist Sivers penetrated to the Tarbagatai Mountains, whilst the mining engineer Sneghiroff penetrated to Chuguchak searching for gold; and in 1828 Humboldt reached the Chinese picket of Baty on the Irtish, collected itineraries from Asiatic traders at Semipolatinsk, and, with the help from these and materials from Chinese sources, made some shrewd guesses at the geography of Sungaria.

In 1871, however, the Ili valley came into possession of the Russians for 12 years, which period was fruitful in explorations in Sungaria. In 1875 Sosnovsky returned from Central China, passing through Hami, Barkul, and Guchen to Lake Zaisan, an account being written by Piassetzky, one of the mission. In 1876 Pevtsoff travelled from the Zaisan to Guchen by way of Bulun Tokoi, near Lake Uliungur; and Potanin's expedition set out from Zaisan to Kobdo, passing by Bulun Tokoi, and in the following year arrived at Hami and Uliassutai. Also, in 1879, Regel travelled from Kuldja, by way of Shikho, to Turfan. The latest of Russian travellers are the brothers Grum-Grjimailo, who have recently returned from a journey to the Sungarian oases of the Tian Shan, which they crossed, and explored the country for 70 miles south of Turfan.

Turning our attention a little farther west, we have in 1821 Bubeinoff, a merchant, travelling from Semipolatinsk to Kashgar, and in 1859 Captain Valikhanoff, in the disguise of a Khokand trader, crossing the Tian Shan by Lake Issik-Kul, and likewise reaching Kashgar; whilst in 1876 we have Kuropatkin's expedition crossing from Ferghana to Kashgar, on a political mission to Yakub Khan, and continuing eastwards through Maralbashi, Aksu, Bai, and Kurla, besides making journeys by the Bedal Pass to Kara-Kol, and through Karashar to Lake Bagratsh.

To these I may add the journey of Dr Seeland in 1886 from Vierny to Kashgar, Aksu, and by the Bedal to Kara-Kol, to whose narrative I am indebted in several directions. Of the Russian scientists to whom we owe information about the mountain district round Issik-Kul (ceded to Russia in 1860 by the treaty of Peking) I say nothing here, but may refer my readers to what I have written in *Russian Central Asia*.

But the Russian who towers above all others, as does Marco Polo among his contemporaries, and to whom we are most indebted for information on trans-mural China, is General Prjevalsky. Whilst on military service in the sea-coast province of Siberia, his first rambles were in the Manchurian forests.

In 1871-3 he made his first great expedition from Kiakhta across Mongolia to Kalgan, whence he turned westward by Huc's route to Kansu, visiting Koko-Nor and the salt marsh of Tsaidam, and pushing southwards to within 500 miles of Lassa. Lack of resources obliged him to turn back. In returning he crossed the Gobi in its widest part between Din-yuan-ing and Urga.

In 1876 Prjevalsky set out from Kuldja up the Yulduz valley, crossing the Tian Shan to Karashar and the Tarim, which he followed to Lake Lob. Then, continuing southwards, he discovered the Altyn Tagh range rising almost precipitously and forming the most northerly range of the Tibetan plateau.

In 1879 he started again, this time well supplied with funds, from Lake Zaisan along the Uliungur, or Urungu, and Bulgun, whence he crossed the desert of Sungaria, passed the salt lake and plain of Barkul, over a pass of the Tian Shan, 8,700 feet high, and descended to Hami. Thence he crossed the desert to Sa-chu, passed over the Altyn Tagh, continued east of Tsaidam, and then descended in a south-westerly direction towards Lassa, which he approached to within 170 miles, but was turned back by the authorities.

In his fourth great journey, 1883-5, Prjevalsky crossed the Gobi from Urga to Ala-shan, through Sining to Eastern Tsaidam. From hence he made an excursion to the sources of the Yellow River, and then marched westwards along a wide valley, which he named "The Valley of the Winds," stretching for 150 miles between the Kuen Lun on the south and the Chaman Tagh on the north, and closed westwards by a range connecting the Kuen Lun and the Altyn Tagh. Prjevalsky crossed the Altyn Tagh south of Lob-Nor, and travelled through Cherchen and Keria to Khotan. Thence he tried to ascend the Kuen Lun, but failed from physical difficulties, as he gave me to understand, and then, turning homewards, followed the rivers Khotan and Aksu to the Bedal Pass and Kara-Kol.

Thus, for accurate and scientific knowledge of extra-mural China, we are chiefly indebted to Russian travellers, but not for the first map of Chinese Central Asia. Peter the Great sent some of his prisoners, taken at Pultava, to Siberia, and among them a Swedish sergeant named Renat, who, tired of nothing to do at Tobolsk, asked to be allowed to take part in the expedition of Bukholtz, sent in 1716 to reconnoitre Sungaria.

The force, however, was captured by Kalmuks, amongst whom Renat lived in captivity 17 years. In similar captivity, in various parts of the country, were several Russian officers, whose description of their journeys, supplemented by inquiries from the natives, gave Muller much of his geographical information of countries bordering Siberia; but to Renat belongs the honour of drawing up the first map, based largely on personal observations, of Sungaria and the Tarim valley.

On his return to Sweden, the map was copied five years afterwards, and has recently been published in St Petersburg, a copy in facsimile now lying before me.

The map is not correct as to astronomical indications, and distances are too great; but these defects are counterbalanced by careful delineation of political boundaries, lakes, rivers, mountains, deserts, forests, towns, the camps of the nomads, and, above all, their royal tents. Some of the 250 Swedish inscriptions are descriptive. Thus, at Issik-Kul we read "here is found iron sand," and in the forest of Ebinor "here are wild camels," whilst at Keria is written "here they find gold."

At the beginning of the eighteenth century, under orders of the Emperor, the Jesuits surveyed China generally, and their map of 1718 was subsequently enlarged in Europe to include the Trans-Caspian country, and published by D'Anville in 1737. After the depopulation of Sungaria, the Chinese Emperor sent there, in 1760, Jesuit missionaries, by whom trigonometrical points were determined north and south of the eastern Tian Shan, and on the south shore of Issik-Kul. Their labours were added to their predecessors' map of China and contiguous countries, after which Klapvoth drew up and published his map of Central Asia, which was in Europe the chief geographical manual of this region until the recent researches and imprints made by the Russians.

We come now to our last source of information,

chiefly English. The way to Sungaria from the East was led by Mr Ney Elias, who in 1872 crossed Mongolia from Kuei-hwa-cheng to Uliassutai, through Kobdo, and thence passed the frontier into Siberia, near Suok, and down the valley of the Katun to Biisk. The last Englishman in Sungaria, known to me, is Mr St George Littledale, who, with Mrs Littledale, made up their caravan, as he informs me, at Zaisan, crossed the Chinese frontier, and shot in the mountains south of Kobdo, whence they continued south towards Kuldja, and, turning back to Chuguchak, re-entered Russia near Sergiopol.

The Ili valley was visited, as I have indicated, when in possession of the Russians, by Ashton Dilke and Schuyler in 1873, Delmar Morgan in 1880, and myself in 1882, but none of us crossed what was then the Chinese frontier, this little sprig of laurel, of being the first Englishman to enter China from the West, being left seemingly for me to cull in 1888.

This brings us, lastly, to Chinese Turkistan, into which Adolf Schlagintweit penetrated in 1857. The first Englishman known to have reached the valley was Mr Johnson, who, in 1865, was engaged on topographical work in Kashmir, and, making his way towards Khotan, was kindly received by the ruler Habibullah. Three years afterwards, in 1868, Mr Shaw, a tea-planter, and Mr Hayward, an explorer, made their way over the Himalayas to Kashgar, and were well received by Yakub Khan, Mr Shaw returning in safety, but Hayward being murdered at Yasin.

In the same year a Russian embassy, under Captain Reintal, arrived at Kashgar. England and Russia were now bidding for the goodwill of Yakub Khan, and the former sent an embassy under Mr Forsyth, with Henderson and Shaw, the trio going as far as Yarkand, whilst, two years later, another Russian embassy, under Kaulbars, was received at Kashgar.

Then was made up, in the following year, Forsyth's second embassy, consisting of between 30 and 40 officers and soldiers, who carefully surveyed routes and collected information of the mountain region between India and the Tarim valley, and made their way from Yarkand round the valley as far as Maralbashi; besides sending native explorers to Khotan, and making excursions to the Pamirs and the mountains north of Kashgar. Their information was printed in a bulky quarto volume, but not published, and has proved to me a valuable storehouse of material for the portion of country covered by the expedition.

And thus matters stood when the Chinese re-conquered the country in 1877-8. In 1879 Mr Ney Elias went to Yarkand on political duty, arranging, among other things, for the passage to and fro of traders from India, whilst in 1882 I met M. Petrovsky at St Petersburg, about to proceed to Kashgar to reside as Russian Consul.

Two years later, however, from 1885-7, Mr Carey, with Dalgleish as assistant, accomplished by far the grandest journey that has been made in Chinese Turkistan. Leaving Ladak, they descended upon Keria, passed along the Khotan river to the Tarim and Lob-Nor; then over the Altyn Tagh and along the Kuen Lun to East Tsaidam, and northward to Hami; then westwards by the high road to Maralbashi, whence they turned south to Yarkand, Mr Carey reaching India after an absence of two years.

In 1887 also were performed two remarkable journeys from Peking by Colonel Mark Bell and Lieutenant (now Captain) Younghusband. Younghusband, as already stated, took the northern route outside the Wall, and Colonel Bell the cart-route, to Hami. Thence Younghusband proceeded by the ordinary road to Toksun, Bell going to the same point by way of Barkul and Urumtsi. From Toksun both followed the same route to Aksu; but thence reached Kashgar, Younghusband through Ush-Turfan and Bell through Maralbashi. Lastly, proceeding to Yarkand, Bell crossed by the Karakoram and Younghusband by the Muz-Tag to Kashmir. Captain Younghusband has since spent a winter at Kashgar, and has broken new ground towards the Pamirs.

Two later travellers in Chinese Turkistan are Major C. Cumberland and Lieutenant Bower, who, in August 1890, crossed the Karakoram, and from Kilian turned westwards towards Sarikol, meeting Captain Grombchevsky, after which they reached Yarkand.

Mr Bower had taken in hand the detection of Dalgleish's murderer (of whom more hereafter), and left for Kashgar; but Major Cumberland was bent on shooting, for which purpose he crossed the desert to Maralbashi, and then turned eastward to Aksu and onwards a certain distance in the direction of Lob-Nor. Returning to Maralbashi, he reached Kashgar, and then proceeded up the Gez defile to the Pamirs, and over into Ferghana, particulars of which are given in his letters on "Sport on the Pamir Steppes," which appeared in *Land and Water*.

Later expeditions of Grombchevsky and Prjevalsky will be noticed hereafter, but having now indicated the principal sources of our information and the stages by which they have become known to us, I shall continue my own narrative of travel through Chinese Turkistan.

CHAPTER XXIV.

FROM AKSU TO MARALBASHI.

Two roads to Kashgar; Northern through Ush-Turfan, followed by Younghusband, 377.—District of Ush-Turfan; its people and capital, 378.—Aksai valley and Kirghese nomads, 379.—Our departure by southern route, 380.—March to Chinese city of Aksu, 381.—Fording the Janart river, and shooting birds, 383.—Ride to Sai-Aryk, 384.—Stormy weather, 385.—Night travel through Chilan to district of Maralbashi, 386.—Sunday at Yaka Kuduk; A Chinese official, 387.—Undesirable companions, 388.—March to Chadir-Kul, 389.—Its birds and buildings, 390.—Pheasants and Podoces, 391.—Scriptures at Tum Chuk, 393.—Arrival at Charwagh, visited by Biddulph for shooting, 394.—Antiquities between Charwagh and Maralbashi, 395.

FROM Aksu to Kashgar we had a choice of two roads,—one through Ush-Turfan, skirting the mountains; and the other through Maralbashi, crossing the plains. Osman Bai, with an eye doubtless to free pasture for his horses, would have been pleased to take the former. He depicted in alluring colours the verdure and cool air of the hills, and on the other hand dilated on the stifling heat and mosquitoes of the plains, together with enforced travel by night to escape the horse-flies. Probably he foresaw also that he would have to purchase fodder from station to station. Inasmuch, however, as my chief interest lay amongst the people of the country rather than pretty scenery, and the southern route was the more populous, it needed but a moment's consideration to decide in its favour.

We may briefly glance, nevertheless, at the northern road. The route from Aksu to Kashgar through Ush-Turfan is about the same length as through Maralbashi, but is not, like the southern route, practicable for carts, the ascents beyond Ush-Turfan being sometimes difficult even for horsemen.

Captain Younghusband followed this route in August 1887, and calls it the pleasantest part of his whole journey. He describes the area between Aksu and Ush-Turfan as level, and cultivated with rice—the best, it is said, in the country—and watered by the Janart and Aksu streams. The latter is crossed about seven miles on the way. Beyond, the traveller passes through Saik, the village of Barin (where clover, barley, and fuel can be had), and along a good road through an inhabited country past Yaz-jigda, Akyar, and the village of Acha-Tag to Ush-Turfan.

Ush-Turfan is the chief town of a district lying northeast of the district of Kashgar, and separated therefrom by a range of mountains running east from the Terekti Pass, and called the Balauti range—the irregular chain of hills which shuts off the Ush-Turfan valley from the plains. The limits of the district are Kakshal on the west and the Aksu river on the east, the Bedal mountain on the north and the Balauti ridge on the south.

The western half of the valley is occupied by the Kirghese pastures of Kakshal, through which flows the Aksai, Tushkan, or Kizil-Kungai river, running down from the valley east of Chadir-Kul, lying at an elevation of 11,000 feet. The population of the eastern end of the valley, which is agricultural, is quoted by Forsyth as living in 2,000 houses. Farmsteads are scattered over the valley, but the principal settlements are Safr Bai, Karawul, Akyar, Acha-Tag, and Aral.

Sheep, cattle, and horses are very numerous, the fine wool of the sheep being woven by the Kirghese for home use, and also exported to Aksu, to which place the trade relations of the valley are said by Forsyth to be limited, though I have met with the statement that the fine wool alluded to makes its way over the Himalayas for the manufacture of the well-known Kashmir shawls.

The capital of Ush-Turfan had formerly a strong little castle, but it was destroyed with the town in 1765, and the people massacred by the Chinese for revolt in favour of a Khoja rebellion. Forsyth calls it an open market town of 800 houses, peopled by descendants of Taranchis, planted here by the Chinese after the massacre. Under Yakub Khan it had a garrison of 300 men. Sunarguloff, in 1877, mentions Mondays and Thursdays as market-days. The present Chinese fortress is situated at the foot of a rocky precipitous hill, about 150 feet high, with a small guard-post at the top. Near the fort are about 50 houses and a row of shops.

From Ush-Turfan, Younghusband continued to ascend the Aksai valley for three days. At seven miles west of the town is Bashagma, whence there branches off a pack-road to the Bedal Pass, put down by Sunarguloff at 15,000 feet above the sea. The main road continues to Safr Bai, whence also goes a caravan road northward over the Bedal Pass to the source of the Narim, and then across the Zauka Pass to Issik-Kul.

West of Safr the valley contracts, and the road

passes for 30 miles through dense forests of poplar, which clothe the river banks. The little farm settlements are for the most part left behind, and the country is now entirely inhabited by Kirghese, amongst whom the traveller must not depend on getting provisions other than mutton.

At the end of three days, presumably from Akchi, Younghusband turned south-west from the valley over the Belowti Pass (11,000 feet), another road continuing up the valley and crossing the range farther west at Saribeli in the direction of Kashgar. The ascent of the Belowti Pass is spoken of as quite easy, whilst the descent brought our explorer into a region that had been traversed by Captain Trotter and Dr Stoliczka, when members of the Forsyth mission.

Descending from the Pass over a stony plain, Younghusband found his way to the Sirt country, which consists of large plains, covered in some places by woods of considerable extent, and surrounded by hills. There were seen also large fields of wheat grown by the Kirghese, who were left behind at Kalti Ailak, 50 miles from Kashgar, where the road quits the hills and descends into the plains through the rich district of Artish.

By this northern route, presumably, the *Tautai* of Kashgar expected me to travel, for it afterwards transpired that he sent a packet of letters to meet me; whereas, for reasons already stated, we had chosen the southern route, and the day of our departure—Tuesday, August 21st—was marked by considerable activity on the premises of Madamin Bai, where many persons assembled to watch our preparations, and to accompany us out of the town.

We did not start till after midday, the Afghans,

Andijanis, and others swelling our cavalcade. After filing through the western gate of the town, called Sabun-Kabuk, we continued along a 15-foot road, embanked from one to two feet, traversing rice-fields, and presently reached a cliff from 20 to 30 feet high. Under this the road became broad and sandy, and in about an hour ascended by a gully to an elevated plain of a sandy clay soil. Riding along, we had a pretty view of the trees and greenery of the oasis below.

That, I told them, was something like England, only they must picture our island green all over, and not with mere patches of verdure and huge deserts between. No doubt they thought it must be a grand country, and consequently its people grand too; for as we met mounted natives who did not at first realise the importance of the encounter, our escort, like new brooms, cleared the way, and shouted ahead, not "Bow the knee!" but "Get down! get down!"—an order that was immediately obeyed, the horsemen standing at attention till the cavalcade had passed.

Thus, after descending again to the cultivated plain, and passing through gardens, huts, and habitations which to besiegers would give cover up to its walls, we came to the Chinese city, where at a wayside restaurant we took a parting snack of refreshment. Monkey-face and Tor-jee had put in an appearance, and accompanied us thus far. They now came forward to bid us good-bye, which they did after their manner, Monkey-face gloomily and Tor-jee with smiles.

Their places were filled by two Chinese soldiers from the *Tautai* of Aksu, and the Russian *Aksakal* also attached to our caravan two men, one of them named Sarim Sak; so that with the *arbakesh* and interpreter, his cart and four animals, together with the mullah and Osman Bai and his helpers, we made a party of about 30 horses and more than a dozen men. At Yengi-shahr our complimentary escort returned, and we had the rest of the afternoon to reach our first station of Choktal, or Chuk-Tal Rabat, which we did about five hours after setting out, and at a distance, it was said, of 40 *li*, or, according to Kuropatkin, 13 miles, from Aksu.

The *serai* where we stayed was an extremely poor one—the *arba* being preferred by one of the party as a sleeping-place—so that we had no inducement to linger next morning, but started a little before seven o'clock; that is, according to my poor watch, which, being a common one for rough travelling, varied sometimes, and was found, on our arrival at Kashgar, to have lost two hours since we left Kuldja. The road, from 20 to 30 feet wide, and lined by trees, all of recent growth, passed through a well-cultivated valley of fertile clay, bordered on the south, a mile distant, by a low cliff of clay, and on the north, five miles away, by barren hills.

Colonel Bell, the only Englishman preceding me along the whole of this route from Aksu to Kashgar, and to whose practised eye I am indebted for many items of information, read to the Royal Geographical Society a paper now before me. He speaks therein of the distance from Aksu to the river Janart as 3 miles, which may mean either that we did not cross at the same spot, or, more probably, the 3 is a misprint for 13.

We had not ridden far from Choktal before we came to the first of several branch streams, each from 100 to 200 feet wide, which were forded. On coming to the main stream, about 300 yards wide, we crossed in a ferry, though the water could not have been very deep, since one poor woman—unable, I suppose, to pay toll, or coming too late—had solved the difficulty by hoisting her garments aloft and wading through.

The Janart rises, as the Sariasi, immediately beneath the southern slopes of Khan Tengri, and, after being joined by several nameless streams in the Tian Shan, runs towards Aksu, where it is joined by another river of that name. After this, the united stream flows for 70 miles till it joins the Tarim.

The Aksu, when in flood, cannot be crossed in *arbas*, for the current is so swift as sometimes to wash horses and passengers away. Where we crossed, the shallow river bed, with banks perpendicular in places and 12 feet high, is about three-quarters of a mile wide, and, what with fording and ferrying, it took us a long time to get over. From the ferry the country in sight down-stream was under cultivation.

The delay in crossing, and subsequent opportunities on the road, gave occasion for shooting, and there were added to my collection two long-billed waterbirds from the river bed; also two sparrow-hawks and a rook, a wood sandpiper *(Totanus glareola)*, a shrike *(Lanius arenarius)*, and a hoopoe *(Upupa epops)*, as well as a specimen of Seebohm's lark *(Alaudula Seebohmi)* and a Kentish ring-plover *(Ægialites cantianus).*

There was a little rain during the morning, which made our ride a cool one, and we stayed for lunch at

* The Kentish ring-plover, called by the Turkis "Chullok," is, according to Dr Scully, "a seasonal visitant to the plains of Chinese Turkistan, arriving about the end of March, and disappearing in winter. It frequents stony ground and efflorescent wastes, always [as I observed] in the neighbourhood of shallow pools of water. When disturbed it appears to take only short flights, but runs very nimbly."

a village called Besharik-Ustan. Thence we marched through cultivated country, well wooded, with abundant pasture, over a road sometimes sandy, and narrowing occasionally to ten feet by reason of rough culverts of trees laid horizontally over the many canals by which the country is irrigated. About five hours from starting we came to Kum-bash, *alias* Gouai-Urten—60 *li*, it was said, from the Chinese town of Aksu—with a station vastly better than the one we left in the morning, and where we stayed for the night.

A march next day of only three hours brought us to Sai- (or Soi-) Aryk. Bell mentions at 20 miles from Aksu a large village of 500 Turki families, called I-crow, where he crossed a stream 50 to 60 yards wide by a rough combination of earthen piers and waterways. I have no note of this village; but we passed half-way, through Ai-kul, situated in a depression, and mentioned by Kuropatkin as marshy in spring.

As we rode through the street I caught sight of a man sitting behind a basket of nectarines, and told Joseph to buy the lot, which he did at the ruinous price of four for a *charik*, or, say, a penny for 35, and better nectarines I think I never ate! We continued onward by a good road lined on both sides, as on the previous stage, with trees, including the willow, poplar, mulberry, and *jigda*, or wild olive ; and in the gardens we noticed the walnut. Here the men were set to butterfly-catching, which they did not enter into with the zest displayed in the mountains by Monkey-face and Tor-jee, though several specimens were secured.

On arriving at Sai-Aryk, which we did by ten o'clock, we took up our quarters in a poor little *serai* once occupied, Muhammad the *Aksakal* told me, by Mr Carey. His luggage, they said, was placed in the room I occupied, a restoration having taken place in the interim. It was a sorry place, however, and soon after our arrival, notwithstanding our being in what is called a rainless region, there came on a violent thunderstorm, with hailstones as large as a starling's egg—the largest, I think, I ever saw.

The rain poured down in such torrents that an old serving-man on the place declared he had never witnessed the like, and the water found its way by the chimney only too freely into my room. This cooled the night temperature indoors to a maximum of 73° and a minimum of 65°; whereas the night before, on my window-sill at Kum-bash, the maximum had reached 10° higher.

The storm cleared the atmosphere, so that our attention was called next morning to the snowy peaks of the Tian Shan, which the map shows to have been 110 miles off, Khan Tengri lying nearly due north. A reason, too, was suggested for the Chinese name, "The Mountains of Heaven," since their base was lost in azure, blue as the vault above, and the snow-tops appeared to float like clouds.

I attempted to photograph this lovely phenomenon, but succeeded in portraying only the maize-field and trees in the foreground. I was more fortunate, however, in securing a good view of the tiny bridge that stretches over a small stream giving life to the village of 130 Turki families, a crowd of whom came out to see what the foreigner with his camera was doing.

We stayed at Sai-Aryk till three in the afternoon to gather up our forces for a march through the night over two stages, on the alleged ground of scarcity of fodder and bad water at the next station. On leaving the village we passed through flooded rice-fields, with many gulls flying about. After several fruitless shots one was secured as a specimen; but my gun failed to bring down what looked like a *birkut* eagle that had descended to the plains.

Within an hour we left cultivation and entered a desert, at first with low brushwood, and then with sparse tamarisk shrubs only. We were at an elevation of 3,500 feet, and at ten miles from Sai-Aryk the soil became saline. Five hours' riding brought me to Chol Kuduk, decidedly tired, so that I was glad to give my horse to Mr Interpreter, and turn into his cart for the rest of the stage. Thus proceeding, we passed through Shor Kuduk (or Shur Kurduck), and at four o'clock in the morning reached Chilan, or Chilian, where the baggage horses had arrived an hour before.

I did not take at all kindly to this travelling through the night, and felt so fatigued that I began to suspect that I was growing less able than formerly to endure hardness. Moreover, at Chilan—a hamlet of 25 poor houses, with a little cultivation—I had a miserable room, and the water was bad, so that I was the less sorry to hear that Osman Bai wanted to start afresh in the afternoon, and do two stages more.

Accordingly, we set out at six, and at dusk I got into the cart, which was less fatiguing than the saddle, but slower, for the road was sandy.

We now entered the district of Maralbashi, the western border of which is a wide sandy desert joining the Kashgar district at Yangi-Awat, whilst to the north it extends to Kalpin, on the Aksu river, and descends southwards to the river of Yarkand.

Towards midnight we came to Jaida, or Jaidi, with a little *chi* grass growing about the station, where were ten huts, peopled in winter; but the inhabitants, except those at the station, were now gone with their cattle to the mountains. Here we stopped to feed the cart-horses, and then plunged into a muddy road, in which the cart stuck, and we found the advantage of having with us a small company to get us out. The ground is here rendered swampy by a stream from the barren and snowless hills from 20 to 30 miles to the north-west.

At 16 miles from Chilan the route became heavy among sand-hills, and at two miles farther on we came upon some species of poplar trees called *tograk*. These, later on, thickened into a wood. Thus we travelled on heavily all through the night, and not until six the next morning did we reach Yaka Kuduk, though the baggage arrived somewhat earlier.

At Yaka Kuduk we spent Sunday, the place consisting of 15 houses, in the midst of tamarisk and *tograk* trees, with a population in winter of 50 inhabitants. There was also a good-sized station with a resident Chinese official of superior appearance, who was well behaved and disposed to be helpful.

I invited him to my room, gave him illuminated cards, tickets, etc., and sold him portions of Scripture. He offered to give me fodder, which I declined with thanks, but submitted to him the question whether the innkeeper was not extortionate in asking seven *chariks* a bundle—that is, seven times the price we had paid for fodder at Aksu. He agreed with me that this charge was excessive, but thought five times not too much, since food had to be imported from afar.

Again, one of the Chinese escort was found to have been feeding his horse at my expense, which perhaps was not unreasonable, and at first I submitted, whereupon his fellow began to follow suit. Upon my mentioning the matter to this official, however, he said the escort could claim nothing from me since they were granted a travelling allowance from their *Tautai*, and anything I might give was a matter of grace.

Both men upon this acknowledged themselves wrong, and undertook to provide in future for their beasts. I had also to call to order one of the Turki *djiguitts* for stealing my nectarines; but, with the exception of these little peculations, and considering what a bad lot Chinese soldiers proverbially are, affairs moved along smoothly enough.

There was, however, another matter in which I had to ask this Chinaman's help. Soon after leaving Sai-Aryk, we overtook in the desert a horseman who turned out to be a policeman, a horsewoman who was his prisoner, and a cart carrying the woman's father, with, I think, some other members of the family.

Salutations were exchanged as a matter of course, and, remembering the loneliness and dangers of the way, it was natural for this small party to try and keep up with ours, which they accordingly did, conversation and jokes flowing apace, and the pipe passing round, in all of which the woman was not backward in taking her part. She was young and good-looking —not yet out of her teens—stylishly dressed and unveiled, and mounted upon a fairly good horse, said to be her own. Joseph told me she was of evil reputation, on her way to the prison at Maralbashi, and then probably to Kashgar to be put to death.

I did not much like this set of companions for my caravan; but, whether I would or would not, when we stopped they stopped, when we moved they moved, and thus we came to Yaka Kuduk, both parties putting up at the one inn of the place. Looking about the yard in the afternoon, I was invited into a room and offered tea, and here was this woman smoking opium. She appeared also from time to time chatting and smoking with my men, of which I took no ostensible notice, until information reached me that a rumour was going about to the effect that this woman was the travelling companion of my servant Joseph.

Doubting whereunto this might grow, and not knowing upon whom the calumny might next fall, I sent for the official and explained the situation, whereupon he kindly cut the knot for me by sending her party another way, and I saw no more of her until inspecting the prison at Maralbashi.

We had heard a great deal of the numbers of pheasants we should see on the way, and at Yaka Kuduk my men came more than once to call my attention to coveys of these birds a few yards only from the station. Next morning I breakfasted on the first pheasant shot by my own gun. For some reason, however, of momentary inconvenience I excused Joseph from dressing the skin; but with the result that, though we more than once saw pheasants afterwards, I did not get one for my collection.

Osman Bai wanted to start again on Sunday afternoon and travel through the night, which I declined, and we left next morning at seven for a four hours' march to Chadir-Kul, passing on the way a ruined fort, built by Yakub Khan. Here Bell, a month earlier, found the horse-flies so troublesome as to render night travel imperative. The heavy sandy track lay through a forest of *tograk*, with occasional ponds, and after 11 miles we passed through a jungle of tamarisks, low shrubs, and trees.

When one speaks, however, of " forests " the reader must not call to mind the density of an Indian jungle, for I rarely saw underwood in Chinese Turkistan so thick as that of a Kentish copse, whilst all the trees I saw put together—they rarely exceeded 12 or 18 inches in diameter—would hardly make such a show of timber as exists in Greenwich Park. I found one of my ornithological acquaintances at the British Museum picturing, in the Tarim basin, dense, boundless forests, providing a resting-place for half the birds of the world. I should rather call the Tarim forests straggling collections of trees, through which one could usually march a cavalry regiment.

Around Chadir-Kul were a few cultivated fields, and *chi* grass was plentiful. There was also near at hand (as the name of the place implies) a lake, formed by the overflow of the stream we had first seen at Yaka Kuduk, and which, from Chadir-Kul, flows southward for a distance altogether of about 50 miles into the river of Kashgar, near its confluence with the river of Yarkand.

Two men were sent to the lake, but in vain, to procure me specimens of fish. Meanwhile I took my gun, and secured a shrike (*Lanius arenarius*), two crested larks (*Galerita cristata et G. magna*), having also shot a few birds on the way, but not so many as report had led me to hope for.

I took with the camera a view, outside the village, of a pretentious clay-built mausoleum of a local magnate, one Osman Ming-bashi, or Captain of a thousand. It consisted of a large domed building with *pishtak*, surrounded by a mud wall with gateway; and as it had been built only the previous year, it was in fair order, and gave one an idea of what the tombs of the rich men of the country are like. A view was also taken of the village street, which possesses nine houses and six *serais*, a Chinese military station or fort, a tiny Buddhist temple beneath a lofty tree, and an earthen mile-post.

Declining again to travel by night, we left Chadir-Kul at four in the morning, which meant rising at the uncomfortable hour of two. Outside the village we ascended among sand-hills, and near a copse sighted a fine cock pheasant, and a few minutes afterwards two deer, the only specimens of this animal that we came across all through the country, and these quickly made themselves scarce.

Of course I could not leave the caravan to stalk them, and had to content myself with a pair of antlers of a maral stag, appropriately purchased at Maralbashi from a man who obtained them four months previously from Tum Chuk, where the original owner had been eaten by a tiger. They are now in the Museum of Natural History at South Kensington.

I shot, however, in the morning an ornithological prize. Professor Newton, of Cambridge, as well as people at the British Museum, had bidden me be on the look-out for a bird comparatively rare in European collections, called Podoces, of which four varieties are known (*Podoces Panderi, P. Hendersoni, P. humilis, et P. Biddulphi*).*

From the illustration and description of *Podoces Hendersoni* in *Lahore to Yarkand*, I make no doubt

---

* This genus, Mr Dresser tells me, is characteristic of the region, being confined to the steppe country, and up to the present time ornithologists are undecided as to where the genus Podoces should be placed. For his own part, he believes it to come nearest to the jays, though very different from them. Hume, in *Lahore to Yarkand*, remarks of Henderson's Podoces that in its external form this species most nearly resembles the choughs; with which, following Buonaparte, he places it, and not with the jays or magpies.

it was this variety of which we saw several between Yaka Kuduk and Chadir-Kul.*

The Podoces are spoken of as habitually fluttering and flapping about in the sand, laving their feathers in it after the manner of fowls, or like some of the Babblers (*Malacocerci*), commonly called in India "dust birds." The Turki name "Kum-tuche" is said to mean "sand bird." Those we saw were always in the desert and sandy places, but I think not always in pairs, as Henderson observed near Sanju.

They moved about from one sand-hill to another, and impressed themselves on my memory by the speed at which they ran. They were slow to rise on the wing, but would lead me a chase for hundreds of yards, and generally succeeded in keeping out of range till I shot my first not far from Chadir-Kul. Mr Shaw, it seems, found them good eating. I did not try them, but my men, regarding the capture as a prize, said that its liver, I think, was used by them as medicine. The only Podoces in my collection that reached England was determined as that of Biddulph (*P. Biddulphi*).

* Dimensions of male bird: length, 11·5; tail, from vent, 4·5; expanse, 18. Description: "The bills, legs, and feet are black; the tail quills (except a white bar), the greater coverts, and the whole top of the head and nape, black, with a metallic purplish-blue lustre; most of the feathers of the head with a minute rufescent white speck at the top. All the primaries with a very broad white bar extending from near the base to near the tip, and, except on the first primary, occupying the outer as well as the inner web. The shafts of the white portion of the feather are, in the first two or three primaries, partly brownish, in the rest white. The whole of the rest of the bird may perhaps be best described as a pale jay colour—that is to say, a mixture of pale rufous and fulvous fawn; with, especially on the back and rump, a vinaceous tinge, and becoming albescent on the chin, cheeks, and lower tail-coverts. The upper tail-coverts are very long, and reach to within an inch from the end of the tail, and are coloured like the back. The wing lining is blackish brown, but the feathers about the carpal joint are creamy white."

At four miles from Chadir-Kul trees give place to brushwood, and the track passes between low sand-hills covered with scrub. Approaching Tum Chuk, we ate excellent water-melons from a garden at the roadside, and after more than four hours' march reached this village of 40 Turki families, or, as my notes say, " 60 houses in the district." Here was some small amount of cultivation, and we saw barley cut, but not carried, though Bell observed wheat being harvested about Aksu on the preceding July 13th. Here I set Joseph to sell New Testaments, which he did so successfully as to need restraining, lest we should not have sufficient for all our journey.

On arriving at Tum Chuk, I was at first disposed to regard the day's march as over; but, as Osman Bai seemed eager to push forward, I gave permission, thinking to get on the morrow a day's shooting at Charwagh, where pheasants were said to be as common as barn-door fowls. Accordingly, we set out at four in the afternoon, and soon approached a long barren range of hills called the Akhur-Tau, stretching across the plain, having a gap through which our track passed nearly at a right angle.

As we went along I was looking and inquiring everywhere, but without success, for the ruins of a very ancient stone city, which Biddulph was told, and Forsyth reports, existed at Tum Chuk. In approaching the range we saw, at the southern end of it, something like the ruins of a castle perched on the top, but too far off to be accurately distinguished. Here and there, too, were farmsteads, and ruins of mud huts all around, showing the place to have been once populous.

The track, among low trees, passed over sand-hills, through the gap in the range, which was of indurated clay, with layers of flint at steep angles. Trees now ceased, and *chi* grass became plentiful, the track winding over a plain, out of which rise low detached hills. The district is watered by several canals from the Kashgar river, all sunk from three to six feet below the surface. Travelling thus, I reached Charwagh at ten, about an hour in advance of the baggage, feeling very tired and not quite well, though a night's sleep seemed to put me right.

On reaching Charwagh (or Chahar-bagh, according to Bell) we had come to the farthest point in this direction reached by members of the Forsyth expedition in 1873. Colonel Biddulph made his way to Maralbashi, and then went on 14 miles farther to Charwagh—a village, he says, of 250 inhabitants—being especially anxious to shoot a tiger, in which he was unsuccessful, though there were said to be many about.

He had good sport, however, shooting deer, and saw the *birkuts*, or trained eagles, take gazelles and foxes. For my own part, my opportunities and desires were less ambitious; but, hearing that pheasants were so plentiful, I wished to get some of their skins, to say nothing of procuring something for my larder by way of change from chicken and mutton.

I therefore obtained as guide a man who was said to know the locality, but who turned out a poor hunter. We saw, indeed, two or three pheasants, but after three hours' tramp we returned to the station, rather tired, and with nothing more to show than a hawk, a rook, a crested lark (*Galerita magna*), and a starling (*Sturnus porphyronotus*).*

---

* Colonel Biddulph, writing to Dr Bowdler Sharpe of the pheasant of this locality (*Phasianus Shawi*), says that it frequents thick grass-

The horses having rested, I left Charwagh at five in the afternoon in the *arba*, the hard track over clay continuing to traverse the *chi*-covered flat. Biddulph mentions, as within a mile of the road hereabouts, a huge black rock, apparently basaltic, with a triple peak, rising to a height of some 2,500 feet above the plain, rugged and quite inaccessible. It is called "The Prophet Ali's footstep," and at its foot on the north side is a tomb of renowned sanctity, at sight of which Muhammadans dismount to utter prayer.

At first our way lay through high grass, tall as standing corn. The district being irrigated by numerous canals, we crossed many bridges, one of which had to be mended before we could do so, and herein our Turki *djiguitt*, Sarim Sak, showed himself a thoroughly capable and hard-working fellow. Beyond the high grass we got among trees, where we were annoyed by mosquitoes. The low hills now receded from ten to fifteen miles to the north, whilst detached hills occurred to the southward, all barren and steep.

At 11 miles from starting we approached the Kashgar river, here 50 feet broad, of which we could not see much, since we no longer had moonlight. Six hours' drive, however, brought us, near upon midnight, to a *serai* in the native town of Maralbashi.

jungle, and, according to the natives, never roosts in trees. Some of the Forsyth party shot specimens between Yarkand and Kashgar, and Biddulph was more fortunate than I in finding it very common at Maralbashi; but he did not meet with the bird west of Kashgar. He reports it as very wild and shy, and running like a fiend, only rising, as a rule, at a considerable distance; so that, as it was almost impossible to retrieve them in the grass unless killed outright, he did not bag more than three in any one day.

CHAPTER XXV.

THE INHABITANTS OF CHINESE TURKISTAN.

Chinese Central Asia and its inhabitants; Manchus in Ili and Pelu towns, 396.—Kalmuks in Sungaria and Karashar, 397.—Kirghese; their anthropological characteristics, diseases, morals, and occupation, 398.—Scarcely subjected by Chinese; Turkish inhabitants of plains, 405.—Their alleged Aryan descent, 406.—Lack of physical strength; The Turks hard-working and honest; Weak points of urban character; Lack of baths; Abuse of narcotics, 408.—Sexual depravity, 409.—Piteous story of a female prisoner, 410.—Degradation of country through Muhammadanism; The Chinese, "strangers and foreigners"; their mandarins and soldiery, 412.—Chinese garrisons and traders; Total population, 414.

THE inhabitants of Chinese Central Asia, or China beyond the Wall, may be roughly enumerated as Manchus and Mongols, Kalmuks and Kirghese, Turks and Tibetans. Confining ourselves here to Chinese Turkistan, I may say that of Tibetans we did not meet, or hear of, a single specimen throughout the country; not even at Khotan, where some writers had led us to expect a few.

Nor do I remember meeting any Manchus, though there had been no lack of them in the Ili valley; also among the Tian Shan Pelu towns are mentioned Manchu cities, as at Barkul, with 1,000 Manchu soldiery, and similarly Kinsu, a small village somewhat farther east,

At Guchen, also, a Manchu town was completed in 1887, to be occupied the following year.

Again, of Mongols proper we saw none; but a certain portion of the country is inhabited by their congeners the Kalmuks. Speaking of the Kalmuks generally, they may be divided into four branches, distributed for the most part over Sungaria. The northern division is located in Khobak and Sarin, east of Chuguchak. The eastern division inhabits the country between An-how-tzien and Balgazi; and the western division is spread over the district stretching from south of An-how-tzien to Bora-Burgusu. This division numbers 40,000 individuals, with 3,900 horsemen.

Lastly, the southern division is found on the river Khuidu-gol, near Karashar, and is the most numerous, mustering 8,100 horsemen, which probably includes the Mongol nomads, sometimes called Hoshoits, of the Kunges valley, some of whom migrated there from Koko-Nor, and are said to number 18,000 individuals, furnishing in the field 1,800 horsemen.

In Chinese Turkistan the only Kalmuk settlement is Karashar; unworthy, Wilkins thinks, of the name of a town, since it consists of one street only, about 500 yards long, with no regular bazaar, but only a few poor and dirty shops without Russian or English merchandise. There are, however, about 250 houses, a caravanserai, and, in the time of Yakub Khan, there existed an elementary school, and two *medresses*, or colleges. In the vicinity are 500 Kalmuk cavalry, and from 1,000 to 2,000 Kalmuk families.

Of the physical and ethnographical characteristics of the Kalmuks I spoke when among them in the Tekes valley; and so completely did we there leave them behind, that on arriving at Aksu we could find none amongst whom to distribute any of our few remaining copies of the Kalmuk Scriptures. I had, therefore, to entrust them to the Russian *Aksakal* to sell them to, or send them by, traders proceeding in the direction of Karashar; and when farther west we failed to meet a single Kalmuk, I sent the last ten copies from Kashgar to General Ivanoff, asking him to distribute them amongst the Kalmuks of Vierny.

We may pass, therefore, to the Kirghese, who in Chinese Turkistan are, almost to a man, dwellers in the mountains. They monopolise the Aksai valley west of Ush-Turfan and the Sirt country, and roam over the mountains north, south, and west of Kashgar as far as the Pamirs. They are much better known to science than their Kalmuk neighbours, and have been closely studied, among others, by Dr Seeland, who, not long before I met him at Vierny, had written a paper on the Kirghese for the *Revue d'Anthropologie*, to which I am indebted for much of my information.*

The body of the Kirghese is vigorous, and endowed

* After an elaborate series of measurements of 40 men and 10 women, Dr Seeland describes the Kirghese as of medium stature and well proportioned; shoulders wide, neck neither long nor thick, chest well developed, the lower limbs straight, hands and feet small, brown skin, and dark hair. Fat subjects are rare; hump-backed and crooked not seen. The head, covered with stiff hair, and cut short or shaven, is very brachycephalous, and more or less pointed, the summit forming a sort of crest. The forehead, especially among the men, is more or less retreating; ears of medium size, with the upper portions standing off from the head, by reason perhaps of the sheepskin busby being pressed down upon them, though this would not apply to the *malakhai*, or travelling sheepskin hood. The cheek-bones are wide apart, but less so, as I myself observed, than with pure Mongols such as Buriats. The nose is prominent, and not too large; the mouth fairly small and well coloured; but the upper lip is ordinarily thick and protruding. The teeth are straight and white; the beard and moustache often lighter than the hair, and rarely thick; and in general the skin is not very hairy, but is supple, and impregnated with the smell of smoke.

with greater organic resistance than that of settled peoples; and the temperature of his blood is higher.

A KIRGHESE IN "MALAKHAI," OR TRAVELLING HOOD.

Cold, heat, hunger, thirst, and all physical sufferings are admirably endured by these nomads. Their vitality is especially observable in the way they bear wounds.

Great gashes, even of the skull, often heal without fever or loss of appetite; and amputated limbs are rapidly covered with granulations, without leaving ulcers, caries, etc.

Sickness occurs among them less frequently than among ourselves. The muscular strength, however, of the Kirghese is less than that of the Russian peasant. In horsemanship both sexes excel, the Kirghese being as firm on horseback as on his feet; but in vaulting and tricks of equitation he is beaten by the Cossack. Again, sight, hearing, and smell are admirably acute, but touch is less developed than among educated persons.*

The extremes of climate and variety of territory frequented by the Kirghese, as well as their manner of life, help, no doubt, to develop the organic resistance just spoken of to cold and hunger, as an illustration of which Seeland quotes an instance of a young Kirghese, in the neighbourhood of Pishpek, buried by accident in snow for 20 hours, his only nourishment being his boots, which he ate down to the soles!

Their indifference to physical suffering may, however, be partly attributable to the feebleness of touch before mentioned. Comparing them with the Gilyaks on the Amur (who I remember struck me, in 1879, as the lowest specimens of humanity I had seen), Seeland thinks sensitiveness to pain more developed among the Kirghese. When he pulled a few hairs out of a Gilyak, the man seemed to heed it no more than a horse seized by the mane as an aid to a mount,

* The Kirghese women resemble the men, but with certain important differences. The stature and muscular strength of the woman are less, but her temperature is higher. The arms are relatively shorter, but her physiognomy is more intelligent and grave. The average weight of the men, tested by Seeland, was 131 lbs., that of the women 110 lbs.

whereas the Kirghese winced. Both can rest quietly in their tents when full of smoke, whence it would

A KIRGHESE BRIDE.

seem that the mucous membrane covering the ball of the eyes is less tender than among ourselves.

From the fact that in Kirghese one word, *kok*, does duty for blue, green, and grey, it has been assumed that they are colour-blind; but this is not the case. Moreover, their sense of smell is such that they scent smoke at distances incredible to a European. They like the perfume of flowers, but are indifferent to what some would call a positive stench.

The Kirghese arrive at puberty at about the same age as Europeans of a temperate climate, but so rarely live beyond 85, that in 1883, at Tokmak, among 82,000 Kara-Kirghese, there were surviving only two men of 86 and 92 respectively. Out of a like number of English, 2,700 attain 85 and upwards.

As for their diseases, scrofula is met with but rarely; and of phthisis, Dr Pchigodski met with one case only in the district of Tokmak in seven years.*

The native methods of treatment, apart from the curious instances named in a previous chapter, include the cure by hunger and water, the patient receiving for a period of from 14 to 60 days nothing but water, with a very little milk, of which mixture some drink from 12 to 14 pints a day; so that to pose like Mr

* Leprosy does not appear to exist. Cancer occurs 20 times less frequently than among settled populations. On the other hand, syphilis among them is endemic, one in 20, perhaps, suffering therefrom. In spring the Kara-Kirghese suffer also from scorbutus. Of infectious diseases small-pox is the most frequent, but its virulence and area have much diminished since the introduction of vaccination. Intermittent fevers are rare or frequent, according to the ground selected for winter encampment. Rheumatism is common, but organic disease of the heart rare; whilst diseases of the nervous system, paralysis, convulsions, and psychosis are very rare indeed. Cases, however, are met with of idiocy and melancholy. Diseases of the organs of sense are not common, except superficial inflammation of the eyes, arising generally from smoke; also growths upon the eyeballs and inversion of the eyelids occur from time to time; but loss of sight, from cataract or atrophy of the optic nerve, as well as loss of hearing, is rare. Chronic diseases of the skin frequently exist, due to lack of cleanliness; for regular bathing is unknown even in summer, though, if a Kirghese chance to be passing a river, he may take a plunge into it.

Tanner and his imitators would scarcely pay among the Kirghese. Intermittent fever is treated by fright. Against chills they have recourse to enforced sweating. For scorbutus they give sour cabbage and *koumiss*, which are, in fact, excellent remedies. To wounds they apply burnt felt, if there is hæmorrhage. They

INTERIOR OF A KARA-KIRGHESE TENT.

also place on the wound powdered tobacco, pour on boiling fat, and sometimes (according to M. Gourdet) cauterise by means of ignited gunpowder.

The temperament of the Kirghese is decidedly sanguine. Their manner of living, plenty of horse-riding, frequent change of place and mountain air, together with the absence of intoxicating drinks, opium-smoking, and the use even of tobacco, seem to engender a happy temperament, and to account for the absence of nervous diseases and melancholy.

And this temperament of the Kirghese is reflected in his moral physiognomy. Among his good qualities must be mentioned integrity, compassion, hospitality, endurance, sobriety, and absence of revenge and cruelty. His defects are idleness, want of forethought, vanity, curiosity, uncleanliness, a certain love of litigiousness, and a great weakness for his neighbours' horses, the stealing of which he mixes up with remembrance of raids in pre-Russian times, when cattle-lifting was regarded as part of the calling of a brave; but this love of equine appropriation is said to be consistent with honesty in other things.

Crime, as we understand the word, is comparatively rare among them. Murder is not common, and suicide seldom heard of; and then generally among women, whose lot is frequently a hard one.*

The Kirghese is before all things a nomad, a shepherd, a tender of cattle; and he thinks it a descent in life when obliged to follow agriculture. This, however, he is gradually learning on Russian soil.†

To judge from the zest with which a number of men and boys rushed into a stream near Issik-Kul to secure

---

* Rape occasionally occurs, but Dr Seeland says that prostitution and unnatural offences are unknown, though the last, in Russian Turkistan, are largely practised by the Sarts.

† In Chinese Turkistan, in the valley west of Ush-Turfan, Younghusband found the Kirghese cultivating the poppy, not for their own use, but as a profitable crop; and in the Sirt country, wheat also and other cereals. Gordon, too, mentions a little scattered cultivation by Kirghese in the Toyan valley and the lower valleys of the Siriks district. Many of these people are also carriers, and transport merchandise over the mountainous country between Osh, Vierny, and Kashgar.

for me specimens of fish, the Kirghese should be keen sportsmen. As a means of subsistence, however, hunting is not much in vogue, though they chase the deer for their horns and foxes for their skins, to the extent that, in 1882, there were killed in the districts of Issik-Kul, Vierny, and Sergiopol 6,000 foxes, worth £1,200, and 400 stags, worth £2,200.*

On Russian soil the Kirghese pay about 12s. a tent as taxes, but the Chinese have not got them sufficiently in hand to exact anything—a cause of trouble to the Russians, some of their subjects crossing the frontier to evade the tax-collector. In fact, the district between Kashgar and Ferghana, and the adjacent Chinese portion of the Pamirs, was said to be hardly in subjection, the Kirghese there regarding themselves as free, and ready upon a favourable opportunity to aid insurrection and descend for plunder to the plains. Nor is pillage of caravans entirely unknown. On my arrival at Kashgar, I met Miss Petrovsky, who, with her brother, had crossed by the Narin route from Vierny, and had been robbed, on Chinese soil if I mistake not; but the occurrence was regarded as rare, the goods were recovered, and the robbers taken into custody.

Having now spoken of the nomad hill tribes of Chinese Turkistan, I proceed to the settled inhabitants of the plains, which I have called Turks to distinguish them from Mongols, Manchus, and Chinese. Some writers call them Uigurs; others Dungans, Taranchis, and Kashgarians; and Shaw—" Tatarise dAryans."

The common opinion seems to be that the Yuechi,

* The slaughter of deer for their horns has, of course, wrought great havoc throughout Central Asia, and I have learned with satisfaction from Mr Littledale that in the neighbourhood of Malo-Narinsk an attempt at preservation is being made by inclosing the animals and as an experiment cutting off their horns when soft.

who, in the second century B.C., were driven from their seats over the Pamirs by the Uigurs, were Aryans. They left behind them a considerable remnant, with whom the Uigurs and subsequent Mongol invaders intermarried. Hence the existing inhabitants of the towns of Chinese Turkistan.

Dr Bellew, who both studied the people locally, and, in his historical sketch in Forsyth's Report, as well as in his *Kashmir and Kashgar*, shows himself widely read in his subject and entitled to speak with authority, supports the foregoing hypothesis by etymological considerations, and others follow his lead.

I am not aware, however, that any history, document, or historical monument affords proof that these primitive inhabitants were Aryans, or that their migration was only partial. At the same time I must allow that just as to an ordinary observer the difference was patent between Buriats and Kirghese, so it struck me among the people of Chinese Turkistan that one oftener saw a nearer approach to a European countenance than was visible, I thought, among natives in Russian Turkistan.

But here again I gladly avail myself of the researches of Dr Seeland, whose journey from Vierny to Kashgar, and thence to Aksu and Ush-Turfan, gave him the opportunity of studying anthropologically the natives of the northern portion of the country, just as the Forsyth mission gave similar opportunity to Dr Bellew to study the natives of the southern portion, especially Yarkand, their observations coalescing at Kashgar.

Dr Seeland's examination and measurements were made upon 30 agriculturists and labourers—25 from the oasis of Kashgar, and five from Aksu and Turfan — and may therefore be regarded as complementary to those of Dr Bellew, only that anthropologically they are far more minute and exhaustive. Dr Seeland wrote an account of his journey, a portion of which, translated into French by our mutual friend M. Gourdet, is before me in manuscript.

The Kashgarian type, he observes, is far from handsome, and Aryan blood among them is, without doubt, reduced to a minimum. The average stature is about 64 inches, chest fairly broad, but generally flat, whilst the back is rounded, from the habit, probably, of sitting cross-legged and leaning forward to balance the body. The muscle of the labourer is well developed, and the constitution generally good, though among the lower stratum of poor in the towns feeble folk are common enough.

As for the head, it resembles that of the Kirghese, thus far at least, that it is strongly brachycephalous, retreating towards the top and little developed at the back. The faces of some presented certain characteristic traits of the Caucasian race, with a thick beard; but, in most subjects, Mongolian characteristics prevailed — projecting cheek-bones, little beard, large nose, thick lips. The colour of the skin is swarthy, but without the yellow tint of the Chinese.

Here and there among the younger women a whitish tint of great delicacy is observable, and it is noteworthy that the women of Kuchar, eastwards, are remarkable for their beauty and fresh complexions. This agrees with what Marco Polo says of the good looks of the women of the eastern part of the country; and the same is mentioned in some of the older Chinese writings, as well as confirmed by a modern traveller, M. Chikhalibekoff.

In the neighbourhood of Maralbashi, Seeland found the Caucasian type of countenance better preserved—

the face oval and regular, mouth straight and good-looking, nose thin, eyes larger than among the Turkish races, and stature taller; whereas in Aksu the Mongolian characteristics were more accentuated even than in Kashgar. The face of the Kashgarians has little or no expression, unless it be of indifference, and is, on the whole, somewhat repellent.

Their physical strength is in no way remarkable, and Dr Bellew more than once points out their incapacity for sustained exertion. Both sexes ride, but generally on donkeys, and equestrian games are not much in vogue.

The settled inhabitants of Chinese Turkistan are, however, beyond doubt hard-working, and gain their daily bread literally by the sweat of their brow; also they are honest, notwithstanding their poverty. Theft is comparatively rare, and throughout the villages the doors are without locks. One is struck also with the probity of the carriers, who often transport merchandise and money abroad of ten times the value of their own possessions, yet nothing confided to them is lost.

On the other hand, among the weak points of urban character in Chinese Turkistan must be mentioned lack of cleanliness, a tendency to the abuse of narcotics, and sexual depravity. Other Muhammadan countries are supplied with baths, but in Aksu there are none, and in Kashgar only one establishment, and that small and badly kept. I myself was thankful to accept from M. Petrovsky the luxury of a Russian bath at the Consulate. Amongst the natives the well-to-do wash at home; the poor, it is said, dispense with washing.

With regard to narcotics, Seeland says that half the proletariat of Kashgar smoke *hasheesh*, or hemp, under various forms, and four or five per cent. of the women eat it in sweetmeats. At Aksu the consumption of *hasheesh* and opium is relatively smaller by about one-half. These poisons are taken at establishments set apart for the purpose, and are smoked in the *chilim*, or pipe of the country, which is filled with a mixture of hemp and tobacco, whereon are placed live coals, the smoke being drawn right into the lungs.

There exist other means of taking narcotic preparations, for which are used, besides hemp and opium, henbane, thorn-apple, and probably, as in Ferghana, nux-vomica. The gaiety produced by these narcotics seems to afford an artificial oblivion, at the expense, of course, of enfeebling the nerves, so that among the townspeople even old men are often seen to burst into tears ; and madness is frequent.

As for the other form of depravity mentioned, it arises partly from emigration of the men, whereby the women, in Kashgar at least, are in excess of men, I was told, by six to one. Hence throughout Central Asia the cheapness of Kashgar wives is proverbial. For four or five shillings one may acquire a " lawful wife"; and if for one reason or another she does not please, divorce is equally easy. Some of the men, Seeland says, change their wives six times a year ! *

---

* There exists among the Sarts another hideous depravity in marrying girls of from ten to twelve years old, and drugging them at first with opium. This testimony was confirmed to me by a man of education resident in Kashgar, and by a second European, who said he had known many girls have 20 husbands before they were capable of becoming mothers ! What sort of progeny results when they become old enough to bear children may be imagined, and indeed seen in the miserable appearance of many of the townspeople. Meanwhile, the lot of the cast-off women is very sad. They cannot obtain daily employment, and their only resource is the making of *mata*, by which to earn a miserable pittance. Others, again, of the unmarried women who cannot obtain husbands have recourse to practices which recall the

The case of the female prisoner whom we overtook on the road will illustrate this, and is worth more than many statements of a general character. When looking over the fort at Maralbashi, I peeped into one of the prison rooms, and there, alone, cleanly dressed, but hiding herself from observation, was the young woman we had seen, and whose piteous tale was afterwards given me as follows :—

Her father, it seems, about ten years before, killed another man, for which he was put in the Chinese prison at Kashgar, whither her mother daily sent her little and pretty child of nine with food for her father. One of the prison officials thus came to notice the child, and made an offer to the mother that if she would give her daughter to him the father should be released.

The mother consented, and for six months the child was abused in the house of her keeper, who, having to go to Peking, and she not wishing to accompany him, sent her home to her father. Then another Chinese official married her and took her to Ush-Turfan for two years, after which her husband put her into a cart and sent her back to Kashgar, whilst he returned to China.

Next, she was married to a Muhammadan Bek, or nobleman, for a year, when he took an additional wife, with whom for three months this one quarrelled, whereupon she was divorced and sent away, and remained free for three months. Then came another Bek, to whom she was married for five months. But he already had a wife of higher grade, from whom at

unseemly things of heathen Rome. In the country districts of Chinese Turkistan, however, these depravities are said not to obtain, each man usually having but one wife, and living permanently with her.

first he kept this one separate, till, bringing them together, and quarrels ensuing, she was again dismissed, at the age of only thirteen, from this her fourth husband.

Then she went home and lived a loose life for a year, her mother being aware of it, but not the father. He, on learning the facts, not only did not forbid her, but, after the mother's death, forced her against her will, and with blows, to pursue an evil life, and basely lived and smoked upon his daughter's gains.

The next chapter in her melancholy career was to be kept by a Chinese officer, and he quarrelled with another man who came to her house, on account of which the woman was exiled to Aksu. Here, again, two men had quarrelled in her dwelling, the result being disastrous to herself; for, at the age of only eighteen, and in spite of her good looks, this poor young creature was on her way to execution.

She herself told this tale to Joseph, in the hope, as I afterwards heard, that I would intercede on her behalf. Amin, too, had seen her seven years before, and, having been born in Kashgar, knew her family sufficiently to corroborate the main facts of the case.

Much of the foregoing, it should be observed, is quite in keeping with being an excellent Muhammadan. Yakub Khan posed as a religious reformer, restored colleges, built mosques, appointed officers to drive the people to prayers, closed licensed houses, and tried to suppress prostitution; yet, according to Kuropatkin, he maintained 300 women, six of whom accompanied him in all his wanderings; and I was told that he absolutely killed by his brutality two of the young girls of his harem, and brought upon himself much indignation thereby.

It would have been pleasanter to have passed over a great deal of what has been written in this chapter, but the reader may thus form an idea to what degree Muhammadanism is capable of degrading a country after centuries of unopposed sway. Other features of anthropological and ethnographical interest among the Turks will be noticed as we travel round Chinese Turkistan, but I pass on now to notice briefly the ruling class among the inhabitants of the country— namely, the Chinese.

The Chinese are as much strangers and foreigners in the Tarim valley as are the English in India; indeed, more so, since the Chinese longest in residence came into the country but yesterday, and I never heard of a mandarin troubling himself to study the requirements, or even to learn the language, of the people he governed.

Moreover, the imperial government at Peking, it seems, acts in a most foolish manner towards the reconquered country, sending thither, not its best mandarins, but those who for some disgrace are thus banished as to a Botany Bay. Hence I was given to understand that the Chinese officials in Kashgar and neighbouring towns are mandarins decidedly below par, educationally and otherwise.

Again, the larger proportion of the Chinese soldiery are but militia, sometimes convicts, or enlisted often at a moment's notice from among the idlers and ragamuffins of the bazaar, and sent off to the colonies for service, where, thanks to bad military discipline, and lawless conduct of various kinds, they become a veritable pest to the localities where they are quartered.

In the Ili valley we were constantly reminded that many of the higher officials came from Manchuria,

CHINESE WOMEN AT KASHGAR.

but I do not remember hearing the like in the Tarim valley. There (beginning east), the 500 soldiers at Tsi-tai-hsien, near Guchen, are said to be from the province of Sz-chuen, and the Guchen garrison consists of 500 braves of Hunan. Again, at Gu-medi are 500 Hunan braves, and 20,000 similarly described are supposed to be posted between Hami and Ili. The garrison of Toksun are called braves from Hunan and Shensi, whilst 1,050 of the soldiers at Kashgar are spoken of as from Hunan, and at Yengi Hissar are 500 cavalry from Shantung.

Besides this military population there are certain Chinese traders, who generally take up their quarters in the forts, and who are mentioned (by Bell), especially in the eastern towns, as settled by hundreds. Thus at Chi-mu-sa are 35 Chinese families; at San-tai, 300; at Szen-i-chien, 130; at Fuh-khan, 130; and at Kashgar, 300. At Urumtsi there are said to be from 500 to 1,000 Chinese shopkeepers from Hunan, Su-chow, and Ping-yang, but living without Chinese wives.

It was this sort of thing repeated, I suppose (to judge from the paucity of Chinese women we saw farther west), in the "Yengi-shahr" of Aksu, Kashgar, Yarkand, and Khotan. The foreign rulers looked always a scanty few among the surrounding natives.

The total population of Chinese Turkistan was estimated by Forsyth at a million, but Bell thinks this too low, and after travelling all along the northern and western portions of the country, and with the advantage of Russian estimates before him, his "two millions" is probably nearer the mark.

Having thus spoken of the inhabitants generally, I shall continue to describe my journey among them.

CHAPTER XXVI.

FROM MARALBASHI TO KASHGAR.

An early welcome, 415.—Call on the mandarin; The bazaar, 416.—Visited by mandarin, 417.—Photography, and consequent excitement, 418.—The fortress and its features, 420.—General character of forts in Chinese Turkistan; Maralbashi, a strategical position; Road southwards to Yarkand, 422.—Dolan shepherds and their underground dwellings, 423.—Departure from Maralbashi, 424.—A trot to Urdaklik, 425.—Caught in a quagmire, 426.—A neighbourhood of wild-boars and deer, 427.—March to Faizabad; Visited by Chinese general, 428.—Features of the town, 429.—Limits of Kashgar district; March to the Yengi-shahr, 430.—March through fortress to old town of Kashgar, 431.

EARLY on the morning of August 30th, at Maralbashi, before I was up, Isa, a Turki *bek*, in the employ of the Government, called to inquire for me and offer his services. He had been advised, he said, of my coming, and had taken for me better apartments at another *serai*, to which he invited us to remove. The baggage, however, being unpacked, and anticipating only a short sojourn, I preferred to stay where I was; whereupon he did his best to make himself useful in other ways.

Of his own accord he asked the Chinese authorities to send me a guard because of the curious crowds forcing themselves into the *serai* to look at the stranger—the numbers being the more increased by my giving

Joseph books and cards to sell—so that at length, in self-defence, the crowd had fairly to be driven out of the yard by a petty officer and two subordinates, who stuck up at the gate an arrow, as an emblem of authority, to signify that I was under the special protection of the magistrate.

In the afternoon I called upon the chief authority, there being two mandarins in the town, a *hsien* and a military. Riding into the fort, and not dismounting until I reached the great man's door, I thought, seemed to perturb some of the Chinese, who came up to me as if remonstrating. But I neither understood nor heeded, and sent in my card. Before the door stood a drum, which if a man strikes at any hour of the day or night the mandarin, whatever he may be doing, is bound to come.

Such is the magnificent theory by virtue of which the distressed may flee to the highest for help; but, inasmuch as the mandarin, under such conditions, usually orders his summoner 100 lashes, and then asks what he wants, the privilege is of doubtful value, and one of which I did not avail myself. It took but a short time, on the appearance of this local potentate, to exchange compliments; after which we proceeded to look about the fort, and permission having been given to visit the prison therein, we found it new, much better than at Aksu, and with few inmates.

On our way to and from the fort we passed through a portion of the bazaar, which is, in fact, the main road, lined by shops, some kept by Turks and some by Chinese. Indian merchants are said to come here *viâ* Yarkand, and stay for a month or two. They bring tea, sugar, pepper, ginger, and cotton goods. Thus, in the shop of an Afghan, I was pleased to read on a piece of muslin " Ferdinand Cohen & Co., Manchester." For 18 yards they asked 5s., whilst for another piece of 10 yards of figured coloured muslin, marked "Graham, Bombay and Calcutta," the price named was 7s. 6d.

In the summer ice is cheap and plentiful, and iced curds and apricots are the order of the day. Iron ore is said to be found in the vicinity, and is roughly smelted ; but it did not give one a lofty idea of local commerce when Isa, the *bek*, represented the getting me small change for five ounces of silver—about a sovereign—as not quite an easy matter. He thought it might be done at 16 *tengas* the *ser* instead of 20—that is to say, at the rate of 16s. for £1 ; whilst another man quoted 15 *tengas* only, but doubted if so much ready cash could be found in the market.

At the time of Colonel Bell's passing through, there was at Maralbashi a barber from Lahore, said to be doing well and contented ; the same, I suspect, who presented himself to me about 12 months later at Kuldja—one Ismail—who said he had been recommended to try his fortune as barber in the Ili valley. He had accordingly come thither from Maralbashi over the Muzart Pass in 24 days, and at a cost from Aksu of 100 *tengas*, or about £1, for each of two horses, and 100 more for expenses. I did not gather, however, that he had improved his position by wandering farther from India, but rather the contrary ; and I heard on the spot of no British subjects at Maralbashi, though Isa said he had known Mr Dalgleish.

When, on the morrow, the chief mandarin returned my visit, I asked whether he had received orders to make inquiries for the murderer of Dalgleish. He replied in the negative, but showed every disposition to meet my wishes, having already promised me two Mussulman attendants to relieve the two *djiguitts* returning to Aksu.

My first wish, after resting for a day, was to start again ; but, for a wonder, Osman Bai desired me to tarry, saying that one of his horses was sick, and I assented the more readily as it was a rainy morning ; also it gave me opportunity to take some photographs, which I commenced from the top of the *serai*.

The neighbouring flat roofs and the straight level of the Chinese fort in the distance presented a dull picture, relieved by one erection only, standing out above the horizon—namely, the so-called Old Tower, the sole building I remember as a possible survival of what Biddulph calls a "palace," built outside the fort by Yakub Khan, who often stayed here on his way to and from Aksu. The views of the bazaar east and west from the gate of the *serai* presented the curious aspect of Central Asian streets shaded with what once were leafy branches, and now looked like brushwood.

Meanwhile the sight of my camera so stirred the curiosity of the crowd that they made a rush for the housetop, which I forbade. It was plain, however, that my Turkish attendants, although officials, and not hesitating to lay their whips on their fellow-countrymen, were very cautious of touching a Chinaman, and, as it soon appeared, with good reason.

I had heard of the outrageous lies a Chinaman can tell, merely to give point to his conversation. On the present occasion one of these rascals, who had, I suppose, been turned back from ascending to the roof, went to the mandarin and told such a tissue of falsehoods as to the treatment he had met with as to make one's hair stand on end. The mandarin sent to ask

TAKING PHOTOGRAPHS IN THE BAZAAR.

whether it was true, and fortunately accepted my denial; but it was easy to see how a Turk would be no match for such a calumniator before a Chinese judge.

Happily the authorities manifested no fear of my revisiting and taking photographs of the fort, which Kuropatkin calls the "third of the important defences of Kashgaria," though I should hardly think it would take such rank now.*

A photograph of one of the four gateways presented an enormous mass of brickwork, 100 feet deep. The gateways are in the centre of each side, and project 40 yards by 60, thus giving flank defence. Within, we mounted the walls by ramps at the gateways, over some of which are covered lodgments, whilst at the angles of the fort are circular projections of about 30 feet diameter, with towers, thus giving a double line of musketry fire.

The fort was originally built by the Chinese, but many of the mud huts within it were probably erected in the time of Yakub Khan; whilst here and there were new buildings, *yamen*, barracks, etc., of a style unmistakably "Celestial," but there were no shops. We nowhere had so good an opportunity of inspecting the characteristics of the Tarim forts as at Maralbashi.

The Chinese seem to be well aware that their tenure is precarious; and remembering how completely their soldiers are outnumbered by Turks, and on former occasions have been butchered, they have

* The fort has faces, according to Kuropatkin, of about 280 yards long, whilst another estimate says 400 yards. The walls are from 15 to 18 feet high, and about as thick, revetted with brick, and surrounded by a dry ditch. The Kashgar river, or a branch of it called the Kizil, flows close under the north face, whereby it would seem possible to flood the ditches. On the east face the village would give cover to besiegers. On the other sides the ground is uneven, but open with easy slopes.

TAKING A PHOTOGRAPH FROM THE ROOF OF THE CARAVANSERAI.

built at each important point we visited (namely, Aksu, Maralbashi, Kashgar, Yengi Hissar, Yarkand, and Khotan, to say nothing of towns farther east) strong inclosures, into which the Chinese population may run and be safe, whilst the Turki towns are left without walls, or nearly so, and the people are deprived of arms. Hence, as one native merchant said to me, "We are as weak as a lot of women."

The fort at Maralbashi should be garrisoned by 350 soldiers of Hunan, some mounted, but the number was 100 short. How they are armed I cannot say, but on examining some of the muskets at the *yamen* I found them marked "Tower," which smacked of the days of the old "Brown Bess." I photographed the interior of the fort from the ramparts, and then placed my camera on the top of the wall for a view of the native town, which has a population, it is said, of about 2,000 Turks.*

The existence of this large fort near so insignificant a village is explained by its situation at the junction of roads which lead to the town of Aksu from Khotan, Yarkand, and Kashgar, thus giving it a position of considerable strategical importance.

Of the track from Maralbashi southward to Yarkand we know but little, four Europeans only, so far as I remember, having travelled that way.†

---

* Biddulph observes that the town is also known as Barchuk and Lai Musjid, having a population of about 1,500 inhabitants, whilst Forsyth mentions 5,000 houses for the whole Maralbashi district, and says that, in the time of the former occupation of the Chinese, they kept here a garrison of 3,000 men, whereas Yakub Khan maintained the post with only 300.

† Benedict Goes did so, and has left us 14 names of places on his 25 days' journey from Yarkand to Aksu. Mr Carey travelled the reverse way, but neither he nor his lieutenant, Mr Dalgleish, in their contributions to the Geographical Society's publications, appears to have given us names of stations between Maralbashi and Yarkand, and of

Carey speaks of a reception, always kindly and hospitable, on the part of the Dolan shepherds in the country round Maralbashi, which Forsyth calls their capital. Bell, however, does not speak of the inhabitants of Maralbashi as different from those of other towns he passed through, nor did I notice any distinctive marks, though Seeland observed about Maralbashi, without being able to account for it, a greater number of countenances of Aryan type.

Forsyth, who met several of the Dolans at Yarkand, calls them an outcast Tatar tribe, whose dwellings were described to him as oblong pits dug in the ground, and roofed with a thatch of reeds supported on poplar beams—miserable hovels, in which the family consorts with its live-stock. This recalls exactly what I saw of the Tatars of the Crimea or Caucasus in 1880. Biddulph reports the Dolans to be descended from prisoners brought from Trans-Oxiana in the eleventh century by Haroun Bugra Khan, and forcibly settled between Maralbashi and Kuchar.

Again, Forsyth speaks of Dolan settlements along the river of Yarkand, where their principal wealth consists of asses, though they have also small herds of oxen and flocks of sheep. They have no agriculture, but carry to the market at Yarkand fuel, potash, coarse desert salt, butter, curd cheese called *suzma*, skins of foxes and birds, and coarse rope made from the fibre of the poplar. Another product of the poplar which they bring is called *toghrago*—a fungous decay from the trunk, sold for ferment in baking. They carry back in exchange cotton cloth, flour, bread, biscuits, boots and shoes, caps, etc.

the four places indicated on Walker's map none appear to tally with those of Goes. The fourth traveller referred to is Major Cumberland.

The Dolans are poor and illiterate, nominally Muhammadans, and without conjugal fidelity.* Physically, they are said to be of inferior race, and their mental capacity is of the meanest. They are short, small of limb, with retreating forehead, and repulsive Tatar features, resembling, Forsyth says, the Tibetans. They talk a dialect of Turki, but among themselves use a language nobody else understands. They are timid, simple, despised, shunning and being shunned by their neighbours.

On the third day I was impatient to start, and gave my men the first call at an hour after midnight, rose myself at two, breakfasted at three, but even then did not get off till nearly four. At first the 30-foot road traversed the well watered oasis, which is said, however, to be poor rather than fertile. Here and there are farmsteads, and then we came to a district of low bushes of tamarisk, sometimes so profusely tipped with crimson as to remind one of lilacs in bud.

About five miles from Maralbashi we crossed the Kashgar river, a sluggish stream here 50 feet wide, and its bed from six to eight feet below the general surface of the land. Beyond, the track ran over an uncultivated country, and, at ten miles, entered a wood of *tograk*, with trees 25 feet high, and 18 inches in diameter. In this wood, during the summer, horse-flies abound. With me it was the first of September, and sufficiently cool to make a shawl acceptable when lying in the *arba*.

* The custom obtains among them, according to Forsyth, that is also reported by Bell to exist among the Mongols, and which Marco Polo recorded of the people of Hami and Caindu, whereby the master of the house, on receiving a traveller, places his wife at the disposal of his guest, and himself retires to a neighbouring hovel until the guest's departure.

Mindful of the date, I was keenly on the look-out for "birds." The clay soil, easily pulverised, and abundance of *chi* grass, seemed to afford good cover, but I do not remember flushing any partridges in the northern part of the country. Two pheasants crossed our path, but not within gun-shot. At a bend of the river, many feet below, I saw a goose or swan, of a kind not familiar to me, but I did not fire because of the apparent impossibility of retrieving the quarry. I knocked over, however, my first hare, one of the few mammals I shot.

Four hours' ride brought us to Shugeh, a distance of 70 *li*—"very tired," says my journal ; whereupon I got into the *arba* and drove 60 *li* along a heavy road, often deep with dust, to Kara-Kuchan (or Kara-Kilchin-Robat), where we arrived at three. The baggage had come about an hour earlier, but minus a large piece of felt, which Osman Bai had left at Maralbashi—the only time, I think, he was forgetful—and for which the officer at the station kindly sent back a message, and it was recovered.

At Kara-Kuchan we spent Sunday, and I indulged in an extra hour or two of bed, with such success that, on rising, I reported myself in the enjoyment, so far as I could tell, of perfect health. That these Sunday stoppages were alike good for man and beast I have not a doubt, though Saturday night sometimes landed us in queer places wherein to spend the day of rest.

Monday morning brought a continuation of the rain that had been falling during the night, so that I did not hurry the men away; whilst for my own part I delayed for nearly an hour more, and then tried the experiment of a trot to Urdaklik (or Urdalick) in three and a half hours, instead of walking with the caravan, which took six.

By way of a change, the road was very muddy instead of dusty, and lay through forest with little undergrowth; but I saw no birds worth shooting. Colonel Bell seems to have been so persecuted here by horse-flies as to speak of this tract of country as worse than the passage of the Gobi; but I was six weeks later, and had no such cause of complaint.

My experiment of a quicker pace so far succeeded that I was less tired than sometimes after proceeding at walking pace; and my early arrival gave me the opportunity for taking photographs of the station, which was typical of the travellers' resting-places hereabouts. Approached from the road, it was a large walled inclosure, about 100 by 150 yards, which could be made to serve as a fortress; and on entering the gate, the first yard was surrounded, or partly so, by rooms, each with doorway and tiny window, suitable for the lodgment of soldiers on the march, or the serving-men of caravans; whilst in the inner yard were rooms for officers or travelling mandarins, with paper windows, a *kang*, a fireplace, and sometimes a table and chair, but nothing more.

We left Urdaklik next morning at seven, and I was proceeding alone over what looked like a little expanse of dried sand, when my horse unexpectedly sank in a quagmire, first to his knees and then to his girths. The farther forward he plunged, the worse it became, till he came to a standstill sufficiently on his side to imprison my left foot. Happily the soil was soft, and on getting off I was able, with the help of the men who had come up, to extricate myself without injury.

After this, at a distance of 40 *li*, we came to a

picket station, Yassa Bulak, or "Wusu Block." About a quarter of a mile before reaching it, the Kashgar river, here about 40 yards wide, is again crossed, this time by a bridge of three spans, 45 paces long, the banks being revetted with timber for some distance up and down the stream.

Here we stayed for rest and refreshment. On the previous night they had told me that wild-boars were making a raid into the neighbouring melon gardens; but the prospect was not alluring enough to draw me out of bed either for shooting or pig-sticking. It was in this neighbourhood, I presume,.that Biddulph stopped at a place he calls Toga Sulookh for a day's shooting, but secured only a specimen of the *djeran* (*Antilopa gutturosa*), nearly resembling the Indian gazelle, except that the horns are rather larger and curved outward, the tips being turned sharply inwards, and making a very handsome head.

At Yassa Bulak I saw many water-birds in a lake, some of them tall waders, like cranes or herons. These I could not approach, but I managed to bring down a snipe. Then I turned into the *arba* for about a third of the way, and after 80 *li* more we arrived at Lungur, forest and sand being plentiful all day, with low brushwood, thorny bramble, and camel-thorn, but no grass; so that at Lungur again we had to pay for fodder seven times, and corn double, the Aksu prices. Joseph, too, having been instructed that the female of a cock was a hen, came to inform me that he had bought a "hen" sheep for 20 *tengas*, or say 4*s*.

The next day's march brought us practically to the end of the desert, through which we had been travelling for many days. The rutty road, over dry alluvial soil, covered sometimes with a thin, hard crust of soda, crackling under foot at every step, and in which horses sank to their fetlocks, was once more alternated with a sandy track, amidst tamarisk bushes and hillocks. Several podoces allured me to a chase that was twice successful; and then we came, after 70 *li*, to Yangi-awat, or Yengi-abad, a village of 30 houses, where cultivation recommenced.

Here we stayed for refreshment, in a small shaded inclosure by the roadside—I think belonging to a mosque. Then I turned into the *arba* to proceed over an easy road, from 30 to 40 feet wide, with good bridges and well shaded by trees, through a well-watered oasis, dotted over with farmsteads, where maize grows luxuriantly, and wheat had been harvested in July. Thus we continued for 50 *li* more, and ten hours from the time of starting arrived at Faizabad.

Forsyth calls " Yangabad " and " Fyzabad " places of 600 houses each. Bell speaks of a few only in the village of Faizabad, but of 450 houses scattered about, and each accommodating two or three families. I did not feel so fatigued as yesterday, and was hardly settled in my room before a high military officer, General Li, called upon me, presenting fuel and fodder.

He was commander, I presume, of the garrison, evidently disposed to be chatty, and invited me to stay over the morrow to dinner, which I declined. He seemed to want all the information concerning me he could get, and not understanding very well, I suppose, the Chinese of my interpreter, sent for Amin, of whom he asked who I was, what amount of attentions I had received from previous mandarins, who had feasted me, and so on.

In the morning he sent messengers urging me to stay, in answer to which I returned him a present, but again declined. Thereupon he came in person, assuring me that there was no lack of oxen and fatlings, that he had plenty of everything, and was ready to kill ducks, fowls, and sheep, and give me a right good dinner. But I had been counting the days when I should end my weary march to Kashgar, and to be delayed four-and-twenty hours for the delights of a Chinese dinner was not to my mind.

He then asked, as a parting favour, a portrait of Queen Victoria, which I happened to possess among my baggage, though not at hand. I promised, therefore, to send it back to him from Kashgar—and was not allowed to forget my promise—by one of the two soldiers he had given me in place of the two men returning to Maralbashi.

These latter, I had heard, each received 200 cash for the double journey; but Joseph had standing orders to see that commissariat affairs went smoothly, and on parting I gave the men presents. Of the two soldiers furnished me by General Li, I despatched one of them in advance to announce my coming (on the next day but one, as I hoped) to M. Petrovsky at Kashgar.

Meanwhile much rain had fallen in the night, and came through my roof, and the roads in the morning were muddy to a degree that beggars description, so that we did not hurry off, and I was successful in taking an excellent photograph of the Bazaar Mosque of Faizabad. With its two minarets and *pishtak* it was the finest building we had seen thus far in the country, excepting perhaps at Aksu.

In the bazaar were exposed, besides melons, abundance of fodder, and cotton cloth, called *mata*, which here costs 8*d*., 1*s*., and 1*s*. 6*d*. the piece of six yards; whilst raw cotton sells at about 4*d*. per lb. I took, also, a view of the Chinese barracks, where is a garrison of 120 Dungan cavalry, and then left Faizabad about nine o'clock.

We had now entered the district of Kashgar, which stretches north to the Ush-Turfan valley, north-west and west to the Russian frontier, and south to Yapchan, whilst the border on the east is desert. Within these limits the population was estimated by Forsyth at 16,000 houses. Of these 5,000 were attached to the city and suburbs, 2,000 to Artosh, and the remainder distributed among a dozen principal market towns, with from 200 to 800 houses each, besides several agricultural settlements.

Our road from Faizabad lay for the most part through fields and gardens with abundance of Indian corn, good grazing land, and plenty of *dhub* grass; but not many trees were to be seen. We rode through several hamlets, coming first to a rest-house at Shafdul, and then pushing forward to Kazangul, 50 *li* from Faizabad, where I rested till the *arba* came up, and then, crossing a rapid stream at 16 miles from Faizabad, drove 50 *li* farther through Gam-i-sang (with good grapes) to a picket called Yaman Yar. Here we stayed for the night, fuel being reported dearer than ever, and rising to six *tengas* per 100 *jing*, or, say, 1s. 3d. per cwt.

It was a relief next morning to feel that we were starting on our last stage to Kashgar, for which we set out at half-past four, and at 30 *li* we came to a resthouse, Yondama, where was a small village, and beyond that a saline soil with little cultivation, a thick crust of saltpetre covering the stagnant pools. Thirty *li* farther on brought us to another hamlet, called Bahrin, and ten *li* more to the Yengi-shahr, approaching which cultivation improves. On the north of the city is an extensive swamp.

The Yengi-shahr of Kashgar is the chief fortress of Chinese Turkistan, and was built in 1838. It measures from 700 to 800 yards square, the eastern side being slightly curved. Outside, on the north and east, there is cover for an attacking party; to the west and south the ground is clear.*

Within the ramparts the city is divided into defensible quarters, and here resides the General commanding the military district, extending as far as Khotan. Here, too, are the artillery depôt, powder magazines, armourers' shop, and both military and civil *yamens*. There are within the town one *Chi Tai* mandarin and one *Chew*, its population consisting of about 200 Dungan, 300 Chinese, and a few Turki families. It is garrisoned by 250 cavalry and 800 infantry from Hunan, with 125 Turki cavalry.

As we approached the Yengi-shahr—impregnable, I presume, to an Asiatic foe—my men were for proceeding at once, without entering the fort, down the broad and excellent 40-foot highway leading to the Turkish town; but I bade them conduct me at all events, whatever became of the baggage, right through the new city, as its name implies; and thus I got a peep at the Chinese, who stared hard at the stranger, and were, I thought, a little disposed to be rude.

* The clay walls are 25 feet high, with a seven-foot crenelated musketry parapet two feet thick. On the east and north are flanking projections of about 50 by 40 yards; and some small towers in the projections and angles give additional flanking defence. There is also a covered way from 30 to 50 feet wide, fronted by a musketry parapet, and a ditch 40 feet wide and 15 deep, with a partial cunette. There are double gateways on the north, east, and south, entering at right angles, the outer being 50 and the inner 100 feet through. Ramps at the gates lead to the top of the ramparts, which are about 50 feet wide.

Here were more Chinese shops built in the style of the Flowery Land, and merchandise of higher pretensions than any we afterwards saw in the old town, though we did not linger, but, having passed out of the gate opposite to that by which we entered, rode along a parade ground and rejoined the main road.

From our last sleeping-place to Yengi-shahr I had driven in the *arba*, and there now remained for us but a ride of five miles northwards, with the Turkish town lying well in sight amidst an oasis of verdure. The road too, by comparison with the way we had come, was full of life and animation, merchants and humbler folk wending their way to or from the old city, as also Chinese officers, with outriders and attendants, helping to make up a lively concourse.

We saw snipe in the marshes adjoining the rapid river, which we crossed by a wooden bridge 100 feet long, in four spans. As we continued between walls and mud buildings, we presently met an *Aksakal* from the Russian Consulate. From him we learned that, expecting us to come by another road, an escort of a dozen horsemen had gone out to meet our caravan.

We were also told that there had been an amiable altercation between the Consul and the Chinese authorities as to who should be my host; the Consul claiming it on the ground of personal acquaintance, and the Chinese on the ground that I was in their country. The latter were allowed to prevail, and I was accordingly taken to a house in the town to be the guest of the Chinese *Tautai*, or General in command.

CHAPTER XXVII.

OUR STAY AT KASHGAR.

Ride to Russian Consulate, 433.—Ascent of city wall, 434.—M. Nicolas Petrovsky and his Consular staff, 435.—His hospitality and intellectual tastes, 436.—Miscarriage of letters; Visited by local authorities, 437.—Taking photographs, 438.—Trade of Chinese Turkistan and its ramifications, 439.—Calls and presents from the *Tautai*, 440.—Visit to prison, 441.—Three homicides, and instruments of torture, 442.—Uncertainty as to route; Thoughts of Kafiristan, 444.—Preparations for Karakoram route; Osman Bai paid off, and three carts engaged; Lack of antiquities in Kashgar, 446.—Ruin of Aski Shahr; Present town of Kashgar; Visit to shrine of Khoja Aphak, 447.—Rifled grave of Yakub Khan, 449.—The Mausoleum, 450.—The Golden Mosque; The Consul's photography and Muhammadan prejudice, 451.

REACHING Kashgar had been for many weeks looked forward to as the attainment of a much-desired goal, not only for the satisfaction of visiting a little-known city, but also because I there expected to find correspondence awaiting me which would help determine my course onwards. I lost no time, therefore, on the day of our arrival in going to the Russian Consulate.

Of cabs in Kashgar there are none, nor public vehicles answering to them, though I believe there are something like omnibuses plying between the old and new towns. The Consul's *calèche* is the only carriage in the city; and of wheeled traffic of any kind there is but little, though occasionally there are seen in the streets rough carts with the clumsiest of wheels made of blocks cut in sections of a circle cobbled together, and groaning and creaking beneath slabs of stone or logs of wood. We had, therefore, to ride, and directed our course across a fruit market near our lodging, and then continued through a street so narrow that two horsemen could not comfortably ride abreast. At the end of this we came to the north gate in the city wall.

This wall, built of mud, is from 1,200 to 1,400 yards long on one side, and, according to Gordon, three miles round. Small projections at close intervals give flanking fire commanding the narrow and shallow ditch. The gate projections (on the north the water gate, and on the south the sand gate) have sides of about 40 by 50 yards; but walls, huts, and ditches outside would give cover to besiegers right up to the town.

The area of the city, according to Bellew, is given at about 50 acres, and, within, a narrow road is kept clear under the steep inner slope of the wall. The ramps, leading up to the top, are barred by doorways; but they were opened to enable us to ascend 25 feet to the parapet, where the mass was 20 feet thick. Here were posts of observation, and rooms built on the wall that might serve for stores and sleeping-places for watchmen.

The view extends from five to ten miles to the north and west to low hills, beyond which, in the latter direction, the fine summits of the Tsung-ling Mountains, already alluded to, form the horizon. The town, 4,060 feet above the sea, on a plain of *loess* about 16 feet thick, and resting on sand, is surrounded by a belt of gardens and fields, but within the view of the city is anything but attractive.

Of the ornaments of an Oriental city, as popularly conceived—marble mosques, stately palaces, and lofty domes—there are none, and the few minarets are of unglazed bricks, devoid of ornament or taste. Instead of sparkling fountains, surrounded by greenery, are visible here and there in a square muddy pools, providing a meeting-place for bathers and water-carriers. Also, in place of cooling colonnades and arabesque-adorned corridors, are seen everywhere the small, crowded, clay-built dwellings of about 40,000 inhabitants.

As in Aksu, the streets, or some of them, are shut off with palisades and closed by night. The courtyards are small, and the houses badly lighted. Window-frames, where they exist, are covered with paper, panes of glass being seen only at the Consulate. Here and there a trader's house may have five or six fair-sized rooms, and the *ne plus ultra* of Kashgar taste is a verandah with a diamond-patterned clay parapet, whitewashed, or painted in gaudy colours. The view over the town, therefore, did not long detain us, and we descended to the Consulate, at a short distance outside the city walls.

I had met M. Nicolas Feodorovitch Petrovsky in St Petersburg in 1882, when he was on the eve of departure for Kashgar, to reside as Consul. On arriving, a native mud hut had been adapted to his needs; but I understood that the Chinese had given, or were to give, a piece of ground whereon a worthy Consulate should be erected for himself and his wife, for Mr Lutch, the dragoman-secretary, and for about 40 Cossacks with their two officers and a *feldscher*, or surgeon's attendant. These, with the exception of a Dutch Roman missionary, M. Hendriks, and a Pole whom he had brought from Russia or Siberia, were the only European residents in Kashgar.

It was, however, pleasant to get back to Western languages, and a real kindness to receive an open invitation to dine daily at the Consulate; for, if Madame Petrovsky found it difficult to provide a variety of food from the meanly-stocked bazaars of Kashgar, it may be imagined that my servants found yet greater difficulty in furnishing me with anything but the plainest fare. One redeeming point was the abundance of excellent fruit. Water-melons were in season at 1*d.* each; also figs, grapes, and autumn peaches —the last large, and 25 for 1*d.* These peaches, sometimes called "cling-stones," are of reddish yellow, firm, or almost hard, and hence "meat" or "food" peaches, in contradistinction to the juicy peaches of summer.

The Consul's library showed him to be a man of intellectual tastes. His books were numerous and well selected, with a good sprinkling of English authors. He had also collected some valuable Turki manuscripts, and had brought with him a set of Negretti and Zambra's meteorological instruments wherewith to establish an observatory. The variations of the barometer, thermometer, etc., were recorded by the Pole just alluded to several times a day. M. Petrovsky delighted in other scientific instruments also, and was not a little pleased occasionally to excite the amazement of his Turki visitors by showing them electrical tricks, whereby it would not be strange if he gained the reputation of being a sorcerer.

The view from the library included the Kizil-su, which runs in two branches north and south of the city to unite at a short distance below. The river bed was wide, but in September the stream looked almost dry. Near at hand, in the garden, was erected a Kirghese tent to serve as a summer-house or reading pavilion; and adjoining the offices was a Russian bath-house, a building I was not a little thankful to use; whilst near at hand were added to the ordinary occupants of a local poultry-yard several turkeys, which M. Petrovsky had imported, and was rearing with success.

To my surprise I learned that the Consul had no letters for me. A packet from India had reached him some weeks before, which he had forwarded to the Chinese Governor-General at Urumtsi, where, in accordance with my first communications, I was expected to go. Of this I heard at Aksu, and not many days before our arrival at Kashgar the *Tautai* had sent off another packet for me, as I have said, thinking to meet me at Ush-Turfan. My packets of money, however, had arrived safely from Vierny, and messengers had been despatched to recover the letters; but I, meanwhile, had to plan as best I could.

The morrow was a day of calls. Before I was up, Lew, Chief of the town, sent his card, with a sack of rice and a sack of maize, and inquiries for my health. There came also a card from Kwang, Chief of the Kashgar district. In reply I sent cards and presents in the afternoon, at which time appeared the brother of our friend Mattie at Suiting, sent by the *Tautai* with his card, two sheep, and a bag of rice. Thus the Chinese were mindful that we should not starve, and I think there were added, besides, chickens and other provisions.

The Russian Consul also paid me a formal call, expecting to find me in a larger house, surrounded by a garden, perhaps in the suburbs, such as the authorities had intimated they should place at my disposal; but, for my own part, I much preferred to be amidst the life of the town, even though in less comfortable quarters.

The next day was Sunday, and I was thankful to rest; but there was no public service to attend. The Consul and his Cossacks had no Russian priest, M. Hendriks and his Polish acolyte had no congregation, and Joseph and I were left to provide our own spiritual exercises.

On Monday it was arranged that I should visit the *Tautai*, and my card was sent early; but his Excellency had gone on the previous day to the new city, and, as it had rained in the evening, had not returned, it not being the fashion to go out in wet weather. I, therefore, took photographs of the bazaar, and saw something of the town—though, sooth to say, it was hard to find buildings worth portraying.

A view was secured of the Festival Mosque, which, in common with other religious buildings, had the merit of being built of burnt brick, with a somewhat lofty gateway; but the whole looked mean and poor. Inside, however, there was a rather fine avenue of poplars, with a broad, well-kept path, and streams on either side, where the mullahs could delight themselves in a cool and shady retreat. Another picture taken was the Pishigeh caravanserai, which, after the rain, presented a street full of ponds and puddles, everything looking extremely dirty.

One could see from the streets some of the principal industries of the people. Here in a shop, open to the dust of the road and the winds of heaven, are exposed pieces of *mata*. There, in another building, sits a workman before a frame on which he is making a carpet. A little farther on is a forge with bellows roaring and sparks flying, and near it a cook-shop with steaming mutton puddings just taken out of the saucepan, and getting nicely seasoned with the dust of the street, whilst on a counter, black and grimy with dirt, is a medley of vegetables, grapes, melons, pieces of meat, wares of sundry kinds, hats, and stuffs. In shops devoted to the last are exhibited pieces of English make, but more of Russian, of common quality, chintzes, handkerchiefs, mirrors, etc.

Besides the shopkeepers there are many pedlars bawling out the excellence of their wares, chiefly eatables; also men with baskets on their heads filled with horse-dung—the principal fuel of the poor. In the bazaar flour costs a halfpenny per lb., and 100 oz. of opium cost 21 oz. of silver. Ice is both plentiful and cheap.

Concerning the trade of Chinese Turkistan generally, I learned from a Russian source that merchandise passes by all four of the routes leaving the country to north, south, and west, the two principal commercial points being Kashgar and Yarkand. Between Osh and Kashgar are employed for transport 4,000 horses a year; between Narin and Kashgar 1,000 horses, 500 camels, and 25 asses; the exports to Semirechia and Ferghana being valued at £150,000, and the imports at £100,000 a year.

This trade was said to be increasing daily, owing to the Russians paying no import duty, and, further, because the residence of a Russian Consul gives the traders a feeling of security, so that they are gradually getting the trade into Russian hands.*

---

* The chief articles of export are *mata* and carpets; but there are no large capitalists, and many of the merchants trade on borrowed

By the next morning the *Tautai* had returned, and I made my way to his *yamen*, with my camera ready. Our party was shown into his private apartments, where, after the usual formalities, and acceding to the few things I asked, the General was amiable enough to pose at the door of his room, whilst I arranged in two rows his 25 retainers, some in Chinese costume with black felt hats, but others, apparently Dungans, with handkerchiefs tied about their heads. After thus depicting the private apartments, I was allowed to photograph the court-house, or tribunal of justice, built of timber beams, having also a table and certain emblems of authority, such as are seen in Chinese public offices, as well as several lanterns.

In the afternoon the *Tautai* returned my call, and that with so much pomp and circumstance as to excite the whole neighbourhood. He was borne in a huge palanquin on the shoulders of perhaps a dozen men, preceded and followed by a numerous suite. In front was a man with a gong, thrumming and shouting to all and sundry to get out of the way, for that the *Tautai* was coming.

capital, for which they pay the lender one-third of the profits. Trade is carried on chiefly by credit and by barter, such currency as there is for large amounts being gold *tillahs* and silver *yambs*.

The trade with Badakshan is small, and not very long begun, and little is done on the way with Shignan or Wakhan. The Badakshanis bring to Yarkand horses, sheep, pistachio nuts, drugs, turquoise, and an inferior quality of precious stones, for which they take back *nasha*, or hemp, gold, and carpets, but not often cotton stuffs. Again, from India, *viâ* Ladak, are brought a variety of cotton goods, coloured muslins, calico, scarves, and cloth, among which are noticeable those of Macdonald of Manchester and Graham of Bombay. To these must be added red leather, drugs, watches, jewellery, knives, and Muhammadan books; but the sale of Indian tea is forbidden throughout Chinese Turkistan. In returning, the traders take with them silk, *nasha*, gold, silver, wool, carpets, and felts.

If any failed to give heed, there were two lictors with whips thick enough to chastise an elephant; whilst next walked two or more executioners with cudgels the length of a broomstick, and, as I have previously described, spatulated at one end, and ready to administer a beating at a moment's notice — a tempting subject for an artist, though I am bound to say I did not, on the present occasion, see either instrument used.

On entering my humble lodging, the great man and his suite filled it to overflowing. The meeting, however, was short, and he was borne away again with the same ceremony as in coming, leaving or sending me as a present four chickens and four ducks. I gave in return presents of a binocular, oleographs, copies of the Scriptures, a watch-chain and compass, my portrait, a plume for his horse's martingale, and a pair of brass rosettes.

I had asked to see the prison, and, next day, went to do so, being taken first to call on the Chief of the Kashgar district. Here, in a garden *kiosque*, I was regaled with light refreshment by a very intelligent Chinaman, who seemed to have met with Europeans in China proper. As regards foreign information, he was head and shoulders above the other officials. He and a young man went with us to the prison. They both seemed to have some knowledge of photography, and even pointed out to me, when the picture was focussed, that one of the lines was out of the perpendicular.

Whether the whole of the prison was shown to me or not I am uncertain. They were some little time before they announced that all was ready, and when we did arrive the place bore signs of being brushed up to its maximum presentability. One part of the building was remarkable, and consisted of a double row of cages of wooden bars perhaps six inches in diameter, suggestive of a menagerie.

Here were three prisoners in a costume that was new to me—namely, Chinese blouses of scarlet cotton cloth. Their ankles were chained together below their trousers, whilst round the neck was an iron band continued down to the waist, and having at the bottom two loops, through which the wrists were secured. Hence it was not only next to impossible to run away, but the hands could not be brought to the mouth.

These men were undergoing four years' imprisonment for manslaughter—the reason, I was told, they were dressed in red. One had served three years, the others two each. In every case the hair and beard were uncut, and their uncombed locks, hanging from beneath sheepskin hats, and in a country where most persons have shaven heads, added much to their miserable appearance.

I asked that the three might be brought out and photographed, first in front of their cages, and then in a little yard close by with their jailor, and two lictors, one armed with a whip and the other with his long cudgel, and both wearing tall sugar-loaf felt hats, adorned in front with a perpendicular tin ornament, and wearing on their breasts square or circular badges of office of white calico inscribed with Chinese characters.

The authorities on this occasion were so amiable that it struck me as a favourable opportunity to ask for some of the prison instruments, offering to pay for new ones as a substitute. Orders, therefore, were given for making a murderer's suit and a lictor's hat, which, needless to say, I preferred to have new; but for instruments I took from the prison collection some small scourges and a policeman's whip for patrolling the streets.

They gave me also one of the iron abominations for confining the neck and wrists; a leather slapper, about as big as the palm, for slapping naughty women's faces, and a wooden stick for beating them elsewhere; together with what might be called a Chinese thumb-screw, or rather finger torture, consisting of sticks to be placed between the fingers and then tightened by means of cords.*

How far these Chinese tortures are generally practised upon the Turkis I do not know, but in the case of the three manslayers I felt perfectly convinced they were dressed for my special benefit. They were said to have been in prison for at least two years, whereas their red clothing looked as if it had not come out of the tailor's hands two hours ago.

When, moreover, I asked to see the other prisoners, and was expected to believe that these three men were all the felons under arrest in Kashgar, my powers of

* Torture is practised, according to Williams, in China, upon both prisoners and witnesses, in prison and also in court. Among the methods employed in court, and reported in the *Gazette*, three are described as legal—namely, boards with grooves for compressing the ankles, round sticks for squeezing the fingers, and the bamboo. Twisting the ears with roughened fingers, and keeping them bent whilst making the prisoner kneel on chains, is illegal; but when the prisoner is contumacious, they sometimes resort to striking the lips with sticks till they are nearly jellied, wrap the fingers in oiled cloth and burn it, suspend the body by the thumbs and fingers, tie the hands to a bar under the knees so as to bend the body double, and chain the prisoner by the neck to a stone. One magistrate is accused of having fastened two criminals to boards by nails driven through their palms, using beds of iron, boiling water, and red-hot spikes [a catalogue, in fact, as bad as the Papal Inquisition], but the Emperor exonerated the magistrate on account of the atrocious character of the criminals.

belief broke down entirely, and I came to the conclusion that the prison had indeed been prepared for my visit. I left in it some Turki and Persian Scriptures for future prisoners, and, after the fashion of the country, gave a little money to the unfortunates, and then made my way to the Consulate for dinner.

I have already intimated my uncertainty as to the route by which to leave Chinese Turkistan. Concerning the approaches to Tibet from Khotan I could learn no more in Kashgar than in England, and reading Dr Bellew's *Kashmir and Kashgar* and the horrors of the Karakoram route did not make me anxious to pass by that way into India.

Mr Wilkins, as already mentioned, had suggested my ascending the Gez defile, crossing the Pamirs and the Baroghil Pass to Chitral, and so into Kafiristan. This, physically, would have been much easier, I presume, than by the Karakoram; besides which I had been in correspondence with a medical missionary in Kashmir, who had expressed his readiness to meet me at Yarkand. He further proposed that we should cross the Pamirs to Wakhan, and enter Kafiristan, whence I happened to know that the people had sent to Peshawur asking that a missionary should come to them. If, therefore, the way opened in this direction, I thought, as I approached Kashgar, it would be my duty to enter.

My friend's "committee" in London had not seen their way to grant my request that he might meet me at Yarkand, but I had a lingering hope that in the interval he might have obtained permission; and, failing that, I wondered whether it would be of any use to take my boxes of medicine, endeavour to make my way to Kafiristan, and on the plea that I understood they had sent for a missionary, and had offered to provide him a house, ask to be allowed to see it, and invite further negotiations.

I had accordingly asked M. Petrovsky to inquire into the possibilities of my reaching Kafiristan; but he completely overturned my air-castles by explaining, more fully than I previously knew, the relative positions and relations of Chitral and Kafiristan; and he said that to enter the latter district would probably mean death.

Perplexed, I anxiously but vainly awaited letters that might come from any of four directions.* Subsequently it appeared that my correspondence travelled by each of these four routes, and eventually I received the whole of it, so far as I know, except one bundle of letters in an envelope, which, after travelling to Kashgar, and back again safely to England, was irrecoverably lost in the post between London and Sevenoaks.

My way, therefore, seemed shut up to the Karakoram, failing the receipt of a telegram which I anticipated might recall me westwards by the Terek Pass; and this M. Petrovsky seemed rather to wish that I might try, no Englishman up to that time having crossed it. He spoke also of the desirability of my visiting Khotan, in connection with which the principal diffi-

* On the 2nd of the month, it seemed, a *djiguitt* was despatched from Osh, who usually reached Kashgar on the 9th; and on the 15th of the month Cossacks set out with money and letters from Narin, and arrived by the 24th. These were the only regular postal communications; but the British authorities at Leh were able occasionally to send letters by chance traders passing through Ladak; whilst, lastly, the authorities in China proper despatched messengers to "the Western Country" as necessity required, who also, by favour, sometimes carried letters to private individuals, their quickest delivery between Peking and Kashgar being two months.

culty seemed the getting there and back again in time to cross the passes before the fall of the winter snows.

I therefore began to make preparations. On paying off Osman Bai, he expressed his willingness to go to Khotan and to India, if I desired ; but for this he asked a prohibitive price, and evidently did not want to go even to Yarkand. At the same time, he was quite effusive in his compliments, asking for a compass as a parting gift, with the observation that the money I paid him would speedily be scattered, but the compass he should wear, and thus at the hour of prayer be reminded of me ever hereafter. He thought, too, it was such an admirable thing for an English gentleman to travel and spend money in the country, and he hoped that I should come again.

Obliged, therefore, to look for a new carrier, I was glad of the assistance of a Turki official, Ibrahim Beg, who found me a man possessing three *arbas*, in which my baggage was to be transported to Yarkand ; but before leaving we were to go out to the locally famous shrine of Hazrat Aphak.

The lack of antiquities in a place that has existed for so many centuries as Kashgar is surprising. From pre-historic times downwards, it appears to have been the capital of the territory and a centre of trade. So early as 94 A.D. we read of its being conquered by the Chinese general Panchao. In the seventh century it was visited by Hiuen Tsiang, who calls it Kie-sha ; and in the eighth century it was conquered again by the Muhammadan warrior Kutaiba. Abulfelda quotes authors with respect to Kashgar of the tenth and twelfth centuries ; and then comes Marco Polo, in whose day it was the seat of a Nestorian bishopric ; but of the " Cascar " visited by him all that now remains is the ruin called Aski Shahr, "the old city," seen a little to the eastwards from the bridge between the present town and fortress.*

The present town dates from 1513, and was built as a fortress by 10,000 men in seven days, under Mirza Abakakar, when he destroyed the ancient capital on the approach of an invading army under Sultan Said Khan. Nearly two centuries later the first mullah king of the country, named Khoja Aphak, died, and in 1693 was buried about two miles north of the city, beyond the Tuman river. The spot has now become a place of pilgrimage; and the shrine of Hazrat Aphak represents the most renowned Muhammadan building, with any pretension to antiquity, in Chinese Turkistan.

When visited by Forsyth, his party were said to be the first Christians allowed to enter its sacred precincts, and I was sufficiently premonished concerning Muhammadan bigotry to know that if I wished to see it, and, above all, to take photographs, I must be on my best behaviour.

On our way, beyond the river, we passed a cemetery. Many of the tombs are covered with domes, or vaulted chambers, open towards the east; and several of these in Forsyth's time were inhabited by ragged and filthy Kalendars, or dervishes, "devoted ascetics and abandoned mendicants," as he calls them, "veritable dwellers among the tombs, impudent claimants of charity from every passer-by, and equally ready

* It consists of a few walls about 24 feet high and 12 paces broad at the top, built of hard clay and gravel. At intervals of 50 or 60 paces are tall, round moles, built of layers of clay and rubble. On the west face are four of these moles standing some 30 feet from the walls, and pierced with horizontal lines of holes, at intervals of about 6 feet. These represent, probably, sockets for rafters to a covered way from the outwork to the fort, giving the archers a flank fire upon assailants.

with curse or blessing, as their loud appeals may require." I imagine their number may have diminished under the Chinese *régime*, for we were not molested by them; and all went well up to our arrival, when I asked to see the Sheikh, or chief mullah of the shrine.

We were shown into a carpeted room, and seated on the floor. Refreshment was quickly brought, and on the

DERVISH SHAH ISMAIL, A KALENDAR OF THE APHAK MONASTERY.

Sheikh's appearing, I began to enlarge upon the long journey I had made from distant lands, whither had spread the fame of Hazrat Aphak, and said I hoped to be allowed to see for myself what had otherwise been learned by reading. I informed him, further, that I, too, was a mullah, and had brought some of our sacred books; that I should like to present to the college the

Bible in Arabic and Persian, and the *Inghil*, or New Testament, in Persian and Kirghese. Upon this the Sheikh accepted the books, and preparations were quickly made for showing me the buildings.

The mausoleum is surrounded by a cemetery, a coveted spot for burial, full of clay tombs, inclosed by a wall and shaded by numerous silver poplars called *tarik*. Walking down the main avenue, we came to a spot of historical interest, where Yakub Khan had been buried. The Chinese, however, on re-entering Kashgar, were not minded that the bones of the usurper should rest in peace. They, therefore, exhumed the body, burnt it, sent the ashes to Peking, and forbade the erection of any monument or descriptive sign over the rifled grave.

This struck me as a good opportunity to begin photographic operations. I said that we had heard of Yakub Khan in England, and asked two of the mullahs to stand and point to the spot where their ruler was buried. Yakub Khan was, of course, in favour with them, since he posed as a good Muhammadan, and it was he, according to Forsyth, who built the college, mosque, and monastery adjoining the mausoleum.

This view taken, I had only to turn my camera round and say how much I should like to secure a view of the eastern side of the mausoleum, the most beautiful of all buildings in Chinese Turkistan. No objection was made, whereupon I proceeded next to take a picture of a local curiosity on the same side—namely, a brick pedestal, on the top of which was a pyramid of *ovis poli*, or wild sheep's horns, such as would delight the heart of an English collector, and the like of which I have seen nowhere else. I next was allowed to photograph the northern face of the building, but was given to understand that the door was locked, and that no one was allowed to enter.

The mausoleum is a rectangular building, with a dome, and on the north side is a *pishtak* over the

AT KASHGAR—MULLAHS INDICATING THE RIFLED GRAVE OF YAKUB KHAN.

principal entrance, and round minarets at the two corners. The walls are faced with blue and white glazed tiles, which, as specimens of Kashi work, are in no way remarkable—in fact, are very poor as compared with the Kashi work of Samarkand. Forsyth saw it, no doubt, at its best, when recently restored by Yakub Khan, and he calls it handsome; but such an expression is permissible only by comparison with the generally wretched buildings of the country.

Near the gateway leading to the mausoleum is the so-called Golden Mosque, with wooden doors, and pillars of carved work. I photographed this, and then made my way to dinner, and told M. Petrovsky of my successes.

"You mean to say that you have taken a dozen pictures of Hazrat Aphak?"

"Yes."

"Well, that is more than I have had the courage to attempt during the six years I have been here!"

But the Consul forgot that when he was photographically inclined, he proceeded to a spot in his *calèche* with Cossacks before and behind, and that he might consider it beneath his dignity, if forbidden, to allow himself to be deterred by Muhammadan prejudice from effecting his purpose; whereas, with me, had they objected, I should have simply packed up my camera and departed, and the wheels of the universe would have rolled on as usual.

To me the incident seemed to show that one need not always be afraid of the alleged bigotry of the Muhammadans, and to illustrate the saying that "one man may steal the cow whilst another dare not look over the hedge."

My remaining days in Kashgar were largely devoted to reducing baggage, and packing my specimens for transport homewards.

CHRONOLOGY

OF

CHINESE CENTRAL ASIA.

(Vol. I. is to be understood, unless otherwise mentioned.)

DATE B.C.		PAGE
2698.	Inventors of Arts and Sciences arrived in China	357
1122.	Singan, capital of Shensi, and, for 2,000 years, of China	324
580.	Supposed flight of Syawush to Afrasiab, near Bokhara . ii.	48
550.	The founder of Buddhism died . . . . . ii.	81
253.	The Great Wall of China built by Shi-Huangti . . ii.	48
200.	The Yuechi deprived of their lands by the Uigurs . ii.	48
163.	The Saka pushed out of the Tarim valley . . . ii.	48
140—86.	The Yuechi driven from their seats by the Hiongnu .	358
139.	The Envoy Chang Kian despatched to the Yuechi for help ii.	49
135.	Chinese Emperor sent Chang Kian against the Hiongnu .	358
126.	The Saka driven farther West . . . . . ii.	48
62.	Emperor Ming-ti despatched a mission to Tokharistan . ii.	81
60.	The Uigurs were conquered by the Chinese . . ii.	49
59.	The Chinese subdued the Hiongnu	358

A.D.		
65.	Emperor Ming-ti sent to India for Buddhist information .	359
73.	The Chinese took Hami and established military colonies.	326
83.	Hiongnu and Uigurs subdued under Panchao . . 358, ii.	49
94.	Kashgar conquered by Chinese General Panchao . 358, ii.	49
142 and 178.	Chinese settlers were colonised in Armenia . .	360
200.	Christianity introduced into Merv	41
202.	Khotan sent elephants to the Emperor of China . . ii.	168
250.	Chi-Ming translated Buddhist writings from Patna . . ii.	82
260.	Fa-hian reached China . . . . . . ii.	82
335.	Chinese subjects permitted to take Buddhist vows . . ii.	82
399.	Chi Fa-hian procured Buddhist writings from India . ii.	83
411 or 503.	The bishopric of Samarkand founded . . . ii.	122

CHRONOLOGY. 453

DATE A.D.		PAGE
420.	The See of Merv was promoted to Metropolitan rank. 41,	ii. 122
445.	A Chinese punitive expedition was sent against Tangut.	ii. 168
461.	The first record of a Chinese embassy to Persia	361
518.	Sung Yun procured MSS. from India. . . . 359,	ii. 83
629.	Hiuen Tsiang travelled to India, etc., to study Buddhism	ii. 83
630.	The Tibetans learned arithmetic and medicine from China	ii. 291
635.	The Missionary Olopan from Syria arrived in China. 361,	ii. 120
639.	Srong-btsan-sgam-po founded Shaldan, afterwards Lassa	ii. 292
712.	Kutaiba conquered Bokhara and penetrated into Ferghana	ii. 50, 208
713.	General Kutaiba crossed the mountains to Kashgar.	360
713—755.	Christian Church recovered its ascendency in China.	ii. 120
714.	See of Samarkand promoted to Metropolitan rank	ii. 122
745.	An edict issued in China concerning Christian temples 361,	ii. 120
781.	Singanfu monument erected by Nestorian Christians.	ii. 120
845.	Persecution of Christians in China	ii. 120
858—1338.	Dates on tombstones in Nestorian cemeteries.	ii. 124
860.	John of Balad ordained by Sergius as Bishop of Merv	ii. 122
878.	Christians formed a large foreign population at Khanfu	ii. 121
888.	Ismail, a Samanid, became governor of Samarkand.	ii. 209
893.	Ismail captured and annexed Taras, or (possibly) Talas.	ii. 209
900.	Joseph was Bishop of Merv.	ii. 122
907.	The Samanid Empire extended from Ispahan to Turfan	ii. 50
988.	Ebed Jesu was Bishop of Merv	ii. 122
1013.	Dharmapala came to Tibet with several Buddhist disciples	ii. 293
1037.	Hasan Bughra Khan succeeded as ruler over Kashgar	ii. 74
1041.	The second introduction of Buddhism into Tibet	ii. 288
1070.	The Kudatku Bilik was written in Kashgar	ii. 133
1135.	The leader of the Kara Khitai took the title of Gur-Khan	ii. 51
1176.	Supposed date of inscription on a rock in the Muzart gorge	247
1220.	The Tarim valley passed under the rule of Jinghiz Khan 366,	ii. 51
1241.	Jagatai died after succeeding his father, Jinghiz Khan	ii. 52
1245.	Carpini proceeded by the Irtish valley to Mongolia.	362
1246—48.	Sakya Pandita visited the Court of Kuyuk Khan	ii. 293
1253.	Rubruquis started by the Syr-daria to Mongolia	362
1254.	Hayton of Armenia proceeded from the Volga to Mongolia	362
1270.	The Sakya-pa lamas became Tibetan rulers for 70 years	ii. 293
1271.	Marco Polo crossed the Pamirs from Badakshan	362
1274.	Water stations established between Khotan and Yarkand	ii. 157
1275.	Marco Polo arrived at Kubilai's Court in China	362
1316.	Monastic life in Central Asia proved by an epitaph.	ii. 129
1328.	Friar Odoric of Pordenone visited Tibet . .	ii. 299
1336.	Pascal, a Franciscan, travelled through Urgenj (Khiva).	ii. 125
1338—42.	Papal Embassy passed through Old Khiva to Peking	363
1339.	William of Modena was put to death at Almalik	363
1342.	Marignolli baptised some of the natives at Hami	326

DATE A.D.		PAGE
1347–63.	Tuglak Timur on the throne in Mongolia	ii. 52
1375.	The Catalan map shows a monastery near Issik-Kul	ii. 129
1377.	Turfan appears first in Chinese annals	334
1383.	Khizr Khoja reigned and enforced the *shariat* on Kirghese	ii. 213
1389.	Tamerlane undertook his last campaign into Moghulistan	ii. 52
1399.	Aksu is described as having three castles	340
1419.	A new route to Hami followed by Shah Rukh's Embassy	363
1447.	The Tashi Lunpo monastery was founded by Gedundub	ii. 294
1513.	The present town of Kashgar was built as a fortress	447
1531.	Said, according to the *Tarikhi Rashidi*, invaded Tibet	ii. 53
1576.	The king of Koko-Nor designated Sodnam "Vadjra Dalai Lama"	ii. 294
1602.	Travels of Goes through Central Asia	364
1624.	Antonio Andrada visited Tibet	ii. 299
1644.	Manchus placed present dynasty on the Chinese throne	156
1645.	The fifth Dalai Lama was made monarch of all Tibet	ii. 294
1655.	The Russians sent their first Embassy to Peking	368
1661.	Grueber and Dorville went from Peking to Agra, *via* Lassa	ii. 300
1678.	Aphak placed as governor at Yarkand	ii. 54
1684.	Russia and China first came to blows on the Amur	369
1688.	Limits of Manchuria defined by Treaty of Nertchinsk	154
1693.	Khoja Aphak, the first Mullah king of Kashgar, died	447
1706.	Joseph d'Asculi, and Maria de Tonn, reached Lassa	ii. 300
1716.	Renat reconnoitred and drew first map of Sungaria	372
,,	Desideri left Lassa	ii. 300
1717.	The Sungarian name of Urumtsi appeared in Chinese annals	331
,,	The Sungarians invaded Tibet	ii. 295
,,	A map of Tibet was submitted to the Jesuits	ii. 307
1718.	Van de Putte made his way to Lassa through India	ii. 301
,,	The Jesuits surveyed China generally	373
1719.	Orazio della Penna reached Lassa through Nepal	ii. 300
1720.	The Chinese army finally conquered Tibet	ii. 295
1740.	Orazio della Penna once more reached Lassa	ii. 300
1755.	Amursana was made ruler of Sungaria	ii. 55
1756.	Sungaria was depopulated by the Chinese	169
,,	D'Arocha determined the astronomical position of Urumtsi	331
1757.	Hami was again placed under the administration of Kansu	327
1758.	The Tarim valley again in the hands of the Chinese	ii. 55
1760.	Christian missionaries were expelled from Lassa	ii. 302
1771.	The Torgout Kalmuks returned to the Ili valley	169
1772.	Deb Judhur invaded Kuch Behar	ii. 302
1774.	Warren Hastings sent Bogle to the Rajah of Bhotan	ii. 302
1778.	Tchuen-yuen wrote *Memoirs of the Western Countries*	368
1782.	The Goorkhas of Nepal appeared before Tashi Lunpo	ii. 295
1783.	Captain Turner was sent through Bhotan to Shigatze	ii. 303
1786.	The Chinese expelled the Goorkhas from Tibet	ii. 307

CHRONOLOGY.

DATE A.D.		PAGE
1792.	To this date the Dalai Lamas were elected by the clergy.	ii. 289
1811.	The Russians began to trade at Chuguchak and Kuldja.	369
,,	Thomas Manning made his way to Lassa.	ii. 303
1813.	The Chinese subsidised Khokand to control the *Khojas*.	ii. 56
1820.	Körös travelled through Bokhara and Cabul to Leh.	ii. 304
1828.	Humboldt reached Baty on the Irtish.	370
1834.	The Dogra troops under Zorawar Sing subdued Ladak.	ii. 296
1838.	Efforts to Christianise Manchuria were begun.	159
,,	Wood pushed up to the Pamirs from Badakshan.	ii. 16
1840.	English missionaries expelled from the Trans-Baikal.	163
1841.	Zarawar Sing plundered the monasteries of Rudok.	ii. 296
1842.	The Chinese re-occupied lost territory and besieged Leh.	ii. 296
1844.	Huc and Gabet made their way to Lassa.	ii. 303
1845.	De la Brunière was murdered on the Amur by the Gilyaks	159
1846.	Seven *Khojas* under Katti Tura took Kashgar.	ii. 57
1851.	The treaty of Kuldja made between Russians and Chinese	ii. 260
1853.	Two Moravian missionaries set out for Mongolia *via* India	ii. 306
1857.	Adolf Schlagintweit penetrated into Chinese Turkistan.	374
1858.	The route was opened between Kiakhta and Kalgan.	161
,,	The Russians took all Manchuria north of the Amur.	155
1859.	Valikanoff, disguised, crossed the Tian Shan to Kashgar	370
1860.	The district round Issik-Kul was ceded to Russia.	371
,,	Government of India employed natives surveying.	ii. 16
1862.	Dungan rebellion broke out in Shensi and Kansu.	ii. 58
1863.	Mr Howell crossed China from Shanghai to Kiakhta.	161
1865.	Yakub Khan arose and posed as a Ghazi.	ii. 217
,,	Johnson approached Khotan from Leh.	ii. 170
1866.	Yakub Khan ruled over Kashgar, Yarkand, and Khotan.	ii. 59
1868.	Shaw and Hayward crossed the Himalayas to Kashgar.	374
1869.	Whyte's *Overland Route from Peking to Petersburg*.	161
1870—73.	The Forsyth Missions from India to Yakub Khan.	374-5
1870.	Das went to Tashi Lunpo to study Buddhism.	ii. 309
1871.	A school was opened in Vierny for baptised Kalmuks.	256
,,	The Ili valley came into possession of Russia for 12 years	370
1871—73.	Prjevalsky's first expedition, from Kiakhta to Kalgan	371
1872.	Yakub Khan received the Mission of Kaulbars.	ii. 60
,,	Ney Elias crossed from Kuci-hwa-Cheng to Uliassutai	374
1873.	Ili valley visited by Ashton Dilke and Schuyler.	374
1874.	Gordon, Trotter, and Biddulph penetrated to Kila Panj	ii. 17
,,	Dalgleish made his way as a trader to Yarkand.	ii. 111
1874—75.	Pandit Nain Sing explored from Leh to Lake Tengri.	ii. 308
1875.	The expedition of Sosnovsky passed through Hami.	370
,,	Yakub Khan received the second Mission of Reintal.	ii. 60
1875—76.	Milne wrote on the Route from St Petersburg to Peking	161
1876.	The Chinese re-occupied Manas and Urumtsi.	ii. 61
,,	Prjevalsky set out from Kuldja up the Yulduz valley	371

DATE A.D.		PAGE
1876.	Pievtsoff travelled from the Zaisan to Guchen	370
,,	Kuropatkin crossed from Ferghana to Kashgar	370
,,	Kostenko was the first Russian author to reach the Pamirs	ii. 17
1877.	Yakub Khan died	ii. 62
,,	Potanin passed through Hami	327
1877—78.	The Chinese re-conquered the country round Khotan	375
,,	Severtsoff visited and wrote concerning the Pamirs	ii. 17
1878.	Siu-Joshive regained Urumtsi for the Chinese	333
,,	Oshanin visited Karategin	ii. 17
,,	Pandit A. K. was despatched to cross Tibet into Mongolia	ii. 308
1879.	Prjevalsky started from Lake Zaisan along the Ulungur	371
,,	Count Szechenyi tried to enter Tibet from Sachu	ii. 310
,,	Regel travelled from Kuldja to Turfan	335
,,	Dr Lansdell crossed Siberia and part of Manchuria	156
1880.	Delmar Morgan visited the Ili valley	374
1881.	Dr Regel explored Darwaz	ii. 17
,,	Russian merchants established themselves at Hami	328
,,	Russo-Chinese treaty on retrocession of Kuldja	ii. 260
,,	Chandra Das and a Lama visited Lassa	ii. 309
1882.	Two French travellers crossed Manchuria to Vladivostock	156
,,	Dr Lansdell visited the Ili valley	174
1883—85.	Prjevalsky crossed the Gobi from Urga to Ala-Shan	372
1884.	Prjevalsky crossed the Nan Shan Mountains to Koko-Nor	ii. 310
1885—87.	Carey travelled round Chinese Turkistan	375
1886.	Dr Seeland journeyed from Vierny to Kashgar and Aksu	371
1887.	Harry de Windt crossed Mongolia	161
,,	Bell and Younghusband rode from Peking to Kashgar	375
1888.	Grombchevsky proceeded from Marghilan to the Alai	ii. 18
,,	Bonvalot, Capus, and Pepin crossed the Pamirs to India	ii. 19
1889—90.	Bonvalot crossed the Tarim desert into Tibet	ii. 172
1889.	Roborovsky's party entered Nia	ii. 174
,,	Grombchevsky, Pievtsoff, Bonvalot, Rockhill, and Lansdell travelling towards Lassa	ii. 311
1890.	Grum-Grjimailo explored the Bogdo Mountains	335
,,	Cumberland and Bower crossed the Karakoram	376
,,	Mr and Mrs Littledale went a second time to the Pamirs	ii. 19
1890—91.	Younghusband made excursions to the Pamirs	ii. 19
1891.	Bower started again to cross Tibet	ii. 312
,,	Cumberland approached the Pamirs by the Gez defile	ii. 45

☞ The Editio Princeps will be limited to the number already printed, of which the type is distributed, and more than a third of the edition sold to America. Early applications, therefore, are invited, which will be attended to in the order received.

RUSSIAN CENTRAL ASIA:

INCLUDING

KULDJA, BOKHARA, KHIVA, AN'D MERV;

WITH APPENDICES ON THE FAUNA, FLORA, AND BIBLIOGRAPHY OF RUSSIAN TURKISTAN.

Illustrated with Photographic Frontispiece; Seventy Engravings; and with Route and Ethnological Maps showing the Afghan Frontier as Marked in New Russian Publications.

IN TWO VOLUMES. DEMY OCTAVO, 1,500 PAGES. PRICE TWO GUINEAS.

By HENRY LANSDELL, D.D., M.R.A.S., F.R.G.S.,

AUTHOR OF "THROUGH SIBERIA."

A journey of 12,000 miles—5,000 by rail, 3,500 by water, and 3,700 on wheels, horses, or camels—through Western Siberia to Kuldja: thence through Russian Turkistan and the Kirghese Steppes to Tashkend, Khokand, and Samarkand. Crossing into Bokhara, the Author travelled through the Khanate as guest of the Emir, floated 300 miles down the Oxus to Khiva, and then continued by a new route across the land of the Turkomans and north of Merv to Krasnovodsk. One of Dr. Lansdell's objects (as before in Siberia) was the distribution in prisons and hospitals of the Scriptures, on the Patriarchal and Persian customs of which the work throws light in references to 350 texts. In 77 chapters the book treats more or less fully of all parts of Russian Turkistan, Kuldja, Bokhara, Khiva, and Turkmenia, down to the frontier of Afghanistan; describes many hundreds of miles of country not previously visited by an English Author; gives 4,300 species of fauna and flora in about 20 lists, with introductions; adds a bibliography of 700 titles, and an index of 5,000 entries.

LONDON: SAMPSON LOW, MARSTON, SEARLE, & RIVINGTON,
188, FLEET STREET, E.C.

CONTENTS.

CHAPTERS.	
1.	INTRODUCTORY.
2, 3.	JOURNEY FROM LONDON TO OMSK.
4, 6, 7, 8, 11, 12.	GEOGRAPHY, ECONOMY, AND ADMINISTRATION OF THE PROVINCES OF AKMOLINSK, SEMIPOLATINSK, AND SEMI-RECHIA.
5, 10, 13, 14.	FROM OMSK TO KULDJA.
9, 20.	HISTORY OF THE RUSSIAN ADVANCE UP THE IRTISH.
15—17.	ETHNOLOGY, ETC., OF THE CHINESE VALLEY OF ILI.
18, 19, 24, 28.	FROM KULDJA TO TASHKEND.
21—23.	THE KIRGHESE AND THEIR PATRIARCHAL CUSTOMS.
25, 26, 29.	METEOROLOGY, GEOLOGY, COMMUNICATIONS, AND STATISTICS OF THE SYR-DARIA AND AMU-DARIA PROVINCES.
27, 41.	THE RUSSIAN ADVANCE UP THE SYR-DARIA.
30, 31.	OUR STAY AT TASHKEND.
32, 35, 37.	FROM TASHKEND TO KHOKAND AND SAMARKAND.
33, 34.	HISTORY AND GEOGRAPHY OF FERGHANA, AND THE PAMIR.

CHAPTERS.	
36, 38, 39, 40.	ANTIQUITIES AND TOPOGRAPHY OF MUHAMMADAN, JEWISH, AND RUSSIAN SAMARKAND.
42—44.	SIBERIAN, PETERSBURG, AND CENTRAL ASIAN PRISONS.
45—48.	FROM SAMARKAND THROUGH KARSHI TO BOKHARA.
49—51.	THE HISTORY, COLLEGES, AND JEWS OF BOKHARA.
52, 53.	THE EDUCATIONAL INSTITUTIONS, POPULATION, CUSTOMS, AND DISEASES OF BOKHARA.
54, 55.	FROM BOKHARA TO CHARJUI.
56—59, 70.	THE OXUS (UPPER AND LOWER, ANCIENT AND MODERN), AND FLOATING DOWN IT.
60.	FROM FORT PETRO-ALEXANDROVSK TO KHIVA.
61—63.	THE OASIS, CAPITAL, AND MOSQUES OF KHIVA.
64—66.	FROM KHIVA TO THE NORTH OF THE KHANATE.
67—69, 71, 72.	DESERT TRAVEL FROM KUNIA URGENJ TO THE CASPIAN.
73.	TURKMENIA AND THE TURKOMANS.
74.	THE TURKOMAN OASES.
75.	THE RUSSIAN ADVANCE TO MERV.
76.	MERV AS ANNEXED.
77.	FROM KRASNOVODSK TO BAKU AND HOMEWARDS.

A LIST, BIBLICALLY ARRANGED, OF 350 TEXTS ILLUSTRATED OR REFERRED TO.
CHRONOLOGY OF RUSSIAN CENTRAL ASIA, FROM B.C. 329 TO A.D. 1884.
MAPS SHOWING AUTHOR'S ROUTE AND REGIONS INHABITED BY PRINCIPAL RACES.

APPENDICES.

A. THE FAUNA OF RUSSIAN TURKISTAN, WITH GENERAL PREFACE, INTRODUCTIONS, AND ENUMERATION OF 3,000 SPECIES; VIZ.: MAMMALIA, 83; AVES, 385; REPTILIA, 33; PISCES, 87; MOLLUSCA, 54; ARANEAE, 146; CRUSTACEA, 52; COLEOPTERA, 556; MELLIFERA, 438; SPHEGIDAE, 183; SCOLIIDAE, 30; MUTILLIDAE, 18; FORMICIDAE, 36; CHRYSIDIFORMES, 54; LEPIDOPTERA, 744; NEUROPTERA, 95; ORTHOPTERA, 74; VERMES, 47.

B. THE FLORA OF RUSSIAN TURKISTAN. A GENERAL PREFACE, WITH NAMES OF 92 FAMILIES AND 1,200 SPECIES IN LATIN AND ENGLISH, ALSO THE LOCALITY AND ALTITUDE WHERE FOUND, AND THE TIME OF BLOSSOM OR FRUIT.

C. BIBLIOGRAPHY OF RUSSIAN CENTRAL ASIA OF 700 TITLES, CHRONOLOGICALLY AND TOPICALLY ARRANGED, WITH ALPHABETICAL LIST OF AUTHORS.

GENERAL INDEX OF 50 PAGES.

bellows and inflate the bed. This appeared greatly to tickle his fancy, though I doubt whether he had used a screw before. To this I added an excellent filter, to preserve his Majesty, I said, from *rishta;* a pair of

THE AUTHOR IN ROBE OF HONOUR, WITH TURQUOISE BRIDLE, PRESENTED BY THE EMIR OF BOKHARA.

mosquito curtains, the like to which I had seen nothing in the khanate; an electro pepper and salt case, presented to me by Messrs. Langton and Son, whose "travelling requisites" I have found so useful, besides

BY THE SAME AUTHOR.

THROUGH SIBERIA.

Illustrated with Engravings and Maps.
FIFTH EDITION. IN ONE VOLUME. 10s. 6d.

[*A few copies remain of the Library Edition at* 30s., *in two volumes, printed on thicker paper, with more engravings, a photographic frontispiece, and an ethnological map.*]

A journey of 8,000 miles from the Urals to the Pacific, on the rivers Obi, Amur, and Ussuri, and by the hire of a thousand horses. The Author travelled privately on an expedition of a philanthropic and religious character to the penal establishments of Siberia, and describes his visits to nearly all its hospitals, prisons, and mines, giving a mass of authentic information concerning the exiles such as has never been published before. The book treats of all parts of the country, as to its geography, natural history, and inhabitants, both Russian and aboriginal; whilst 3,000 miles of the Amur and Ussuri are here described by an English Author as an eyewitness for the first time.

Extracts from 200 Notices of the English, Irish, Scotch, American, Australian, French, Finnish, German, and Swedish Press.

The Times. (*One column.*)—"The reader will . . . find in Mr. Lansdell's volumes all that can interest him about Siberia."

The Athenæum. (*Five columns.*)—"With the exception of Mr. Mackenzie Wallace's 'Russia,' the best book on a Russian subject which has appeared of late years is Mr. Lansdell's 'Through Siberia.'"

Fraser's Magazine. (*Thirteen pages.*)—"His testimony . . . is simply the best that exists." O.K. . . . (a *Russian* writer.)

The Academy. (*Four columns.*)—"We are of opinion that 'Through Siberia' is much more entertaining, and certainly more readable, than many novels."

The Church Times. (*Two columns.*)—"Englishmen have every reason to be proud of this work; for it . . . can only result in making the name of our country more honoured and respected than any mere victory of arms would do."

Church Missionary Intelligencer. (*Four pages.*)—"It is altogether different from even the higher class of books of travel. It teems with information of every possible kind."

Harper's Monthly Magazine. (*One column.*)—"Since the time of Howard, no one has given us so full and fair an account of Russian prisons as is now presented to us by Mr. Lansdell."

Revue des deux Mondes. (*Twelve pages.*)—"Qu'on n'aille pas s'imaginer après cela que M. Lansdell soit un fanatique . . . Il estime qu'une sage philosophie et une piété sincère ne sont irréconciliables ni avec la belle humeur ni avec ces honnêtes petits plaisirs que assaisonnent la vie."

The Baptist. (*Two columns.*)—"A man who undertakes to set matters in a true light before the eyes of the world deserves the gratitude of all parties. This Mr. Lansdell has done."

The Guardian. (*Two columns.*)—"It touches upon political and social questions of great interest, and offers information upon the internal administration of the Russian empire, which is not readily obtained elsewhere."

LONDON: SAMPSON LOW & CO., 188, FLEET STREET, E.C.
AMERICA: HOUGHTON, MIFFLIN, & CO., BOSTON.
GERMAN TRANSLATION: HERMANN COSTENOBLE, JENA.
SWEDISH TRANSLATION: ALBERT BONNIER, STOCKHOLM.
DANISH TRANSLATION: O. H. DELBANCO, COPENHAGEN.

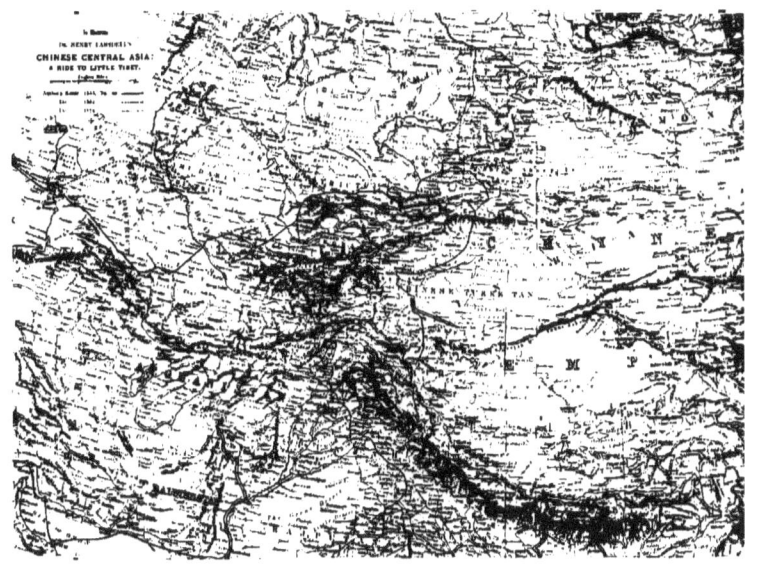

www.ingramcontent.com/pod-product-compliance
Lightning Source LLC
Chambersburg PA
CBHW051158300426
44116CB00006B/354